INDUSTRIAL POLICIES FOR PACIFIC ECONOMIC GROWTH

Edited by
Hiromichi Mutoh
Sueo Sekiguchi
Kotaro Suzumura
Ippei Yamazawa

ALLEN & UNWIN   Sydney   London   Boston
In association with
The Pacific Trade and Development Conference Secretariat
The Australian National University

HC
79
.I53
I53
1986

© Hiromichi Mutoh, Sueo Sekiguchi, Kotaro Suzumura and Ippei Yamazawa 1986

This book is copyright under the Berne Convention.
No reproduction without permission. All rights reserved.

First published in 1986

Allen & Unwin Australia Pty Ltd
8 Napier Street, North Sydney, NSW 2060 Australia

Allen & Unwin New Zealand Limited
60 Cambridge Terrace, Wellington, New Zealand

George Allen & Unwin (Publishers) Ltd
18 Park Lane, Hemel Hempstead, Herts HP2 4TE England

Allen & Unwin Inc.
8 Winchester Place, Winchester, Mass 01890 USA

National Library of Australia
Cataloguing-in-Publication entry:

Industrial policies for Pacific economic growth.

 Bibliography.
 Includes index.
 ISBN 0 04 330381 1.
 ISBN 0 04 330380 3 (pbk.).

 1. Industry and state—Pacific Area—Addresses, essays, lectures.   2. Pacific Area—
Industries—Addresses, essays, lectures.   3. Pacific Area—Economic conditions—
Addresses, essays, lectures.   I. Mutoh, Hiromichi.   II. Pacific Trade and
Development Conference. Secretariat.   III. Pacific Trade and Development
Conference (15th: 1985: Tokyo, Japan).

338.9'009182'3

Library of Congress Catalog Card Number: 86–071943

Set in 10/11.5 pt Plantin by Graphicraft Typesetters Ltd., Hong Kong
Printed in Hong Kong by Dah Hua Printing Press Co., Ltd.

INDUSTRIAL POLICIES
FOR PACIFIC ECONOMIC GROWTH

Contents

v

PART III   INDUSTRY SECTORAL STUDIES

PART IV   THE REGIONAL ASPECTS OF INDUSTRIAL POLICIES

PART V   CONCLUSION

Tables

Figures

Contributors

Hiromichi Mutoh	Japan Economic Research Center, Japan
Sueo Sekiguchi	Osaka University, Japan
Kotaro Suzumura	Hitotsubashi University, Japan
Ippei Yamazawa	Hitotsubashi University, Japan
Mohamed Ariff	University of Malaya, Malaysia
Richard E. Caves	Harvard University, USA
H. Edward English	Carleton University, Canada
R.G. Gregory	Australian National University, Australia
Hal Hill	Australian National University, Australia
David Hughes	Australian National University, Australia
Hideki Ide	Kobe Gakuin University, Japan
James Jordan	Australian National University, Australia
Ai Tee Koh	National University of Singapore, Singapore
Robert Lawrence	The Brookings Institution, USA
Ching-ing Hou Liang	National Chengchi University, Taiwan
Kuo-Shu Liang	National Taiwan University, Taiwan
P.J. Lloyd	University of Melbourne, Australia
Frances McCall	Ministry of Finance, Japan
Donald D. McFetridge	Carleton University, Canada
Chong Hyun Nam	Korea University, Korea
Masahiro Okuno	University of Tokyo, Japan
R.B. Suhartono	Agency for Industrial Research and Development, Indonesia
Masu Uekusa	University of Tokyo, Japan
Lawrence J. White	New York University, USA
Mu Yang	Chinese Academy of Social Sciences, People's Republic of China

Preface

This volume presents the papers written for the Fifteenth Pacific Trade and Development (PAFTAD) Conference, held in Tokyo on 26–29 August 1985.

The theme of the conference was 'Industrial Policies for Pacific Economic Growth'. The conference attempted to enhance understanding of the theoretical issues and the historical circumstances supporting industrial policies, as well as to analyse policies adopted by nations of the Pacific region.

The first part of the conference explored the identification and definition of the various manifestations of industrial policy. Part I of the volume makes it clear that while an industrial policy that is coherently articulated and consistently applied may not exist in any country, governments undertake a range of measures to encourage the development of particular industries at the expense of others; a range of measures that, it was suggested, can be thought of as de facto industrial policy. Part II examines the industrial policies of some Pacific developed countries (the United States, Europe and Canada), the role of industrial policies as part of the growth strategies of developing countries (Taiwan and the 'big four' members of ASEAN), and finally the important case of the industrial policies of Japan.

Part III looks at a number of industries that are particularly important for the developing countries of the region: iron and steel, textiles and clothing, automobiles, and petrochemicals. Part IV discusses regional aspects of industrial policy with reference to ASEAN and the interesting case of China. It was here that generalisations were attempted about industrial policy, and this section details perhaps the most interesting and challenging questions discussed at the conference: does the history of industrial policy in Japan provide a model for the developing countries—or, for that matter, for the United States? Does the stage of economic development affect the choice of policies adopted and their likely success?

The conference was organised by the Fifteenth PAFTAD Conference Organising Committee, comprising Saburo Okita and Kiyoshi Kojima (advisors), Hisao Kanamori (chairman), Hiromichi Mutoh, Sueo Sekiguchi, Kotaro Suzumura, Michihiro Ohyama, Motoshige Itoh, Masu Uekusa and Ippei Yamazawa, in association with the Japan Economic Research Center. It was assisted by advice from the International Steering Committee of the Conference Series, comprising Kiyoshi Kojima, Saburo Okita, Seiji Naya and Hisao Kanamori in Japan; Lawrence B. Krause and Hugh Patrick in the United States; Narong-chai Akrasanee in Thailand; Peter Drysdale (Director of the PAFTAD Secretariat) and Ross Garnaut in Australia; Mohamed Ariff in Malaysia; Wontack Hong in Korea; Filologo Pante in the Philippines; Bruce Ross and Sir Frank Holmes in New Zealand; H. Edward English in Canada; and Augustine Tan and Lim Chong Yah in Singapore.

We are grateful for financial support from the following organisations: the Asian Development Bank; the Ford and Asia Foundations; the Rockefeller Brothers Fund; the National Institute for Research Advancement, Japan; and the Australian National University.

For the convenience of readers, and especially busy readers, a summary of the chapters and discussion has been prepared, which constitutes the final chapter of the book. Robert Gregory has also written an informative overview of the conference, which appears as the introductory chapter of the volume.

We acknowledge with gratitude the contributions of various people to the preparation of the final version of the manuscript. The integrated summary of the chapters and discussion that constitutes chapter 15 was written by David Hughes from the chapters themselves, from direct transcripts of the discussion, and from summaries prepared by James Jordan and Frances McCall. David Hughes also compiled the index. Heinz Arndt and Hal Hill acted as editorial consultants, in particular for chapters 13 and 11, respectively. Janet Healey edited the complete manuscript for accuracy and consistency of style. Kim-lan Ngo and Minni Reis wordprocessed the manuscript from original typescripts in various states of imperfection.

Hiromichi Mutoh, Sueo Sekiguchi, Kotaro Suzumura and Ippei Yamazawa
September 1986

1 Overview

R.G. GREGORY

There is no doubt that industrial policy generates considerable interest. Hardly a month goes by without the announcement of a new conference or the publication of a new paper on the topic. There is also no doubt that most economists feel uncomfortable with the concept of an industrial policy. There seem to be no natural or agreed boundaries to what should be encompassed within the area; nor is it even clear that there should be a body of theory that is especially tailored for industrial policy problems. In chapter 3 of this volume Richard Caves goes so far as to say that industrial policy 'is a category of policy measures searching for an analytical framework or, less kindly, a political slogan in search of respectability'. Others, such as Brian Hindley, have suggested that this vagueness is one reason for the popularity of industrial policy:

> From a political point of view, this very lack of precision in definition is a major attraction of support for industrial policy. Such support is a means of signalling a preference for industrial vigour over industrial stagnation and, more important, of signalling a willingness 'to do something' to obtain the one and avoid the other without being specific about what that something is. (Hindley, 1984:278)

Why then bring together a range of papers on such a topic? What objectives could such a conference hope to achieve?

First, it is important to document what industrial policy is in practice. As Caves suggests in chapter 3, and as is made clear in a number of other chapters in this volume, while an industrial policy that is coherently articulated and consistently applied may not exist in any country, it is nevertheless true that governments undertake various measures to encourage the development of particular industries at the expense of others; measures that, as Lawrence White suggests in chapter 10, can be thought of as a de facto industrial policy. These actions—ranging from import quotas to state ownership of the steel industry—are usually not trivial. Furthermore, there are many who argue that greater investment in industrial policies will achieve faster economic growth.

This volume contains chapters on the industrial policies of developed countries (the United States, Europe and Canada); the role of industrial policies in the growth strategies of developing countries (Taiwan, China and the ASEAN countries); and finally—the fascinating special case—the industrial policies of Japan. The conference also looked at a number of industries that are particularly important for the developing countries of the region: iron and steel, textiles and clothing, automobiles, and petrochemicals.

The second objective, and one that was more difficult to achieve, was to learn about industrial policy by juxtaposing these topics. Could progress be made on such questions as these: does the history of industrial policy in Japan provide a model for the developing countries, or for that matter for the United States? Does a country's stage of economic development affect its choice of policies and their likely success? Is it possible to describe the characteristics of good and bad industrial policies in a way that is useful for policy decisions? A wide range of responses to these questions is possible, and potentially a lot may be gained from bringing together economists who operate in very different economic, political and social environments.

Finally, the essays focus primarily on the Pacific Basin, which is one of the most interesting regions in the world. It encompasses countries from all income levels. It also includes two of the giants of world trade, Japan and the United States; the world's fastest growing economies, Taiwan, Korea and Singapore; and the nation with the world's largest population, China. The Pacific Basin area is forecast to be the fastest growing economic region in the world over the next fifteen years. It is of concern to everyone whether there are likely to be changes in the industrial policies of different countries over the next decade or two that will enhance or retard these growth prospects, and whether the revival of protectionism might become a problem. The Pacific Basin is an area of vital interest to all the participants.

This overview begins with a number of comments on the relationship between economic theory and industrial policy, a topic which, explicitly or implicitly, was always present in the discussions of various papers. A commentary on the country and industry studies follows, and the final section offers a number of concluding remarks.

ECONOMIC THEORY AND INDUSTRIAL POLICY

The conference began with two excellent papers, one by Masahiro Okuno and Kotaro Suzumura (chapter 2), and the other by Richard Caves (chapter 3). These papers developed an analytical framework that might be applied to industrial policy. The framework adopted by both papers was essentially that which would apply to trade policy. It was static and neoclassical, with very little explicit emphasis on the growth process. Both papers suggested that industrial policy be defined as those policies 'undertaken with the object of changing the allocation of resources among industries' (Okuno and Suzumura).

Much time was devoted to discussing appropriate frameworks for the analysis of industrial policy. In particular, there was a general feeling among many participants that, although economic theory as it relates to industry policy is evolving at a rapid rate and is an exciting area of research, the focus and evolution of the theory are not quite appropriate for a thorough understanding of the realities of industrial policy. Some of the apparent reasons for this disquiet are described below.

The role of externalities

The principal rationale for industrial policy developed by these theoretical frameworks is that of positive externalities—those economic advantages flowing from an activity that cannot be adequately appropriated by those producing the activity. Where some of the benefits generated by an industry are difficult to appropriate, it is assumed that the private return will be less than the social return. The correct process for developing efficient industrial policy that emerges from this analytical framework is clear: identify the source of the positive externality; identify the appropriate policy instrument to deal with the source of the externality; assess the costs as well as the benefits of intervention; and act if there is a positive rate of return from the intervention.

But this idealised decision process seems to bear little resemblance to industrial policy in practice. The lack of correspondence between the theory and the practice does not seem to arise because it is difficult to identify and measure externalities, even though, as Paul Krugman remarked, 'external effects by their very nature, leave no paper trail of market transactions by which they can be measured, and thus are likely always to be elusive'. Rather, the lack of correspondence arises because, in practice, the process of developing an industrial policy is obviously not about externalities as they are commonly conceived; it is clear from the industry and country studies that industrial policy is about other things. I find myself very sympathetic to Robert Lawrence's (chapter 7) description of industrial policies as not related to the efficiency of resource utilisation, as described in the theory, but as 'a response to the conflict between the market's allocation of resources and the values and objectives of the political system'.

This proposition was illustrated many times in the various studies presented to the conference. With respect to iron and steel, for example, Chong Hyun Nam points out in chapter 11 that in many countries the iron and steel industry is nationalised, and that in these instances industrial policy is therefore applied very directly. In addition, many developing countries have assiduously fostered the development of an indigenous steel industry. Nam, however, is unable to explain either of these important developments in terms of externalities. He suggests, probably correctly, that the steel industry has been encouraged because it supplies vital inputs to a wide range of industries, because it will replace imports, and because it is believed to create employment. Externalities associated with the industry and as understood by economists are not mentioned. Every reason offered for the policy appears to be against increasing the efficiency with which resources are utilised. Thus policy towards the steel industry makes no sense in terms of the theoretical models that may be used to justify intervention.

The economic theory of externalities and the reality of industrial policies seem to be almost completely disconnected, except in the negative sense that the theory suggests quite clearly that most industrial policy is inefficient, and is justified, in Caves's words, by 'dubious propositions'. There seems no good reason why industries that have thick value-added slices or are large suppliers of inputs should enjoy special government assistance. The net result is that in broad terms economic theory has failed to provide much of a guide for the policy that has actually evolved.

Empirical research: is there a need for more pragmatism?

This disconnectedness between the theory and the reality poses a serious problem about how to respond. Should particular instances of industrial policy be opposed at every opportunity on the grounds that the policies, a priori, inevitably involve an inefficient use of resources? Should a more humble stance be adopted—can so many governments be so wrong so often? Or should a pragmatic, open and ad hoc approach be followed? All these responses can be found in the chapters of this book. Many discussants, however, endorsed the sentiments expressed by Mohamed Ariff and Hal Hill in chapter 5:

> The fundamental point should be stressed that government intervention has been an important element in the past and will be a critical determinant of future performance. The issue is not whether the ASEAN governments will or should intervene. The experience of the Asian newly industrialising countries—Hong Kong excepted—and Japan refutes the notion that intervention and rapid growth are incompatible. Rather, the focus is on the implications of various forms of intervention for industrial growth.

It seemed to me, listening to the evolution of the discussion at the conference, that to a large extent the most interesting research in the future would flow from an approach like this, an approach that stressed empirical research and was closely related to particular examples of policy. It may be too much to ask that particular industrial policies be directly linked to growth performance in the aggregate; but it should be possible to quantify the extent of the interventions, who gains and who loses, and so on. There seems no substitute for empirical work to relieve the tension between economic theory and the reality of industrial policy.

Hill and Ariff also stress another idea that gained some support: that 'it is not so much the extent as the type of regulation that is significant'. In their view, intervention should be market-facilitating rather than market-inhibiting. Most participants seemed to know what they meant—at least heads were nodded—but the idea was not developed in any great depth. A similar idea arose when the proposition was discussed that in a future, more hostile world trading environment there may be a second round of import-replacement policies among the countries of the Pacific Basin. A number of participants made the point that there is a range of policies that can increase the domestic stimulus to growth, all of which are better than import restrictions and are not blatantly biased against international trade. These other policies—the provision of infrastructure, housing, education, and so on—are less discriminatory between industries, and presumably, in the minds of those suggesting them, are market-facilitating rather than market-inhibiting.

It was at this point that Kiyoshi Kojima suggested a similar idea: that the justification for industrial policy in developing countries is not market failure but the *lack* of markets. The governments of developing countries see themselves as *creating* markets and overcoming a range of growth-inhibiting factors—social, economic and political—by the indirect instrument of encouraging manufacturing. The notion of encouraging markets does not fit easily into the theoretical framework propounded by Okuno and Suzumura and Caves.

The idea that there are some types of regulations that facilitate economic development and others that do not—separate from the usual arguments of externalities and public goods—was never developed to any degree, although many of the participants quite clearly subscribed to the idea. If the proposition is true, the characteristics of good and bad government interventions should be explored further, as such information is of vital practical and theoretical importance. A careful reading of the chapters suggests that some individual policies have worked well—the Chrysler bailout, for example (although White may not agree)—but that other policies, such as those directed towards the clothing and textile industry in the United States, have generally not succeeded. At this stage, however, there has been no systematic analysis of the characteristics of good and bad policies that can guide policy in advance of the decisions being made. The terms market-facilitating, market-inhibiting and market-creating all need further refining.

Can there be a universal theory of industrial policy?

In a similar vein, some participants thought that to define industrial policy as those policies *undertaken* to change the allocation of resources among industries missed much of the point. Changing the allocation of resources among industries will certainly be the outcome of policy, but it does not seem to be the explicit objective. It might be more productive, in attempting to understand industrial policy, to think of it in more direct and precise terms—as a range of policies aimed at promoting exports, creating employment, dispersing populations, extending indigenous control, and so on. In this way the analysis could become less abstract and the nature of the empirical work to measure costs and benefits more closely related to what appear to be the actual objectives of policy.

At various times during the conference many participants expressed the view that there could not be a universal theory that could be applied either to explain industrial policy or to discriminate between good policy and bad. This important judgment was made in the very first session by Okuno and Suzumura:

> ... unlike fiscal and monetary policies, industrial policy probably does not lend itself to the formulation of a universal theory. The relationship between government and business and the legal institutions that provide the arena where industrial policy functions differ substantially from country to country, so that a policy that makes complete sense in one country may be a mystery in a different social and legal context.

And furthermore:

> ... the stage of economic development of a country, or of a particular industry, should be taken into consideration in judging whether the implementation of a category of industrial policy or a specific policy measure is legitimate and justifiable.

Some of the Japanese participants seemed to place a strong emphasis on this way of looking at the problem. As Nobuyoshi Namiki remarked, 'Industrial policy is an historical phenomenon and therefore we need to consider this essential nature'.

The conference never quite came to grips with this idea, which seemed to have very little support from the participants from developed countries. Both the Australian and the New Zealand participants, however, recognised that during the economic development of their own countries there had been periods when it was widely believed appropriate to pursue active industrial policies based on tariffs and import replacement, and that those periods seemed now to be virtually over. It was unfortunate that the idea was not developed further, since it was never really clear whether its proponents believed that the *theoretical* justification for industrial policies changes with the level of economic development, or whether the observed policies change in response to the changing level of development—that is, whether the statement was about what does happen or what should happen.

This general discussion prompted the notion that if industrial policy is studied across a wide range of countries and over time there are obvious links that run from the stage of development of the economy to the nature of the industrial policy, although the tendency has been to stress the links that run the other way, and to regard industrial policy as exogenous. In attempting to understand the phenomenon it may be more sensible to place greater emphasis on the endogenous nature of industrial policy, and to ask how the economic, social and political system produces a given range of measures that come to make up industrial policy? Perhaps the attempt should be to discover how attitudes towards industrial policy change during the development process.

It was fairly obvious that many participants did not like the idea of economists spending too much time exploring these terrains, commenting that they belonged in the realm of the political scientist. Yet if economists are to offer advice on industrial policy and write sensibly about the phenomenon, the process by which policy evolves must be understood; it cannot be left to others, and the increasing number of economists who are developing an interest in models of political choice should be a welcome development. At this conference Tsurihiko Nambu began to explore the role of bureaucracies in determining the nature of industrial policy (see Nambu, 1986). Nambu's approach was very exploratory, but he offered comments on the different bureaucratic styles of the United States and Japan and the role of industrial policy in the high-technology industries.

Nambu's contribution led to a vigorous discussion about the role of bureaucrats. Lawrence Krause saw them as an effective lobby group for more government intervention, on the grounds that industrial policy increases their power. But Frank Holmes remarked that in Australia and New Zealand it is a particular group of powerful bureaucrats—those from the Departments of Treasury and Finance—who form the strongest group in favour of deregulation and limiting the extension of industrial policies. All bureaucrats do not have the same degree of self-interest. In Holmes' view, and I agree, it is politicians who tend to favour more active industrial policies, rather than bureaucrats; indeed, I suspect that bureaucrats tend to be a restraining influence in most countries.

Finally, although there was no agreement about whether it is possible to have a universal theory of industrial policy, neither was there any dissent from the proposition that once development has been achieved 'the guiding principle of industrial policy should be to liberate private incentives from the bureaucratic, regulatory and protective measures adopted (presumably with good reason) in the infant stage' (Okuno and Suzumura). This point will be picked up again later.

COUNTRY AND INDUSTRY STUDIES

It is useful, in the first instance, to think of industrial policies as being either defensive or positive. A defensive policy is one designed to prevent too rapid a decline in an industry, whereas a positive policy is designed to encourage a particular industry to develop and grow. Defensive policies are discussed here largely in the context of the developed economies.

Defensive industrial policies

Over the past ten years the rate of growth of national product in most industrialised countries has fallen considerably, without a commensurate decline in either the growth of labour productivity or the growth of the working-age population. The result has been rising unemployment. Between 1970 and 1979, the unemployment rate in the total OECD area increased from 3 per cent to 5 per cent. In 1984 unemployment was 8.2 per cent, and was hovering around its highest level since the depression of the 1930s. In addition, the

Figure 1.1 Manufacturing employment as a share of total civilian employment, selected countries

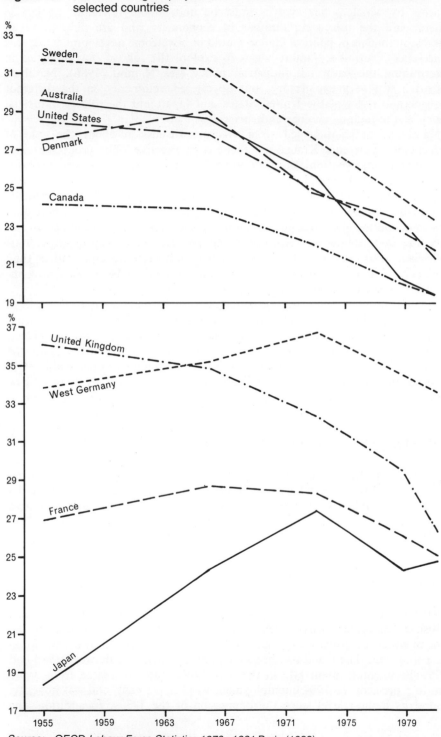

Source: OECD *Labour Force Statistics 1970–1981* Paris (1983)

manufacturing sector has increasingly been losing its share of employment (Figure 1.1), and particular industries—footwear, clothing, textiles and steel— have been subject to large increases in import competition.

Of course, there is nothing special about the manufacturing sector's share of civilian employment. It should not be an objective of economic policy, and variations of the share, by themselves, would not be expected to generate intense interest. It is when a sudden change in employment shares is associated with slower economic growth and rising unemployment that people begin to search for causal connections.

Much of the discussion of defensive industrial policy takes place in the context of attempts to slow down the rate of employment loss in an industry. It was suggested by a number of participants, such as Peter Lloyd, Richard Caves and Robert Lawrence, that it may be useful to think of society as recognising that workers have some, but limited, property rights in their jobs. These property rights become firmer as the length of service in the job increases. Accordingly, it is to be expected that society will be responsive to political pressures to slow down those economic adjustments that involve large job losses in particular sectors of the economy.

There is considerable empirical evidence that is consistent with this view. In most developed economies the expected average completed job tenure of those employed is quite long, typically around fourteen to sixteen years. According to the OECD (1984) the expected job tenure of employed persons in eleven OECD countries varied between thirteen years for Australia and 23 years for Japan. Long job tenure is a necessary but not a sufficient precondition for societies to develop the notion that there should be property rights in jobs.

It is also true that most of the job turnover observed in developed countries occurs among workers with very short job tenure. For example, in Australia, the United States and Canada about 50 per cent of those who have been employed in their present jobs for less than twelve months will leave during the next year, whereas for those employed for fifteen to twenty years in their present jobs the annual rate of leaving is about 13 per cent. This behaviour is also consistent with the view that property rights in jobs are recognised. Property rights that strengthen as the length of service increases lead to labour turnover rules such as last-hired-first-fired.

In Australia, where average job tenure is almost identical to that in Canada and the United States, most workers appear to believe that they will not lose their jobs. During the economic booms and slumps in Australia over the past ten years the proportion of workers who have regarded their jobs as safe has remained remarkably constant at about 80 per cent (Gregory, 1986). Consequently, any structural change leading to large job losses that extend to the core workforce—those with long tenure—must be expected to lead to pressures for job protection, since widely held expectations have not been fulfilled.

Yet it is not clear in the medium term to what degree defensive industrial policy in developed countries has protected jobs. The chapter by Lawrence offers a number of comments on this point. Presumably the Chrysler bailout in the United States saved many jobs for particular workers (see Lawrence, chapter 7; White, chapter 10), but in other instances the industrial policy instrument was clearly not appropriate if job protection for particular workers was an important objective. As Lawrence points out for the textile industry, 'the United States began the 1960s with one group of people who needed protection because they worked in textiles in the northeast but ended the decade with another group who needed protection because they worked in textiles in the south and west'. Policy protected the stock of jobs to some degree, but not the jobs of particular workers—those who might be thought to have property rights in their jobs.

Similar considerations seem to apply in Australia (Lloyd, chapter 9). Import quotas were introduced in 1975 for textiles, footwear, clothing, and auto-mobiles. These quotas are still in place ten years later, and yet it is unreason-able to suppose that society would recognise property rights in jobs to this degree. Furthermore, after ten years only about 24 per cent of the original labour force is likely to be employed with the same firm. Import quotas applied as an instrument to protect particular jobs are very expensive. Lloyd describes these quotas as *ineffective*, in that they are not closely tailored to the objective of facilitating structural change, and *inefficacious*, in that producers and consumers will respond in a number of ways to reduce their impact. He points out that restricting the flow of imports of textiles and clothing into New Zealand and Australia has not protected jobs, because the substitution of capital for labour has continued in the face of a slow output growth to reduce the level of employment. In most countries the same phenomenon is observ-able. Lloyd notes that 'the decline [in jobs] due to rising imports is quite small . . . and is swamped by the effect of increases in labour productivity'.

Some idea of the cost of these quotas can be obtained in the following way. First, assume that the only purpose of the quotas introduced in 1974–75 was to protect the job property rights of those employed in that year. Then, divide the subsidy equivalent of the quotas for selected years since 1974–75 by an estimate of the number of original workers in each year who remain with the firm that was employing them in 1974–75. Each year some workers will leave their jobs, and this number can be estimated from the average rate of job leaving in the manufacturing sector as a whole for each job-tenure category. The calculations are given in Table 1.1. Column 1 lists the subsidy equivalent of the quotas for each year as a fraction of value added. Column 2 lists the level of employment each year, and Column 3 provides an estimate of the proportion of the workforce in each industry that has remained with the original employer of 1974–75. Column 4 allocates the subsidy equivalent of the quotas to these original workers. Column 5 lists the subsidy per original worker as a proportion of the average wage in each year.

In a very short time the subsidy per original jobholder becomes very large. Three years after the introduction of the quotas in textiles, clothing and footwear the subsidy per original jobholder is three-quarters of the average wage. By 1982–83 the subsidy is approximately twice the wage. Similar results occur in the motor vehicle industry, where the subsidy per original worker increases for a similar reason to that given by Lawrence. The quotas begin by

Table 1.1 Implicit job subsidies for long-tenure workers in Australian industries protected by import quotas

	Net subsidy equivalent of import quotas as a fraction of value added (per cent) (1)	Annual employment (in thousands) (2)	Proportion of 1974–75 workers employed with same employer (per cent) (3)	Net subsidy equivalent per 1974–75 worker with same employer ($A) (4)	Net subsidy equivalent per 1974–75 worker with same employer as a proportion of the wage (5)
Textiles, clothing and footwear					
1974–75	0	133.5	100	0	0
1977–78	31	118.3	58	5 977	0.75
1982–83	36	102.5	31	25 507	2.11
Transport equipment					
1974–75	0	147.3	100	0	0
1977–78	7	134.9	58	1 918	0.19
1982–83	14	121.0	31	11 866	0.67

Sources: ABS *Labour Mobility* Australia, February 1979, Cat. No. 6209.0; *Manufacturing Establishments: Summary of Operations by Industry Class* Australia, 1982–83, Cat. No. 8202.0; IAC 'Australian Trade Classified by Industry 1968–69 to 1981–82' Industries Assistance Commission Working Paper, March 1985, and data supplied to author

protecting one set of workers, and eight years later largely protect a different set, since few of the original workers have remained with their original employers.

These calculations raise the question of whether defensive industrial policy can really be about property rights for *individual* workers in their jobs. It might make more sense to think of the property rights as belonging to the union, that is, to the stock of workers currently in the industry irrespective of their job tenure.

Some insights into the relationship between industrial policy, job protection and the political process can be found in Lawrence's survey of the economic principles and political practices of industrial policy in the United States and Europe. He lists five economic principles that should be observed when developing an industrial policy: that market failure must be established; that the correct policy instrument must be chosen; that the focus should be on long-run issues; that industrial policy should not be used for employment purposes; and finally, that there should be no attempt to reverse fundamental market forces. He goes on to remark that these principles are 'often scarcely recognisable in the actual practice of industrial policy'.

There seemed to be fairly widespread support for Lawrence's principal conclusions. He suggests that 'where policies genuinely supplement market forces, they may do some good (and are unlikely to do much damage); on the other hand, policies that try to reverse (or significantly delay) market behaviour will be extremely costly, and may actually be counterproductive when viewed in terms of their own objectives'. He also concludes that, apart from the textiles industry, industrial policy in the United States has been fairly successful in dealing with declining industries in that it has slowed down the rate of adjustment but not avoided it.

In Europe industrial policy has not been so successful in dealing with declining firms. This may be because governments subsidise particular firms, which enables those who receive the benefits from industrial policy to organise easily and to exert political pressure to avoid having to adjust to changing comparative advantage.

Here is a good example of the need to understand the political process: a firm-specific policy instrument appears efficient; it is well targeted, and therefore likely to focus on the relevant group of workers. Yet in the longer term the instrument can be less efficient than a more broadly based measure because, as a result of the political process, the firm-specific measures are more difficult to remove.

Positive industrial policies

Many have called for positive industrial policies in the United States, Canada and Australia. In the United States the call seems intimately related to two issues. First, as mentioned earlier, the macroeconomic policy mixture has generated an exchange rate that has severely reduced the competitiveness of many industries. Most of the industries adversely affected seem to be those in which comparative advantage would be expected to weaken over the next ten years. The strong dollar has brought these adjustments forward in time and to some degree concentrated their effects. The trade adjustments that are occurring seem to be the natural outcome of the macroeconomic policies adopted. If there is concern, the macroeconomic policies should be changed; developing a new arm of economic policy to solve these problems is unlikely to be successful.

The second issue is the relative strength of the United States in high-technology industries. But its lead in many areas seems to be narrowing, and fears of loss of leadership, de-industrialisation and loss of general business dynamism have grown. Here there may be a stronger case for industrial policy if the gap between private and social returns can be identified and if policy can be changed so that the returns to government intervention exceed the costs. Even very careful analysis, however, fails to demonstrate the existence of a problem (Krugman, 1984b).

Of course, positive industrial policy is not necessarily about increasing the degree of government intervention in the economy. In Canada, for example, there is a vigorous debate about the benefits that would flow from a bilateral free-trade arrangement with the United States, and industrial policy there constitutes an attempt to reduce intervention in trade flows. English and McFetridge (chapter 4) describe the evolution of this debate from the very successful United States–Canada automotive pact of the 1960s through to the present. They frame the debate as one between 'engineering' comparative advantage and accepting comparative advantage as given, and their judgment is that industrial policy in Canada is increasingly being based on market signals and on leaving the choice of economic activities with the private sector. Those who stressed the need for government intervention in support of Canadian technology, management, and the exportation of processed and manufactured products appear to be losing ground. There is evidence for the validity of this judgment not only in the growth of support in Canada for the liberalisation of trade with the United States, but also in the changing Canadian attitude towards foreign investment, which is now seen in a more positive light. These trends in Canada are very similar to those in Australia, New Zealand and China.

In many ways the most interesting issue in the Canadian case is the extent of the gains and losses that would flow from a bilateral free-trade arrangement. The estimated 10 per cent of GDP attributed to Harris and Cox (1984) seemed very high to a number of participants, but there was not enough time to discuss the issue. Nor was there time to canvas the trade-diversion aspects of such a policy, which may be very important for other members of the Pacific Basin area.

Canada also provides an example of the difficulties associated with an industrial policy based on picking winners. Successive oil-price crises led to an increased emphasis on the production and processing of natural resources and the pursuit of megaprojects, but at today's energy prices these projects appear to be mistaken.

Similar difficulties associated with picking winners could be perceived in the paper on the petrochemicals industry by Ai Tee Koh (chapter 12) and the ensuing general discussion. Towards the end of her essay Koh discusses the short history of the petrochemicals industry in Singapore. Singapore has been attempting to move out of labour-intensive activities towards more capital-and-technology-intensive activities, and, Koh claims, 'the petrochemicals industry, with its characteristics of scale economies, high capital investment, dependence on sophisticated technology and low labour intensity, appears to fit this criterion'. Most contributors to the discussion were pessimistic about the prospects for the petrochemicals industry in oil-importing, less developed countries, and particularly so with regard to the Singapore petrochemicals complex. As one person remarked, if Japan cannot succeed in such a high-technology industry, other countries without feedstocks should beware.

The fact that many governments do not pursue a well-articulated industrial policy does not mean that a policy does not exist. In chapter 10 White introduces the notion of a de facto industrial policy, taking the United States motor vehicle industry as an example. He discusses the rapid turnaround of that industry over the 1970s, from relative prosperity to depression as Japanese imports increased dramatically and the government responded with import-restraint programs and the Chrysler bailout, and then back to a comparatively prosperous phase. White is very critical of the policy initiatives. He documents the consumer costs, comments adversely on the voluntary export restraints that allowed Japanese car producers to capture the rents from the restriction of trade, and is concerned about the precedents set by the Chrysler bailout. It is clear that there have been costs associated with the intervention by the United States government but, by comparison with other countries such as Australia, the United States government has so far contained those costs well below what might have been expected. In Australia the response to increased imports during the early 1970s was to impose import quotas, which not only froze the import share of the domestic automobile market at 1974–75 levels but has also been associated with an increase in the nominal tariff from around 35 per cent in 1974 to an estimated tariff equivalent of the import quotas of about 85–90 per cent during 1983–84.

It is in the developing countries, however, that positive industrial policies have been important, and are more likely to be important in the near future. One of the most spectacular examples of what can be achieved from international trade is the rate of economic growth in Taiwan, described in chapter 6 by Kuo-shu and Ching-ing Hou Liang. Taiwan's industrial policy was inward-looking during the 1950s, but after 1961 the emphasis changed to an outward-looking, export-oriented industrialisation program. The transformation of the economy that occurred was extraordinary. In the Liangs' words,

> The compound annual rate of growth in the index of manufactured output, 11 per cent during the period 1955–60, accelerated to 21 per cent during the period 1965–70. ... the share of manufactured products in total exports rose from 28 per cent in 1960 to 77 per cent in 1970. ... Manufacturing employment rose by 9 per cent a year in 1965–70, while real wages increased at a rate of 6.6 per cent.

Taiwan is obviously among the most successful of countries in terms of fast economic growth. But it presents many puzzles to be understood for those interested in the relationship between industrial policy and economic growth.

First, as in Japan, the emphasis on export growth and the remarkable success that was achieved were largely accompanied by various measures to restrict the flow of imports. Although import restrictions were liberalised over the period discussed, quantitative restrictions still applied to about 40 per cent of items in 1970. There is a tendency to discuss inward-looking and outward-looking policies as though they are alternative regimes, but in many developing countries both types of policies are often pursued at the same time. The export success seems to occur despite the implicit tax imposed by the import-substitution programs that are often in place.

Second, other aspects of the marketplace in Taiwan are subject to a significant degree of government control. In his comments, Wontack Hong emphasised the range of restrictions on the financial markets. The Liangs also mention the incentives to strategic industries, low-interest loans, the right to retain earnings of up to 200 per cent of paid-in capital, the right to delay the start of a five-year income-tax holiday by up to four years, and so on.

When such directly interventionist policies are proposed for Canada, the United States and Australia, they do not find widespread support among most economists (see, for example, Krugman, 1984b). Why is that? Did Taiwan succeed despite these policies? Did the policies succeed because Taiwan has a particular economic, political and social system theat ensured their success although in most other countries they would fail? There is a lot more work to be done before these questions can be answered.

The conference was very fortunate to have a paper by Mu Yang describing and analysing China's economic development and policy since 1949. Many of the policy changes and current trends in China reflect some of the trends in other parts of Asia. There was the initial emphasis on the development of heavy industry—a tendency that is observable in other countries that are attempting to develop iron and steel industries. There is also the present emphasis towards achieving a greater degree of deregulation and a closer integration into world trade. There is a readjustment under way, an open-door policy that was supported by the commentators. In real terms the average annual growth rate of China's exports has been around 14 per cent for the past six or so years, and China will obviously create an increasing presence in international trade in the Pacific region.

Ariff and Hill in chapter 5 provide an exceptionally good survey of industrial policy and performance in the four larger countries of ASEAN—Indonesia, Malaysia, the Philippines and Thailand. The industrial policy objectives of the four countries are remarkably similar: the generation of employment, the regional dispersion of economic activity, the encouragement of indigenous small enterprises, and the favoured treatment of heavy industry and manufactured exports.

The authors conclude that the success of industrial policy in ASEAN is somewhat mixed. The increase in manufactured exports has been impressive and they believe that government policy has been central to this success. The performance of state enterprises is probably not so good, although state enterprises have been concerned primarily with non-economic objectives. The interventions in heavy industry and large resource projects also do not look promising.

In chapter 13 R.B. Suhartono traces in more detail the evolution of industrial cooperation in ASEAN. The development of policy has been slow and pragmatic, and did not begin until ten years after the establishment of ASEAN in 1967. To a large degree, and especially during that first ten years, many of the participants have seen ASEAN as a political force rather than as a natural grouping of countries for economic integration. The result has been that ASEAN has adopted 'a cautious and step-by-step approach' to economic cooperation, leaving the final goal unspecified.

From these two papers, and from the comments of Narongchai Akrasanee, the conclusion is unavoidable that a loose economic arrangement is probably in ASEAN's interests. These four countries are so diverse in income levels and so relatively small in economic terms that they have a lot to gain by fostering trade with the rest of the world and a lot to lose by significant trade diversion, although Akrasanee made the important point that the political cohesion and power of the group *require* some economic integration.

To conclude, the discussion turns to Japan. In many respects Japan holds the centre of the industrial policy stage. As Hugh Patrick remarked, 'If any nation is popularly considered to have had a successful industrial policy then certainly Japan is it'. Furthermore, Japanese economic growth has been so fast that its industrial policy may conceivably be a role model for all; its early industrial policies may provide guidance for developing countries, and its later ones may serve as models for Europe and North America.

Uekusa and Ide (chapter 8) suggest that Japanese industrial policy can be usefully divided into three periods: postwar reconstruction; the years of high economic growth—the 1960s to the early 1970s; and the period since the oil crises.

During the early years of the first period, policy focused on decreasing market concentration and assigning special priority to key industries such as coalmining, electricity and steel manufacturing. Then, in the latter half of the 1950s, the focus shifted to a new set of industries—synthetic fibres, plastics, petroleum refining, machinery, automobiles and electronics. These industries were fostered by special tax treatment, low-interest loans, and allocation of foreign exchange, and they were also protected by tariff and non-tariff barriers.

During the second period trade liberalisation was pursued, and industrial policy advocated a shift towards industries with higher value added. At the same time Japanese labour productivity grew at a rate of around 8 per cent a year.

By the third period industrial policy had changed dramatically as the emphasis shifted from 'maximum economic growth towards the broader objective of comprehensive improvement of social and economic performance'. The objectives of industrial policy had become less well defined. In addition, the increasing importance of Japanese industries in international trade was creating policy tensions abroad, and this, combined with the trade and capital-market liberalisation that had occurred at home, had weakened the ability of the Japanese government to implement policy.

Japan's industrial policy during this third period does not sound all that different from industrial policy in Europe; it is increasingly being directed towards declining industries, structural adjustment, the control of pollution, and other social objectives. As one commentator suggested, by far the largest share of government resources and consumer costs are allocated defensively to ameliorate income losses and to buy votes: 'This policy is certainly not growth-inducive, technology-enticing, efficiency-orientated, or even helpful of structural adjustment.'

The discussion of Japanese industrial policy at the conference was wide-ranging, and the following views seemed to emerge.

It was clear that Japanese industrial policy had changed a great deal over the years, and that the growth emphasis, in terms of directly encouraging 'winners', had declined. Increasingly, Japan's industrial policy seems to be converging with the policies of other advanced industrial countries, particularly in Europe, as income support for particular groups—farmers and small businessmen—and intervention to reduce the social costs imposed by declining industries are becoming more important.

In addition, most participants were unwilling to attribute a large proportion of Japan's economic growth to industrial policy. Instead, many discussants emphasised economic competition within Japan, the role of the private sector and the high savings ratio. It was clear, though, that these were very much ad hoc judgments, as there was no systematic discussion or consensus about the nature of the growth process in Japan.

Although there was agreement that industrial policy was *not* the key to Japanese economic growth, it did not seem possible with the available evidence to go much further than this. In terms of the frameworks constructed by Okuno and Suzumura (chapter 2) and Caves (chapter 3), Japanese industrial policy was not about clearly identified externalities. Does it follow then, as is suggested by the theoretical papers, that Japan's industrial policy actually reduced the growth rate? No one seemed to know, although many participants thought that the rapid postwar reconstruction of Japan's economy would not have been possible without so much government intervention.

Quite a few of the Japanese participants were sceptical about the degree of independent influence that many non-Japanese writers had attributed to the Ministry for International Trade and Industry. The Japanese participants emphasised that the ministry was only part of the process and that, with Japanese firms controlling the information flow, perhaps those being regulated had to some degree captured the regulators. Some of the discussion here was very reminiscent of the Chicago view of regulatory agencies.

Most discussants also felt that the power of industrial policy to enhance growth, or at least not to inhibit growth unduly, is greater when nations are followers. When per capita income levels are relatively low the problem is to pick the direction in which the economy will evolve within a fairly well known history and set of markets and technology, but once a country approaches the frontiers the process of picking winners becomes more difficult. It seemed to follow from this view that in the future Japan's industrial policy will be seen to be less successful than it was in the past.

Finally it was noted that, whether industrial policy was growth-enhancing or not, Japan's economic history certainly contained a number of clear failures. Special mention was made of the difficulties experienced in facilitating structural change in the textile industry.

CONCLUDING REMARKS

The advantage of a conference that includes so many countries covering a wide spectrum of economic development is that it leads to discussion of much larger questions than is the usual fare. These conferences tend to bring home clearly the role of history and the importance of different political and social systems. What then has been learnt?

First, it is striking to see how many developing countries seem to see industrial policy, that is, selective measures to advantage one industry over another, or just measures to encourage manufacturing in general, as part of the development process. Often these measures are accompanied by protection of the home market, as in the early history of industrial policy in Japan, Australia, New Zealand and Taiwan. There seem to be strong economic and political forces generating such an outcome, forces that are not well understood or even deeply analysed. No clear understanding emerged of why protectionism is such an important part of industrial policy, even when, as in Japan and Taiwan, there is also a strong emphasis on export-led growth strategies.

Second, the interventions of industrial policy are not closely related to the externalities of economic theory. They seem to be largely justified by what Caves calls 'dubious proposals'. The typical justifications offered are that the industry generates employment, that it produces a large share of value added, and that it is a large supplier of inputs. There also more subtle variants of the 'dubious proposals'—that an industry should be encouraged because it has a high labour-productivity growth, because it is a risky venture, because it is disadvantaged by poor infrastructure, and so on. And yet, despite these 'dubious proposals', almost all countries feel the need to go down this path. Economic theory will be lacking as long as it cannot explain this important economic outcome. Why is it, if the theory is correct, that it does not have more influence on policy?

Third, to a large degree industrial policy in developing countries seems to be about anticipating where the market would have led the industrial structure in any event. It is as though the object of much industrial policy in developing countries is to bring *particular* industry developments forward in time—to change slightly the order in which industries develop in the belief that the overall growth process will thereby be accelerated. Why this should be done, and what advantages are to flow from the procedure, is not clear. Within the theoretical frameworks developed early in the conference there seems no case for such a policy. The discussions rarely emphasised a difference across industries or sectors between private and social rates of discount.

One possible explanation for bringing forward the development of particular industries may be the belief that the political forces for an industrial policy are very strong and cannot be denied. If so, the best strategy from the viewpoint of resource efficiency is to attempt to channel these social and political forces into producing an outcome as close to the unfettered-market outcome as possible: to put the point in a negative way, to design an industrial policy that does the least possible damage to efficiency, or, as Lawrence describes it, to design an industrial policy that follows the market. It is interesting to conjecture whether Japan's industrial structure would have been all that different without its industrial policy.

Fourth, if the economic theory of industrial policy as discussed in the early chapters of this book captures the essence of the process, most interventions in the name of industrial policy should retard growth and injure economic efficiency. Yet I did not detect among most commentators who study the economic development of countries a *strong* presumption that Japan's economic growth was significantly retarded by its industrial policy. Nor did there seem to be a clear assumption that Taiwan dissipated a significant fraction of its growth opportunities by government intervention. Rather, my reading of the papers and the discussions suggests that most participants thought the industrial policies of Japan and Taiwan contributed positively to their growth. That said, it was also clear that most participants were anxious to suggest that the contribution of industrial policy to economic growth had been exaggerated by many earlier writers.

The proposition that so many market interventions did not reduce growth in Japan and Taiwan inevitably generates a tension with economic theory. As Paul Krugman commented at one stage, if the conceptual framework is correct then quite clearly Japan and Taiwan succeeded *despite* rather than because of their industrial policies. For this conference, and for all those interested in industrial policy, nothing is more important than resolving this tension. Is it true that the industrial policies of Japan and Taiwan did not reduce their growth rates? As was to be expected little progress was made. What is needed is more aggressive empirical research that attempts to document the outcomes of particular policies.

Fifth, although on the one hand the industrial policies and on the other hand the high rates of economic growth of Japan, Taiwan and Singapore were there for all to see, there was no general support for adopting similar or more interventionist policies in the developed countries. Indeed, the emphasis in most of the papers was on the opposite strategy (English and McFetridge, Lawrence, Lloyd, White). It was generally believed that industrial policy in the developed economies should be directed towards less regulation and less direct government intervention. There was no generally shared belief among the participants that the United States could do better by emulating Japan's industrial policy.[1]

Sixth, most participants did not support existing defensive industrial policies. Although all were sensitive to the social costs that are often associated with the rapid rundown of an industry, it was generally believed that these policies are too often ineffective—they do not protect the right people—and that the political process generally finds a great deal of difficulty in winding the programs down at an appropriate rate. As a general rule, temporary import quotas or firm subsidies are not temporary enough.

Seventh, with regard to the future, all participants were concerned with the possible rise of protectionism and the development of inward-looking growth strategies. It was a unanimous view that increasing restrictions on international trade flows would hurt all, but particularly the smaller and poorer countries of the region.

PART 1
THE CONCEPTUAL
FRAMEWORK OF INDUSTRIAL
POLICIES

2 The economic analysis of industrial policy: a conceptual framework through the Japanese experience

MASAHIRO OKUNO AND

KOTARO SUZUMURA

Recent years have witnessed an upsurge of interest in industrial policy in general, and Japanese industrial policy in particular. There seem to be at least two distinct reasons for this phenomenon. On the one hand, the recent decline in the rate of productivity increase in the advanced market economies has motivated some people to be concerned about industrial policy, and particularly about policy interventions in the supply side of the economy. On the other hand, the prima facie success of Japan's industrial policy in promoting postwar recovery and the ensuing rapid economic growth has served for some people as a sure proof of the efficacy of industrial policy as a model of development strategy.

Partly as a reflection of these different perceptions, one person's definition of industrial policy is often quite different from another's, so that Hindley's (1984:277) sweeping criticism is not altogether unfounded: '[T]he term "industrial policy" has an entirely spurious sound of precision. Over the past ten or fifteen years, the term has become a portmanteau catchword for that broad range of governmental actions which directly affect the structure of production in an economy.' With this state of the art in mind, the first item of business should be to establish an analytical definition of industrial policy, and this is what the second section of this chapter attempts to do.

The second general point to note is that, unlike fiscal and monetary policies, industrial policy probably does not lend itself to the formulation of a universal theory. The relationships between government and business and the legal institutions that provide the arena where industrial policy functions differ substantially from country to country, so that a policy that makes complete sense in one country may be a mystery in a different social and legal context. The conceptual framework of this chapter has been shaped by a study of Japan's industrial policy since the second world war, and readers should keep this background in mind.[1]

Third, it should be noted that if several countries are employing industrial policies simultaneously, the strategic interactions between their policies will add an interesting dimension at the international trade level. That said, however, this chapter will be concerned exclusively with Japan's industrial policy in isolation, leaving aside the game-theoretical analysis of strategic interdependence. There is nevertheless a rather wide field to be covered.

THE DEFINITION OF INDUSTRIAL POLICY

Industrial policy is defined here as the totality of governmental policies undertaken with the object of changing the allocation of resources among industries from what it would otherwise be, or intervening in the industrial organisation of a specific industry, in order to enhance a country's economic welfare when unrestricted functioning of the competitive market mechanism is seen to fail in serving that end.[2] In other words, industrial policy is concerned with complementing the competitive market mechanism, rather than substituting for it, when its autonomous functioning is failing to maximise economic welfare.

Industrial policy, as conceptualised above, may usefully be divided into three principal categories: the development of new industries (T1); intervention in specific aspects of industrial activities in general (T2); and adjustment assistance for ailing or declining industries (T3). T1 and T3 are self-explanatory; T2 includes such policies as extracting foreign monopoly rent (T2a), reorganising or modernising an existing industry (T2b), and regulating the degree of competitiveness within an industry by improving competitiveness or regulating 'excessive competition' (T2c).

On the other hand, a specific instrument of industrial policy may be classified by two criteria: whether it is non-discriminatory (C1); and whether it is pecuniary or regulatory (C2). Discriminatory measures are those that can, at least potentially, provide favourable treatment for a particular firm or group of firms within an industry, while non-discriminatory measures are those that apply to all firms within an industry. Some policy measures provide pecuniary incentives, such as direct subsidies and grants, various special tax treatments and government-assisted loans, and tariffs and quotas; other measures, such as governmental licensing, prohibition and approval of cartelisation, operate through legal restrictions and/or administrative guidance. Needless to say, few specific measures fall into only one of these categories. Patenting for an invention, for example, is non-discriminatory viewed as a system, but a single patent is discriminatory taken in isolation. Patenting is also a regulatory measure, but it provides pecuniary incentives as well. Nevertheless, these criteria can be useful in answering the questions posed below.[3]

The economic analysis of industrial policy, as conceptualised here, has three parts:

1   to identify the conditions that lead to market failures and necessitate the implementation of industrial policies in the T-categories;

2   to examine and rank the appropriateness of the various policy measures, in terms of achieving the objectives of each category of industrial policy; and

3   to weigh the welfare cost of market failures (which underlie the need for

industrial policy) against the welfare cost of industrial policy per se and its after-effects, in order to judge whether the net effect of adopting industrial policy is favourable from the viewpoint of economic welfare.

Before further discussion, several points should be clarified. First, the present definition of industrial policy—that it is concerned with the enhancement of economic welfare in the presence of market failures—is rather restrictive. This is because the purpose is to frame the discussion of industrial policy within the standard theory of welfare economics and applied microeconomics, the intended merit being the transparency and communicability of the resulting analysis of industrial policy. On the other hand, this approach excludes industrial policies designed to pursue 'non-economic' objectives (for example, self-sufficiency for reasons of national security). Also excluded are several policies that are effective in enhancing economic welfare as long as there is no underlying market failure; to cite just one example, a policy of maximum tariffs, which would enhance one country's economic welfare at the expense of another's, is not included. The extent of the resulting lacuna in our treatment is uncertain, but sufficiently interesting topics remain within the scope of this chapter.[4] Furthermore, the policies covered by our definition are widely acceptable and theoretically justifiable, whereas other policies are more difficult to rationalise.

Second, the stage of economic development of a country, or of a particular industry, should be considered in judging whether the implementation of a category of industrial policy or a specific policy measure is legitimate and justifiable. Conceptually, three stages of development may be distinguished: infancy (S1), maturity (S2), and decline (S3). An industrial policy that may well be quite legitimate when a country (or an industry) is in the infant stage may become hardly justifiable when the country (or industry) reaches maturity. The basic contention here is that during the mature stage the guiding principle of industrial policy should be to liberate private incentives from the bureaucratic, regulatory and protective measures adopted (presumably with good reason) in the infant stage, unless there are clearly identified factors leading to paralysis of the competitive market mechanism. This observation applies equally to the stage of decline. It follows that an industrial policy of the type T1 is naturally associated with the S1 stage of development, and T3 with S3. Whether policy types T2a–T2c are naturally associated with S2 is more debatable. Indeed, such an association, if pursued too mechanistically, might become a straightjacket that would deprive the analysis of empirical relevance. Nevertheless, if carefully applied it could be of value.

Third, the leverage a government may have with which to pursue an industrial policy changes over time, partly reflecting the level of economic development. Several mandatory control measures that are within a government's discretion in a premature market economy become unavailable in a developed economy in the international context.[5] Thus the leeway in assigning policy measures to each (admissible) category of industrial policy may in fact be quite narrowly circumscribed.

Fourth, attention should be paid to the political costs and after-effects of an industrial policy. It often happens that industrial protection, once introduced, is hard to abolish. Especially in the case of public assistance towards ailing and declining industries, therefore, protection may simply prolong an adjustment process that is unavoidable anyway. Furthermore, to favour one industry by giving it protection is to discriminate against others, so that there should be a crystal-clear justification for a protectionist policy in terms of economic welfare. If a decision to protect one industry at the cost of disadvantaging others is made in accordance with the relative strengths of the political groups behind the respective industries, the cost of such protection would be quite high because of the equity question involved. In addition, the fact should not be glossed over that even within a protected industry an equity issue exists: more often than not, protection works in favour of larger companies within the industry, giving an impetus towards further concentration.[6] If this is the case, the welfare cost of having a less competitive market organisation should also be taken into account.

It is well beyond the scope of this one chapter to present a fully developed analysis of industrial policy, covering all the relevant topics, along the lines described above. The purpose here, therefore, is to summarise some of our findings in order to illustrate the nature of the analysis we are seeking to develop. The following discussion covers the development of a new industry, the extraction of foreign monopoly rent, and the regulation of 'excessive competition' within an industry.[7]

THE DEVELOPMENT OF A NEW INDUSTRY

The most typical category of industrial policy is probably the development and promotion of a new industry. The standard theory of international trade policy describes this as infant-industry protection.

An infant industry, by definition, is an industry that currently cannot survive in free-trade conditions without protection, but will acquire a competitive edge against foreign competitors by accumulating production experience ('learning by doing') and/or employing economies of scale if it is temporarily protected during the initial stage of development. Standard theory holds that the protection of such an infant industry can be justified only under somewhat stringent conditions (see Corden, 1974:ch.9; Johnson, 1970; Kemp, 1960; and Negishi, 1972:ch.6).

To begin with, for the required protection to be really temporary it is necessary that the industry in question should in fact eventually become self-sustaining. Furthermore, the social benefits from the industry when it is mature should more than compensate for the social costs incurred in protecting the industry in its infancy. However, this double criterion, which is known as the Mill-Bastable test, is a necessary but not a sufficient justification for protection. If firms within the industry can appropriate the benefits of the learning process, there is, in principle, no need to protect them socially, since they can make up for their initial private losses by their future private profits.[8]

On the other hand, if the outcome of the learning process spills over to other firms, including latecomers, the firms that sustained the initial losses may be unable to compensate properly for them in the future, so that the output of the industry may be less than is socially desirable, or the industry may not even get started. In short, non-appropriability of the outcome of learning-induced technological progress and accumulation of knowledge constitutes a legitimate reason for protecting infant industries.[9]

Even when the learning process and its outcome are internal to firms, so that they can directly control the process and exclusively appropriate the benefits of it, there is still a clear case for protecting infant industry provided that the country in question is 'large' in the jargon of international trade theory.[10] Suppose that the expansion of output by a present-day infant industry reduces the international relative price of its product in the future. Then, even if the firms' private calculus (after taking into account the appropriable benefits from learning-by-doing) went into the red, the falling international price would increase the consumer surplus, which might well cancel out the social costs of covering the firms' initial deficits. If this is in fact the case, protecting a present-day infant industry may yield a higher overall level of economic welfare.

Besides these well-known reasons for protecting infant industries, there are several other justifications for promoting the development of a new industry. Two of these are discussed below: Marshallian externalities,[11] and scale economies and information.[12]

Marshallian externalities

It is argued above that there is a case for protection when the outcome of learning is external to the firm (that is, non-appropriable). Consider, in contrast, a case where the process of learning is external to the firm. Unlike the internal process of learning (on-the-job training), where the outcome depends on the productive activities of the firm itself, the external process of learning (Marshallian externalities) is such that the outcome depends on the output of the industry as a whole, the effect of an individual firm's output being reckoned as negligible. In other words, a firm operating in an industry governed by Marshallian external economies (or diseconomies) experiences an external downward (or upward) shift in its average cost curve when the output of the industry expands.[13]

To illustrate how the presence of Marshallian externalities allows the introduction of industrial policy, consider a country producing two goods, X and Y, using a single factor of production, say labour. Assume that X (or Y) is characterised by Marshallian external economies (or diseconomies), whereas an individual firm's production function is subject to constant returns to scale. Let $A(X)$ and $B(Y)$ denote, respectively, the unit costs (in terms of labour) of producing X and Y. By assumption, $A'(X) < 0$ and $B'(Y) > 0$ are obtained.

To simplify matters further, assume that the elasticities

$$a(X) = A'(X)X/A(X), \quad b(Y) = B'(Y)Y/B(Y) \tag{1}$$

are constant (say a and b), and that they satisfy $-1 < a < 0$ and $b > 0$. If L denotes the total available labour force, the production possibility frontier (PPF) is given by the locus of (X, Y) satisfying

$$A(X)X + B(Y)Y = L \tag{2}$$

It is easily verified that the shape of PPF, thus defined, is as shown in Figure 2.1. Note also that the social rate of transformation (SRT) and the private rate of transformation (PRT) at (X, Y) are given, respectively, by

$$SRT(X, Y) = (1 + a) \, A(X)/(1 + b) \, B(Y) \tag{3}$$

and

$$PRT(X, Y) = A(X)/B(Y) \tag{4}$$

so that we obtain

$$PRT(X, Y) = c.SRT(X, Y), \text{ with } c = \frac{1 + b}{1 + a} > 1 \tag{5}$$

Note, finally, that the production of X increases (or decreases) with a decrease (or increase) in the production of X if $PRT(X, Y) < p$ (or $PRT(X, Y) > p$) holds true, where p denotes the relative price of X in terms of Y.

The small-country case

Suppose, first, that this hypothetical country is small and is facing an international relative price p. There are three long-run equilibria in this economy, namely A^*, B^* and C^* in Figure 2.1, of which A^* and C^* are stable whereas B^* is unstable. Once A^* is somehow established, therefore, there is no private incentive to move towards C^*, which is in fact much better than A^* in terms of economic welfare.[14] To realise C^*, however, an industrial policy may be applied in such a way as to induce the production of X to rise above X_{B^*}. Once this critical point is surpassed, private incentives may be relied upon to expand the production of X up to X_{C^*}.

If, as shown in Figure 2.2, the autarchic equilibrium output of X, namely X_{F^*}, is large enough, then the above objective may be met by a temporary prohibition on imports of X. This policy measure may be found particularly attractive because it enables the government to avoid an otherwise inescapable budgetary outlay. Note, however, that the success of this scenario hinges on

Figure 2.1 Production possibility frontier: small-country case

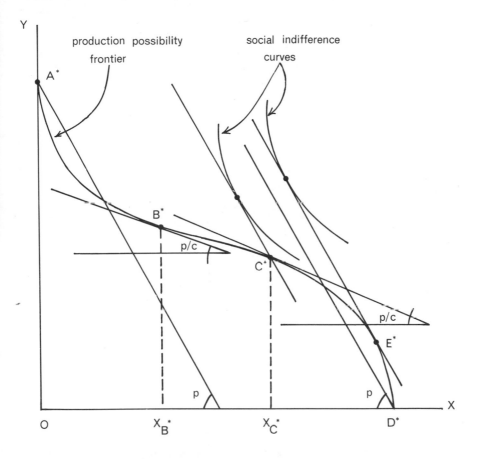

the existence of a large domestic demand for X, since otherwise domestic producers would be unable to survive after trade liberalisation. This proviso seems particularly relevant for developing countries.

The large-country case

In the case of a large country, it is assumed for the sake of simplicity that there are two identical countries with homothetic social indifference curves. Figure 2.3 shows the world production possibility frontier (WPPF), of which the dotted part may be unrealisable by private incentives. Since the two countries have identical and homothetic preferences, they can be aggregated to form the world indifference curves. The term E^* denotes the world equilibrium, where $PRT(X_{E^*}, Y_{E^*})$ coincides with the marginal rate of substitution in consumption.

Figure 2.2   Autarchy equilibrium

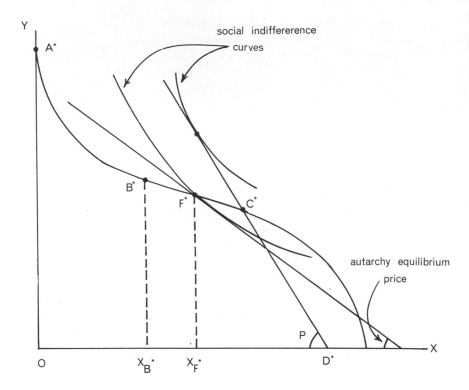

At E*, the first country (C1) specialises in the production of X and the second country (C2) in the production of Y. As a result, the budget line of C1 lies above that of C2, so that C1 enjoys higher economic welfare than C2 does. Since the two countries are identical in every respect, there is no intrinsic reason why C1, and not C2, should enjoy higher economic welfare. One factor that may make the difference is the existence of an industrial policy in one country that has the effect of promoting an industry with economies of scale in the form of Marshallian external economies. If such a policy is pursued by one country in advance of others, the alert country with the aggressive policy stance may appropriate the benefits of international trade.

According to the above analysis, Marshallian externalities will provide a justification for protecting infant industry. But it remains to be shown exactly what economic factors or combination of factors will generate Marshallian externalities. The mere knowledge that the presence of Marshallian externalities constitutes a rationale for industrial policy does not help in designing the policy itself. The following section describes one possible economic mechanism that creates Marshallian externalities.

Figure 2.3   Production possibility frontier: large-country case

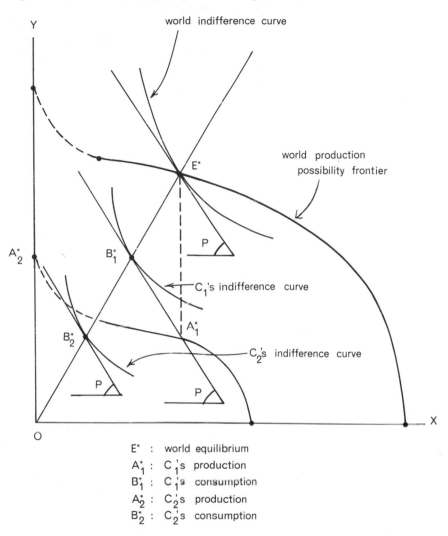

E* : world equilibrium
A_1^* : C_1's production
B_1^* : C_1's consumption
A_2^* : C_2's production
B_2^* : C_2's consumption

Scale economies and information

One of the alleged virtues of perfectly competitive markets is that prices convey all the information needed by all individual agents to formulate their strategies. By contrast, in oligopolistically competitive markets the informational content of prevailing prices falls far short of what oligopolistic agents need to determine their most effective strategies: information about the price elasticities of market demand, the strategies adopted by other agents, and the potentialities for growth of the markets, to cite only a few salient factors, are needed as well. Furthermore, the difficulties, in terms of both cost and accuracy, of collecting, processing and using this information will be compounded if there are other industries that are related (as output users or input suppliers) to the industry in question. Such a task would almost certainly be much beyond the capability of a single firm. This simple fact, coupled with the scale economies at the firm level that constitute the underlying reason for oligopolisation in the first place, provides another reason why industrial policy is needed to promote an industry characterised by economies of scale at the firm level.

Consider, for example, an oligopolistic industry that supplies various industries with inputs. The demand for its products comes from upstream industries, the properties of which are determined by such factors as the demand and supply characteristics of competing industries. Obtaining information about these factors, which can hardly be conveyed by prices, requires substantial economic resources and not many firms, acting with only private incentives, would be motivated to collect this information for themselves. On the other hand, the extent to which each firm utilises the potential merit of scale economies is constrained by the size of demand: the division of labour is limited by the extent of the market, as Adam Smith has put it.[15]

Suppose, now, that the output of this industry somehow expands. The resulting price reduction, which is made possible by scale economies, would make this intermediate product more attractive than competing inputs and improve the cost position of the upstream industries, thus enlarging the derived demand for the product. This induced expansion of the derived demand would generate a further decline in the price, thereby bringing about a further expansion of the derived demand. If the firm can only foresee this positive-spiral effect correctly, it will be able to expand its output and activate the spiral. It is precisely the informational problem explained above that prevents firms from expanding their output voluntarily, and reaping the fruits from it.

In such a situation, industrial policy can improve economic welfare. If the government plays a role in providing an opportunity for interrelated firms to communicate information so as to form a more accurate prediction about potential markets, that may well help to activate the positive spiral.[16]

Some qualifying and clarifying comments should be made at this point. First, by its very definition an infant industry should be able to mature into self-sustaining adulthood in an internationally competitive environment and repay the social costs of protection within a reasonable time. The choice of industry to be protected on the basis of the infant-industry argument should be carefully made with this prerequisite in mind.

Second, the choice of industrial policy measures is often affected in reality by government budget considerations. More often than not, tariffs and non-tariff barriers to trade are invoked to protect domestic industries from international competition, even if a production subsidy would be the first-best policy measure. This is most likely because a production subsidy requires additional government revenue to support itself, whereas tariffs and non-tariff barriers do not. In view of the distortions that would be created by having to raise this extra tax revenue, the inclination towards tariff and non-tariff measures might even be economically justifiable. In any event, it is important to rank possible policy measures, as there are usually many alternatives that are both possible and effective.

Third, industrial policy in general and development promotion policy in particular often raise the delicate issue of distributional equity. As a concrete example, consider the development promotion policy to capture Marshallian externalities that was discussed earlier. In the small-country case, whatever policy measure is used, a transfer of income from consumers or taxpayers to producers on the one hand, and from the present to the future generation on the other, is inevitably involved. In the large-country case, the serious equity issue involved is that between countries. Whichever country is moving ahead of the other to secure an industry with Marshallian external economies will enjoy a higher level of welfare. Development promotion policy in such a situation might therefore spark off future trade conflicts.

Fourth, it is important to note that, unlike the situation in a world of perfect competition and constant returns to scale, where import protection can never serve to promote exports, import protection does promote exports in a world of oligopolistic interaction and economies of scale, as Krugman (1984b) has forcefully shown. The present analysis of import protection should be understood with this important qualification in mind.

THE EXTRACTION OF FOREIGN MONOPOLY RENT[17]

Consider a commodity whose market in a country is monopolised by a foreign firm. If a home firm somehow succeeds in establishing a duopoly position vis-à-vis the foreign firm, three important changes will be introduced.[18] First, the price of the commodity will fall, which will increase the consumer surplus in the home country. Second, the profit earned by the home firm will add to the home country's economic welfare. Third, the profit earned by the foreign firm will be smaller than the previous profit under monopoly. In short, by establishing a home firm with a competitive edge against the foreign firm, a country can extract part of the foreign monopoly rent, thus enhancing domestic economic welfare.

Needless to say, a foreign monopoly would not just sit and wait in such a situation: it would try to prevent the entrance of the home firm, unless giving tacit approval somehow became more profitable than preventing entry. This consideration naturally suggests a possible role for industrial policy: the promotion of a home firm as a countervailing force against a foreign monopoly.[19]

Consider a homogeneous-output Cournot duopoly model consisting of a foreign firm f and a home firm h. Let x_f and x_h denote, respectively, the output of the foreign firm and that of the home firm. Let $F(x)$ be the inverse demand function for the commodity in question, and let $C_f(x_f)$ (or $C_h(x_h)$)

denote the foreign firm's (or home firm's) cost function. The profit function of the foreign firm, $\pi_f(x_f, x_h)$, and that of the home firm, $\pi_h(x_f, x_h)$, may then be written as follows:

$$\pi_f(x_f, x_h) = F(x_f + x_h)x_f - C_f(x_f) \tag{6}$$

$$\pi_h(x_f, x_h) = F(x_f + x_h)x_h - C_h(x_h) \tag{7}$$

Throughout this section it is assumed that $F'(x) < 0$, $C_f'(x_f) > 0$, $C_f''(x_f) > 0$, $C_h'(x_h) > 0$ and $C_h''(x_h) > 0$ hold true.

Suppose each firm expects that the other firm will not change its output in response to the change in its own output. Under this Cournot-model hypothesis, the reaction functions $R_f(x_h)$ and $R_h(x_f)$ may be defined, respectively, by

$$\frac{\partial}{\partial x_f} \pi_f(R_f(x_h), x_h) = 0 \tag{8}$$

and

$$\frac{\partial}{\partial x_h} \pi_h(x_f, R_h(x_f)) = 0 \tag{9}$$

Figure 2.4 depicts these reaction functions and a Cournot-Nash equilibrium E^0 in this market, the latter being determined by the intersection between $x_f = R_f(x_h)$ and $x_h = R_h(x_f)$. Throughout this section it is assumed that $x_h = R_h(x_f)$, as well as $x_f = R_f(x_h)$, slopes downward, with the absolute value of its slope being less than one, which guarantees the stability of E^0. The two upward curves shown in Figure 2.4 are the home firm's iso-profit curves, the lower one being associated with a higher profit level.

If the home government introduces a production subsidy at a rate s, the home firm's profit function changes to

$$\pi_h^s(x_f, x_h) = F(x_f + x_h)x_h - C_h(x_h) + sx_h \tag{10}$$

from which is obtained a modified reaction function $x_h = R_h^s(x_f)$:

$$\frac{\partial}{\partial x_h} \pi_h^s(x_f, R_h^s(x_f)) = 0 \tag{11}$$

It is easy to see that $x_h = R_h^s(x_f)$ lies uniformly to the right of $x_h = R_h(x_f)$, like the dotted line in Figure 2.4. The introduction of a production subsidy therefore shifts the Cournot-Nash equilibrium from E^0 to E^s. It then follows from the stipulated assumptions that:

1 the home firm's (or foreign firm's) output increases (or decreases);

2 the aggregate output increases, so that the equilibrium price decreases;

Figure 2.4 Cournot-Nash equilibrium

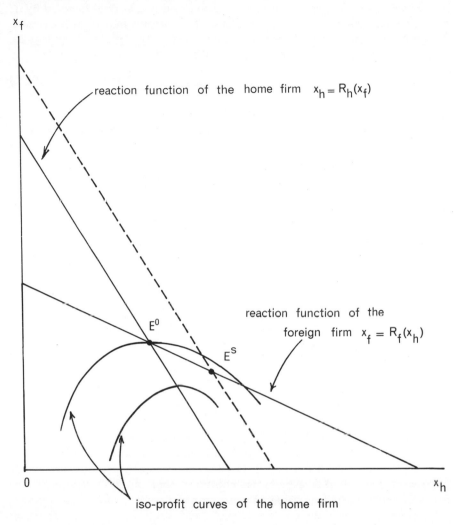

3 the home country's economic welfare increases unambiguously as long as home production does not exceed home consumption.[20]

The first and second of these conclusions are obviously valid. To verify the third, note that the home country's economic welfare (W_h) consists of consumer surplus and social profit (that is, private profit minus the social cost of protection). Let the variables representing the no-subsidy equilibrium E^0 (or the cum-subsidy equilibrium E^s) be indexed by a superscript 0 (or s), and let $\Delta x_f = x_f^s - x_f^0$, $\Delta x_h = x_h^s - x_h^0$, and $\Delta p = p^s - p^0 = F(x_f^s + x_h^s) - F(x_f^0 + x_h^0)$.

Note that by virtue of conclusions 1 and 2, $\Delta x_f < 0 < \Delta x_h$ and $\Delta p < 0$ hold true. If s is small enough, and if the home consumption at E^0 is denoted by d_h^0, it is easily ascertained that a change in consumer surplus may be approximated by $-d_h^0 \cdot \Delta p$, and the change in social profit by $\{p^0 - C_h'(x_h^0)\} \cdot \Delta x_h + x_h^0 \cdot \Delta p$. This gives

$$\Delta w_h = (x_h^0 - d_h^0) \cdot \Delta p + \{p^0 - C_h'(x_h^0)\} \cdot \Delta x_h \tag{12}$$

from which the third conclusion follows immediately.

Of the many criticisms of these arguments, the two most important are the following. First, when an industry produces differentiated products and rival firms compete in terms of prices rather than quantities, it is taxation on the domestic firm that will increase the country's economic welfare. Second, if entry is free there will be no monopoly rent, and the whole argument breaks down. And if entry is not free the argument may still break down, even when the strategic reasons for deterring entry are explicitly introduced.

In order to answer these objections, strategic entry deterrence is introduced into the model above. Note that the movement from E^0 to E^s, which is induced by the home government's subsidisation policy, is beneficial to the home country but detrimental to the foreign firm, because the foreign firm's profit then declines. What can the foreign firm do to prevent this?

Naive price limitation—setting prices strategically low so as to discourage potential entrants by the gloomy prospect of low profitability—would not work, because once a potential entrant dared to come in despite the price limitations, the domestic firm's best response would be to abandon price limitation and share the market with the new entrant at the higher price. The potential entrant would behave in full awareness of this *ex post* rational adjustment by the incumbent firm, so that price limitation would not in fact limit entry.

The gist of this argument is that price is a variable that may be changed at will if doing so turns out to be *ex post* rational. An effective entry-preventing strategy should be such that, once adopted, it becomes a commitment by the incumbent firm, so that a potential entrant cannot but take the incumbent firm's intention at its face value. An example of such a *credible commitment* by the incumbent firm is the construction of fixed-capital equipment. Once constructed, such equipment constitutes sunk costs, which are irrecoverable.

To analyse the entry-preventing behaviour of the foreign firm along these lines, the model must be modified to allow for the existence of fixed costs (sunk costs).

Figure 2.5 delineates a response function in the presence of fixed costs. An upward-bending curve is an iso-profit curve for the home firm *in the absence of fixed costs*, where profit equals fixed costs; in other words, it is the zero-profit curve of the home firm *in the presence of fixed costs*. If the foreign firm produces more than x_F^I, it is to the home firm's advantage to stay out of the market, so that the reaction function of the home firm in the presence of fixed costs becomes the kinked curve shown in Figure 2.5.

Figure 2.5   Reaction function in the presence of fixed cost

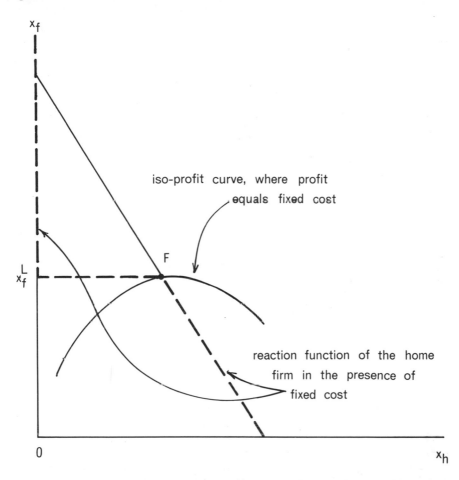

Figure 2.6 is obtained by applying the same consideration to the foreign firm. The figure delineates the entry-preventing behaviour of a foreign firm, where E^S is a Stackelberg equilibrium with the foreign firm (or the home firm) being the leader (for follower), and π_f^S (or π_f^L) represents an iso-profit curve for the foreign firm corresponding to E^S (or corresponding to the entry-preventing output x_f^L). Since π_f^L is higher in this case than π_f^S, the foreign firm will prevent the home firm's entry by committing itself to the fixed-capital equipment corresponding to x_f^L instead of allowing the home firm to enter and becoming a Stackelberg leader.

In a situation like this, the home government may help the home firm to enter this market by providing, for example, a capital subsidy on fixed costs. The home firm's private fixed costs will thus be curtailed, so that the foreign firm's output where the home firm's response function becomes kinked (x_f^L)

Figure 2.6   Entry-prevention by the foreign firm

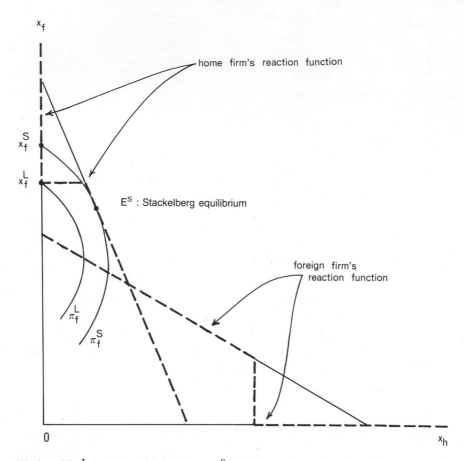

will rise. If x_f^L becomes higher than x_f^S, the home firm may be able to enter the market, because it is now to the foreign firm's advantage to live with a Stackelberg equilibrium E^S, rather than preventing the home firm's entry by committing itself to a productive capacity x_f^L.

Will this subsidisation policy be justifiable in terms of economic welfare? Since the social profit of the home country is positive at E^S, the focus must be on the effect on the level of consumer surplus. It is clear, then, that the home country's economic welfare will be improved only if the market supply after the home firm's entry is not less than it was before the home firm's entry. To the extent that this condition is likely to be satisfied, industrial policy may contribute to the enhancement of economic welfare by encouraging the entry of the home firm as a counterbalance to foreign monopoly.

Finally, it should be noted that the above policy will improve the foreign country's consumer surplus, although it will necessarily decrease foreign monopoly rent. Therefore, the foreign country's economic welfare will not necessarily decrease. In other words, an industrial policy of this type is not necessarily harmful to the foreign country.

THE REGULATION OF 'EXCESSIVE COMPETITION'

Except possibly in the infant-industry stage, the guiding principle of industrial policy should be to make the best possible use of the competitive market mechanism by liberating private incentives from bureaucratic regulations, unless there are identifiable dysfunctions of the market mechanism. Throughout the postwar period, one of the alleged dysfunctions of Japan's market mechanism, which has been invoked in rationalising intervention in the organisation of several industries, has been 'excessive competition'.

To those accustomed to the standard theory of welfare economics and industrial organisation, the very term 'excessive competition' sounds rather dubious. As Baumol (1982:2) has put it,

> ... the standard analysis leaves us with the impression that there is a rough continuum, in terms of desirability of industry performance, ranging from unregulated pure monopoly as the pessimal arrangement to perfect competition as the ideal, with relative efficiency in resource allocation increasing monotonically as the number of firms expands.

Reflecting this indoctrination, there is 'a widespread belief that increasing competition will increase welfare' (Stiglitz, 1981:184). How on earth can competition ever be 'excessive'?

This question becomes at least partly answerable if it is rephrased as follows. Consider an imperfectly competitive industry where the home firms are earning above-normal profits. If 'a widespread belief' to the effect that 'relative efficiency in resource allocation [increases] monotonically as the number of firms expands' is correct, the profit-induced entry of new firms will always improve welfare. Examining whether this conjecture is valid may verify whether competition can ever be 'excessive'.

With this purpose a homogeneous-output Cournot oligopoly model with free entry has been analysed. Left to themselves, potential competitors will enter the industry until the profits of the marginal firm are zero. Let the number of firms existing in this long-run equilibrium be called the 'equilibrium number of firms'. On the other hand, two concepts of the 'socially optimal number of firms' are introduced. In an industry analysis such as this, it is natural to adopt net market surplus, which consists of consumer surplus and producer surplus, as the criterion of optimality. Depending on the extent to which the government can regulate the behaviour of firms, a 'first-best' and a 'second-best' optimality may be defined. In the first-best case, the government has a powerful leverage against firms in that it can impose marginal-cost pricing; in the second-best case, the government has to accept the profit-maximising behaviour of firms as a constraint. It may be said that a number of firms are first-best optimal (or second-best optimal) if they maximise the first-best market surplus (or the second-best market surplus).

Contrary to what is suggested by the expression 'a widespread belief', the equilibrium number of firms demonstrably exceeds the first-best number of firms by as much as the latter exceeds unity; similarly, the equilibrium number of firms exceeds the second-best number of firms by as much as the latter exceeds unity. These excess entry theses, which are proved in Suzumura and Kiyono (forthcoming), seem quite robust, casting doubts on the universal validity of Stiglitz's 'widespread belief' and suggesting an economically meaningful interpretation of the term 'excessive competition'.[21]

It is sometimes claimed that what is called 'excessive competition' (in investment) in Japan is concerned not with the welfare effect of an increase in the number of firms within an industry but with the socially 'excessive' aggregate investment within an oligopolistic industry. It is also claimed that 'excessive competition' in this sense develops in industries characterised by heavy overhead-capital expenditure, homogeneous output, and oligopolistic competition.[22] Is there any reason why such 'excessive competition' should be expected to develop in an oligopolistic industry?

The best analytical way to answer this question seems to be to construct a model incorporating these three features, and to examine whether such a model generates an intrinsic tendency towards socially 'excessive' investment in fixed capital.

Such an analysis has been conducted by the authors (Suzumura and Okuno, 1985), using a two-stage model of oligopolistic competition. In the case of linear inverse demand function, the competitive level of investment in fixed capacity is demonstrably 'excessive', in the sense that it unambiguously exceeds the socially first-best level as well as the socially second-best level so long as there are no fewer than three competing firms within the industry. In the case of a constantly elastic inverse demand function, the same 'excessive investment' thesis essentially holds true so long as the number of firms within the industry exceeds a critical level determined by the elasticity of inverse demand.

Why is it that oligopolistic competition generates this tendency towards 'excessive competition' in investment? The basic reason seems to be that oligopolists can secure higher profits by committing themselves to larger capacity, with the result that they tend to invest more in productive capacity.

Even if the 'first-best' and/or the 'second-best' government can in principle improve economic welfare by regulating entry and exit or by intervening in oligopolistic competition in investment, that does not necessarily justify intervention by a down-to-earth government in industrial organisation. Indeed, there are at least two reasons for assuming that intervention by the Japanese government has aggravated the competitive situation within industries.

First resorting to anticompetitive arrangements, mainly cartels, has been quite frequent in postwar Japan. Especially during the recession, the Japanese government has selectively approved cartels with the purpose of alleviating recessionary problems and rescuing firms from temporary difficulties. Banking on this relief by industrial policy, firms could take more risks and engage in sharper competition than they would otherwise voluntarily have done, just as 'motorcars are traveling faster than they otherwise would *because* they are provided with brakes' (Schumpeter, 1942:88). In short, safety measures undertaken in the name of industrial policy might have been a factor accelerating severe competition among oligopolistic firms.

A second problem arises from the criterion adopted by the government for administrative or allocative purposes in direct controls, administrative guidance, or cartelisation. More often than not, this criterion has been geared squarely to the relative share of existing productive capacity or the current market share of the incumbent firms. Reckoning on this 'share' principle in allocating, for example, import quotas or mandatory authorisation of new production facilities, each firm would try to surpass the others and secure priority in the future, thus creating sharper competition than would otherwise be the case.

A DISCLAIMER

To conclude this chapter, the authors would like to record a disclaimer in view of the sharp warning by Dixit (1984:15):

Vested interests want protection, and relaxation of antitrust activity, for their own selfish reasons. They will be eager to seize upon any theoretical arguments that advance such policies in the general interest. Distortion and misuse of the arguments is likely, and may result in the emergence of policies that cause aggregate welfare loss while providing private gains to powerful special groups.

This chapter has shown in several contexts that, from the point of view of economic welfare, industrial policy is justified, at least from the single-country perspective. The purpose of doing this is emphatically not to help vested interests find convenient support for their claims but to identify arenas for careful and serious future analysis. Our hope is that this chapter will contribute to a more balanced understanding of what industrial policy is about, of its potential for improving economic welfare, and of its possible dangers in view of its often inequitable nature.

3 Industrial policy and trade policy: a framework

RICHARD E. CAVES

Industrial policy has emerged as a category of economic policy only in recent years. By my reading, it evolved during the postwar recovery efforts of the continental Western European countries, which were the first to take up the idea that the market, left to its own devices, does not necessarily produce the best allocation of resources among sectors of the economy. Early suspicions about the source of difficulty centred on problems of information and coordination—whether decentralised investment decisions might fail to take into account their own pecuniary externalities and tend to over- or undershoot the allocations that could be calculated by an all-knowing coordinator. By the time this policy fashion reached Britain in the 1960s, the era of Sputnik and the vogue of science had arrived. The need for extended intervention in the economy (a 'white-hot technological revolution') was accepted, mainly on the evidence that the British economy was not doing well compared with its European competitors. The inference was drawn that an economy that was perceived to be consistently underperforming its peers needed something pervasive in the policy line—and industrial policy would fill the bill.

The turn of the United States to assume this posture came in the 1970s. It was fuelled, again, by the public perception that the economy's performance was trailing that of its international competitors, and again the box labelled 'industrial policy' was opened to receive whatever contents the political process might contribute. The recent report of the President's Commission on Industrial Competitiveness took a relatively placid and neoclassical view of the issue, but many other American observers have called for elaborate new styles of intervention in the marketplace.

If this brief caricature of history is not too inaccurate, industrial policy is clearly not a contrivance of academic thinkers. It is a category of policy measures searching for an analytical framework or, less kindly, a political slogan in search of respectability. Economists of traditional persuasion have greeted it with little enthusiasm, taking in essence the view that either it is something we have known all along or it is wrong. Yet even from that traditional stance, industrial policy poses a number of issues for analysis. Normatively, it raises the question of whether newly identified market distortions call for fresh analytical treatments. Positively, it must be asked what

42

policies will be selected by economic actors in the political sphere when they are invited to maximise their welfare by selecting something that can be labelled industrial policy.

This chapter reviews the uses of the concept of industrial policy and its relation to the more familiar conclusions about policy of the theory of international trade. Industrial policy and trade policy are in fact closely related, and popular arguments for the application of industrial policy turn out to overlap substantially the traditional arguments for intervening in international trade. Associating industrial policy with trade policy has the advantage not only of recognising this important analytical affinity but also of invoking a normative issue that has been central to trade policy and should be central to the consideration of industrial policy: when does a policy designed to attain some national objective impair the welfare of a country's trading partners, and when do they benefit?

INDUSTRIAL POLICY: THE CONCEPT, ITS USES AND ABUSES

Industrial policy is defined here as any policy designed to change the allocation of resources among sectors in a national economy. The breadth of that definition flags the problem of treating industrial policy cogently: there is so little that it leaves out.[1] Reasonable coherence can be achieved only by restricting the discussion to those policies adopted primarily to affect the activity level of some sector, and omitting those (such as corporation income tax) for which this result is incidental. Even with that restriction, the category includes everything from agricultural subsidies through competition policy to regulations on industrial pollution.

The neoclassical perspective

It will be useful to establish the relevant neoclassical core of analysis before proceeding to new issues. Market forces are expected to deliver the wrong scale of output in an industry if there exists some externality or distortion such that the marginal private and social values of the resources committed to the industry are unequal. Putting aside monopoly (and competition policy) for the moment, the relevant distortions turn on external economies or diseconomies and industry-specific distortions in input prices. External economies or diseconomies cause the marginal social value of a sector's output to differ from its marginal private value to the output setter. As will be shown, it is important whether the difference is pertinent to the nation or the world as a whole. Input-price distortions giving rise to excess supply or demand are especially relevant to the optimality of the speed of adjustment in the short run. Tax/subsidy correctives of the relevant marginal inequivalence are the 'standard fix' for both externalities and price distortions.

Political decisionmakers commonly seize upon trade policy as a readily available way of enlarging the output of an industry that has been forced to contract. If it is assumed for the moment that the industry's output is indeed suboptimal, a familiar result (for example, Johnson, 1965) shows that the use of, say, a tariff to enlarge domestic production is a second-best remedy, because it effects an undesirable contraction in domestic consumption at the same time as it accomplishes its stated goal of expanding domestic production. In this case a domestic production subsidy is the first-best solution. The same theorem, of course, applies to trade controls as correctives for non-optimal levels of domestic consumption: a tariff to discourage the consumption of 'luxury' goods raises their domestic production to undesirable levels. In this context a tariff should be used only to remedy an inequivalence between the marginal cost and the benefits of trade flows themselves. The obvious example (from the viewpoint of the single nation) is a tariff to maximise the nation's benefits from exploiting its monopoly/monopsony power in world markets.

Some dubious proposals

From this perspective, most observers have taken a negative view of the many calls for expanded industrial policy in the United States and other industrial countries (Schultze, 1983). Enthusiasts for industrial policy claim to identify many sources of non-optimal domestic production that involve no analytically cogent marginal inequivalence but rather a casual confusion between productivity in some narrow sense and the most productive use of society's scarce resources, which is the object of the marginal-equivalence policy rule. These calls for expanding selected sectors have been called 'industrial fetishism', and they include some of the following simple fallacies.

The first is that a country should expand (or protect) those industries that pay high wages or employ highly skilled labour, because the wages of skilled workers exceed those of unskilled workers. For skill-intensive industries, the question is whether the compensation differential exceeds the return to investment in human capital that should differentiate skilled from unskilled wages. Although vocational training is probably an important locus of resource misallocation in many economies, it is not obvious that the problems involved are remedied by incentives to expand the outputs of skill-intensive industries.

A variant of the preference for protecting skill-intensive sectors holds that high-wage industries should be promoted, and this is the second fallacy. The issue in this case is why the wages are high: if they are not a reward to human capital or a reflection of a temporary disequilibrium, they presumably reflect a monopoly of labour. As Krugman (1984b) points out, an industry with inflated wages may produce too small an output and may contract inefficiently in the face of increased foreign competition, but any case for policy intervention to expand the industry's output is valid not because the inflated wage rate is itself desirable but because policy can partly offset the resource misallocation that it produces.

The third fallacy is that industrial policy should favour industries with 'thick' value-added slices, that is, with value added making up a large proportion of sales. This preference seems to rest on a simple mercantilist misconception that the expansion of such an industry will create extensive employment opportunities for the nation's stock of production factors. However, the appropriate question is where the factor stock will be used, not how much is required per unit of any given industry's gross sales. Unless input markets are subject to distortions, earning $100 of national income by turning $300 of purchased inputs into $400 of salable output is just as good as earning $100 by turning $100 of inputs into $200 of outputs.

Fourth, the brightest cynosure of industrial policy has, of course, been made up of sectors that are growing rapidly or exhibit high levels of technology or research intensity. This preference in some guises represents a simple confusion, but in others it does raise substantial problems of policy. The confusion originates in the assumption that the market does not provide enough resources for fast-growing sectors. That committing resources today can capture enlarged rents in the future in a fast-growing market is, of course, exactly what entrepreneurs bet on, and there is no obvious mechanism by which they undercommit resources *ex ante*.[2] Sometimes the preference for promoting growing sectors rests on a preference for productivity growth itself, which raises the question of the origins of the productivity growth. It may be associated with the innovation process, which in turn incurs failures due to externalities and the familiar issues of access to proprietary knowledge (see the following section). But to the extent that productivity gains result from investment within the enterprise that is not subject to externalities, the fact that an industry enjoys rich opportunities for productivity growth does not itself indicate a market failure unless there is good reason for thinking that entrepreneurs underestimate the potential but the government does not.[3]

These examples could be extended, but they all make the same simple point: that sectoral preferences, unless backed by some specifically identified externality or other market failure, typically represent little more than simple mercantilist confusions.[4]

VALID PROBLEMS OF RESOURCE ALLOCATION AND INDUSTRIAL POLICY

Discussions of industrial policy have identified three types of unsatisfying performance that involve genuine problems of market failure, and may indeed call for policy correctives. One of these lies in externalities associated with research and proprietary knowledge, the second in international competition in oligopolistic markets, and the third in processes of adjustment.

Research and proprietary knowledge

A long history of discussions of property rights in industrial knowledge has clarified the problem that resides here. In general, it is expected that the producer of knowledge should be able to appropriate all the rents that are generated, if socially optimal investments are to be made in innovative activities. However, full appropriation is normally (that is, in the absence of perfect price discrimination by the owner) second-best, in that it results in the knowledge (or the output embodying it) being sold to users only at a price exceeding its marginal cost. It is widely accepted that a patent grant of limited duration is the best compromise, trading off the underprovision of innovative effort against the loss of welfare from the monopoly pricing of proprietary innovations. This optimum pertains to global welfare, in the sense that it encompasses gains to all the producers and consumers of knowledge and assumes that in general they are weighted equally. The degree to which the international patent system actually attains this global second-best is considered below.

These principles can be applied in a straightforward fashion to any policies designed to offset the underprovision of industrial knowledge from a purely national viewpoint. If each member firm of a domestic industry can protect its proprietary knowledge, either through patents or by keeping its discoveries secret, then no problem arises for national policy. Similarly, industrial policy can make no contribution if knowledge diffuses freely around the world. Domestic firms thus have an incentive to underprovide it, but so does each single country as a whole. Any one country will rationally choose to ride free on the research investments of others, and the resulting problem of resource allocation can be solved only at a global level. The opportunity for national public policy comes in the intermediate case, where the research outlays of domestic firms have externalities for other domestic firms, but lesser externalities (or none at all) for firms located abroad. Domestic innovative effort should then be promoted to the point where the marginal gain to the nation from the external benefits of innovation offsets the difference between the private benefits and costs of innovative activities.

While restrictions on trade have no direct role in promoting the best possible provision of innovative effort, they are effective (if not necessarily ideal) for promoting another sort of proprietary knowledge—that associated with learning by doing. As Krugman (1984a) points out, the existence of an activity that generates learning-curve gains may constitute a case for tariff protection (or production subsidies) to maximise national welfare. Indeed, this may be the most cogent formulation that can be given to the classic infant-industry case for the restriction of imports. If benefits from learning by doing accrue only within the company, it presumably internalises the benefit and prices its output in the short run in recognition of the gains yielded by each unit of output on day t in terms of lower production costs for all subsequent units of output. If the learning curve affects the national (but not the global) industry, individual producers set their short-run outputs without taking account of all national benefits, and policy intervention is again warranted. A tariff on competing imports may suffice, although a production subsidy is first-best. If learning is diffused internationally, of course, the activity will be underprovided globally, but the single nation does best by riding free on other producers' investments in knowledge.[5] In short, correct policy toward learning-curve effects depends on conditions of appropriability in the same way as externalities associated with research and industrial knowledge.

International oligopoly

The second new and valid problem of market failure that has been stressed in discussion of industrial policy is that of international oligopoly. Recent contributions on this subject were preceded by an extensive literature that recognised the conflict between national and global interests in competitive international markets. The focus of recent writings has shifted from the problem of national monopoly to that of oligopoly and international market rivalry. However, the older literature remains a useful background to the new developments. If a country has monopoly over an export (or monopsony over an import) that is not fully exploited by domestic suppliers (or buyers), the government has an incentive to impose a tariff as a first-best remedy. In the case of the export, a second-best solution is to monopolise the domestic industry (second-best because of the resulting distortion in domestic consumption). A tariff may be beneficial against a monopolistic supplier of imports even if the monopolist has constant long-run marginal costs, because a tariff that shrinks the domestic demand for monopolised imports can cause the monopolist to reduce his price (Katrak, 1977).[6] The best policy response to a foreign monopoly may, however, be a subsidy on imports rather than a tariff: the subsidy becomes appropriate either if the monopolist enjoys decreasing marginal cost or if the domestic-demand curve is such that the monopolist's price for imports falls by more than the unit subsidy (Brander and Spencer, 1984).

New theoretical developments in the literature address international oligopoly and strategic behaviour—chiefly situations in which a domestic producer or oligopoly group faces similar competitors in the world market. The analytical results in all these cases flow from the fact that the income of the home nation includes any profits that domestic producers earn from foreign markets, so that national income can be increased by any policy that enlarges national producers' share of world sales and profits, unless the benefits are offset by losses arising from the distortion of domestic consumption of the commodity in question.

This literature includes a number of specific models. Some of them focus on the possibility that the government can effect commitments for its national duopolist (say, through a subsidy to the firm's research and development activities) that manoeuvre the national champion into a position of Stackelberg leadership over its foreign rival (and away from a symmetrical Cournot equilibrium). If the two duopolists sell only in a third market and the government can effect a commitment that the firm itself cannot effect, the national welfare is increased by the excess of Stackelberg-leader profits over Cournot profits. The relevance of this case for policy depends, of course, on whether governments in fact enjoy any advantages that firms do not when it comes to making commitments. The modern theory of entry deterrence in fact points to a rich assortment of investment-type outlays that can yield first-mover advantages (deterring a potential competitor, in this literature; but also reducing the set of opportunities of an incumbent rival). Governments, on the other hand, lack instruments that allow them to make credible, binding policy commitments. As Harry Johnson once remarked in the context of host governments' dealings with multinational companies, a government can promise that it will not expropriate, but is cannot credibly promise that it will still be in power six months later.

The other cases of policy for international oligopoly put aside the scope for commitment and simply raise the question of whether the government can fruitfully intervene to improve the national firm's position in a Nash equilibrium. Quantity being the variable upon which duopolists react, a subsidy to the domestic firm's output causes the foreign duopolist to contract output, which raises the national duopolistic profit and thus the national welfare. However, in a duopoly with price reactions the case comes out the other way, with a tax on the domestic producer being required to cause a cutback of output by the foreign producer (Eaton and Grossman, 1984). This difference between the cases of quantity and price reaction is rather subversive for the policy relevance of these models of profit-shifting, because the mode of oligopolistic reaction is not among the readily observable attributes of a market.

In conclusion, modern model-building has identified new theoretical roles through which industrial policy can manoeuvre the domestic producer(s) into a more favourable position in an international oligopoly. The stringency of the information requirements of these cases, however, invites pessimism about their direct empirical application. Still, the proposition stands out clearly enough that governments can usefully intervene to raise national welfare by tilting the oligopoly bargain to shift rents toward the national income. An example is Japan's apparent success in reducing the market price of international technology licences by restricting the number of Japanese companies allowed to enter into negotiations with foreign licensers (Peck, 1976).

Somewhat lost from sight in this discussion is the global interest in a coordinated competition policy that forces the 'international duopoly' to sell at a price equal to marginal cost. To put it another way, the national discrepancy between marginal social and private value (profit-maximising price minus actual price) is not the same as the global discrepancy (price minus marginal cost). This problem is discussed later in this chapter.

Failures in the adjustment process

Another possible source of market failure is the process by which resources are reallocated among industries in response to international disturbances. Earlier research on this subject (for example, Mussa, 1978) suggested that, with positive costs of adjustment, rational expectations concerning future prices,

and only a single source of friction, private allocation decisions would correspond to socially ideal ones, and that public intervention to effect the reallocation of capital from declining to expanding sectors could make no positive
contribution to welfare.[7]

Neary (1982) showed, however, that this conclusion fails to hold if the
economy suffers from several sources of stickiness in the reallocation process,
such as inflexibility of wages in the short run and capital embodied in sector-
specific plant and equipment or subject to reallocation costs. The adjustment
process, then, may involve phases of 'immiserising reallocation' in which
private decisions lower real national income, because of the combination of
two sources of allocative inefficiency. Neary showed that, in order to eliminate
the difficulty, the government needs instruments with the power to control the
speeds of adjustment in both the capital market and the labour market. The
optimal general policy is likely to call for subsidisation of the movement of
capital but, if the speed of wage adjustment cannot be affected by policy, then
the optimal second-best policy will in many cases imply a reduction in the
speed of capital adjustment. This is more likely the slower the speed of
adjustment of wages and the smaller the potential for input substitution
between capital and labour. Rational expectations do not avert the need for
policy because wage rates, even if perfectly foreseen, do not reflect the social-
opportunity cost of labour.[8]

The issue of failures in the adjustment process is related to the question of
whether private information failures may impair the dynamic allocation of
resources—the old question of 'indicative planning'. Economists have recently
tended to treat this as one of the fallacious bases for industrial policy, pointing
out that it amounts to expecting the government to pick 'growth stocks' more
effectively than the private sector is able to do. Furthermore, the private sector
of an advanced industrial society expends considerable resources gathering
information in attempts to predict accurately the marginal productivity of the
resources committed to various sectors. Nonetheless, it is not possible to be
dogmatic about the general efficiency of private decisions on intersectoral
allocation, for at least two reasons. First, the public-good character of information implies that it can be privately overprovided in pursuit of speculative
returns (Hirshleifer, 1971), and that in principle pre-emptive public provision
could be superior. Second, when the addition of resources to a sector involves
entrepreneurs racing to make commitments and obtain first-mover advantages,
the movement to equilibrium can involve inefficient sequences of excess or
deficient capacity. But that possibility still leaves copious room for doubt
whether governments can forecast better, and, even if they can, whether they
are able to impose their forecasts on private investment decisions without
finding themselves running cartel operations.

THE POLITICAL ECONOMY OF INDUSTRIAL POLICY

The framework for analysing industrial policy should include the political
economy surrounding it. One reason for this is the prevalence among the

objectives advanced by the proponents of industrial policy of economic goals or criteria that have no recognisable relationship to national economic welfare, but that may be explicable in terms of non-economic preferences concerning the economy's sectoral composition. The other reason is that choices of public policy can sometimes be explained as the result of rational actors maximising their welfare through allocations determined by the political process— allocations that in general will not serve to maximise national welfare. In the case of tariffs, economists have come to accept that differences in the tariff protection levels obtained by industries seem to reflect differences in their structural access to the political process. The same proposition seems likely to hold for other instruments of industrial policy.

Models of political choice

A variety of approaches have been put forth to explain political decisionmaking economically on the basis of rational actions by individual political actors or cooperating groups. These include the familiar models of voting in national elections or geographic representation. They also include lobbying by interest groups interacting with politicians or bureaucrats.

These models of public choice have proved successful in explaining tariffs and other policy choices. They may, however, miss important bases for the industrial policies that have been chosen, especially in the United States. For instance, it is well known that industrial policy in the United States and Europe tends to support the losers rather than aid the winners among industries facing international competition. The conventional vote-maximising model of political behaviour implies that a government will enact any measure that a majority of voters perceive to provide benefits to themselves in excess of the cost to them in taxation. Such a model is consistent with helping losers if a taste for a collective good is assumed—that is, the sense that fellow citizens are being treated fairly in the light of their reasonable expectations. Equivalently, the public sector may provide last-resort insurance against economic disasters that the public views as being visited unfairly upon the victims.[9]

If the political process balances perceived equities in this fashion, several otherwise puzzling aspects of aid to losers can be explained. Why should economic disturbances emanating from imports bring political assistance when an equivalent domestic disturbance would not?[10] Why should the public readily support assistance to industries whose unionised employees command above-median incomes? A few examples may be noted of symmetrical penalties imposed on 'undeserving' winners, such as those who enjoyed capital gains from increasing energy prices. The argument here is not that this political process of balancing equities is the only concept of rational political action that is useful for explaining the orientation of United States and European industrial policy towards aiding losers; for example, Lawrence (chapter 7) points to the role of industries' sizes in determining the terms under which they are aided, and other commentators stress the role of bureaucratic preferences.

However, it can be argued that a collective sense of equitable treatment explains features of public choice that are otherwise obscure.

In the nations of Western Europe, more than in the United States, assistance to losers seems to focus mainly on the preservation of jobs, and this points to another concept that seems useful in explaining the propensity of the industrial policies of these economies to aid losers. As Houseman (1985:ch.4) suggests, a great deal of public policy can be characterised as conferring on workers limited property rights in their jobs. These rights are never unlimited in time, nor do they necessarily guarantee the complete preservation of real incomes at levels previously attained. But they do treat a person's job as an endowed asset that warrants limited compensation if it is lost or protection if it is threatened. Because neoclassical economics has generally been unsympathetic toward such a property right, it should be noted that it can be given a straightforward analytical interpretation. Assume that a person obtains certain non-marketed satisfactions that are attached to the job, the workplace, or a place of residence that is contingent upon the particular job. Then loss of the job entails not just the conventionally recognised cost of retraining and relocation but also an increase in the cost of obtaining the previous bundle of non-marketed satisfactions.[11]

Implications for industrial policy

If these elements of collective equitable treatment and job property rights do characterise the political process surrounding industrial policy, there are a number of implications for both national and international policymaking. At the national level, a policy of supporting the losers is to be expected, and expectations about any systematic policymaking aimed at identifying and backing winners must be lowered. It is implied, however, that the support for losers will be limited in time and amount; the thrust of policy intervention is to delay adjustment processes rather than to forestall them permanently. This implication matches rather well such patterns as the use of voluntary export quotas to curb the expansion of imports' share of the domestic market but not to fix it permanently. The normal turnover of employees may set a limit on the rate at which adjustments in a sector's level of activity and employment can proceed without triggering intervention to sustain workers' property rights in their jobs.[12]

That public policy preserves limited property rights in jobs and otherwise serves a collective interest in equitable treatment seems the most important implication of collective goods for explaining industrial policy, but it is not the only one. The economically specious arguments for industrial policy listed earlier may indeed constitute some claim for coherence along this line. Breton (1964) argued that middle-class voters may gain utility from the knowledge that the economy's sectoral mixture is one that provides a rich array of middle-class jobs—skilled labour, research, middle management, and other non-production activities. Such a collective preference is consistent with elec-

toral support for measures to promote or preserve high-wage, high-skill industries and those supporting substantial research activities. Thus, industrial
policy may be called upon to serve the collective interest of the middle class in
the sectoral composition of the economy.

INDUSTRIAL AND TRADE POLICIES AND INTERNATIONAL RELATIONS

It has been proposed that industrial policy can be regarded either as a conventional normative area of economic policymaking at the national level or as a
behavioural phenomenon that can be explained by the choices of national
policies made by political actors. Either way, it affects policymaking at the
national level towards both sectoral activity levels and international trade.
Most bases for industrial policy, both normative and behavioural, imply that
the first-best policy is governmental intervention by means of tax/subsidy
measures to affect sectors' levels of activity in either the short or the long run.
Affecting sectoral allocations through tariffs or subsidies on international trade
is for most purposes second-best.[13] The prevalence of this second-best
approach is not difficult to explain. If political decisionmakers perceive a
substantial shadow price on sources of government revenue, a tax incentive
will be preferred to a subsidy even at some welfare cost. If a sector is to be
enlarged (or its shrinkage averted), a tariff on competing imports has an
obvious attraction over a subsidy on domestic output, especially if application
of the subsidy cannot be confined to the margin. By extension, expanding a
sector through subsidising exports becomes preferable to subsidising all of its
output, including that sold on the domestic market, especially if export demand is highly elastic.

Whether national governments select first-best or second-best policies, international ramifications must be expected. Except in special cases (see, for
example, Brander and Spencer, 1981), a production subsidy (tax) increases
(decreases) net exports of the affected sector, just as does a tax (subsidy) on
imports or a subsidy (tax) on exports. As United States public policy keenly
recognises, all of these measures, when taken in a large country, have similar
qualitative effects on sectoral production levels in other trading countries.
Industrial policy therefore raises essentially the questions of the international
coordination of policies that have stood before the General Agreement on
Tariffs and Trade since the second world war.

International coordination: the general issue

Whatever pessimism may be felt about the international coordination of economic policy, it is still worth knowing where significant payoffs could be
achieved, however difficult it may be to attain them. Presumably no problem
arises with policies that have favourable effects on the perceived welfare of the

country imposing them and inflict no harm on other countries: they will be put into effect. The substantial cases calling for international coordination are those where one country's policy exerts a spillover effect, favourable or unfavourable, on the perceived welfare of another country or countries. A standard approach to this problem is to assume an initial Cournot equilibrium in which each country has set one or more policy instruments without taking acount of their effects on the foreign country's welfare (the two-country case is stressed, for simplicity), or of the possibility that it will retaliate.

The analysis of international policy coordination then follows as an application of bargaining over externalities in a market setting, but with the constraint noted that it is awkward to arrange direct pecuniary compensation between sovereign nations, so that barter in policies is a potential route to mutual gains. Policy spillovers may take either negative or positive forms. Suppose that the first country's welfare has (at the margin) a negative effect on the second country's welfare, and that the second country has no property right in freedom from such effects.[14] The standard theory identifies the second country's preferred option as a bribe to effect a reduction of the policy's intensity to the point where the diminished losses to the second country from the spillover at the margin just offset the diminished benefits to the first country from the policy. With a positive spillover, the exactly correct bribe expands the policy to the point where the second country's spillover benefits at the margin match the first country's loss of opportunity from 'overkill'.

Another useful frame for bargaining over policies is a barter setting with two symmetrically positioned countries, each plying a policy instrument that imposes spillovers on the other. Efficient policy trade is then the counterpart of a mutually beneficial shift from a Cournot equilibrium to one that is Pareto-optimal, and it may involve a marginal increase or decrease in either country's instrument, depending on the sign of the spillover. Each country's gross benefits from policy trade take the form of increased welfare for the second country, say, a function of unit increases in the first country's policy beyond the Cournot level that it would select on its own, when the spillover is a positive one. For a negative spillover, the benefits repose in the increases in the second country's welfare that stem from unit reductions in the intensity of the first country's policy from its Cournot level. The benefits to the first country from changes in the second country's policies are analysed symmetrically. These benefit functions may be conceived as giving rise to offer curves that delineate the opportunities for mutually beneficial policy trade that is analytically identical to the neoclassical model of two-country barter in goods.

Applications to industrial policy

These analytical approaches to policy spillovers are at once familiar and too abstract to enrich the preceding analysis greatly. Yet they do have important practical implications for the international coordination of policy. Consider, for example, the rounds of tariff reductions that have occurred under the aegis of the General Agreement on Tariffs and Trade. Assuming that pre-negotiation tariffs represented legitimate choices for national political systems, the successive rounds of international negotiations (such as the most recent Tokyo Round) can be thought of as policy barter to cut back these tariffs and curb negative spillovers that has taken the form of worsened terms of trade for the tariff-setting country's trade partners. Economists obsessed with the belief that few tariffs make any contribution to the tariff-setting country's own welfare have resisted this behavioural interpretation of the tariff-bargaining process, yet it elucidates many features of the GATT multilateral trade negotiations.

Consider policy spillovers in the light of the substantive issues of industrial policy identified earlier in this chapter. International oligopoly poses the simplest problem, in that the profit-shifting policies proposed for national industrial policy are entirely redistributive between countries and in themselves have no effect on global real income. Although countries have not responded in any obvious way to these new theoretical invitations to seek rents from their neighbours, there is a well-established practice of exempting from a country's competition policy any national monopolies or cartels seeking to extract rents from foreign markets (Auquier and Caves, 1979). One might hope for a GATT-type agreement that each country enforce its competition policy evenhandedly with respect to the benefits it will yield to domestic and foreign buyers. This arrangement would not generate equiproportional benefits for every trading country, but neither do multilateral tariff reductions under the GATT; and both procedures offer a rough likelihood that the gains to each country, from global reductions in allocative inefficiency, will more than offset any curtailment of the rents it obtains from foreigners.[15]

International interests in research and development and in proprietary learning pose more complex issues. In the case of research and development, the international patent system already provides a limited assignment of property rights to nationals who devise patentable inventions, with countries that accord patent rights to foreigners forswearing the spillover benefits that they could otherwise obtain by freely copying foreigners' innovations. Thus, to the extent that the universal patent is the best available compromise for rewarding inventive effort, the patent system has already devised a global solution that keeps nations from fencing over rents and spillover benefits from individual inventions. However, this global solution really describes only the arrangement among the leading industrial countries, for nations outside this group typically choose to some extent to ride free by according property rights in patentable innovations only to their own citizens.

Obviously not every industrial country benefits proportionally from the international patent system, and some may not on balance benefit at all. That is, they might gain from free-riding on other countries' innovations even if other industrial nations were to retaliate by denying patent privileges to their own citizens. Nonetheless, the system works rather like the GATT-negotiated tariff reductions to pursue a global optimum on the mutually accepted assumption that its benefits are proportionally distributed.

A new issue under the banner of industrial policy is raised by the attempts of nations to manoeuvre their home producers into priority in the discovery of patentable innovations or similar proprietary assets such as learning-curve knowledge. These have spillover effects in the opportunity-cost sense that one nation's investment in supporting its national industry precludes foreign countries' access to the potential rent stream. The international interest here lies in averting the waste of resources in competitive rent-seeking.[16] There may also be gains in minimising the world's real cost of output, in so far as industrial policy manoeuvres a national producer other than potentially the most efficient into the 'lead' position. (This case is particularly clear in regard to learning-curve benefits.) However, making this global interest prevail against national policy is not easy, for exactly the reason revealed by the international patent system. In any particular innovation race, an efficient solution requires that the 'best' producer (the most skilful inventor, the lowest-cost manufacturer when all learning gains have been obtained) bribe others to let it go ahead. Compensation could conceivably take the form of a binding commitment to limit the price–cost margin on the efficiently produced innovation or output, but credibility and enforcement problems make this unlikely. The only practical prospect seems to be the same type of compromise as is embedded in the patent system, which is to assume that commercial victories will be spread more or less proportionally among the main industrial countries so that governments mutually agree to maintain a hands-off policy.

Problems of efficient adjustment in the short run also have potentially important ramifications for international policy coordination, although their structure is not so readily predicted. An industry that optimally delays the contraction of its i industry can generate either negative or positive spillovers abroad. Perceived negative spillovers arise if the i industry abroad is also subject to excess capacity. Positive spillovers obtain should the foreign country's expanding industry avert overshooting and excessive entry into industry i by investors with biased expectations. Because such effects are short-term and specific, international coordination requires a framework for continuing coordination rather than a definitive international resolution. A framework may be imagined that embraces intertemporal policy trading, with the first country tolerating an adjustment-related trade restriction by the second country at one time, on the understanding that the second country will reciprocate on a future occasion. The lower the correlation over time between countries' levels of unemployment, the better is the prospect of such balancing.

PART II
COUNTRY STUDIES OF INDUSTRIAL POLICIES

4 Industrial policy: the Canadian case

H. EDWARD ENGLISH AND

DONALD G. McFETRIDGE

After a brief discussion of the definition and recent history of industrial policy in the Canadian context, this chapter is developed under three principal headings: the role of trade policy as the foundation of industrial policy; complementary short-term adjustment policies; and longer term structural policies. The chapter ends with a short summary of Canada's industrial policy options.

BACKGROUND

Definitions of industrial policy vary with the perspective of the analyst or policymaker. The focus of the Fifteenth PAFTAD Conference was that of the economist, and thus the conference was concerned primarily with policies that affect the allocation of resources among industry sectors and may shift that allocation over time. The economist's normative criterion, whether explicit or implicit, is primarily related to efficiency. Although economists recognise that resource allocation policies may also affect the equity and the prospects for stability of an economy, these often receive less stress than considerations of efficiency, in part because of the difficulty of identifying and measuring such effects.

However, those responsible for public policy decisions often place greater emphasis on equity and short-term stability, and even on political factors that are not easily related to any economic criterion. The task of the economist then becomes to identify and measure the costs associated with departures from more efficient allocation and use of resources, and perhaps to suggest alternative, less costly ways of achieving those objectives.

The purpose of this chapter is to indicate the distinctive nature of these industrial policy choices in the Canadian economy, and to describe, and in part explain and assess, the choices that have been made in the decade or two since industrial policy became more fashionable.

What is distinctive about the Canadian case? In the first place, Canada—like Australia—displays the special characteristics of industrial policy in economies that are resource-rich and historically heavily dependent on exports of resource-based products. Such economies cannot have comparative advantages in that wide range of secondary industries for which resource inputs are much less important. This imposes an important constraint on policymakers, who are tempted to judge the success of industry by its export performance, or who uncritically apply infant-industry protection to all manufacturing industries. The problem in these circumstances is how to satisfy the criterion 'as efficient as possible' instead of the criterion 'as large as possible', the former criterion implying a very different choice of industrial policy. The problem is more complex but somewhat analogous for resource-rich developing countries—for example, Indonesia.

Another distinctive feature of both the Canadian and Australian economies that affects industrial policy is the role of federalism in structural policies. In the Canadian case, constitutional responsibility for natural-resource development is preponderantly provincial, though the federal government has a significant role in agriculture and saltwater fisheries, and, through its policies on transportation, tax and trade, can exert considerable leverage on the resource industries. Property rights are also constitutionally a provincial responsibility. The potential for federal–provincial conflict in policies affecting the allocation of industrial activity has encouraged the federal government to rely on these indirect levers, along with the promotion and regulation of banking institutions. While these federalism issues cannot be fully explained in this chapter, it is essential to recognise the constraints they impose on the choice of federal industrial policy. These distinctive features of the Canadian economy help to explain the origins of industrial policy in Canada.

In the nineteenth century, Canadian industrial policy was based on the absolute necessity of achieving and maintaining access to international markets for Canadian resource products. It was during this period that the National Policy was adopted in Canada—a mixture of westward (mainly agricultural) development based on railway-building and immigration, and manufacturing development in Central Canada (Ontario and Quebec) behind a higher protective tariff. This policy provided the basis of Canadian industrial policy right up to the second world war. The result was that the Canadian economy was in part meeting an international competitiveness standard and in part deliberately sheltered from it. But as the economy grew, so did the market base for the protected sector, and protection began to impose a growing cost. After 1945 it became increasingly evident that protected consumer-goods industries were inefficiently structured, and if rationalised would be able to achieve greater plant and product-line economies of scale on the basis of the larger Canadian domestic market.[1] Thus the protective system that had been deemed essential in an earlier era was now a deterrent to adjustment. By the early 1960s these circumstances were being described and analysed by academic economists, and were soon affecting policy thinking in Canada (see Daly, 1968; Eastman and Stykolt, 1967; English, 1964).

The industrial policy debate that emerged in the 1960s had two principal features. First, it was argued that a significant part of the problem was heavy dependence on foreign direct investment, both in some high-risk resource sectors and in manufacturing, especially those high-profile sectors where technology and marketing advantages and related property rights provided inducements for foreign parent firms to build branch plants behind Canadian tariff barriers. This debate focused on the relative importance of policies to limit or regulate foreign-controlled enterprises, as against tariff and similar policies that permitted and encouraged them to operate in ways that might not accord with the Canadian public interest.

Second, the debate became increasingly focused on whether policy that served the regional interests of Ontario and Quebec in secondary manufacturing was imposing an unnecessary burden on the outlying provinces, in respect of both their ambitions for more processing and manufacturing and their suspicion that protection of manufacturing in the industrial centres unnecessarily raised prices and did not encourage the cost reductions that scale economies might now make possible.

Consequently, the definition of industrial policy adopted during the subsequent decade focused almost exclusively on manufacturing. In June 1972 the Honourable Jean Luc Pepin, Minister of Industry, Trade and Commerce, described industrial strategy in Parliament as follows:

> ... proper planning by government (federal) for the optimum coordination of policies and decisions, on the use of all productive resources, in order to achieve defined (and accepted) social and economic goals. The strategy must embrace all sectors of economic activity from resources to services, but must emphasize manufacturing and processing.

The minister's use of the word 'federal' is a significant indicator of awareness of provincial sensitivities. The stress on policy affecting manufacturing has continued to the present. However, there were times during the 1973–83 period when the government seemed ready to abandon the secondary sector as a lost cause in the face of the rapid rises in food and energy resource prices that so strongly favoured investment in areas of traditional strength for Canada.

But what new policies were actually adopted during this period? Modern industrial policy in Canada probably began with the signing of the Canada–US automotive pact, or with the duty-remission schemes that led up to it. By the early 1960s the government had accepted the view that the principal industries were not achieving economies of scale within a protected domestic market context. The nature of the automotive pact reflected a perceived need for direct government intervention to set standards by which the industrial adjustment that flowed from it could be evaluated. These standards included a necessary minimum value added to be produced by Canadian branch operations of foreign firms, and a target share of North American production to be met by each branch operation, on the basis of the Canadian market share in its sales in the United States and Canada. Canadian subsidiaries also enjoyed the privilege of duty-free imports of automotive products, while Canadian consumers still had to pay duties on automobiles made in the United States.

In terms of economic growth the automotive pact was very successful indeed, reducing unit costs in Canadian plants to United States levels by tailoring production to the North American market (Reisman, 1978). Its problems related to the fact that it was a single-sector deal, which led to distortion in the manufacturing sector, partly through the higher wages generated by the improved productivity and protected profits it made possible; other manufacturing industries found their competitive positions weakened by this upward pressure on labour costs and other inputs.

The automotive pact contributed to at least one other important debate, that about 'truncation'—the claim that foreign-controlled manufacturing discourages research and development in the host country, since these as well as other staff and management functions are frequently attached to the head office.

The automotive pact raised three questions that have been central to the subsequent debate on industrial policy. To what extent is the liberalisation of international trade essential to an effective industrial policy? What kinds of transition arrangements are needed? Is foreign control of some Canadian industries a force enabling or handicapping the rationalisation process?

The general concern about inefficiencies in industrial structure that was addressed by the automotive pact gave rise to the federal government Task Force on the Structure of Canadian Industry. The report of the task force (1968) incorporated the findings of the academic studies mentioned earlier, and recommended government action to enhance competition in Canada through freer trade, stronger competition law and fuller disclosure requirements for large companies (notably the wholly owned subsidiaries of multinationals).

At the time the government was concluding the Kennedy Round of GATT negotiations, and was committed to giving priority to multilateral negotiations as a means of liberalising trade. This meant that no other action on trade policy could be contemplated (or for that matter seemed necessary to the government).

At about the same time the government requested a special review of competition policy by the Economic Council of Canada. This resulted in the *Interim Report on Competition Policy* (1969), which stressed the efficiency-promoting role of such policy. This was the beginning of continued efforts during the 1970s to make the legislation on combines, mergers and other restrictive practices more effective and relevant to the needs of the Canadian economy. The same period witnessed efforts to improve the disclosure laws, notably through the Corporation and Labour Unions Returns Act.

But there was also a growing interest in more interventionist policies respecting foreign-controlled industry. Neither critics in government nor outsiders were satisfied that a policy environment involving competition-inducing trade liberalisation and competition laws could deal with the impact of foreign control. Out of this concern arose two related industrial policy approaches of the 1970s: the screening of foreign-controlled investment, and the call for an industrial strategy in which the government would directly foster more Canadian research and development and export activity.

The former approach was supported in a second government task force report, called the Gray Report after the main ministerial proponent of screening (Government of Canada, 1972). The Foreign Investment Review Act was passed in 1974, establishing under the authority of the Foreign Investment Review Agency a process for screening new takeovers and, later, investment in new lines of business by established foreign-controlled firms. The object was to determine whether any new takeover was of significant benefit to Canada, and to negotiate with the prospective buyer so as to enhance such benefits. In the following decade the agency passed many hundreds of proposed takeovers, approving about 90 per cent of each year's cases considered in the early 1980s.[2] However, as Steven Globerman (1980) and others have concluded, it is doubtful whether the added benefits were enough to compensate for the costs entailed in the administration of the scheme and the uncertainty of the outcomes.

In any event, the new Canadian government (elected in September 1984) has substantially modified the agency, converting it into Investment Canada with more emphasis on stimulating foreign investment and power to review only very large or, it might be surmised, high-profile takeovers.

During the middle and late 1970s, the main focus of debate seemed to shift somewhat towards a contest between those who stressed trade liberalisation as a cornerstone for public policy and those who stressed the need for direct government intervention in support of Canadian technology and management so as to encourage Canadian exports of specialised processed and manufactured products. This debate seemed to polarise around reports and studies by two government agencies—the Economic Council of Canada, and the Science Council (see French, 1980).

In 1975 the Economic Council issued the report *Looking Outward*, which argued for substantial and comprehensive trade liberalisation and stated that this might be based not only on the traditional multilateral negotiations but also on a bilateral agreement between Canada and the United States. On principles related to those behind the automotive pact, it was claimed that a bilateral arrangement would enable Canadian manufacturers to rationalise their operations through specialisation and two-way trade within the North American continent, and would thus strengthen Canada's capacity to compete in world markets also.

The Science Council and some of its staff studies took the view that, mainly because of the branch-plant phenomenon, freeing of trade would mean that the large multinationals would have insurmountable advantages over Canadian-owned firms, and that the result would be a further (and perhaps irreversible) truncation of Canadian industry (Britton and Gilmour, 1978). In this view, trade liberalisation would have to be preceded by government measures to stimulate Canadian industrial technology, and Canadian firms would require help in developing and marketing any distinctive products resulting from this support. Some authors argued for the need to provide incentives to multinational firms to assign 'world products mandates' to their Canadian branches (Bishop and Crookell, 1985).

It is not surprising that policymakers concerned with measures to preserve the health of the industrial economy found it difficult in the context of the events of the late 1970s and early 1980s to prescribe interventionist measures with any conviction as to their longer-run reliability. Nevertheless, the traditional piecemeal approach included elements of both trade liberalisation and industrial-technology incentive approaches. The Tokyo Round of GATT negotiations ended in 1979, and this time Canada was committed to greater reductions of tariffs affecting more manufactured goods than in previous rounds (Stone, 1984:64–65; Whalley, 1985). On the other hand, many Canadians felt that non-tariff barriers were handled with limited effectiveness, and it was argued that a new approach to reducing these obstacles might be necessary (Grey, 1981). Many incentives for research and development and exports were put in place during the 1970s. To longstanding tax credits for research and development expenditures were added grant programs designed to pick winning firms and back them well beyond the invention and innovation stages into the development and marketing phases. Export credits have been mainly of the conventional kind, primarily supporting trade with third world countries where it was deemed necessary to match the financial services offered by competing countries. These will be discussed later in this chapter.

At present, however, the favoured form of industrial policy seems to be that based on market signals and growing support for the trade liberalisation option, together with the kinds of adjustment and incentive policies that leave choice in the hands of the private sector. The details of this option will be specified in the following two sections.

THE ROLE OF TRADE POLICY IN CANADIAN INDUSTRIAL POLICY

Historically, as noted above, trade policy has always played a leading role in the microeconomic policy of Canadian governments. Since 1947 this policy has rested on a commitment to multilateral negotiations under GATT auspices. The Canadian government today remains committed to participation in the GATT's effort to remain relevant and effective by tackling some of the non-tariff-barrier issues, especially those related to agricultural trade and relatively labour-intensive manufactures, and more generally by creating a stronger framework for negotiating with developing countries and overcoming the barriers to trade in services (Stone, 1984).

Over the past ten years, Canadian industry and government have increasingly recognised that a more extensive and systematic use of bilateral arrangements with the United States can play a role highly complementary to that of the GATT, as well as contributing new approaches and stimuli that could be relevant to future GATT negotiations (Lipsey and Smith, 1985).

When the concept of bilateral free trade with the United States was given significant support by the Economic Council in 1975, the leaders of the Canadian government of the day took little notice. Seven years later, the Standing Senate Committee on Foreign Affairs came out strongly in favour of a Canada–United States free-trade arrangement (Standing Senate Committee on Foreign Affairs, 1982). While the views of the Canadian Senate have limited influence on those of the Cabinet, a year later the government issued a Review of Foreign Trade Policy, in which it acknowledged the comprehensive free-trade arrangement as an option, along with another, more cautious alternative, sectoral free trade (Department of External Affairs, 1983; see also Hart, 1985). In this same period, leading business groups, including the Canadian Chamber of Commerce and the Canadian Manufacturers Association, gave positive support to free trade between Canada and the United States. Early in 1985, the new Canadian government issued discussion papers showing a distinct leaning towards comprehensive liberalisation of trade with the United States.[3] Then, in September 1985, Prime Minister Mulroney announced in the House of Commons that he had asked President Reagan to open negotiations on such an arrangement.

The emphasis on 'assured access' is based on perceptions such as the following, taken from the Standing Senate Committee document of 1982:

A major trading nation like Canada cannot fail to be concerned about its international competitiveness. Canada's record is, in fact, spotty: strong in freely traded resource products, in processing and in a few manufacturing sectors, but relatively weak in most areas of secondary manufacturing . . .

. . . a growing number of witnesses from the private sector have recognized that bilateral free trade could offer manufacturing industries opportunities to specialize and achieve economies of scale, which could be translated into higher rates of productivity.

. . . If the government were to set the goal of achieving free trade with the United States, and the US Administration were to respond with a show of interest, companies would immediately begin to calculate the impact and adjust to the potential new market situation. As the CMA [the Canadian Manufacturers Association] pointed out to the Committee, most businesses would try to adapt as quickly as possible to a free trade environment if they thought it was coming.

It is clear that the basic argument for this approach is founded on industrial policy objectives, together with a view that the traditional gradual evolution of multilateral trade will not by itself offer a sufficiently reliable opportunity to achieve the same enhancement of domestic productivity, especially in these crucial years of slow recovery in the world economy.

The main advantage of a comprehensive bilateral arrangement is that it is expected to give Canadian industries assured access to the large United States market, putting Canadian producers on approximately the same basis as their United States competitors. To achieve this, it would be necessary to cover the principal non-tariff barriers affecting Canadian exports to the United States (that is, to get 'national treatment' on purchasing policies and so on). Apart from enabling the kind of rationalisation of traditional industries that the automotive pact has afforded that sector, the access would be especially valuable to new sectors and smaller and medium-sized firms with innovative products. Both the research and development and the launching costs could thus be spread over a much larger market. If in the first year or two a new product can expect to gain only a fraction of 1 per cent of the market, it would probably make the crucial difference for many firms if that were a percentage of the North American market, or even of that portion of it closest to the Canadian producer's plant. This is one of the reasons why the Federation of Independent Business, which represents smaller firms, and most of the smaller high-technology companies, favour a Canada–United States bilateral trade arrangement.

The alternative, the sectoral free-trade approach that was pursued by the previous Liberal government, placed strong emphasis on the rationalisation of established sectors and the promotion of some smaller high-technology concerns. But the main economic problems with bilateral sectoral deals are, first that in most cases the benefits to the two countries would be asymmetrical; and second that including only a few sectors would distort the allocation of resources and impose burdens on the sectors not covered, as the automotive pact did. The benefits would have to be large to justify this additional cost, but there is serious doubt about whether this would be the case unless most of the larger sectors were included, a fact which would in turn complicate the negotiations (and raise the transaction costs) in the search for reciprocal deals that would achieve an aggregate balance of benefits.

Then, of course, there are the political difficulties associated with the incompatibility between sectoral arrangements and the GATT, and the requirement to compensate third parties (see Hart, 1985).

The case for a comprehensive Canada–United States trade deal has been supported by a number of estimates of its prospective economic benefits. From the work of the Wonnacotts reported in 1967, which estimated the benefits of Canada–United States free trade at approximately 10 per cent of GNP, to the 1984 study of Richard Harris and David Cox, which arrived at a very similar estimate, the lesson is clear: the benefits should greatly exceed the costs. In May 1985, a study by Richard Lipsey assessed all this evidence from the vantage point of a senior policy analyst not previously committed to a position in the debate, and concluded that a conservative estimate of the benefits could place them in the range of 5–7 per cent of GNP (Lipsey and Smith, 1985:ch.3). The greatest concern, both economically and politically, becomes adjustment costs and the identification of the adjustment process that is most likely to minimise the burden of such costs.

Before addressing these matters directly, there is good reason to add a word on some of the implications for Pacific economic relations of any serious bilateral deal between Canada and the United States. Trade diversion is always a matter for concern when regional groups are being formed. The fact that 65–70 per cent of Canadian trade is with the United States suggests that trade-creation effects will be dominant. Furthermore, there is reason to believe that a successful Canada–United States arrangement would help Canada to accommodate imports from other sources, and thus to reduce its restrictions on overseas trade. Canada and the United States could be encouraged to act together to support the liberalisation of non-tariff barriers affecting other countries, including voluntary export restraints and other quantitative restrictions on labour-intensive manufactures. It could also make Canada a more attractive place for direct investment by Japan and thus, at least moderately, increase Canada's share of Japanese investment in North America. Above all, it should give Canadian producers a better foundation for the development of export capacity in specialised manufactures and an enhanced ability to penetrate the challenging markets of the Western Pacific, and therefore to accept with more political grace the manufactured products of Japan and other East Asian countries.

ADJUSTMENT POLICIES

The relationship of adjustment policy to industrial policy is straightforward. The former assumes change based on either priority policies or market forces that cannot, practically speaking, be controlled. Industrial policy encompasses both the priority policies and their complementary and supportive adjustment measures. Of course, adjustment policies can exist in the absence of any explicit industrial policy. They are traditionally proposed as ways of adapting to inevitable technological change or shifting comparative advantages within the world economy. In the context of a policy based on trade liberalisation, and therefore acceptance of international market discipline, adjustment policy acquires more focus.

Canadian adjustment policies date mainly from the 1960s. The first trade-related program of this sort was attached to the automotive pact (the Automotive Adjustment Assistance Program of 1965–76). The General Adjustment Assistance Program of 1967 was designed to deal with the effects of the Kennedy Round of tariff cuts. Both these programs involved loans to firms and assistance to workers. Both were used, but neither achieved a high profile in the buoyant macroeconomic environment for adjustment that prevailed up to 1971.

In the more difficult times that followed the 1973–74 oil crisis, and particularly in the recession of the early 1980s, the automobile industry asked for and received government support under the Enterprise Development Program, which supports high-risk and innovative investments and adjustment activities that aim to increase efficiency. The program began in 1977, and by 1983 over Can\$100 million had been granted to companies in the automobile sector. Since 1981 additional funds have been made available under the Industrial and Labour Adjustment Program. Originally designed to help communities with long-term dislocation problems caused by large layoffs, this program was enlarged to cover all automotive parts companies.

In 1984 a new Industrial and Regional Development Program replaced the Enterprise Development Program and the Industry and Labour Adjustment Program. Under the intensive combined pressures of the losses and unemployment generated by the recession and the continued success of Japanese competition, Canadian governments (federal and provincial) also engaged in expensive ad hoc competition with federal and state governments in the United States to induce the Ford company to build a plant in Ontario instead of Ohio. Direct and indirect support worth about Can$100 million was considered 'necessary' (Trebilcock, 1985).

As for dealing directly with Japanese competition, since 1975 the government had operated a duty-remission scheme for firms not covered by the automotive pact, designed to induce sourcing of parts in Canada. Nevertheless, in 1981 it was deemed necessary to 'complement' adjustment by 'voluntary' export restraints, though, to be fair, these restraints were made politically inevitable by the imposition of similar restraints by the federal government of the United States. Ultimately, Canadian consumers have had to bear most of the cost of this hotchpotch of adjustment and adjustment-avoidance mechanisms, while Japanese manufacturers have enjoyed higher prices to compensate for a lower volume of sales. Canadian consumers have been partly compensated by the entry of the Korean Hyundai company into the Canadian market. Since Korean cars attract lower duty rates under the generalised system of preferences, they have a discriminatory advantage over Japanese cars.

The Textile and Clothing Board was established in 1971, and has continued to examine and make recommendations on ways of making these industries more viable in the face of growing import competition, mainly from the newly industrialised countries but also from other developing nations. The 1971 Act that founded the board also gave the government new authority to impose restrictions on textile products likely to cause or threaten serious damage to Canadian producers. Global quotas were immediately imposed, using Article XIX of the GATT (on safeguards) as their authority.

After the Multi-Fiber Agreement of 1973 took over from the Long-Term Arrangement for cotton, Canada's restraint program operated in conformity with its rules, and the number of agreements with exporting countries and the range of products covered declined somewhat between 1971 and 1975. However, this changed dramatically in 1976 when the Canadian government imposed quotas on almost all imports of clothing, mainly as part of a vain effort to prevent the election of a separatist Party Quebeçois government in the province where much of the clothing industry is concentrated. At first these were imposed under GATT Article XIX, striking at all imports from developed as well as developing countries. Under pressure to change this, starting in 1979 Canada switched to bilateral quotas for the larger exporting countries. Nearly as comprehensive as the global quotas, these arrangements discriminated much more against third world countries. These quotas have been repeatedly renewed or extended, and cover about 90 per cent of Canadian imports of clothing and 10 per cent of total textile imports.

In 1981, a new report from the Textile and Clothing Board was tabled. However, the government avoided the report's most restrictive recommendations, and introduced a new adjustment program, managed by the Canadian Industrial Renewal Board. Since its foundation the board has allocated about Can$270 million to the textile, clothing and footwear sectors over five years.

This money is intended to assist the creation of new employment opportunities in communities heavily affected by industrial development, and to help workers take advantage of these opportunities. The board has chosen to stress the support of firms with potential, a three- to five-year plan for renewal, and a commitment to reinvest 75 per cent of profits to the plan. To this program over Can$100 million has been allocated. The board has also assigned funds to seven vulnerable areas in Quebec and Eastern Ontario, the allocation of about Can$40 million going mainly to smaller or medium-sized businesses with projects for modernisation and productivity improvement. Labour adjustment grants are also given in the forms of portable wage subsidies and mobility and training assistance, but use of these opportunities has been limited, presumably because of the recession, which limited alternative opportunities, and the relatively lower mobility of unskilled clothing and footwear workers.

In the past two years the Import Tribunal (formerly the Anti-Dumping Tribunal) and the Textile and Clothing Board have had to make judgments on the future of quotas as their termination dates approached. One encouraging sign is that these boards have been asked for the first time to take consumer interests into account in their deliberations on trade restrictions. Unfortunately there is little evidence as yet that the work of the Canadian Industrial Renewal Board or that of the older tribunals will lead to a new commitment by the government to true adjustment.

Michael Trebilcock (1985) has concluded that policy for this sector has repeatedly stressed primary resort to protection, secondary resort to firm subsidies, and limited labour adjustment policies as a last resort. He refers to this as 'policy inversion', since precisely the opposite order of priority would impose a smaller cost on the economy and reduce the long-term misallocation of resources. This order of priorities has been especially evident in the past ten years, reflecting the tendency to resort to costly protection and subsidy rather than real adjustment in periods of high unemployment. The fact that other countries have followed similarly inappropriate policies partly explains the political choice, but does not justify it in terms of economic sense or longer term political wisdom (Stone, 1984:110).

There have been other government programs to assist specific sectors, including shipbuilding, the Cape Breton coal industry and the high-technology sector. The first two are not especially significant for any discussion of trade adjustment. The question of the high-technology sector and policy affecting it is addressed later in this chapter. Evidence on ad hoc firm-oriented support as a feature of the new protectionism may be found in Biggs (1981).

The scepticism about present Canadian adjustment programs can readily be related to their lack of connection to any commitment to preserve or achieve free trade, or to some clearly defined approximation of it. This is why many have come to feel that adjustment that takes place within the context of a Canada–United States free-trade arrangement could be more meaningful. Four areas of policy seem relevant to such an arrangement: the period of adjustment; the macroeconomic environment; assistance to labour or firms faced with adjustment; and non-financial structural adjustment policies—

specialisation and export agreements, control of foreign investment, and so on.

One of the recognised characteristics of any substantial regional free-trade arrangement is that it involves a period of some years during which specified tariff and non-tariff barriers are phased out. This period will normally cover the time required for restructuring or modernising capital. The European Community originally adopted a twelve-year transition period; however, this turned out to be too long, and the later internal tariff reductions were speeded up. It has usually been suggested that eight to ten years might be an appropriate period for establishing a Canada–United States free-trade regime. In addition it has been suggested in discussion since the 1960s that Canada would be justified in asking for a transition period longer than that for the United States, on the grounds that Canada has more adjusting to do (Lea, 1963). In view of the opinions business leaders have expressed concerning the probability of immediate action by many businesses to reorganise their production arrangements, a period of three to four years for the United States and six to eight years for Canada would be enough to permit smooth adjustment, and would be less likely to delay the process than an excessively long period.

The question of the macroeconomic environment is of great potential importance. As suggested elsewhere in this chapter, the more buoyant an economy is, the easier adjustment will be. This is because alternative jobs are available to absorb workers laid off from industries whose products are being replaced by imports. On the other hand, there can be an advantage to a slack labour market if the change in trade policy is important enough to generate substantial new export opportunity and investment in restructuring. This is most likely to occur in the case of a Canada–United States free-trade arrangement over the next few years. Thus fiscal and monetary policy that provides further scope for the private sector to employ idle resources and a lower cost of capital may generate a rather sharp rise in spending and employment.

The most recent Canadian budget (23 May 1985) promises a strong supply-side stimulus to investment, but by itself it also reduces demand significantly by reducing both government and consumer spending. It can only be effective if renewed buoyancy in the United States economy or a significant Canada–United States trade initiative, or both, would provide enough business investment to compensate for the decline in consumer spending caused by higher taxes. In these circumstances, a rate of Canadian recovery higher than elsewhere in the developed world might be expected, and an environment for adjustment that could be close to ideal.

The other macroeconomic policy element that is important to adjustment is the exchange rate. With a flexible exchange rate, such adjustment is in principle easier, since any short-term surge in imports could be balanced by a lower Canadian dollar. Given the transitional phasing out of trade barriers, however, it is likely that the largest changes in the short run would be in capital flows. The level of investment that might follow from the announcement of a Canada–United States agreement might cause a substantial new inflow of private capital (and/or a reduced outflow of Canadian savings). This could drive the Canadian dollar upward, imposing a higher import cost on the transition process. Measures such as a temporary federal–provincial agreement to limit public borrowing abroad might be wise under these circumstances.

Financial adjustment assistance measures for workers and owners of capital are in principle desirable to make adaptation to a new industrial structure easier and more politically acceptable. However, the problem of identifying efficient policy has been illustrated in reference to the experience of the past. Assistance to firms is unlikely to be required provided that financial institutions can supply adequate venture capital, or that it is available internationally. If the investment climate is as buoyant as the macroeconomic policy conditions above would suggest, pressure for financial support for weaker companies is much less likely to be applied than in recent years, and presumably could be resisted.

Assistance to labour is a much greater challenge to policymakers. Significantly, the most successful adjustment experiences have been those associated with the automotive pact and the Kennedy Round tariff reductions. This is partly because of the macroeconomic circumstances of the time, but also, surely, because in the case of the automotive pact the trade arrangement itself stimulated the economy. In a general free-trade arrangement with the United States the labour adjustment necessary would be greater; but it should be noted that the labour-intensive industries would not be affected as much as they would be by a multilateral trade liberalisation.

The approach to worker adjustment policies has been analytically refined in recent years, and Canada's contribution to this analysis has been substantial (Glenday et al., 1982). The discounted future benefits of trade liberalisation should be set against all private and social adjustment costs, and if (as is expected in the Canada–United States case) the costs are lower, workers should be compensated accordingly. When the compensation levels are assessed, some uncertainties about the estimates, and perhaps some inducement to voters in order to mobilise support for liberalisation, might justify more generous compensation than conservative estimates would suggest. Glenday and his co-authors discuss three kinds of worker assistance:

1 financial assistance for specific firms to prevent or delay large permanent lay-offs, with the amount of assistance based on the short- and long-run efficiency costs of the lay-offs;

2 compensation to cover the income losses of laid-off workers;

3 re-employment promotion programs to find employment and improve job quality for workers laid off as a result of trade liberalisation (or similar events), which would reduce short-run private costs.

One or more of these programs could be adopted, depending on their efficiency. The reasons given for focusing policies on adjustment to trade liberalisation as such seem to rest on the political inducement required to accept the policy change and the administrative efficiency of a less general policy, a general policy being unnecessary because other sources of change are more gradual and easily accommodated.

Commenting on existing adjustment programs, the Glenday study notes that they are mainly worker-training and manpower-mobility grants. One question that can be raised about these is whether retraining can be carried out as efficiently through public programs as by new employers, since the private benefits to the employer concerned would often be close to the social benefit generated.

The Labour Adjustment Benefits Program, initiated for textile workers in 1971 and extended to footwear and tanning workers in 1974, provides workers with two-thirds of their previous wage until retirement age. The Glenday study observes that the level of benefits in this case is generous in relation to the estimates of income losses, but that the criteria for eligibility seem restrictive.

It is noted that adjustment assistance in the United States under the 1974 US Trade Act used more relaxed eligibility requirements, after the experience with the criteria employed under the 1962 Act.

There are, of course, many national manpower policies and programs already in place in Canada, most of which are not designed specifically for adjustment to trade policy changes. These include Unemployment Insurance, the Industrial Adjustment Service (a consulting service for firms and workers), the Canada Employment Centres (for job placement), various training programs (under the National Training Act of 1982 and its predecessors), and the Canada Mobility Program (to help workers to relocate).

Certain problems with any Canadian transition to a substantially free-trade system, especially one involving the United States, have generated a call for particular policy prescriptions for non-financial adjustment (English, 1979). Two of these will be addressed here: specialisation and export agreements, and special controls on foreign investment.

The former relate to the perceived need to assist restructuring by permitting agreements that would normally be subject to investigation and possibly prosecution under the competition laws. The need to permit companies to form specialisation agreements arises out of the production structure that has characterised a number of manufacturing industries, where each firm has been producing too wide a variety of products, models or brands of products. To achieve line economies under free trade, specialisation in a few lines by each firm might be necessary. While much of this could happen without an exception being made under the law, a temporary exemption (say for ten years) might hasten the adjustment process. If international competition is stimulated by trade liberalisation, such agreements need not lead to collusive oligopolistic prices to the consumer. Similarly, export agreements would permit firms to open joint export outlets in the United States, which might be attractive for enterprises not previously active in the United States market. Again, this suspension of the law might be temporary.

In both cases it might be necessary to negotiate a provision in any Canada–United States treaty that permitted firms based in the United States a similar temporary exemption under United States law for specialisation and export agreements involving their Canadian subsidiaries. Otherwise they might face antitrust prosecution.

The support for policies specific to foreign-controlled firms under free trade arises out of this fear that such firms might not act in accordance with Canadian national interests under a free-trade regime. However, such fears largely rest on grounds that suggest those firms would not act in their own best interests. If the circumstances for continuing to produce in Canada are favourable, why should they behave differently from Canadian-owned enterprises? The expectation that they might do so seems to rest on observations of past behaviour under conditions that would no longer prevail under free trade. For example, branches of some United States firms did not in the past have the right to export to the United States, but in these cases United States trade barriers and/or Canadian unit costs made such exports unlikely on economic grounds, and the circumstances that could prevail under an assured access arrangement would differ substantially. Firms would have a period of transition in which to determine what would be the economically ideal adjustment strategy. Perhaps Investment Canada might be charged with monitoring the responses of foreign firms in the adjustment or transition period, and have some right to intervene in asset-disposal procedures should firms decide to move out of the Canadian market within that period.

LONGER TERM STRUCTURAL POLICIES

The discussion so far has focused on the benefits to Canada of freer trade and on the adjustment policies that should accompany trade liberalisation. But industrial policy is generally regarded as encompassing more than trade and adjustment policies; it also includes what might be called structural policies, the intent of which is to effect long-term changes in the composition, nature and location of productive activity.

Among the policy instruments that have been used to bring about structural change in Canada are transportation policy (particularly subsidised freight rates), competition policy, industrial technology policy, and export-promotion policies (particularly subsidised export financing).

There is, of course, considerable debate about whether the pursuit of these policies has been productive. What is relevant here is whether structural industrial policies can be productive in a free-trade environment, and, if so, what form they should take. The answers may depend on the characteristics of the national economy. Policies that are productive for large economies like Japan and the United States may not be productive in the context of the smaller advanced economies (Canada, Australia) or newly industrialised countries (Singapore, Korea, Taiwan).

The following discussion attempts to determine the appropriate form for one class of structural policies, those relating to the development and acquisition of new industrial technologies, in the context of an advanced economy such as

Canada operating in a free-trade environment. It begins with a brief description of the Canadian record in this area, and then analyses the policy options available.

Technological innovation: the Canadian record

Canada has not been among the world's main sources of new technologies. Patents granted to Canadian nationals have represented less than 0.5 per cent of worldwide patenting activity in recent years.

Canadian spending on research and development amounted to about 1.3 per cent of GDP in 1981, which puts Canada in roughly the same category as Norway, Denmark, Italy, Australia and, by some measures, the Netherlands. Canada's ratio of research and development expenditure to GDP is much lower than the ratios in the United States, West Germany, Sweden and Switzerland. However, the differences between Canada's ratio of non-defence research and development expenditure to GDP and those of the United States, Britain and France are relatively small.[4]

Approximately 55 per cent of the present Canadian research and development effort takes place in industry. This represents an increase of some 14 percentage points since the 1960s, and has partially alleviated the historical concern that too much of Canada's research and development goes on in government laboratories and too little in industry. Canada carries out a greater fraction of its research and development in industry than do the Netherlands, Norway and Australia, but continues to trail the United States, Switzerland, West Germany, Japan and France in this regard (McFetridge, 1985; Statistics Canada, 1984).

Canada has been more important as a user of technology than as a source, continuing to award more than 5 per cent of all patents granted worldwide. Canada is more important as a place to patent than West Germany and the Netherlands, as important as France, and nearly as important as Britain (Ellis and Waite, 1985).

Although there has been some dispute about this, the weight of the evidence is that, holding the mode of transfer constant, Canada acquired new technologies from abroad at least as fast as the Western European countries, taken as a group, during the period 1960–80. There is also evidence, however, that Canada's position in the transfer order is slipping. Canada is now much less likely to be the first foreign recipient of new United States technologies than was the case twenty years ago (McFetridge and Corvari, 1985).

The evidence on domestic diffusion rates is fragmentary, but there is a school of thought to the effect that the diffusion of new technologies within Canadian industries tends to be slower than is the case with their foreign (principally American) counterparts, and that this is a consequence of tariff protection. It is said, and there is some evidence to support this view, that Canadian producers are neither large nor specialised enough to make profitable use of the latest technologies. According to this view, trade liberalisation would encourage—if not force—a rationalisation of domestic production, which would, in turn, make it more economic for Canadian producers to use the latest manufacturing techniques (Daly and Globerman, 1976; Economic Council of Canada, 1983).

The 'bottom line' as far as innovation is concerned is the rate of growth of total factor productivity. Canada's productivity growth record was acceptable by international standards during the 1960s, but has been rather poor since then. While there are various explanations of both the slowdown in productivity growth and Canada's apparently poor relative performance, it is the explanations in terms of energy, cyclic factors and specific sectors, rather than the innovation stories, that are most convincing (Denny, 1985; Helliwell et al., 1985).

Canadian public policy towards technological innovation

Government support for technological innovation in Canada takes the following forms: industrial research and development subsidies and tax incentives; procurement policies, including research and development contracts; acquisition of new technology and incentives and assistance; and government research and development and university support.

Subsidy programs for industrial research and development have existed in one form or another since 1962. As a general rule, they provide cash grants of up to 50 per cent of the cost of specific research and development projects.[5] Federal research and development grants totalled Can$268 million in the fiscal year 1983/84 (Statistics Canada, 1983). Recently, some of the larger grants have been accompanied by a 'memorandum of understanding', under which the recipient, often a large multinational such as General Electric or Pratt and Whitney, makes certain guarantees concerning exports, value added and employment in return for assistance.

Canada has experimented more widely than any other nation in the world with research and development tax incentives, a special incentive of some sort having been in effect continuously since 1962 (McFetridge and Warda, 1983). The present form of incentive is a tax credit (which is taxable) equal to 20 per cent of annual research and development expenditures of either a current or a capital nature. Small businesses are eligible for a 35 per cent credit, which is refundable in the event that the taxpayer has insufficient taxable income to make use of it.

Canada is one of the few nations to allow capital expenditures for research and development purposes to be written off in the year they are incurred. It also maintains relatively liberal carry-forward and carry-back provisions. In sum, in terms of its statutory provisions Canada's tax treatment for industrial research and development is more generous than that of virtually any other industrialised country (McFetridge and Warda, 1983:63–77).

Canada recently terminated a short experiment with a transferable tax-credit scheme.[6] Some have estimated the tax-revenue losses to the government as a consequence of this scheme at close to Can$2 billion, or 40 per cent of total research and development spending. The problem with the scheme was that it allowed the sale of tax credits on research and development that had not yet been performed. Frequently it was never performed, leaving the government as an unsecured and disappointed creditor.

Canada has made much less use of research and development contracts, which totalled Can$190 million in 1983–84, than other countries, such as the United States. It is frequently suggested that government procurement could be used to much greater effect as a means of stimulating research and development (Statistics Canada, 1983).

Since 1972 government departments have been under instruction to contract out all new mission-oriented research and development, but there is little evidence of compliance with this directive; the proportion of federally funded research and development carried out within federal laboratories was the same in 1982 as it had been in 1971 (Task Force on Federal Policies and Programs for Technology Development, 1984).

Specific assistance for firms wishing to acquire new technologies is provided by the National Research Council under its Technical Information Services program. The council, in cooperation with provincial research councils, maintains a field staff of industrial technology advisers which numbered 121 in 1984.

Recent initiatives in this area include the establishment of six technology centres by the province of Ontario to disseminate new technologies to Ontario firms in the areas of microelectronics, robotics, computer-aided design and computer-aided manufacturing, resource machinery, farm machinery and automotive parts (see Bhanich Supapol and McFetridge, 1982). The Science Council of Canada has also proposed the augmentation of Canada's network of science attachés, which numbers six at present, with the objective of obtaining better intelligence on foreign technological developments (Science Council of Canada, 1985).

Some 21 per cent of Canada's research and development effort continues to take place in government laboratories. Despite some significant successes such as the development of rapeseed (Canola), which yielded a rate of return of 101 per cent, these research operations have come under increasing criticism for their bureaucratisation and lack of relevance (Task Force on Federal Policies and Programs for Technology Development, 1984). Considerable effort has been devoted in recent years to transferring both research findings and ongoing projects from government laboratories to industry.

The support of innovation in small open economy: some alternative directions

For Canadian policymakers there are three questions to be answered. How much support should be granted to technological innovation? What kind of innovative activity should be supported? What form should the support take?

The amount of support allocated to technological innovation will obviously depend on national economic goals. If the goal is efficient use of resources, government investment in or support for technological innovation should be guided by considerations of the social rate of return. Assistance for technological innovation should be allocated in such as way that private rates of return are reflective of, if not equal to, social rates of return. The traditional view has been that the social rate of return on innovative activity will exceed the private rate of return because the benefits of innovation are not entirely appropriable by the innovator and because innovation is risky and the social cost of risk-bearing is less than the private cost.

Policy prescriptions have generally focused on the inappropriability (spillover) problem. In this regard, the appropriate amount of assistance will be equal to the excess of the benefits appropriable by domestic nationals over the benefits appropriable by domestic innovators.

It is reasonable to expect that the smaller the country involved, the smaller will be the proportion of spillover benefits accruing to domestic nationals. If this is the case, the ideal level of assistance to innovative activity will be proportionately smaller in a small country. Indeed, it may be in the interest of very small countries, perhaps including Canada, to 'free-ride' on the innovative efforts of larger countries. This implies an absence of assistance to indigenous innovative activity, and may also involve some attenuation of the property rights of foreign innovators.[7]

In some cases there may be large domestic spillover benefits. An example is what Richard Nelson has called 'applied generic research' relating to resources that are specific to Canada or with which Canada is disproportionately well endowed; for instance, research in various aspects of agriculture, forestry and mineral extraction. As Nelson also points out, support for generic research has the additional merit of allowing for disinterested scientific assessment of alternative projects and methods (Nelson, 1982; Nelson and Langlois, 1983). As subsequent discussion will indicate, this is not true of other types of research and development activity.

In recent years economists have questioned the proposition that, left to itself, the market necessarily generates too little innovative activity. It is entirely possible that rivalry for innovators' rents will result in duplicative, premature or hurried innovative efforts, and that all appropriable rents will be dissipated as a consequence. Under these circumstances the interests of society are served by discouraging rather than encouraging innovative effort (Dasgupta and Stiglitz, 1980).

Whether there is too much or too little innovative effort from a social point of view will depend on the circumstances. It has been suggested that too much effort may have been devoted to the development of proprietary technologies and not enough to basic and applied generic research. The implication is, again, that assistance should be concentrated on basic and applied generic research in areas of particular national interest rather than on the development of proprietary technologies. Nelson (1982) points out as well that the governance of research in the field of proprietary technologies is necessarily compli-

cated by the difficulty of obtaining disinterested scientific assessment; knowledgeable parties also have considerable wealth interest at stake.

An alternative view is presented by the neo-Schumpeterians. This view,
popularised in the United States by Bruce Scott (1984) and in Canada by R.G.
Harris (1985), is that a nation can and should 'engineer' its own comparative
advantage. This involves a systematic policy of pre-emptive innovation followed by a rapid movement down the learning curve, which results in an
enduring cost advantage over potential entrants and a continuous stream of
worldwide monopoly rents.

As Michael Spence (1984) has noted, even under an ostensibly free-trade
regime governments can assist this process by subsidising proprietary innovation, providing temporary guarantees for the domestic market (through procurement, competition and regulatory policies), and providing concessionary
export financing.

Competition for Schumpeterian rents is privately attractive. Harris (1985)
argues, in addition, that it is socially efficient to encourage it and that governments of small countries have a special interest in doing so. Schumpeterian
competition is to be encouraged, in his view, basically for infant-industry
reasons. The benefits of moving down the learning curve accrue, in part, to
domestic labour, thus generating a potential externality. Moreover, the
Schumpeterian rents earned by a small country are extracted largely from
foreigners. The implication is that small countries have a special interest in
encouraging Schumpeterian competition in products in which the successful
innovator occupies the strongest proprietary position.

The neo-Schumpeterian view can be questioned on a number of grounds.
Krugman (1983, 1984b) discusses many of the conceptual problems involved.
Rivalry to pre-empt international market niches may be carried to the point
where all participants are reduced to their respective opportunity costs; that is,
ex ante rents—and hence the net advantage of participating in Schumpeterian
competition—will be nil. Moreover, there is little evidence that the benefits of
learning are either significant or confined to 'high-technology' activities; nor is
there any evidence that these benefits accrue to domestic workers rather than
foreign workers or domestic investors or that, in the absence of state intervention, domestic workers and investors would not take their mutual dependence
into account.

The practical problems include the requirement that the government of a
small country actively target assistance or pick winners. The policy implications are far-reaching, including the active suppression of domestic and foreign
competition with targeted firms.[8] The records of countries that have tried to
pick winners—that is, to support proprietary technological innovation—have
been assessed by Nelson (1982) as unambiguously disastrous. Furthermore,
Trebilcock (1985) has pointed out that a policy of picking winners complicates
the administration of industrial adjustment policies. In particular, governments find it difficult both to disengage themselves from targeted firms that
have failed and to avoid supporting declining firms that present themselves as
potential winners (the so-called breathing-space rationale for support).

The discussion to this point has focused largely on the type of indigenous innovative activity that a small country should support. In this regard the weight of the evidence favours the support of applied generic research in areas related to Canada's natural-resource endowment. It has been suggested that public policy has tilted too far toward indigenous research and development, and should be oriented more to supporting the acquisition of technology (Daly and Globerman, 1976; Economic Council of Canada, 1983). As noted, there is now considerable explicit assistance for acquiring technology in Canada, along with implicit assistance in the forms of accelerated depreciation and tax credits on new equipment. Moreover, it is not obvious that there is a significant technology-acquisition externality with which to justify this assistance. While much remains to be learned about the process of adopting technology, the tentative conclusion would have to be that a further orientation of assistance towards diffusion is unwarranted.

OPTIONS FOR INDUSTRIAL POLICY

For a medium-sized advanced economy such as Canada's the centrepiece of industrial policy is trade policy. The evidence is fairly clear that, at least in a Canadian context, trade liberalisation under the GATT and bilateral deals such as the Canada–United States automotive pact have resulted in specialisation and longer production runs, and consequently a more efficient manufacturing sector. The evidence is that even more dramatic gains can be obtained by moving towards more comprehensive free trade with the United States. There are also persuasive arguments to the effect that further trade liberalisation is a necessary if not sufficient condition for improving the record of Canadian industry in both management and the acquisition of technology.

Industrial adjustment policies will necessarily accompany changes in trade policy. There is reason to argue, however, that there will be a continuing role for policies to support industrial adjustment after the completion of trade liberalisation. These policies can be used to assist the victims of unanticipated changes in technology or world markets. They can be justified on ethical (fairness) grounds; on political grounds, as payments to those who would otherwise obstruct beneficial change; or on economic grounds, as a kind of human-capital insurance. As the literature on positive adjustment rightly emphasises, assistance should be structured so as not to retard adjustment as tariffs, quotas and firm-specific subsidies (bailouts) have often done. There is much to be said for focusing assistance on individuals rather than firms or industries and making it conditional upon some form of adaptive behaviour such as retraining.

Trade liberalisation reduces the scope for policies designed to alter national industrial structure. In a small country, trade liberalisation serves as a partial substitute for domestic competition policy. Transportation, export or other subsidies designed to assist certain firms, industries or regions are likely to be proscribed, or at least constrained, by the provisions of any free-trade arrangement. Indeed, these measures will come under increasing scrutiny from abroad whether trade is liberalised or not. Probably some of this assistance will continue in less measurable forms, such as the use of loss-making government enterprises or regulatory cross-subsidisation. Even here, however, the scope for engaging in significant unobservable subsidisation over the long term is extremely limited.

It has been argued that even under an ostensibly free-trade regime a nation can alter its industrial structure (engineer its comparative advantage) by pre-emptive entry into new markets characterised by learning or experience curves in production. In this case government support may be confined to the early stages of the process (research and development and initial market guarantees), and may not be effectively countered by other countries.

Given the strong theoretical and practical objections to the pursuit of this type of strategy, the tendency of governments to give competing subsidies to research and development suggests that some international effort to consult and if possible to limit such practices might be appropriate. While support for research and development with significant domestic spillover benefits is warranted, public support of commercial (proprietary) research and development should generally be avoided, except through the formulation of appropriate patent, copyright and trademark legislation. Here too the international implications must be accommodated, especially for a smaller industrialised economy seeking to play a role in exporting technology-intensive products.

5 Industrial policies and performance in ASEAN's 'big four'

MOHAMED ARIFF AND HAL HILL

The economies of the four larger ASEAN countries—Indonesia, Malaysia, the Philippines and Thailand—grew very rapidly in the 1970s, and even in the more subdued international environment of the 1980s all except the Philippines have recorded above-average growth. Industrialisation has been an important element in this performance. Since 1970 manufacturing has been the 'leading sector' in all but the Philippines, in the sense that manufacturing output has grown faster than that of agriculture, industry in aggregate, and services. Although not comparable with the extraordinary records of the four Asian newly industrialising countries, manufacturing growth in ASEAN's 'big four' has been very rapid by international standards. Even the relatively sluggish Philippines manufacturing sector has grown faster than that of the middle-income developing countries as a whole. The manufacturing sectors in Malaysia and Thailand grew at more than twice the rate for this group, while output growth in Indonesia was more than three times the average, albeit from a very small base.

There are important similarities among these four countries. They are members of an increasingly important and influential political association; they have many industrial policy objectives in common; the past decade has witnessed important changes in the structure and market orientation of their manufacturing industries; compared with many developing countries they are reasonably open economies with limited state ownership (at least in manufacturing); and finally, they share, to varying extents, problems of access to markets in developed countries.

However, there are also significant differences among them. The Philippines was the first ASEAN country to vigorously promote import-substituting industrialisation. Beginning in the 1970s its volume of manufactured exports grew rapidly, and these manufactured exports—mainly labour-intensive products—closely reflected its comparative advantage. But the export growth of the 1970s and the ambitious plans for industrial restructuring in the early 1980s were overtaken by the serious economic and political crisis that emerged in 1983. Malaysia is a small, well endowed and relatively prosperous country that is rapidly losing its comparative advantage in labour-intensive manufacturing as real wages increase. Consequently, its manufacturing sector is on the threshold

81

of radical restructuring. Indonesia is the least industrialised of the four, and its manufacturing sector is arguably the most heavily protected and regulated. Although (per capita) industrial output and exports are significantly lower, it is now embarking on an ambitious second round of import substitution. Thailand, also something of a latecomer to industrialisation, has experienced rapid industrial growth and is now emphasising several large resource-based projects.

In the 1970s the policy environment was an important stimulus to industrial growth and transformation and, in all these countries except Indonesia, to manufactured exports. Indeed, the objectives of industrial policy in the four are remarkably similar: all emphasise the goal of industrialisation for its own sake, as well as heavy industry, resource processing, manufactured exports, small industry and indigenous enterprise.

Industrial policy will be a critical determinant of future economic performance in these countries. Several of them, having experienced a phase of rapid, labour-intensive growth, are now actively promoting a more diversified industrial structure. This policy reappraisal raises many important questions: how are the (in some cases) conflicting objectives to be resolved? Is there any danger of a headlong and premature push into heavy industry? Should the emphasis on manufactured exports be maintained and extended? What is the scope for increased domestic processing of resources and resource-based industrialisation? Important questions also arise concerning the policy tools: what are the desirable levels and forms of protection? What role should state enterprises play? What is the appropriate mixture of regulatory policies?

The range of policy issues and the particular circumstances of each country are such that this chapter cannot answer all these complex questions. Rather, it seeks to identify some of the more important issues that must be considered in their resolution. The task is somewhat simpler than it might be because, as noted, the four have many common policy objectives. The first section provides a brief overview of recent industrial performance, emphasising in particular the changing structure of industry and the growth of manufactured exports. The second section examines various aspects of the policy environment, including the factors underlying the transition to a more outward-looking industrial sector, and looks at the trade and regulatory regime. In the third section the economic implications of government intervention are analysed, also in the light of stated policy objectives. Some concluding observations are offered in the final section.

RECENT INDUSTRIAL PERFORMANCE

Although all four countries experienced rapid growth in industrial output and exports in the 1970s, in other important respects they form a heterogeneous group (Table 5.1). The recent performances of Indonesia and the Philippines, in particular, deserve comment.

Table 5.1   ASEAN: comparative indicators of industrialisation

	Indonesia	Malaysia	Philippines	Thailand
Production[a] (value added)				
Percentage of GDP, 1982	13	18	25	19
Percentage of agriculture, 1982	50	78	109	83
Value per capita (US$)	75	326	192	148
Annual real growth, 1971–82 (%)	15	9	6	10
Exports[b]				
Broad definition				
Value per capita, 1982 (US$)	18	399	78	90
Annual real growth, 1972–82 (%)	13.3	13.1	12.1	13.6
Percentage of total exports, 1982	12.6	47.8	78.3	64.4
Narrow definition				
Value per capita, 1982 (US$)	5	163	52	37
Annual real growth, 1972–82 (%)	29.1	21.9	25.9	21.3
Percentage of total exports, 1982	3.6	19.6	45.8	26.3

Notes: a Current price data unless otherwise stated
             b The broad definition corresponds to ISIC 3, based on an ISIC-SITC concordance; the narrow definition refers to
                SITC 5–8, excluding 68 (plus 931 for the Philippines); Malaysian data refer to 1981.

Sources: ASEAN–Australia Project and Australia–Japan Centre Data Bank, Australian National University; Asian Development
             Bank *Key Indicators of Developing Member Countries of ADB* Manila: ADB (1984); World Bank *World Development
             Report* Washington, DC (various annual issues)

Indonesia possesses the largest industrial sector of the four in absolute terms, but by far the smallest on a per capita basis. In the mid-1960s, after 30 years of virtual stagnation, it was one of the least industrialised of the large developing countries (McCawley, 1981). Subsequently, manufacturing has grown very rapidly—in the 1970s almost matching that of Korea—but Indonesia's share of manufacturing in GDP is still well below those of the rest of ASEAN (excluding Brunei) and comparable middle-income developing countries.

By contrast, the Philippines has been by far the poorest performer, although it was the first of the four to cross the threshold at which manufacturing output exceeds that of agriculture and although its share of manufacturing in GDP is the highest. Both these phenomena reflect its early and prolonged period of import substitution. But despite good export growth and respectable performance for most of the 1970s, over the past few years—and even before the present crisis—growth has been declining and the share of manufacturing in employment and output has shown little change.

The growth of manufactured exports in the four countries has generally been impressive, whatever definition is adopted (see Table 5.1).[1] Indonesia again stands out from the other three, in that it recorded the fastest growth rate (using the narrow definition). But its level of manufactured exports is extremely low, either as a proportion of total exports or on a per capita basis: per capita, its manufactured exports are less than 5 per cent of Malaysia's, and their share in total exports is less than one-sixth that of the Philippines.

Rapid production growth has been accompanied by important structural changes. A simple index of structural change within each country's manufacturing sector during the 1970s reveals a strong association between output growth and the value of the index.[2] Indonesia has the highest index and the Philippines the lowest; for all but the Philippines the index is at least comparable with those of the fast-growing Asian newly industrialising countries.

The compositions and changing structures of the manufacturing sectors are illustrated in Table 5.2. (For more details see Appendix Table A1.1, column 1.) Food, textiles, chemicals, and metal and machine products are generally the principal industry groups, but there have been significant changes in their relative importance since 1971. Three of these changes warrant attention.

The first concerns food products, which in 1971 were the most important group of manufactures in all four countries. In Indonesia their share declined very sharply during the 1970s, and the Philippines and Thailand experienced smaller declines, while Malaysia registered an increase. Statistical problems partly obscure the real trend,[3] but the decline in Indonesia appears to be the result of its very limited industrialisation in 1971 and its less developed agricultural processing industries. The second change concerns the increased importance of (non-food) resource-based products. The most prominent example is Indonesia's petroleum sector; wood-processing and other chemicals (particularly fertilisers) are other examples. The third is the expanding share of machinery and equipment. Two quite separate policies have been responsible: all countries have developed their automobile industries, offering very substantial protection; and the assembly of electronics components has flourished, especially in Malaysia's free-trade zones.

It is useful to examine these structural changes in a little more detail, with reference to the main industry groups and their characteristics. Two classifications shed light on these changes: that of UNIDO (1979) into light and heavy industry, and a factor-intensity grouping based on the dominant or location-determining production inputs (Table 5.3).

The first classification, while somewhat lacking in analytical content, illustrates the increasing diversification of manufacturing in ASEAN. In all four countries the share of heavy industry has risen, a significant trend given the policy emphasis now being accorded these industries. Heavy industry consists of two fairly well defined subgroups: processing activities (paper and pulp, chemicals, non-metallic minerals and basic metal goods); and engineering and assembly activities. The latter group—sometimes referred to as capital goods (ISIC 38)—consists of more (skilled) labour-intensive activities, whereas the former requires relatively larger inputs of physical capital and resources. The shares of both subgroups have risen for all countries except Malaysia, where the increased importance of heavy industry is due entirely to engineering and assembly activities.

The second classification offers more scope for testing the theory of dynamic comparative advantage, which hypothesises a shift away from resource-based activities and labour-intensive manufactures as capital–labour ratios rise (see Garnaut and Anderson, 1980; Krueger, 1977). Trends in the relative importance of the main factor-intensity categories, using a classification developed by Krause (1982) and subsequently extended by Tyers and Phillips (1984), pro-

Table 5.2   ASEAN: distribution of manufacturing value added

Code		Indonesia (1982)	Malaysia (1981)	Philippines (1980)	Thailand (1982)
31	Food, beverages, tobacco	23.9	23.0	29.9	30.0
32	Textiles, garments, leather	10.4	7.1	11.5	19.8
33	Wood and wood products	6.5	8.8	5.5	3.0
34	Paper and paper products; printing	2.0	5.4	4.4	3.6
35	Chemicals and petroleum products	34.8	19.7	20.4	17.5
36	Non-metallic minerals products	4.8	6.1	4.2	6.7
37	Basic metals	1.8	2.4	10.2	1.4
38	Fabricated metal products; machinery	15.3	26.8	13.2	13.5
39	Miscellaneous products	0.3	0.7	0.7	3.7

Sources: Indonesia—Biro Pusat Statistik *Statistik Industri 1982* (Industrial Statistics 1982) vol. 1, Jakarta (1984); Malaysia—
            unpublished data, Department of Statistics (the assistance of Ms F. Rani in extracting the data is gratefully
            acknowledged); Philippines, National Census and Statistics Office (1983); Thailand—World Bank (1983a:117)

Table 5.3   ASEAN: the changing structure of manufacturing (percentage of total manufacturing value added)

	Indonesia		Malaysia		Philippines		Thailand[a]	
	1971	1982	1971	1981	1971	1980	1971	1982
By industry characteristics[b]								
Light industry	71	45	62	53	60	53	66	61
Heavy industry	29	55	38	47	40	48	33	40
—processing	(24)	(39)	(25)	(20)	(29)	(34)	(23)	(26)
—engineering and assembling	(5)	(15)	(13)	(27)	(11)	(13)	(10)	(14)
By factor intensity[c]								
Intensive in								
—agricultural resources	59	45	41	36	46	36	54	45
—mineral resources	5	8	9	7	12	12	2	6
—unskilled labour	23	17	9	22	19	22	22	28
—human capital	10	22	30	24	18	24	11	17
—technology	3	8	11	10	6	6	11	4

Notes: a The factor-intensity classification for Thailand refers to 1974 and 1979 and omits ISIC 353–54; comparable data
            for 1971 and 1982 are not available because of the limitations of Industrial census data.
         b This classification, derived from UNIDO (1979), is as follows: light industry—ISIC 31, 32, 33, 342, 355, 356, 390;
            heavy (processing) industry—ISIC 341, 351, 352, 353, 354, 36, 37; heavy (engineering and assembling)
            industry—ISIC 381.
         c This classification follows that of Krause (1982), as extended by Tyers and Phillips (1984).

Sources: As for Table 5.2

vide some confirmation of the theory. There has been a significant rise in the
share of labour-intensive manufactures in Malaysia (indicating also that to
classify the electronics components industry as heavy industry is somewhat
misleading) and, to a lesser extent, in the Philippines and Thailand. However,
the decline in this group in Indonesia, taken with the increased share of
human-capital-intensive industries in most countries, suggests that domestic
policy interventions have also been very important. This conclusion is supported by the fact that the theory is a better predictor for the less distorted

Malaysian and Thai economies, and for exports, where there is less scope for government intervention.

As noted, the growth of manufactured exports has been one of the most impressive aspects of economic development in all four countries, although in Indonesia it occurred only recently and from a tiny base. Several factors explain this rapid growth. These include policy reforms and export incentives, the establishment of export-processing zones, the liberal international trading environment at the time of the policy reorientation (for all but Indonesia), the emergence of international subcontracting arrangements, the relocation of activities from the industrially more advanced newly industrialising countries owing to high wages and quotas imposed by developed countries, and improved physical and human infrastructure. The growth of labour-intensive manufactured exports (textiles, garments, footwear, furniture, toys, travel goods, electronic components, and so on) has been fast in all countries, but especially in Malaysia and the Philippines (Figure 5.1).

Indexes of revealed comparative advantage illustrate the growth and changing composition of exports. The index, which is associated with Balassa (1965), measures the share of a commodity (or group of commodities) in a country's exports relative to that of the world. Although the index is subject to well-known limitations (see Bowen, 1983), especially as an indicator of comparative advantage, changes in it are at least indicative of trends in export specialisation. Table 5.4 presents the indexes of these four countries for the

Figure 5.1   ASEAN: exports of unskilled-labour-intensive manufactures, 1962–82

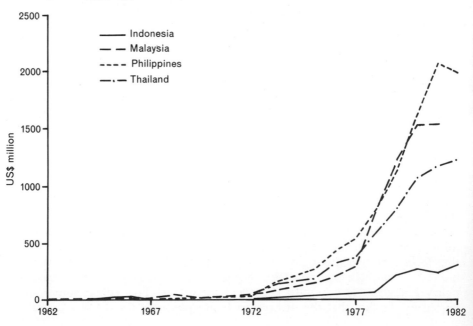

Table 5.4 ASEAN exports: indexes of revealed comparative advantage by factor-intensity categories

	Indonesia			Malaysia			Philippines			Thailand		
	1962	1972	1982	1962	1972	1981	1962	1972	1982	1962	1972	1982
Exports intensive in												
—agricultural resources:												
primary products	2.1	2.1	0.7	2.2	3.1	3.0	2.9	3.5	2.7	3.0	3.6	4.5
—agricultural resources:												
manufactures	*	0.1	1.9	0.2	3.3	2.3	3.6	4.1	3.4	0.2	1.0	1.3
—mineral resources:												
primary products	2.9	4.3	3.4	0.8	0.6	1.1	0.8	1.6	0.6	0.6	0.4	*
—mineral resources:												
manufactures	*	*	*	0.2	0.1	*	*	0.3	0.7	0.6	1.3	2.3
—unskilled labour:												
manufactures	*	*	0.1	0.1	0.2	.3	*	0.2	3.8	*	0.4	1.7
—technology:												
manufactures	*	*	*	0.1	*	0.1	*		*	*	*	0.1
—human capital:												
manufactures	*	*	*	*	*	0.1	*		*	*	*	*
All manufactures	*	*	*	*	0.2	0.3	*	0.2	0.8	*	0.2	0.5

Notes: Factor-intensity categories are based on the classification of Krause (1982), as extended by Tyers and Phillips (1984), with some minor modifications.
    *—Index is less than 0.1.

Sources: ASEAN–Australia Project and Australia–Japan Research Centre Data Bank, Australian National University

five groups of manufactures together with the non-manufacturing resource-based groups.

Three main conclusions emerge from the data. First, the primary specialisation in all four countries remains in resource exports. In most cases the index exceeds unity for the two resource groups, although there has been an overall decline in specialisation. Second, the increasing importance of manufactured exports is clearly evident. In 1962 the index for manufactures in total and for each of the five categories was negligible in all but one case (agricultural-resource-intensive manufactures—mainly wood products—in the Philippines). By the early 1980s, however, manufactures were of considerable relative importance. The indexes exceeded unity for unskilled-labour-intensive manufactures in all countries except Indonesia; those for resource-based manufactures also rose. Third, the limitations of the index notwithstanding, the trends in specialisation were broadly in accord with each country's changing comparative advantage. This conclusion is illustrated by the growth of the labour-intensive and resource-intensive groups, and by the extremely low values for technology-intensive and human-capital-intensive manufactures.

How do the level and structure of industrialisation in these four countries compare with those in other countries of similar sizes and levels of development? The results for the 1970s, prepared by UNIDO (1982), are broadly as would be expected (see Appendix Table A1.1). The first indicator (column 2), which is analogous to the indexes discussed above, is the share of a given industry group for each country relative to its shares for comparable countries. Of greatest relative importance are the resource-based industries. This is especially so for Indonesia, where four of the five 'largest' industries fall into this category. In the other countries the resource-based and labour-intensive industries are the most significant. In only one case (Malaysia) does the index exceed unity within the metal and machinery industries (ISIC 37 and 38); the exception—electronic components—is, as noted, a very labour-intensive activity.

The second indicator (column 3) is the relative degree of industrialisation. Following the Chenery-Taylor analysis, it shows value added in each industry group adjusted for the country's population and per capita income. The value of the index for manufacturing as a whole also confirms a priori expectations. It is well below unity for Indonesia, reflecting its limited industrialisation before 1970 and its large mining sector. By contrast, the higher value for the Philippines reflects the effects of its early push for industrialisation. A similar pattern of inter-industry variations emerges, with resource-based activities being especially important. The ratios for a number of labour-intensive industries are quite low, however, which suggests that there is considerable scope for promotion of these activities.

Two further aspects of industrial structure should be mentioned. The first concerns ownership. Data on the importance of state enterprises are seriously deficient. The most comprehensive are those for Indonesia in the mid-1970s, which indicate that state enterprises accounted for a little over 20 per cent of value added in the organised manufacturing sector. In other countries the share is likely to be smaller, although under Malaysia's New Economic Policy

Table 5.5   ASEAN: importance of foreign investment in manufacturing

	Indonesia[a]	Malaysia	Philippines	Thailand
Year	1980	1977	1978	1977
Stock of foreign investment				
—value in US$ million	2432	433	530	198
—as percentage of manufacturing				
value added	28.7	16.5	8.8	5.4
Year	1974/75	1978	1970	
Percentage share of				
foreign-owned firms in				
—employment	10	34	7	na
—gross value of output	21	44	na	na

Notes: a Firms employing twenty or more workers
         na—not available

Sources: *Stock of foreign investment*: Indonesia—K.W. Thee 'Japanese Direct Investment in Indonesian Manufacturing'
          Bulletin of Indonesian Economic Studies 20, 2 (1984:90–106); other countries—United Nations Center on
          Transnational Corporations *Salient Features and Trends in Foreign Direct Investments* (GT/CTC/14) New York:
          UNCTC (1983)
          Stock as percentage of manufacturing value added: World Bank *World Tables* (3rd edn, 2 vols) Washington, DC
          (1984)
          Percentage shares of foreign-owned firms: Indonesia—Biro Pusat Statistik; other countries—United Nations Center
          on Transnational Corporations *Transnational Corporations in World Development* (third survey) New York: UNCTC
          (1983)

and after the 'bailout' of large financially distressed firms in the Philippines in the early 1980s, the distinction between private and state firms is somewhat blurred.

The four countries have been large importers of capital—each averaging in excess of US$1 billion annually in the early 1980s—although foreign direct investment has usually accounted for substantially less than half the total (Hill and Johns, 1985: Table 1). The manufacturing sectors have been the main recipients of foreign equity capital in all these countries except Indonesia. The evidence, although in some cases out of date, suggests that foreign investors have been of considerable but not overwhelming importance in each country (Table 5.5). Relative to the size of its manufacturing sector, Indonesia has the largest stock of foreign investment. But these figures overstate the importance of foreign investment in Indonesia for various reasons; on the basis of employment and output shares, the level of foreign investment is relatively higher in Malaysia. In any case, such an aggregate picture obscures the importance of foreign firms in particular industries. Consistent with the theory of foreign investment, foreign firms have located more intensively in areas where they can exploit their firm-specific advantages. Extensive investments in export-processing zones and in such industries as automobiles and chemicals are cases in point.

The second aspect of industrial structure in these four countries is the changing size distribution of manufacturing firms. The process of industrialisation is characterised by a shift from predominantly cottage and small industry to larger economic units. (See Anderson [1982] for a summary of the extensive literature on the subject.) The data for ASEAN broadly confirm this trend. Small firms are of considerable importance in all four countries. In the

1970s more than three-quarters of the industrial establishments in Indonesia, the Philippines and Thailand employed fewer than five workers; in Malaysia the proportion was more than half (Bruch and Hiemenz, 1984). The shares of these firms in employment and output are, of course, quite small, and the process of consolidation into larger units is also evident. Within ASEAN this process is most apparent—and best documented—in Singapore, where, between 1965 and 1982, small firms (variously defined as those employing 10–19 or 10–49 workers) roughly halved in importance. A similar trend is emerging in Malaysia. In Indonesia and the Philippines the data are less complete, but the same generalisation appears to be valid.

INDUSTRIAL POLICIES

All four of these countries have promoted their industrial sectors to some extent. Initially this promotion took the form of import substitution; subsequently, more outward-oriented strategies have been adopted. The nature of these early policies and the rationale for the transition are well known and need not be recounted in detail.[4] Indonesia and the Philippines embarked on an import-substitution strategy partly in response to a severe foreign-exchange crisis in 1949. Extensive controls and quotas for the following two decades imparted a strong domestic-market bias, which was not fundamentally altered by a brief episode of liberalisation in the 1960s. Indonesia, in contrast to the other three, introduced few systematic and sustained programs to promote industry before the late 1960s. A range of measures were introduced in the early 1950s, but these were largely unsuccessful and were subsequently overtaken by the general economic deterioration after 1957. By 1965 much of the very small 'factory' sector was in state hands.

Malaysia and Thailand maintained their historically open economies well into the postwar period. Initially tariffs were primarily for revenue purposes. The belief—which was especially strong in Malaysia—that the main beneficiaries of tariffs would be non-indigenous business groups inhibited the adoption of more protectionist policies. Malaysia experienced a fairly mild period of import substitution, with primary reliance on tariffs, beginning in the late 1950s. Systematic manufacturing protection commenced in Thailand at about the same time, and, though more extensive than in Malaysia, was still lower than it was in the other two countries.

The reorientation of policy towards exports began around 1970 in Malaysia, the Philippines and Thailand, and a decade later in Indonesia. A number of factors contributed to the change: disappointment at the poor record of import substitution; the spectacular demonstration effect of the four Asian newly industrialising countries; the changing climate of intellectual opinion (not least within international development organisations); and, especially for Indonesia, a sharp decline in real commodity prices (in this case petroleum). It would be misleading to characterise the transition as being simply from import substitution to export promotion, however. Rather, the reorientation has resulted in a—sometimes awkward—mixture of policies, encouraging, on a selective basis, both import-substituting and export-oriented activities.

The promotion of exports is just one of a range of industrial policy objectives in each country.[5] Despite their differences in political institutions, history and levels of industrialisation, all four emphasise a remarkably similar combination of objectives. Moreover, these objectives tend to be very general and all-embracing, to the extent that some are directly contradictory. The list, common to all four countries to some degree, includes the promotion of exports; the encouragement of small industry and labour-intensive activities; greater regional dispersal of industry; 'industrial deepening', including the development of resource-based industries and high-value-added ('high-technology') activities; higher levels of domestic processing in export-oriented resource industries; the development of a more efficient industrial sector; and the extension of indigenous control over industry, especially in Indonesia and Malaysia.

It would be an enormous task to examine the nature and economic effects of such a wide range of policy issues, each of which receives a somewhat different emphasis in the four countries. A selective approach is necessary. The fundamental point should be stressed that government intervention has been an important element in the past and will be a critical determinant of future performance. The issue is not whether the ASEAN governments will or should intervene. The experience of the Asian newly industrialising countries—Hong Kong excepted—and Japan refutes the notion that intervention and rapid growth are incompatible. Rather the focus is on the implications of various forms of intervention for industrial growth.

Protection policies[6]

The intensity levels of protection have varied considerably, as have the instruments used. Malaysia, especially, and Thailand have adopted modest protection regimes with considerable reliance on tariffs. By contrast, Indonesia and the Philippines have erected substantial import barriers, and tariffs have not been the main instrument of protection (although the intention of the recent reforms in the Philippines was to reduce protection in general and reliance on non-tariff barriers in particular). To this general assessment of protection policies, two qualifications should be attached. The first is the existence of smuggling, which erodes protective barriers, especially for goods that are high in value and low in volume (mainly consumer goods). As might be expected, smuggling is most extensive in the two more inward-looking, archipelago states, Indonesia and the Philippines.

The second concerns exchange-rate policy, which has been a particularly contentious issue in Indonesia. Before 1966 the rupiah was usually substantially overvalued, but after the oil price increases, an altogether different problem emerged in the form of the 'Dutch disease'. The effect of the commodity boom was a real appreciation of the rupiah and a squeeze on the non-oil tradable

Table 5.6   ASEAN: simple averages of tariff rates for manufactures, 1978 (per cent)

SITC code		Indonesia	Malaysia	Philippines	Thailand	ASEAN
5	Chemicals and related products, nes	26.8	19.2	41.1	28.1	30.5
6	Manufactured goods classified chiefly by materials	37.9	14.9	52.0	32.0	27.4
7	Machinery and transport equipment	18.0	10.7	23.0	18.0	14.2
8	Miscellaneous manufactured articles	49.9	19.0	68.9	37.8	35.8
	Overall	33.0	15.3	44.2	29.4	25.5

Note: nes—not elsewhere specified.

Source: R.M. Bautista 'The 1981–85 Tariff Changes and Effective Protection of Manufacturing Industries' *Journal of Philippine Development* 8, 1 & 2, 1981, pp. 1–20

goods sector, including much of manufacturing.[7] A similar effect, although less pronounced, was present in Malaysia. By contrast, the Philippine peso has generally been overvalued, maintained by a range of foreign-exchange and input controls.[8]

Severe data problems confront a quantitative comparison of protection regimes. The simple averages of nominal tariff rates for 1978 suggest that the Philippines is the most protectionist of the four, both in aggregate and for manufactures (Table 5.6; manufactures are defined as SITC 5–8). Then follow Indonesia and Thailand, with Malaysia substantially behind the other three. While these data confirm general expectations, they are deficient in two important respects. One is that they refer to nominal rather than effective protection rates. The other is that they do not take account of extensive non-tariff barriers. To obtain a more comprehensive picture, it is necessary to refer to a plethora of estimates of protection in each country. The results (summarised in Appendix Tables A1.2–5) should be interpreted with great caution. Because of differences in classification systems, coverage and methods of computation, both intertemporal and inter-country comparisons are exceedingly difficult.

Three general features of protection in these countries emerge from these studies. The first is that there is an enormous dispersion in the effective rates of protection, from in some cases negative to in other cases several hundred per cent. This is so for all four countries, even Malaysia, where the aggregated data obscure much of the dispersion. The range for Indonesia is very large, and is understated in the latter two estimates because the effects of most non-tariff barriers are not captured.

Second, the structure of protection displays a 'cascading' pattern. Low or even negative effective protection is conferred on capital goods, while consumer goods and activities at higher stages of fabrication generally receive substantial protection. While this is not apparent in all cases, it is suggestive of 'made-to-measure' protection, given the initial emphasis on consumer goods in the import-substitution phase. This structure may be expected to change during the second round of import substitution, which is directed at capital and intermediate goods.

A final observation is that effective protection appears to have risen in the early and mid-1970s, and thereafter declined somewhat. This is especially so for Indonesia and the Philippines, although it is true that there are severe data problems in the former case, and that policy reforms remain incomplete in the latter. More confidence may be attached to the reliability of the data for Malaysia and Thailand.

The regulatory environment[9]

Protection is just one form of intervention, and one of the more visible forms. An assessment of government intervention in ASEAN countries must take account of the plethora of regulatory agencies and licensing requirements and the manner in which they operate. Although these forms of regulation raise somewhat different policy issues and are not easily quantifiable, their economic implications are at least as important as those of protection policy. Moreover, as the Asian newly industrialising countries illustrate, it is not so much the extent as the type of regulation that is significant. Within ASEAN the contrast between Singapore on the one hand and Indonesia and the Philippines on the other is particularly evident. In Singapore government expenditure as a proportion of GDP is significantly higher, and there are extensive controls. But such intervention frequently takes the form of 'market-facilitating' regulation to achieve policy objectives, rather than 'market-inhibiting' regulation in the form of restrictions and controls.

One attempt to assess the extent of regulation is the World Bank's (1983b) 'distortion index', which attempts to measure government-induced deviations in the prices of foreign exchange, factor inputs and products from their scarcity values. The estimates for the four ASEAN countries were all substantially below the simple average for a sample of 31 developing countries. Such exercises are at best suggestive, however, since much regulation takes the form of non-price intervention, the extent of which is not easily measured.

Government regulations impinge on virtually all facets of industrial activity in the organised sectors of the four countries. Perhaps the most important regulatory bodies are the investment boards,[10] both because fiscal incentives must be licensed with these boards and because such licensing confers 'official' status on firms, which facilitates dealings with the rest of the bureaucracy. Many other regulatory authorities are also important. These generally include the ministries of industry, trade (both internal and external) and labour, and agencies for the environment, social security, urban zoning, securities and exchange, local government, and antitrust activities. In addition, and of even greater significance in some cases, there is a great deal of industry-specific regulation, such as local-content plans for the automotive and appliance industries.

Generalisations regarding the regulatory systems are difficult, in part because of the unpredictable nature of government intervention. Regulations generally confer substantial discretionary authority on the implementing agencies. Hence the effects of intervention may differ from the original intentions.

As with protection, there are considerable inter-industry variations in the extent of regulation in all four countries. As with protection also, recent trends suggest a moderation in the intensity of regulation, especially in Indonesia and the Philippines. Important changes began in the Philippines in the late 1970s, affecting trade controls and Board of Investment procedures, including the notorious 'overcrowding' provisions. The Indonesian reforms were introduced more recently and seem to be more comprehensive.

State enterprises present a special case of intervention. These operate in all four countries in the usual areas (public utilities, transport, and so on), and some also compete directly with private firms. The motives for their establishment have generally been similar to those of regulation in general, in addition to the—generally unsuccessful—objective of generating government revenue. There are no clear statistical indications of their role and importance. All four governments have, to some extent, embraced the objective of privatisation, but the evidence is mixed. In the Philippines, the country in which state enterprises have historically been of least importance, there was an extensive rescue operation for several large, financially weak firms in the early 1980s. This was reflected in a sharp rise in the importance of 'corporate outlays' in the government budget. In the first half of the 1970s this item accounted for less than one-third of a modest capital budget; by 1980 and 1981 its share of a much-expanded capital budget exceeded 50 per cent (Canlas et al., 1984). The Indonesian government has promoted privatisation, but the distinction between many state and private firms is somewhat blurred. Similar moves in Malaysia have been overshadowed by the promotion of heavy industry, in which quasi-state enterprises play an important role.

Foreign investment and technology transfer

All four governments have adopted relatively liberal policies towards imports of capital and technology. Foreign investment is generally administered by the investment boards, which, as well as administering general regulatory controls, usually impose three main requirements on foreign firms. First, they often exclude foreign firms from certain sectors, for example, the media, land ownership, and some services; second, there are usually minimum local-equity requirements (which, however, are generally waived for 'pioneer' or exporting firms); and third, there are stipulations that management and ownership be progressively localised. Not infrequently, governments have intervened in response to nationalist demands for control over foreign investment,[11] but there are also important economic issues concerning the distribution of gains between foreign investors and domestic welfare.

A more recent form of intervention concerns technology flows. All these countries except Indonesia have established regulatory authorities to monitor and approve licensing agreements, control of which is exercised through investment boards and central banks (Santikarn, 1984). The intention is to supervise all such agreements, although in practice those between non-affiliated firms (that is, firms in which there is no foreign equity) are difficult to administer. Government controls over imports of technology and capital have been imposed for similar reasons. In addition, in the case of technology, intervention is predicated on the notion that the international market for technology is inherently imperfect and that government regulation strengthens the bargaining position of local licensees. The belief that such agreements may be a means of circumventing taxation and foreign-exchange controls has been a further reason for intervention.

Fiscal incentives

The four countries offer a range of investment and export incentives. The introduction of investment incentives corresponded broadly with the establishment of investment boards in the 1960s. The principal elements of the packages are similar, including tax holidays or reductions, investment allowances, import-duty exemptions, and provisions for carrying losses forward. Initially they were introduced in a largely ad hoc fashion, and reflected industrial policy goals in only the broadest sense. As government policy emphasis in the region has moved from protection to promotion, incentives policy has become more discriminating. Indonesia has recently abolished a wide range of incentives in the context of a thorough reform of its fiscal policies. Malaysia, also, is undertaking a wide-ranging review of its incentives package.

Export incentives have been another element of industrial promotion, although in some cases—Indonesia, especially, but also the Philippines—they were introduced after investment incentives were in place. Export incentives have generally been implemented in a partial sense; rather than constituting a systematic reform of the general bias against exports, they have taken the form of particular measures, often on an industry-specific basis. The most common measure has been putting export firms on a free-trade footing (partially, ignoring exchange-rate considerations) by establishing export-processing zones or duty-rebate schemes. Other policies include preferential access to credit and the removal of foreign-equity and some labour controls.

SOME ECONOMIC IMPLICATIONS OF INDUSTRIAL POLICIES

Governments have played an important role in the generally impressive performance of the ASEAN economies. In most cases they have provided reasonably stable and secure economic and political environments. They have also helped by investing in physical infrastructure and training. Moreover, in spite of complex and cumbersome bureaucratic controls, they have maintained relatively open economies with predominantly private ownership. Government policies have, in addition, contributed to the growth of the manufacturing sector. The purpose of this section is to examine the effects of industrial policies in some detail, in the light of the stated policy objectives, and to consider the desirability of some of these objectives.

A useful framework within which to assess these issues is the standard structure–conduct–performance model of industrial organisation. There are surprisingly few studies in this area for ASEAN,[12] reflecting in part the neglect of industrial economics in the region's universities. There are both conceptual and empirical problems associated with the application of this model to the four countries: data (especially time-series) constraints are serious; manufacturing growth has been very rapid, giving rise to dynamic lags and related problems of measurement; foreign and state ownership are important in some industries, and 'industrial groups' are ubiquitous (but industrial data are usually at firm or even plant level); and international trade is typically more important than it is in large developed countries, and its effects are not easily incorporated into modelling exercises (Caves, 1980). These difficulties do not necessarily render the standard model invalid, however. It is reasonable to assume—and the few empirical studies confirm this—that less competitive structures are likely to be associated with poorer industrial performance.

Export growth

Government policies have been central to the rapid export growth in these countries, but the promotion of exports has not been a costless exercise, nor have policies always achieved their stated objectives. In the first place, the structure of protection in some of these countries has discriminated against export industries, both sectorally (agriculture is generally more export-oriented than manufacturing but receives less protection) and within manufacturing. The Philippines is a case in point. Tan (1979:170–71) draws attention to the negative correlation between export orientation and effective protection within manufacturing in the mid-1970s. Data constraints preclude an examination of this issue in Indonesia, but it is plausible to draw the same conclusion. Exchange-rate overvaluation—notably, again, in the Philippines—has had a similar effect.

This conclusion requires qualification to the extent that exporting firms may operate on a virtually free-trade basis. Export-processing zones have been one means of achieving partial trade reform, especially in Malaysia and, to a lesser extent, the Philippines. These zones do, however, require substantial public investment. Recent research (Spinanger, 1984; Warr, 1985) reaches no definitive conclusions about their social profitability. The many Malaysian zones appear to be a productive form of investment. By contrast, the principal Philippine zone (Bataan) is not, and the small Jakarta zone is at best marginal.

Of more importance than the zones, in all but Malaysia, is a range of rebates and draw-back schemes. Like export-processing zones, they are very much a second-best solution to trade reform. To the extent that they do not require large public outlays, they might be a preferred policy. But surveys suggest that firms, particularly those with foreign equity, favour the zones, perhaps because geographic separation facilitates smoother customs procedures and confers a general sense of security.

In any case, these schemes do not necessarily provide full compensation for the anti-export bias of the trade regime. For one thing, their operation is affected by the general regulatory environment. In Indonesia and the Philippines, firms incur considerable costs in operating these schemes, and these costs are exacerbated for small exporters by the presence of substantial pecuniary economies of scale in dealing with the bureaucracy (McCawley, forthcoming). Moreover, recent surveys reveal that many firms do not regard these incentives as particularly important, nor, in some cases, do they believe that the considerable expense incurred in obtaining them is justified. This may be one reason for the absence of a strong inter-industry association between export performance and export incentives.[13]

State enterprises

State enterprises have frequently been established for 'non-economic' reasons—to redress ethnic imbalances in ownership, to promote regional diversification, and to control core industries—as well as for the usual economic objectives. The limited data on their performance suggest that, with a few notable exceptions—see for example, the glowing report on PUSRI, the Indonesian state fertiliser company (World Bank, 1983b)—very few are profitable: their rates of return on assets are very low, some incur substantial losses, and many receive some form of budgetary support. Moreover, in cases where they compete with private firms their performance is usually inferior.

Financial-performance data for state enterprises must be interpreted with caution, however, for at least two reasons. The first is that profitability provides little indication of economic efficiency. State enterprises are often monopolies, or operate in heavily regulated industries. In addition they receive subsidies, many of which (for example, credit guarantees, preferential procurements) are not easily quantifiable. Second, it is necessary to take account of the institutional constraints under which state enterprises operate. Not infrequently, multiple (and sometimes conflicting) objectives are imposed, the firms have limited commercial independence, and the link between reward and performance is very weak.

Although all four governments are nominally pursuing the goal of limited privatisation, the particular policy issues differ somewhat. In the Philippines the principal concern is the removal of many large corporations from the public sector, following extensive (and indirect) nationalisations in which public equity has been substituted for loan defaults to government banks. In Indonesia and Malaysia, government enterprise is being used to fulfill the objectives of heavy industry, and also to reduce their demands on government budgets. Promoting an objective of dubious economic viability through enter-prises with a mixed performance record does not augur well for many of these projects.

Small-scale industry

It has already been noted that small firms are of considerable, although generally declining, importance in each country. All four governments have instituted special programs of technical and financial assistance for these firms. While these programs may be justified on the grounds of employment genera-tion, regional dispersion or the development of entrepreneurship (Chee, 1984a), the general policy environment often has the effect of discriminating against these firms. Bruch and Hiemenz (1984: ch.9) provide the most thorough support for this proposition, and the following paragraph draws on their conclusions.

A range of policies, which are in principle scale-neutral, contribute to this outcome. Government controls over the capital market, ostensibly designed to provide access to finance for both large and small firms, often have the effect of excluding small firms from the formal credit market, for well documented reasons. This appears to be especially true in the Philippines and Indonesia, despite the existence there of small credit programs. The regulatory environ-ment has also tended to have similar effects. Licences bring powerful rents to their holders, and it is generally the larger firms, whose owners are better connected and more able to comply with official requirements, that benefit from them (McCawley, forthcoming). Larger firms may also be helped by the structure of protection: Bruch and Hiemenz (1984) conclude that there is some evidence to suggest a positive correlation between effective protection and the share of large firms in an industry. Finally, one means of promoting small firms—subcontracting—has produced indifferent results in all four countries, partly because it is the small, fragmented and protected industries on which enforced subcontracting programs have been imposed (Hill, 1985; Odaka, 1983).

Generation of employment

This objective, as already noted, is emphasised in the plans of all countries. It has been translated into policy through the priority rankings of the investment boards, as well as through specific measures such as Malaysia's Labour Utilisa-tion Scheme. As with the promotion of small industry, however, government policies often have the opposite effect, for at least three reasons.

The first is the general discrimination against small firms, which, because they are usually more labour-intensive, produces a similar bias against the generation of employment. Second, there are the effects of incentives pack-ages; while these may, in principle, be factor-price-neutral, in practice many have a capital-cheapening bias, which induces firms to adopt excessively capital-intensive techniques.[14] Third, the general bias against exports militates against labour absorption, in the sense that export-oriented industries tend to be more labour-intensive than import-competing industries. (Krueger [1983] synthesises the results of numerous case studies, including those for Indonesia and Thailand.) There may also be an inverse relationship between labour intensity and effective protection, although Rhee (1983) was unable to find support for this proposition in any of the four countries.

Regional dispersal of industry

The trade and regulatory regimes are generally regarded as having exacerbated the concentration of industry around capital cities. This is particularly the case in the Philippines, where the predominance of industries based in Manila more or less coincided with the push for import substitution. Indeed, a recent study has found that a proxy for the effects of the trade regime was one of the explanatory factors in firms locating around Manila (Pernia and Padcranga, 1983). The system of regulation is likely to have been especially important in determining the location of footloose manufacturing activities. The plethora of licensing requirements and customs precedures and the need for access to policymakers are all conducive to siting firms in capital cities. Zoning regulations, such as the ban on erecting new factories within 50 km of Manila, frequently have the effect of simply creating industrial satellite towns.

Nevertheless, the effects of these policies on regional development should not be overstated. The superior infrastructures and skilled labour forces of the capital cities are probably of greater importance. The evidence, moreover, suggests that, in aggregate, trade and regulatory policies have not had a great effect on the regional distribution of industry. The strongest concentration around a capital city occurs in the traditionally open economy of Thailand, whereas such concentration is quite modest in Indonesia, which has the most regulated and protected industrial sector.[15]

Foreign investment and the transfer of technology

Government controls over technology-licensing agreements and foreign investment have produced mixed. results. In the former case, an information dissemination function is justified. Government involvement may also strengthen the bargaining power of potential local licensees in the dealing with intransigent suppliers of technology. Moreover, as Peck and Tamura (1976) have demonstrated in the case of Japan, governments may intervene to restrain competitive bidding for lucrative licensing contracts in internationally oligopolistic industries. There has been no systematic evaluation of the operation of ASEAN agencies for regulating the acquisition of technology. It has been suggested that these agencies have achieved substantial savings through government-supervised negotiations (see Bautista [1980] for the Philippines), but verification would require comparison with unregulated markets.

Foreign-investment controls may have hastened the process of localisation and encouraged the introduction of more appropriate products and technologies. But numerous case studies—especially in Indonesia—have concluded that training requirements, local participation in management and controls over domestic trade arrangements are widely flouted. Moreover, there is some evidence (again in Indonesia) to suggest that foreign firms have generally entered highly protected industries, thus enhancing their scope for earning above-normal profits. The benefits to the domestic economy from foreign investment are more likely to be maximised if markets are competitive and the bureaucracy is efficient. (See Dorrance and Hughes [1984] for an elaboration of these issues.)

Heavy industry

The role of heavy industry is perhaps the most contentious industrial policy issue in the four countries. Beginning in the late 1970s all governments began to promote these industries, on a selective basis, through a combination of import protection, financial inducements and direct state investment. In evaluating these programs, a number of observations are relevant.

First, as already noted, heavy industry has been expanding without (and in some cases despite) government intervention. Although the terminology and statistical classifications are somewhat inappropriate—especially in the case of Malaysia—a good deal of the expansion has taken the form of ancillary production units, service workshops and so on, which are essential to an efficient manufacturing sector. Second, it might be argued that a static view of comparative advantage, with heavy reliance on labour-intensive activities, may miss important elements in the industrialisation process. There are dynamic externalities in the process of 'learning by doing', it is alleged, that are not easily amenable to conventional analysis, and planners may need to anticipate changing comparative advantage. Third, protectionist pressures in developed countries may hasten the transition to heavy industry because of market-access difficulties for labour-intensive exports.[16] Finally, it has been argued in the region, heavy industry must be promoted if these countries are to develop a capacity to absorb and assimilate advanced imported technology, especially if this technology is inappropriate to the factor endowments of labour-abundant economies.

The promotion of heavy industry raises many complex issues. Two other industrially advanced Northeast Asian economies—China and Korea—have modified their plans for the development of these industries on a large scale. Much heavy industry is intensive not only in physical capital—presumably not an obstacle, since this is an internationally mobile factor—but also in technology and skilled labour. The four ASEAN countries typically spend less than 0.5 per cent of their GDP on research and development (in contrast to about 2 per

cent for most developed countries), which provides little basis for the development of a high-technology infrastructure. This is especially so as an increasing
number of these industries are experiencing rapid changes in design and
technology (Pack, 1981). Plants embodying 'state of the art' technology may
become outmoded and inefficient within a very short time unless there is a
capacity to innovate and update.

Nor do changing international circumstances provide an encouraging basis
for the promotion of heavy industry. The range of technologies available in the
international market has expanded rapidly. Whereas twenty years ago the
United States and a few OECD countries were the principal exporters of
technology, first Japan and then several advanced developing countries have
since emerged, resulting in a more competitive market—and one with greater
choices in terms of design, factor proportions and so on—for off-the-shelf
purchases of technology (Contractor, 1981). In addition, depressed markets in
a number of industries (for example, steel and certain petrochemicals) have
resulted in exports by efficient producers on a marginal-cost basis.

There are other reasons for proceeding with caution. For one, the record of
the infant-industry justification for promoting heavy industries is not particularly encouraging, as experience in countries as diverse as India and Brazil has
demonstrated (Bell et al., 1984). For another, many of these activities are
scale-intensive, which, in the relatively small ASEAN markets, will result in
higher production costs unless export markets are developed. The heavily
promoted motor vehicle industry is a case in point. In all four countries
(Singapore, notably, has abandoned the industry) the local markets are small
and extremely fragmented and there is little prospect of exports. Thailand has
nineteen plants producing approximately 70 models of passenger cars and
commercial vehicles. The new Malaysian car—the Proton Saga, produced
under the auspices of the government's Heavy Industry Corporation (Chee,
1984b)—is unlikely to be economic with an annual output of 40 000 units and
high local content. Indonesia, the region's largest market (155 000 vehicles in
1983), has no fewer than 40 assemblers and 140 models (Hill, 1984).[17]

The consequence is that many large projects, from aeroplanes in Indonesia
to cars in Malaysia and steel in the Philippines and Indonesia (in the former,
temporarily deferred), are likely to require substantial support, in the form of
either made-to-measure protection, direct subsidies or financially assisted state
enterprises. They may also inhibit export growth, to the extent that basic
industries are established that require downstream users (who are likely to be
more export-oriented and labour-intensive) to source domestically. Moreover,
they may, for a substantial period, entail increased dependence on foreign
capital, technology and expertise, even though one of the reasons for promoting heavy industry has been to foster self-reliance.

Nevertheless, the ASEAN governments have displayed a good deal of flexibility in industrial policymaking, and for this reason the final number of
uneconomic projects may be quite modest. The activities of Malaysia's Heavy
Industry Corporation were curtailed in 1983 following large government and
trade deficits. In Indonesia various large projects were deferred in 1983 after

the decline in real oil prices. Several of the contentious eleven main industrial projects in the Philippines have been shelved because of the present crisis. The Thai government, also, is proceeding cautiously with its Eastern Seaboard Development Program. Ultimately, heavy industry projects must be assessed individually. A number of resource-based processing activities (see the following section) and a range of engineering and assembly activities (see Oshima, 1984) lie within ASEAN's actual or 'potential' sources of comparative advantage. An optimistic scenario would envisage a strategy that encourages training and local research and development capacity; that promotes industry selectively, avoiding activities requiring advanced scientific knowledge and rapid design changes (see Pack, 1981); and that ensures continued pragmatic and flexible economic management.

Resource processing

The development of resource-based processing industries is also being emphasised in all four countries. These industries encompass a diverse range of activities, from simple agricultural processing to extremely capital- and energy-intensive mining operations. Nevertheless, the rationales for their promotion, in ASEAN and elsewhere, are broadly similar. There is a desire to increase domestic value added from resource-exporting industries; onsite processing may, by reducing weight, lead to savings in transport cost; the belief is widespread that processing activities are competitive industries that have been hampered in the past by artificial barriers such as administered shipping prices and tariff barriers that escalate with the level of processing; and developing countries (especially those with lower population densities) may be more willing or able to accept the environmental costs that such processing frequently entails.

It is not possible to examine these issues in any detail. Roemer's (1979:167) observation that 'resource-based industrialisation has been advocated more than it has been analysed' remains a valid assessment of much of the debate. Recent surveys of the issues do, however, point to a number of general conclusions for the ASEAN 'big four'.[18]

First, the case for onsite processing involving energy-intensive activities is likely to be strengthened by the ready availability of energy sources other than oil (because of transport-cost savings). Coal, hydroelectric power and natural gas have all been utilised in recent energy-intensive projects, including the huge hydro-powered Asahan alumina plant in Indonesia and Thailand's natural-gas-based petrochemicals complex. Second, these four countries possess a number of resources for which the weight reductions from processing are especially significant; these include timber (important in all four countries), alumina (Indonesia) and copper (the Philippines). Moreover, technological advances, such as the continuous casting of metals, may in some cases tie fabricators more closely to processors (examples include copper refining and alumina smelting). Finally, there is still considerable scope for improving the processing facilities for a range of agricultural products.

There are few detailed published studies of resource-processing projects in ASEAN. Both Indonesia and Malaysia have increased their petroleum-refining capacity rapidly in recent years, but the economic viability of these investments has not been disclosed. The huge Asahan plant is believed to be economic—because of the availability of very cheap power—but few details are available. A recent examination of tin processing (Lim, 1980), an industry present in all but the Philippines, has suggested that domestic processing may not be economic, at least for the industry's chief product, tin-plate. This is because tin is not the main input (iron ore is more important) and because capacity utilisation is a crucial determinant of viability. But for other tin products, where scale economies are less significant and tin is a more important input, such processing may be viable. Similarly, a careful evaluation of a copper-smelting project in the Philippines (Emerson and Warr, 1981) suggests that it is at best only marginally socially profitable, and that the results of the study are subject to considerable uncertainty. Another case in point is the development in the region of primary steel-manufacturing capacity. The huge requirements of capital, technology and skilled labour, together with the very large economies of scale, raise serious questions about the desirability of these projects (Oshima, 1984).

CONCLUSION

Manufacturing output grew rapidly in all four countries during the 1970s and, although the growth rates declined in the early 1980s, there are prospects for continuing good performance in these countries, except for the Philippines. Two aspects of the recent manufacturing growth have been emphasised here. The first is the transition towards a more diversified manufacturing sector, including the development of processing and machine-goods industries. The second is the emergence of a more outward-oriented manufacturing sector; manufactured exports have grown rapidly and, in all but Indonesia, they constitute a significant proportion of all merchandise exported.

Industrial policy has been an important element in this performance, in the maintenance of political stability in most countries, in the provision of general infrastructure, and in the introduction of a range of specific measures. Government intervention is extensive in all four countries. This chapter argues that it is not so much the amount as the type of intervention that is important. Much of it takes the form of efficiency-inhibiting regulation, which often contributes little to a range of other objectives, such as the generation of employment, regional development and the promotion of small-scale industry.

Manufacturing in ASEAN is now at the crossroads. Apart from the Philippines, where the immediate problem is to overcome the present serious financial crisis, the principal issues concern the impending second round of import substitution and the continued growth of manufactured exports. Manufacturing performance in the coming decade will largely depend on the policies adopted towards these issues.

6 The industrial policy of Taiwan

KUO-SHU LIANG AND CHING-ING HOU LIANG

Economic conditions in Taiwan during the early postwar period were similar to those in many resource-poor, low-income developing countries: the country was overpopulated and the natural rate of growth of its population exceeded 3 per cent a year; the domestic market was small; inordinate military needs competed with development projects for scarce resources; and the economy suffered from chronic balance-of-payments deficits and violent inflation (Jacoby, 1966:118; Lin, 1973:30–31).

As can be seen in Appendix Table A2.1, manufacturing activity accounted for 11 per cent of NDP in 1952, while 38 per cent of NDP originated in the primary sector. In the same year exports accounted for 8 per cent of GNP, and in 1955 the share of manufactured exports in total exports was only 7.6 per cent. Industrial policy in Taiwan has had to cope with problems in order to encourage investment and accelerate structural transformation.

This chapter explains and attempts to understand more fully that Taiwan's economy will be able to overcome adversity and grow steadily, provided that its industrial policies remain well adapted to the changing internal and external economic conditions. The first section briefly highlights the success of export-led industrialisation in Taiwan. The second part explains the challenges the economy faces in the 1980s and examines the government's industrial policy for achieving growth and productivity gains in a changing economic environment.

EXPORT-LED INDUSTRIALISATION IN TAIWAN

The reconstruction of the Taiwanese economy began in earnest in 1949, a year that witnessed the relocation of the central government on the island. Economic development from the end of World War II to about 1960 was characterised by efforts to promote growth in the agricultural sector, coupled with import-substituting industrialisation.

A broad base for economic development was created by the land reforms carried out from 1949 to 1953 (Tang and Liang, 1973:116–17). The positive role played by the agricultural sector in Taiwan offers a sharp contrast to the experiences of many of the other less developed countries, where lack of agricultural development has acted as a drag on industrial and general economic development.

Prewar production levels were by and large restored during the years 1948–51, and United States economic aid was resumed in June 1950, after the outbreak of the Korean War. Taiwan was the beneficiary of a substantial aid program. A total of US$1444 million had been appropriated over the period 1951–65, amounting to US$10 per capita a year. Aid played an important role in helping to control inflation in the early 1950s. In addition, were it not for United States aid, Taiwan's trade gap would have become a serious limitation on its economic development until the early 1960s. United States aid broke this bottleneck by augmenting foreign-exchange resources and sustaining the importation of necessary inputs that complemented domestic labour and other investment components. The share of United States aid imports in total imports remained above 30 per cent until 1961, but declined rapidly thereafter (Liang and Lee, 1974:296–99).

The diversification and expansion of industrial production placed primary emphasis on the domestic market. The government adopted a multiple exchange-rate system and strict import controls during this period. Such measures increased the profitability of import substitution, and were partly responsible for the doubling of manufacturing production during the period 1950–58. The changes in the relative importance of the primary and manufacturing sectors reflect the structural transformation that is expected to accompany economic development. By 1960 manufacturing activity accounted for 17 per cent of NDP, and the compound annual growth rate of manufacturing employment exceeded 4 per cent throughout the 1950s.

Changes in the terms of trade between the agricultural and non-agricultural sectors during the 1950s clearly show that the intersectoral terms of trade became highly unfavourable to agriculture (Lee, 1971:91). The primary-product-exporting sector appeared to bear the burden of the import-substitution policy. For instance, import substitution of textiles received full official blessing by providing the necessary raw materials to the manufacturers through United States aid imports and by restricting imports of finished goods (Lin, 1973:61–63).

The simple and relatively easy phase of import substitution appeared, however, to reach its limit relatively quickly in a narrow, protected domestic market. It was recognised that only an outward-looking or export-oriented industrialisation strategy could sustain a high rate of economic growth in a small island economy such as Taiwan, and a series of policy reforms were undertaken from 1958 to 1961. The overvalued currency was devalued, and the complicated exchange-rate structure was simplified and, in June 1961, was finally unified. The laws and regulations governing investment and imports were liberalised. The emphasis of trade strategy shifted from strict import controls to export promotion. The economic indicators shown in Appendix Table A2.1 clearly reveal that economic performance in the 1960s and the early 1970s improved notably as compared with that in the 1950s.

Export incentives in Taiwan comprised rebates of customs duties (including defence surtax and harbour dues) and commodity tax on imported raw materials;[1] exemption from business and related stamp taxes; a deduction of 2 per cent of annual total export earnings from taxable income, and a 10 per cent tax reduction for manufacturing, mining or handicrafts corporations exporting more than 50 per cent of their output;[2] retention of foreign-exchange earnings for the importation of raw materials and machinery without having to go through the procedures for the application for foreign exchange, together with the privilege of selling such import rights to other firms;[3] special low-interest loans to provide financing for pre-shipment production and the importation of raw materials; and export insurance by a government organisation. Such manufactures as textiles, canned mushrooms, canned asparagus spears and citronella oil formed trading organisations to control production and exports through export quotas and unified quotation of export prices. Direct subsidies for exports were devised by a few industries, such as cotton-spinning, steel and iron, rubber products, monosodium glutamate, wool and fabric, and paper and paper products, financed through the manufacturers' associations concerned. These schemes amounted to private levies on domestic sales, or on materials used to manufacture products for domestic sale, with corresponding bounties on exports.[4] Exports were also assisted by government and semi-government agencies for export inspection, managerial, technical and trade consultation services, market research, and participation in international trade fairs. Moreover, exports have been assisted by the creation of tax-and-duty-free export-processing zones since 1965. The zones were erected to encourage investment in processing and assembling such exportables as electronic products, garments, and plastic products. The Export Processing Zone Administration representing all the relevant administrative offices of the government is responsible for managing the zones, and has greatly simplified the procedures for registration, import and export licensing, and foreign-exchange transactions.

The growth of manufactured exports, coupled with rising domestic demand, accelerated the pace of industrialisation. The compound annual rate of growth in the index of manufactured output, 11 per cent during the period 1955–60, accelerated to 21 per cent during the period 1965–70. Underlying the acceleration of manufacturing-output growth, the share of manufactured products in total exports rose from 28 per cent in 1960 to 77 per cent in 1970. Moreover, the rapid development of labour-intensive export industries permitted economic growth to be more labour-absorptive and equitable. Employment and real wages in manufacturing revealed the clear trend of an accelerated increase in the 1960s and the early 1970s. Manufacturing employment rose by 9 per cent a year in 1965–70, while real wages increased at a rate of 6.6 per cent. Taiwan is also one of the few developing economies to achieve an impressive growth record under relative price stability in the 1960s.

Between 1952 and 1984, the volume of exports grew at an average annual rate of 15.9 per cent (Appendix Table 2A.1), accompanied by continuing shifts in the composition of exports. As shown in Table 6.1, in the first half of the

Table 6.1 Taiwan: major export commodities, selected years (per cent)

	1953	1955	1960	1965	1970	1975	1980	1984
Agricultural products								
Rice and paddy	10.6	23.3	3.1	9.1	0.1	—	0.3	0.1
Bananas	2.4	3.1	3.7	10.8	2.2	0.4	0.1	0.1
Processed agricultural products								
Sugar	67.2	49.9	44.0	13.1	3.2	5.0	1.2	0.1
Tea	5.3	4.4	3.7	2.0	0.9	0.4	0.1	0.1
Canned pineapple	1.9	4.2	4.8	3.8	1.4	0.3	0.1	—
Canned mushrooms	—	—	—	4.3	2.2	0.9	0.5	0.2
Canned asparagus spears	—	—	—	2.3	2.4	1.5	0.7	0.2
Manufactured products								
Plywood	—	0.1	1.5	5.9	5.5	2.5	1.9	0.9
Textiles	0.1	0.9	11.6	10.3	13.0	11.5	8.2	6.3
Cement	0.7	—	0.7	1.9	0.8	0.1	0.1	0.3
Clothing and footwear	0.8	1.4	2.6	4.9	19.9	16.4	14.4	13.7
Plastics products	—	—	—	2.6	5.1	6.5	7.4	7.9
Electrical machinery								
and appliances	—	—	0.6	2.7	12.8	14.7	18.2	21.6
Machinery	—	—	—	1.3	3.4	3.6	3.8	3.8
Transportation equipment	—	—	—	0.4	0.9	2.2	3.2	4.0
Metal products	—	—	0.6	1.1	2.0	2.5	4.4	5.7
Basic metals	0.8	1.6	3.7	3.6	4.6	2.3	2.0	2.4
Total exports	100.0	100.0	100.0	100.0	100.0	100.0	100.0	100.0

Source: Inspectorate General of Customs (PRC) *The Trade of China* (various issues)

1950s two staples, sugar and rice, dominated Taiwan's exports, accounting for
more than 70 per cent of the total. The share of these commodities had fallen
to less than 1 per cent by 1984, and their places had been taken by manufactured goods.

The leading manufactured exports have been electrical machinery and appliances (mainly telecommunications equipment), clothing and footwear, textiles, and plastic articles. Over the years 1965–84 rapid growth was achieved
in exports of electrical machinery and appliances, transportation equipment
and metal products. Structural changes in the pattern of exports over the
period reflect movement into products with higher value added.

In turn, the decline in traditional agricultural exports was accompanied by
the emergence of new export-oriented agricultural products, of which canned
mushrooms and asparagus spears were the most notable examples in the late
1960s. The emergence of these new export crops was largely explained by the
provision of incentives and government aids, including the availability of
overseas market information as well as technical assistance.

Taiwan provides an example of an economy going with its comparative
advantage and reaping the gains from trade, as postulated by the traditional
theory of international trade. On the whole, Taiwan's exports were of low
capital and skill intensity. At the same time, factor intensities varied considerably with differences in export markets. While exports to developed countries
were relatively labour-intensive and of low skill intensity, exports to less
developed countries were relatively capital-intensive as well as skill-intensive.

The resulting pattern of trade conforms to expectations, since Taiwan's factor endowments place it in a position somewhere between the developed and the less developed countries (Lee and Liang, 1982; Liang and Liang, 1978).

Taiwan also provides an example of a highly successful export-led industrialisation drive. The expansion of manufactured exports has contributed not only to efficient industrialisation by permitting specialisation according to comparative advantage and stimulating technological improvement, but also to higher living standards as well as improved income distribution through the expansion of employment in manufacturing that 'pulled' workers from low-paying jobs in the agricultural sector to higher paying manufacturing employment and helped to raise wages. It is noteworthy that female workers played an important part in the economic development of Taiwan as the rapid growth of labour-intensive export industries induced the large-scale entry of women, mostly young and unskilled, into manufacturing.

The industrial and trade policies aimed at reducing domestic distortions and encouraging labour-intensive production for export have created profitable opportunities and thereby encouraged capital accumulation and financial deepening.[5]

The most important measure aimed at financial growth was to offer savers a positive real rate of return, so that financial deepening advanced progressively as wholesale prices stabilised in the 1960s (Appendix Table A2.2). The ratio of M2 to GDP increased from 28.5 per cent in 1961–65 to 37.8 per cent in 1966–70. M2 deflated by the wholesale price index, which represents the real lending capacity of the organised banking sector (McKinnon, 1973:114), multiplied by 2.4 during this period. The strengthened liquidity position provided an important base from which credit expansion of the commercial banks could proceed. The net assets of domestic banks as a percentage of GDP increased from 9.7 per cent in 1961–65 to 12.3 per cent in 1966–70. The relative price stability contributed not only to the financial growth observed, but also to the rise in measured net private savings.

It should be noted that corporate bonds and the market value of stocks outstanding as a percentage of GDP have not revealed an increasing trend during the period under review. One of the principal characteristics of corporate finance in Taiwan is a low proportion of bond financing and a correspondingly heavy dependence on bank credit.

Broadly speaking, an inward orientation that expands manufacturing industries directed towards the domestic market tends to set in motion many forces that can have adverse effects on efficiency and growth over the longer term, namely, high protection, price distortions, the prevalence of sellers' markets, domestic inflation, financial shallowing, social tension, and discouragement of foreign private investment caused by strict controls on imports and foreign-exchange payments. Conversely, placing greater importance on export competitiveness by making increased use of the price mechanism and reducing price distortions is indicative of outward orientation. With a quicker payoff in terms of productivity, labour absorption, export earnings and financial deepening, outward orientation would be the more desirable strategy (de Vries,

1967:11–14, 46–47, 55–56). A viable industrialisation scheme must go beyond import substitution and gain access to markets abroad on a competitive basis. Firms that have to live with foreign competition must change the product composition of their exports in response to changes in world market conditions, whereas inward orientation entails establishing a more rigid economic structure.

INDUSTRIAL POLICY IN THE 1980s

From the beginning of the export drive in the early 1960s until the middle of the 1970s, outward-looking policies for industry and trade were essential for the steady growth and the remarkable structural transformation of Taiwan's economy. Other factors contributing to a climate conducive to the conduct of business were political stability, a reasonably well-educated and hard-working labour force, weak labour organisation, an active private sector, the trust between government and industry, and the commitment of the pragmatic bureaucracy to the acceleration of economic development.

However, the turbulent decade of the 1970s witnessed two oil shocks, one in late 1973 and another in 1979. The recovery of the economy after the first oil shock was rapid, and could be primarily attributed to the timely implementation of the economic stabilisation program in early 1974, the continuous growth of manufactured exports with an increased proportion of exports being directed to the oil-producing countries (see Appendix Table A2.3), and the high rate of gross domestic capital formation through large government investment projects in economic infrastructure and in heavy and petrochemical industries.

The second oil shock unfortunately aggravated the widespread adverse effects of the first. The growth rate of GNP and the volume of exports declined sharply. The slow growth of the industrialised countries reduced the demand for manufactured exports. Export competitiveness was eroded with the appreciation in the value of the US dollar, to which the NT dollar was virtually tied. Protectionist sentiment resulted in higher and more widespread trade barriers. Rising real wages threatened Taiwan's ability to compete with new exporters of labour-intensive products. Meanwhile, the prices of many products of the domestic heavy and petrochemical industries remained higher than world market prices. Business confidence was eroded by stagnant demand for exports, high real interest rates, lower profits, low capacity utilisation in many industries, and economic uncertainties. As a consequence, the real growth rate of gross fixed capital formation fell sharply, from 15.7 per cent in 1980 to 3.7 per cent in 1981, and even became negative in 1982 and 1983.

In 1984 the Taiwanese economy once again experienced simultaneous rapid economic growth and price stability as a result of booming export trade. The growth rate of real GNP rose from 7.5 per cent in 1983 to 10.9 per cent in 1984. The wholesale price index had risen by only 0.48 per cent over the previous year, and the consumer price index had actually slipped by 0.03 per cent. With total exports reaching a value of US$30 billion in 1984, the Republic of China is now the world's eleventh-largest exporter. However, it should be noted that growth rates have shown a clearly decreasing trend since the latter half of 1984, because United States demand has been levelling off. The growth rate of real GNP in the first half of 1984 was 12.4 per cent, but it slowed down to 10.9 per cent in the third quarter and to 8.0 per cent in the fourth quarter, and slipped further in 1985, to 6.2 per cent in the first quarter and 5.3 per cent in the second quarter. There is a sense of crisis, particularly within the business community, a feeling that the recent slowdown in economic growth is not just a part of cyclical downward movements in economic activities. Many industries appear to be facing difficulties and revealing structural weaknesses and changes in the global environment.

The economy of the Republic of China has had to adjust to changing domestic and external conditions. It is presently at a crossroad and its present problems of structural adjustment are the result of the very success of past development efforts. Real wage rates have risen considerably in recent years, and the era of relatively stable real wage rates and unit labour costs is over (see Appendix Table A2.4).

Years of comfortable living appear to have dulled the entrepreneurial spirit. Slow growth and low inflation have combined to make it tough for business to make profits. Companies that went deeply into debt in order to invest heavily in real estate in the hopes of making quick and easy profits have been in trouble. The shift to slower growth and stable prices now demands that businessmen re-examine and reshape their policies for production, financing, investment and marketing. To remain competitive, they will have to take drastic measures to cut costs, control quality, diversify products and manage debts. Capital spending plans must be geared to increase productivity and quality rather than expand capacity.

Industry has not always been in a position to effect adjustments unaided. Many firms have not even been sure which way to move to improve their technological base. The role of industrial policy is to provide information on the direction of changes in industrial structure, help to remove structural rigidities, coordinate with macroeconomic policies so that industry can adapt to new conditions and perform more efficiently, and promote the flow of resources to the activities where they can be most productively employed (Jaffe, 1984:11).

The government of Taiwan has recognised that new directions have become imperative, and created the Economic Reform Committee in May 1985 to review the economy, identify constraints on new growth opportunities, and make feasible proposals within six months for a badly needed modernisation of the legal and institutional framework of the entire economic system and a restructuring of the economy. Whether the economy of the Republic of China can successfully restructure its industry and attain the high rate of economic expansion that it has experienced in the past will depend to a great extent on its success in implementing technology transfers, diversifying export markets, and liberalising imports and foreign-exchange controls so as to reduce the of protectionism.

Technology transfers in export-led industrialisation

Using a modified form of the Cobb–Douglas production function, the Council for Economic Planning and Development has estimated that the rate of exogenous technical progress was 4.5 per cent a year during the period 1962–78. It dropped to 2.9 per cent a year during the period 1979–81. Technical progress is an indispensable factor in sustained economic growth, and the economy has been beset with difficulties because of the slowdown in the rate of technical progress over recent years.

By far the most important determinant of technical progress is the continual inflow of foreign technology through imported capital goods. Modern technology in Taiwan is embodied in machinery and equipment imported from abroad. Export-led industrialisation gives rise to a more rapid rate of capital formation and technical progress by financing the importation of capital goods through rapid export expansion. It also creates learning effects for local entrepreneurs in developing marketing and design capabilities. The pace of export-led industrialisation will, in turn, be facilitated by technical progress (Lee, 1981:12–13, 128). From this standpoint, the government and industry leaders have felt uneasy about the recent dive in investment in machinery and equipment.

Table 6.2 shows overseas Chinese and foreign investment during the period 1978–84. The contribution of direct foreign investment has not been of overriding importance in the Republic of China, apart from a few manufacturing sectors such as electronics and electrical appliances, and to some extent chemicals (Ranis and Schive, 1985:106).

Export-oriented foreign firms seem to use more labour-intensive techniques than their local counterparts in the same industry (Schive and Yeh, 1982). Given the footloose nature of export-oriented direct foreign investment, investing firms adapt their techniques to local circumstances to take full advantage of the low labour cost. Technology transfers normally focus on training within the firm as well as outside, extending to the suppliers of inputs and the users of final products. Taiwan Singer was a good example, showing how direct

Table 6.2   Taiwan: overseas Chinese and foreign investment, 1978–84 (million US dollars)

	1978	1979	1980	1981	1982	1983	1984
Investment in arrival	68	69	109	87	79	112	120
Reinvestment of profits	23	51	62	60	46	50	88
Total	91	120	171	147	125	162	208

Source: Investment Commission, Ministry of Economic Affairs (PRC) *Statistics on Overseas Chinese and Foreign Investment, Technical Cooperation, Outward Investment, and Outward Technical Cooperation, Republic of China* foreign investment helped local firms to improve the quality of parts suppliers and the sewing machine industry in general (Ranis and Schive, 1985:124–29).

Increasing emphasis on technical transfer is both an opportunity and a necessity. The interesting feature of the data shown in Appendix Table A2.4 is the discontinuation of past trends in real wages and labour productivity. The rise in labour productivity accelerated and unit labour costs remained unchanged or even declined in the 1960s. This undoubtedly strengthened the competitive edge of Taiwan's labour-intensive manufactures in the world market. However, the absolute size of the agricultural labour force began to decline in 1969 as the outflow rate accelerated in the late 1960s, and the era of relatively stable real wage rates and unit labour costs came to an end. Failure to recognise the dynamic nature of comparative advantage will freeze capital, labour and other scarce resources in industries where opportunities are declining, and lead to the neglect of advantageous new export opportunities.

The government cannot ignore the seriousness of adjustment problems when important industries lose international competitiveness. For instance, the textile and clothing industries exemplify many of the issues involved in trade between industrialised and newly industrialising countries. Quantitative restrictions on imports have encouraged producers to move into fashionable products with higher value added so as to maintain export earnings. However, the viability of these industries has been at stake. Inadequate technology and skills have hindered progress in bleaching and dyeing. Success in producing fashionable textiles requires a sensitive response to shifts in preferences, the ability to produce in small lots with a very tight delivery schedule, and precise quality controls, none of which is an easy task. Furthermore, recent adjustment problems have become very serious because structural difficulties have been exacerbated by a cyclical downswing and by the regulation of trade.

Some of the defensive measures taken in the recession years to provide special assistance to companies in trouble have resulted in the perpetuation of an inefficient allocation of productive resources and have aggravated problems of overcapacity. Government policy needs to be more adjustment-oriented and must encourage improved responsiveness by industry to new challenges and opportunities. A number of traditional labour-intensive industries, such as cotton textiles, footwear, toys and canned foods, must improve their competitiveness through modernising, phasing out excess capacity and shifting to new product lines.

Industrial policy in Taiwan has been striving to restructure the economy by switching the focus of industrial development from unskilled-labour-intensive manufactures and capital-and-energy-intensive heavy and chemical industries to high-technology areas. The government encourages the transfer of appropriate technology and the upgrading of manpower skills. The concept of 'strategic industries' includes two broad categories: machinery manufacturing, and the information and electronics industries. These industries are skill-intensive at a relatively low capital intensity, and energy-saving. In addition, they support the automation of other industries and accelerate the economy's rate of increase in productivity. They will be next in line for the achievement of a high rate of export expansion as the growth of experience and capacity in manufacturing permits the economy to move beyond simple, labour-intensive types of production.

It is no easy task to foster the growth of the machinery and electronics industries and expand their shares of world trade. Machinery is skill-intensive, unlike process industries such as cement, steel and chemicals, where production is machine-paced and the technology is embodied mainly in imported equipment. However, the scales of operation for most firms in Taiwan are small and most produce a wide spectrum of products instead of concentrating on a few components. As a result, they are poorly adapted for the efficient production of machinery. Productivity has also been hampered by a high turnover of labour. In most cases product design is imitative because of the lack of research and development capability. Supplies of materials such as special steels, ceramics and electronics still lag behind. Machinery produced by small companies is being sold without credit, and after-sales services are inadequate.

The electronics industry is very tightly ruled by technological change, and Taiwanese producers are still very much in the business of assembling components and computer peripherals, with high-technology inputs being imported. Some producers may not be able to survive unless they enter into close subcontracting arrangements with large international corporations. Most software is provided by the hardware suppliers, and little attention is being paid to the development of software packages.

Concerted efforts should certainly be made to promote successful development of the strategic industries. Incentives to these industries take the form of low-interest loans, the right to retain earnings of up to 200 per cent of paid-in capital, and the right to delay the start of the five-year income-tax holiday by up to four years. The government is also encouraging the establishment of venture-capital firms to promote high-technology ventures and technical upgrading. However, adequate financial mechanisms, such as supplementing the share of unlisted ventures in the over-the-counter securities market, must be created to stimulate the provision of risk capital for new ventures.

Table 6.3 indicates a generally increasing trend in approvals for technical cooperation projects and royalty payments in recent years. Technical cooperation provides an important channel for the transfer of technology. But recent cases, such as McDonald's hamburgers, Kentucky Fried Chicken and Procter and Gamble's toothpaste plant, have not been in the high-technology domain. In order to move faster in pursuit of a share of the world market for high-technology products in the 1980s, the government has set the target for research and development spending by the government and public and private enterprises at 1.2 per cent of GNP by 1985, and 2 per cent by 1989 (Executive Yuan, 1982:32). However, national research and development expenditure remains at a low level, as shown in Table 6.4.

High-quality manpower with basic academic training in science and technology is Taiwan's most important and abundant resource. Many foreign firms investing in Taiwan have reaped substantial rewards in the forms of energy-

Table 6.3 Taiwan: approved technical cooperation projects and royalty payments, 1978–84

	1978	1979	1980	1981	1982	1983	1984
Approved technical cooperation projects	110	133	143	124	144	141	168
Royalty payments (US$ million)	52	69	86	95	99	95	122

Sources: Central Bank of China *Balance of Payments, Taiwan District, the Republic of China*; Investment Commission, Ministry of Economic Affairs (PRC) *Statistics on Overseas Chinese and Foreign Investment, Technical Cooperation, Outward Investment, and Outward Technical Cooperation, Republic of China*

Table 6.4 Taiwan: national expenditure on research and development as a percentage of gross domestic product, 1978–83

	1978	1979	1980	1981	1982	1983
National expenditure on research and development as a percentage of gross domestic product	0.30	0.42	0.55	0.76	0.70	0.73

Source: National Science Council (PRC) *Survey of R & D Activities, Republic of China*

saving, substitution of materials, upgrading of manufacturing processes, and equipment design and modification resulting from research, development and engineering work by Chinese scientists, engineers and technicians (Li, 1983:4).

The Hsinchu science-based park began operations in September 1981. Its establishment is a bold step by the government to lead industries into the domain of high technology. The park will span 2100 hectares centred around two national universities, technology research institutes and research laboratories. Investors in the park are provided with land and buildings at low rentals and guaranteed a tax holiday of five consecutive years within the first nine years of operation, exemption from import duty, and freedom to structure capital and repatriate profits. The operation of the park has contributed to the flowback of Chinese talent from overseas. Computer components, telecommunications equipment, carbon fibres, laser equipment and biochemicals are already in production.

All these efforts are aimed at broadening the industrial base, expediting technology transfer and restructuring industry and exports in favour of products with high value added. However, the transition from highly labour-intensive products to skill-intensive products is not an easy process. It is very difficult to keep up with the rapid technical progress in these products, and Taiwan has to compete in markets dominated by the oligopolistic producers of the industrialised countries.

Technology transfers in high-technology areas are risky. A system of 'socialising' the risk has to be developed, with the government shouldering a portion of the risk by providing some research and development funds and start-up capital and encouraging collaboration among university research centres and business. This expanded technological research cooperation will optimise scarce skilled personnel and facilities and reduce both the financial and the intellectual costs. At the same time, macroeconomic measures must complement industrial policy, which takes into account the important micro-economic differences among different sectors.

The Economic Reform Committee has recommended cuts in business and personal income tax, reduced interest rates and the conduct of foreign-exchange market intervention by the Central Bank to avoid unduly affecting international price competitiveness and to dampen seasonality. It also recommended tax simplification; relaxation of foreign-exchange controls; reduction of the average nominal tariff rates to 15–20 per cent by 1991; replacement of the 'positive' list with a 'negative' list of commodities subject to import controls, as well as of activities eligible for overseas Chinese and foreign investment; the abolition of such requirements as to export a minimum portion of a foreign company's output, or to use a certain amount of locally made components; financial deregulation; and a fundamental reform of the financial system. The chief objective of these recommendations is to achieve a better functioning market economy. Taiwan must create a more open and competitive domestic economy in order to make its manufacturing sector fit and lively, encourage small firms to expand, attract multinational firms to secure the benefits of technology transfers, and restructure the industrial base to make industries more income-elastic and high-value-added.

An interesting case is the recent attempt by the government to encourage foreign direct investment and promote more efficient production of lower priced cars and enlarge the components industry base; the aim is to boost the domestic market as well as to compete internationally. There are indications that the incentives for foreign investment become less effective the greater their complexity and the more frequently they are altered. The direct foreign investment that has taken place in countries that have followed a more open development strategy has been in general more in line with the country's comparative advantage (World Bank, 1985:129).

Financial reform, diversification and liberalisation

The experience of Taiwan confirms that the industry and trade sectors have been dynamic and that government policies have been flexible enough to deal with the internal and external challenges. The success of outward-oriented industrialisation has resulted in a growing export surplus. Table 6.5 shows that Taiwan's export surplus as a percentage of GNP widened from minus 1.2 per cent in 1980 to plus 12.7 per cent in 1984. In the same year the foreign reserves held by the Central Bank of China were equivalent to eight months of imports.

The export surplus represents more domestic savings than domestic investment or positive net foreign investment, which is rather unusual for a newly

Table 6.5 Taiwan: key indicators of the significance of the export surplus, 1980–84

	1980	1981	1982	1983	1984
Export surplus as a percentage of gross national product	−1.21	2.08	5.26	8.98	12.66
Export surplus as a percentage of imports	−2.23	4.13	11.59	19.99	26.93
Foreign assets of the Central Bank as a percentage of imports	12.63	24.48	44.42	54.95	66.97

Notes: The data for the export surplus, gross national product and exports are based on the national income statistics; import figures are from customs data. Foreign assets of the Central Bank are twelve-month averages.

Sources: Central Bank of China *Balance of Payments, Taiwan District, the Republic of China*; Department of Statistics, Ministry of Finance (PRC) *Monthly Statistics of Exports and Imports, the Republic of China*; Directorate-General of Budget, Accounting and Statistics *National Income of the Republic of China*

industrialising country. In fact Taiwan exports its savings in very large amounts to the United States to help to finance the United States budget deficits, notwithstanding the continuing quarrel over the trade imbalance.

In 1984 gross domestic investment was only 21.4 per cent of GNP, while gross national savings amounted to 34.2 per cent of GNP, generating a huge export surplus. The difference between domestic savings and investment has accumulated mainly in the form of short-term foreign financial assets. The Republic of China is a newly industrialising country that has still to maximise its static and dynamic allocative efficiency, and yet as much as 13 per cent of GNP was transferred abroad and not used for domestic economic activities in 1984.

One reason for the extensive transfer of domestic savings abroad may be the inadequate and outdated financial regime, which has failed to function as an efficient intermediary between savers and investors.

The Cathay financial scandal made it clear that the failure of financial institutions causes damage that extends far beyond the financial sector. Since the processes of market restructuring and regulatory reform have remained incomplete, the Economic Reform Committee has recommended financial deregulation and a fundamental reform of the financial system.

The essential function of financial regulation is to ensure the soundness of the financial system while providing individual financial institutions with the maximum possible freedom to foster the efficient allocation of financial resources by promoting competition and innovation. An analogy may be drawn with driving on a freeway at a high speed: not only must the driver obey the traffic regulations, he must also constantly check the brake to ensure safety. However, if the car is made of very thick steel plate, it may be safer but the speed will be down. By the same token, financial regulation must respect market discipline as well as recognising the cost of excessive regulation.

The Economic Reform Committee has recommended the easing of restrictions that have proved unnecessary or counterproductive. The regulations should be designed to put more emphasis on enforcing market discipline and sticking to the principles of sound banking. It is recommended that the bank examination process be improved, the regulatory structure streamlined, capital requirements strengthened, disclosure improved, and reporting requirements reinforced.

The Banking Law and the Central Bank Law stipulate that the Central Bank prescribes the ceiling for bank deposit rates and approves the range of bank lending rates as proposed by the Bankers' Association. Not surprisingly, these controls have spawned evasions and innovations. Corporations have circumvented the lending-rate floor by issuing commercial papers and bankers' acceptances to fund large sums in the money market at rates even lower than the bank deposit rates under the present situation of excess liquidity caused by the huge export surplus, high domestic savings and underinvestment. The Economic Reform Committee has recommended not only reduction of the bank rates to bring them more into line with the market-clearing equilibrium rates, but revision of the Banking Law, the Central Bank Law and other regulations governing interest rates, in order to deregulate bank rates completely in due course.

Most of the domestic banks are state-owned and subject to the onerous regulations of numerous government agencies. The most troublesome regulations are the very difficult standards and procedures for writing off bad loans: not only can a small mistake cost a loan officer an 'administrative penalty' in the civil service grading system; he may also be personally liable to pay off bad loans. The Economic Reform Committee has recommended the enactment of a special law to control government banks with minimum state interference and to avoid any resemblance to a government bureaucracy. The regulation of banks should be based on the Banking Law regardless of government or private status, and the government should exercise authority only in the capacity of a shareholder. The Economic Reform Committee also recommends allowing the entry of new private banks to promote competition and avoid excessive concentration of banking power.

In order to equip the financial system to meet the challenges of financial deregulation and international competition, the Financial Subcommittee has recommended the enactment of a law governing mergers among and conversions of financial institutions so as to restructure the financial system. Financial institutions need to be allowed to apply for mergers or conversions in the future, if mergers or conversions can improve efficiency and strengthen sound banking. They may also be able to exploit economies in the provision of financial services, maintain an adequate supply of credit facilities for medium-sized and small businesses and avoid excessive concentration, as well as protecting the interest of shareholders.

Since the gains to the economy as a whole from the development of money and capital markets are considerable, the Economic Reform Committee has recommended that instruments with high credit standing in the money market be diversified; that prudent criteria be established to evaluate the credit ratings of the issuing companies of commercial papers and bankers' acceptances; that new entry of bills finance companies be allowed; that the interbank market functions be improved; that the responsibilities of the Securities Exchange Commission and the Stock Exchange be more clearly defined; that rules to clearly define fair trading practices be adopted; that inspections of brokers and traders be strengthened and market behaviour monitored for irregularities; and that accounting and disclosure requirements for listed companies be improved.

The foreign-exchange market in Taiwan has been composed exclusively of non-speculative exporters and importers and covered-interest arbitragists. Financial transactions in foreign exchange are still not permitted. McKinnon (1979:143) points out that such a market is necessarily unstable, since exchange rates can move continually in the same direction.

It has to be noted that, with a huge trade surplus, there is pressure for the NT dollar to appreciate against the US dollar, since the supply of foreign exchange exceeds the demand. In order to avoid further appreciation of the NT dollar against the US dollar, the Central Bank has been discreetly intervening to steady the NT dollar. The ceiling on the long-term position of the authorised banks with respect to cumulative foreign-exchange holdings was removed in August 1984 to alleviate the upward pressure on the NT dollar as well as to make the authorised banks' portfolio management more sophisticated. However, the continuous accumulation of foreign exchange has exposed the banks to more and more foreign-exchange risk.

The US dollar rose phenomenally against most other currencies from the end of 1979 until the Group of Five decided in late September 1985 to intervene in foreign-exchange markets to lower the dollar's value. To maintain a fairly stable exchange rate against the US dollar, the NT dollar had to appreciate against the European currencies and the Japanese yen, reducing export competitiveness in those markets and concentrating exports more and more on the United States market. Taiwan's exports to the United States amounted to almost half of its total exports in 1984 (see Appendix Table A2.3), and have been heavily concentrated on textiles, footwear, machinery (mainly machine tools) and miscellaneous manufacturing. Taiwan has also been the largest beneficiary of the United States Generalised System of Preferences, with US$3.2 billion of its products gaining duty-free entry to the United States in 1984. Taiwan must recognise the danger of United States protectionism, and must change its export composition and diversify its markets by seeking other important trade partners.

Broadly speaking, the relative importance of domestic supply and foreign demand in determining the rate of growth of a country's exports will vary according to its share in the export market. The greater the country's share, the more probable it is that its exports will grow more or less in line with the growth in foreign import demand for the products it exports. The smaller its share, the more important is its ability to produce for export at prevailing world prices (Maizels, 1986:168). If Taiwan is to sustain a rate of export growth at something like the pace of recent years, the need to expedite the diversification of its markets and product composition is obvious.

In addition, the world economic environment and the prevailing limitations on trade by the developed countries argue in favour of a trading and industrial development strategy supporting a more balanced or widespread expansion of exports from a broad array of manufacturing subsectors, instead of a sudden large spurt in a few traditional exportables that are important sources of employment in developed countries. Sectoral diversification of exports could proceed hand in hand with a substantial increase in intra-industry trade, for instance, specialising in some kinds of machinery and equipment and importing others, producing cars and electronic appliances and importing parts and components for assembly (World Bank, 1984a:xii). Emphasising intra-industry trade through increased import liberalisation and expanding exports over a broad front would defuse the tensions that spring up when trade is one-sided, and resources would be used more efficiently in line with comparative advantage.

Import and foreign exchange controls and restrictions have been relaxed considerably in recent years. During trade talks held in early October 1985 in Washington, the Republic of China promised to lower tariffs on 192 items; to substantially ease restrictions on imports of United States cigarettes, beer and wine; to open up the domestic market to United States insurance companies and other service industries; to widen the scope of foreign banks' operations; and to make chemical and pharmaceutical products eligible for patent protection. Parallel talks were held in Taipei in late October on the protection of rights in intellectual property. The United States government subsequently announced that Taiwan had been removed from a list of countries to be investigated by the Office of the US Trade Representative for alleged unfair trade practices.

Taiwan's strong balance-of-payments position would permit trade liberalisation and the substantial easing of foreign-exchange controls. The Economic Reform Committee has recommended freer gold transactions and the replacement of the tedious reporting procedures for gold carried by tourists into the country with the imposition of an import duty on gold bullion. It has also recommended the replacement of the prior licensing or approval system with a reporting system to simplify the procedures for commodity imports and exports, as well as those for miscellaneous overseas payments of firms within a certain limit. In addition, it is recommended that forward-cover facilities be extended to services and capital transactions.

The setting of the new exchange rate will be influenced by the mixture of the associated policies for opening the domestic market to more imported goods and foreign investment, even though the purchasing-power-parity exchange-rate indexes provide a base for identifying the direction of the change in the appropriate exchange rate. However, the government has a tendency to overstate the steps it has taken in liberalising imports. Not only are there restrictions on particular sources of origin and on the status of applicants; there is also a reluctance among minor bureaucrats to give up their restrictive powers, which manifests itself through unjustifiable reinterpretations of the policies they are charged with enacting. In order to avoid the disruptive effects of substantial exchange-rate revaluation, and to appease protectionist pressures and improve Taiwan's standing with the United States, there are strong needs for trade and foreign-exchange liberalisation. It is desirable to carry out the liberalisation of import restrictions and the reform of the tariff structure on the basis of a program made public in advance to permit firms to make preparations. Trade liberalisation will lower the cost of exports through reduced prices for imported machinery and raw materials, provide a spur for improvements in productivity and trigger accelerated adjustment among industries that have to compete with imports. It may also lead to better treatment for exports in foreign markets through bilateral negotiations to obtain mutual concessions in the present world trade environment, where selective protectionism is often applied arbitrarily. The liberalisation of foreign-exchange control will stimulate more efficient use of and increase the demand for foreign exchange, alleviating upward pressure on the NT dollar. As pointed out by McKinnon (1984:479), liberalisation of the capital account of the balance of payments comes last, following the liberalisation of foreign trade and the domestic capital market. With its huge export surplus, Taiwan must make better use of its foreign-exchange earnings for foreign investment abroad.

A number of enterprises in the Republic of China have reached the position of making overseas investments and running multinational business. Outward investment by local enterprises has been gradually expanding since the late 1970s. The motives for a company to undertake foreign investment include the need to extend foreign markets because local markets are limited; to maintain competitiveness in the international marketplace in the face of constantly rising local wage rates, which make the manufacturing of standardised products at home less competitive; and to avoid tariff and non-tariff barriers under prevailing international trade protectionism. Outward investment was mainly in electrical appliances, chemicals and textiles in the United States and Southeast Asian countries. The emergence of multinationals in the Republic of China is a recent phenomenon. Foreign investment in manufacturing seemed to be an effective method of heading off protectionist action in the United States and other markets.

Finally, the rapid growth in world trade in the 1960s and the early 1970s has now been replaced by slow growth and increasing protectionism in industrialised countries against manufactured exports from developing countries. As growth has slowed down in industrial countries, fewer new jobs have been created. It has become more and more difficult to resist the lobbyists from industries that have been in secular decline.

Countries facilitating structural adjustment permit a more liberalised attitude to trade policies, while countries refusing to let their economic structures adjust are forced to adopt protectionist tactics. Selective protection is often applied arbitrarily and with rather more vigour to diplomatically weak countries than their trade offences may justify (Turner and McMullen, 1982:264). For example, the European Community's Generalised System of Preferences excluded Taiwan, quotas were sometimes unilaterally determined, and the market access of Taiwanese products to the European Community has been on terms inferior to those for goods from other countries. As shown in Appendix Table A2.5, quota restrictions are widely applied to Taiwan's textile exports. It is estimated that the Jenkins textiles-quota bill, passed in early October 1985, will cost Taiwan US$1 billion in sales of textiles and clothing, and the loss of 70 000 to 80 000 jobs.

Protectionism is both inefficient and costly for industrialised countries. Its effects are threefold (Jenkins, forthcoming; Turner and McMullen, 1982:18–23).

First, a scarcity value develops that is added to the cost of goods, with domestic consumers paying higher prices for imports. Cartel pricing creates a transfer from the importing nation's consumers to the exporting nation's authorised suppliers. Many studies clearly show that the cost of the restraints has outweighed the value of jobs saved. It also encourages bureaucratic regulation and control, and foreshadows a long-term decline in economic viability.

Second, it does somewhat cushion the domestic industry from price competition, but the domestic industry usually does not reap the anticipated benefits because higher prices encourage the entry of unrestricted new exporters and imports from the more restricted sources are replaced by imports from other suppliers.

Third, it creates an incentive for foreign producers to improve the quality of their products and aim for higher value added per unit exported, causing then to compete more directly with manufacturers in industrial countries, who traditionally produce in the higher quality ranges of these products. Hence, domestic producers may find that they face an increase rather than a decline in competition from imports in the higher quality ranges. Moreover, because a quota increases the relative cost of low-quality imports, there is an incentive for domestic producers to manufacture the low-quality goods that were previously imported.

All these protection-induced effects have tended to undermine the objectives of import control. Given the economic losses involved for industrial countries, the preferred policy would be to eliminate bilateral quotas and rely on tariff protection accompanied by an adjustment program for labour, even though adjustment is never easy and requires considerable political courage.

The economic performance of the Republic of China is determined by the pace of its export growth, which, in turn, depends to a great extent on market conditions in the industrial countries. The easing of protection in these countries will be a welcome blessing. If protectionist resistance persists all countries will lose, but those heavily reliant on trade will be especially seriously affected.

SUMMARY AND CONCLUSIONS

Economic conditions in Taiwan immediately after the war were similar to those in many resource-poor, low-income developing countries. The industrial policies pursued until the late 1950s were those typically associated with an import-substitution strategy. The multiple exchange-rate system and strict import controls favoured industrial expansion oriented towards the domestic market.

However, the relatively easy phase of import substitution reached its limit quite quickly, and the government introduced a series of major policy reforms during the period 1958–61. The currency was devalued, the exchange-rate structure was unified, investment and import regulations were liberalised, and policy emphasis shifted from import control to export promotion. The marked changes in the commodity composition of exports over time are evidence of successful export-led industrialisation.

From the beginning of the export drive until the middle of the 1970s, these outward-looking policies were essential for the remarkable structural trans-formation of Taiwan's economy. Taiwan has illustrated the traditional theory of international trade by following its comparative advantage and reaping the gains from trade. The rapid expansion of labour-intensive manufactured exports contributed to industrialisation by permitting specialisation according to comparative advantage and stimulating technological improvement. It also improved living standards and income distribution by creating new employment and a rapid increase in real wages.

The prospects for sustained economic growth became less favourable in the turbulent years of the late 1970s and the 1980s, and the very success of the development methods of the past is causing the present problems of structural adjustment. Slower growth and low inflation have made it difficult for businesses to survive. Drastic measures are necessary to cut costs, control quality, diversify products and manage debts so as to stay competitive. However, industry is not always able to adjust without help. The role of industrial policy is to remove structural rigidities, to coordinate with macro-economic policies to help industry to adapt to new conditions and perform more efficiently, and to promote the flow of resources to activities where they can be most productively employed.

The domestic and international economic environments have been changing more quickly in recent years, and industrial policy must be flexible in response to these changes. In recognition of this, the Economic Reform Committee was established in May 1985 to review the economy, identify constraints on new growth opportunities, and make proposals for restructuring the economy and modernising the legal and institutional framework of the entire economic system. Whether the economy of the Republic of China can attain the high rate of economic expansion experienced in the past will depend largely on whether it can transfer technology, diversify export markets and liberalise imports and foreign-exchange control so as to reduce the risks of protection-ism.

Technology transfer is both necessary and opportune, since abundant man-power with basic scientific and technological training is Taiwan's most important resource. The present industrial policy has been striving to reform the economy by focusing industrial development on high-technology areas: approvals for technical cooperation projects and royalty payments have shown a rising trend in recent years, research and development efforts have been stepped up, and the Hsinchu Industrial Park was opened in 1981. All these efforts aim at broadening the industrial base, expediting technology transfer and restructuring exports in favour of high-value-added products. However, the transition from labour-intensive to skill-intensive products is not easy; it is very difficult to keep pace with the rapid technological progress in these products. The risk involved in the transfer of high technology must be to some extent socialised, and industrial policy in this area must be complemented by macroeconomic measures. Taiwan can now boost domestic demand through investment projects, tax cuts and interest-rate reductions, measures that are unlikely to run into inflation or balance-of-payments problems in the short term.

Despite the dramatic rise of the US dollar against most other currencies from the end of 1979 until late September 1985 the NT dollar has remained quite stable against the US dollar. This has allowed the NT dollar to appreciate against other currencies, which has concentrated exports more and more on the United States market. Taiwan's exports to the United States have been heavily concentrated in protected sectors, and it will be necessary for Taiwan to change the composition of its exports and diversify its markets.

As well as market diversification, the global economic environment and the limitations on trade by industrial countries argue for a strategy of expanding exports over a broad front of the manufacturing subsectors, rather than increasing exports of a few traditional items that are important sources of employment in industrial countries. In combination with import liberalisation, this strategy would ease the tensions of one-sided trade and employ resources in line with comparative advantage.

Although the Republic of China is a newly industrialising country that has yet to maximise its allocative efficiency, as much as 13 per cent of its GNP was transferred abroad as export surplus in 1984. One reason for this may be that the inadequate and outdated financial regime has failed to function as an efficient intermediary between savers and investors. The fundamental reform of the financial system recommended by the Economic Reform Committee has become a pressing need. Trade and foreign-exchange liberalisation is also necessary to avoid the disruptive effects of revaluation and to appease protectionist pressure and improve Taiwan's standing with the United States. Any program for liberalising import restrictions and reforming the tariff structure should be publicised in advance to allow firms to make preparations. Trade liberalisation will lower the cost of exports, improve productivity and accelerate adjustment in industries that compete with imports, and may lead to better treatment for exports through bilateral negotiations to obtain mutual concessions. The liberalisation of foreign-exchange control will promote more efficient use of foreign exchange and increase the demand for it. One way for Taiwan to make better use of its foreign-exchange earnings would be overseas investment in manufacturing, which seems to be an effective way of heading off protectionist action in the United States and other markets.

It is economies like the Republic of China, which is heavily dependent on export growth, that stand to lose most from the persistence of protectionist policies in industrial countries. But protection is also both costly and inefficient for industrial countries. The effects are threefold: a scarcity value develops, foreshadowing a long-term decline in economic viability; new entrants are encouraged; and producers in the developing countries are forced to aim for higher value added per unit exported. These effects have tended to undermine the objectives of import control, and it would be preferable to eliminate bilateral quotas and rely on tariff protection, accompanied by a labour-adjustment program, even though adjustment is difficult and demands political courage.

The most important lesson of this chapter is that trade strategy and industrial policy must be adjustment-oriented and coordinated with macroeconomic policies. Industrial policy must be foresighted; it should not be simply a reaction to situations that are out of control. A more open and competitive domestic economy will promote a healthy manufacturing sector and speed up the restructuring of industry to make the best of Taiwan's comparative advantage. At the same time, the easing of protection will make the much-needed structural adjustment less costly.

Taiwan and Korea are often cited as the most successful cases of export-led industrialisation, and the two economies have much in common. Each possesses a well-educated and hardworking labour force. Neither is endowed with abundant natural resources. Both underwent a lengthy development process under the colonial rule of Japan, during which they accumulated considerable investments in infrastructure and education. Both have inherited the Confucian tradition, with its emphasis on education, frugality and kinship. Both have to maintain a high level of military spending in the face of hostile regimes. In recent years both have been under intense pressure from the United States to open up their markets at a development stage much more vulnerable than that of Japan when it began to liberalise. Rapid trade liberalisation will reduce the trade gaps between them and the United States, although Japan may benefit more than the United States. Finally, the development of high-technology and high-value-added industries, through private initiatives and accelerated technology transfers from abroad, is the cornerstone of both their hopes for sustained high growth.

Despite these similarities, a few differences between them have become apparent. First, Korea has accumulated a large external debt, while Taiwan has kept its debt–service ratio at around 4 per cent since the 1970s and has emerged as a net creditor with a very high rate of national savings. It may be said that Taiwan has run too great a trade surplus and accumulated too much in foreign-exchange reserves, while investing too little in industrial modernisation and economic infrastructure. Second, at least 25 per cent of GNP in Korea today is controlled by about 50 family-owned conglomerates, while the Republic of China is a country of small and medium-sized enterprises. Third, Korea has been adopting a rather more balanced policy of promoting healthier medium-sized businesses, while Taiwan's principal concern is to encourage small and medium-sized businesses to expand.

However, apart from such structural defects as local enterprises being generally run by individuals or families and the financial regime remaining inflexible and conservative and hindering the exploitation of scale economies, the Chinese are staunch individualists; each wants to be boss, which is in sharp contrast to the 'group-think' mentality of Japan and Korea. With eager young entrepreneurs and well-educated engineers, Taiwan may be able to promote the transition of its economy to high-technology areas, provided that the government takes adequate measures to assist these ventures by providing venture capital and developing marketing capabilities.

7 Industrial policy in the United States and Europe: economic principles and political practices

ROBERT LAWRENCE

'Industrial policy' denotes all policies designed to affect the allocation of resources between and within sectors of the economy. Thus the scope of this discussion will be vast, encompassing the complete array of microeconomic policies.

Two paradigms, the economic and the political, provide strikingly different perspectives on the conduct of these policies. In the economist's paradigm, allocative policies may be required to complement market forces when market failure occurs because of monopolies, externalities or public goods, or where market institutions have not been established. Economic theory also lays out a set of principles about when and how such intervention should take place. First, even if markets fail, government policy may be inappropriate if it is likely to make matters worse. Second, when intervention does take place, the instruments chosen should achieve their objectives in the most precise fashion possible; for example, tariffs that distort both consumer and producer choice are less efficient than employment subsidies in maintaining employment levels in a particular sector.[1] Third, structural policies are long-range policies; in general they should not be used to maintain aggregate demand and employment, and programs must be sustained over considerable periods of time if they are to attain their objectives. Fourth, these policies should not be used to reverse fundamental market forces: if for example, a developed country loses its comparative advantage in labour-intensive and standardised commodities, it is unlikely to regain it. Government policies may facilitate adjustment to such developments, but should not be used to resist them. Finally, intervention should be aimed at the margin and designed to compensate for market failures wherever they occur in the economy.

However, these principles, as Richard Caves indicates in chapter 3, are often scarcely recognisable in the actual practice of industrial policy. Although the rhetoric refers to facilitating adjustment, actual industrial policy deviates from the economic paradigm in terms of objectives, instruments, time horizons and assumptions about how markets function. Most industrial policies do not aim to complement market adjustment with the object of maximising aggregate output. Rather, they are a response to the conflict between the market's

126

allocation of resources and the values and objectives of the political system. The political paradigm dictates that, instead of simply maximising aggregate economic welfare, industrial policies be used to maintain productive capacity as an end in itself, to preserve capital, to enhance technological capabilities, to increase national prestige, to redistribute income, to reinforce job property rights and to support regional employment. The instruments chosen are frequently not those that are, in principle, appropriate for achieving stated objectives, but rather those available and convenient for historical and institutional reasons. The distinction between macroeconomic and structural policies is frequently ignored—structural policies are often used in an effort to maintain employment. Policies often focus on particular sectors or firms rather than particular market failures. And finally, policymakers place great faith in the capacity of government policies to reverse market processes, and believe that market failure is common while government failure is rare. The attitude is epitomised in the French socialist slogan, 'there are no dying industries, only outmoded technologies': industry problems are usually interpreted as the result of unfortunate and avoidable blunders that can be overcome by modernisation and a modest amount of government support.

No matter how fervent their attachment to free-market principles, governments in the major developed economies inevitably succumb to political pressures to intervene, and do so by means that frequently violate the principles of 'positive adjustment'. Thus, despite its liberal rhetoric, the Reagan administration participated in the Chrysler rescue plan, used quotas when tariffs would have accorded with market principles in offsetting foreign subsidies on steel, sanctioned a tightening of restrictions in the Multi-Fiber Agreement for textiles, reintroduced quotas on sugar, and obtained voluntary export quotas on Japanese automobiles (Reich, 1983a). Similarly, the German government, despite its commitment to the social market doctrine, has permitted a secular increase in overall subsidy levels and large-scale subsidies to individual rescue cases. As Stephen Wilks (1984:462) has noted, the rescue of AEG-Telefunken Actien Gesellschaft 'constituted a turning point, a crisis in a huge company whose problems were symptomatic of organisational, managerial and technological failings and could not be explained away as the product of a declining sector' (see also Donges, 1980).

These observations suggest that no positive analysis of industrial policies can ignore political considerations. Indeed, an adequate positive analysis of industrial policy is more likely to be provided by a political scientist than an economist. Moreover, it is not the role of economists to question the desirability of non-economic social objectives—values should be taken as given. It is, however, within their domain to identify the costs of achieving these values, explore whether they are mutually compatible, and evaluate the efficiency of the policies directed towards them.

It would take many studies to analyse the full array of industrial policies in the major European economies.[2] A treatment such as the present one must inevitably be impressionistic and partial; even to describe all the policies simply would be beyond the scope of this chapter. The primary focus here will be on policies towards declining industries. The most striking message to emerge from this analysis is that, where policies genuinely supplement market forces, they may do some good (and are unlikely to do much damage); on the other hand, policies that try to reverse (or significantly delay) market behaviour will be extremely costly, and may actually be counterproductive when viewed in terms of their own objectives. In an nth-best world, political compromises will be required; the real issue is the extent to which they can be made compatible with positive adjustment.

The first part of this chapter, therefore, discusses the impact of historical traditions, economic status and political institutions on the nature of the industrial policies pursued in the United States and Europe, and the second part is devoted to a consideration of their efficacy.

THE BACKGROUND TO INDUSTRIAL POLICY IN THE UNITED STATES AND EUROPE

Early in the period since 1973 the United States and the major European nations passed through both the initial and the maturing stages of development described by Okuno and Suzumura in chapter 2. Integrated into the world economy, they have sophisticated sets of financial institutions and productive and competitive industries. Their democratic political systems are highly developed and a wide array of interest groups can affect policy outcomes. They share problems relating to completion of the industrial development characterised by the rapid growth of heavy industry and infrastructure, and they are involved in the transition towards services and knowledge-based industries. In both regions virtually the same industries are experiencing particular difficulties: clothing, textiles, footwear, steel, automobiles, machine tools and consumer electronics (although shipbuilding, which has been heavily supported by defence spending in the United States, is conspicuously absent from the American list). Similarly, the industries of the future are the same: chemicals, electronics, aerospace and precision instruments.

Structural change in these economies has not been much more extensive since 1973 than it was during the earlier postwar period; it has, however, become more difficult, both because of the slow-growth environment in which it has occurred and because of the nature of the industries adversely affected.[3] Rising unemployment has vastly increased the adjustment costs of dislocation, while slow growth and declining productivity have increased the burdens of financing that adjustment. The capital-intensive industries adversely affected tend to have large plants, relatively high wages and large numbers of employees. The difficulties of their employees are particularly prominent, since these industries tend to be important to regional economies and associated with industrial prowess, and their plight entails considerable loss of specific human capital for workers and of profits for capitalists. The following discussion focuses on the responses in the United States and the major European economies to the problems of these declining sectors.

INDUSTRIAL POLICY IN THE UNITED STATES

The great strength of the United States economy is its flexibility as judged by virtually every indicator: firm births and deaths; worker mobility between jobs, industries and regions; relative and absolute wage flexibility; and highly developed capital markets and entrepreneurial traditions. The weaknesses are mirror images of the strengths: the difficulties in pursuing centralised and coordinated policies; and the problems of providing economic security and assisting the poor.

The pluralistic system of government in the United States has determined the nature and form of government intervention. The process of government is highly fragmented. The United States Constitution deliberately created a system of checks and balances within which a wide variety of groups, operating through diverse channels, may affect outcomes. This implies great difficulty in implementing policies that fail to reflect a broad national consensus. And, even where such a consensus does exist, opposition groups have a considerable capacity to use the legal process to inhibit radical change.

A second impediment to sustained structural intervention is the lack of continuity in leadership; Eisenhower is the only postwar president to have completed eight years in office, and congressional elections every two years keep the time horizon of policy short. And unlike the position in other major industrial economies, where governments may come and go but civil servants remain, each new president appoints a fresh group of managers to operate his executive branch.

While United States citizens enjoy a variety of civil rights, the system of economic rights is considerably less extensive than in Europe. The government strives to achieve full employment, but it does not guarantee individuals the right to be employed in their current jobs regardless of their economic value. For the most part, employers are free to dismiss their workers and close their plants without government sanction.

Unless they fulfil a self-evident public purpose (like rail companies, financial institutions or defence contractors) industries or firms that fail because of purely domestic competition have little recourse to federal assistance. Such responses to decline as nationalisation, subsidies and cartels, which are quite common in other developed economies, remain unusual in the United States. Government-sponsored technological development has emphasised defence and space, and while this research has yielded several important breakthroughs of commercial value in electronics and aerospace, these have been incidental to the goals of the programs.[4]

The United States has been a frontier economy during the postwar period, which makes future patterns of development extremely difficult to forecast and promote. Accordingly, the government has had virtually no role in overall structural planning. Similarly, the pluralistic nature of the system makes strategic and even coordinated strategies extremely difficult to pursue. Rather than direct leadership and mobilisation of policy, the United States relies on general systems of rules and indirect price signals.

Political pressures make it difficult to implement selective programs with specific goals. As Charles Schultze (1983) has pointed out, the model cities program, which was to concentrate large amounts of resources in a few key urban regions, was successively diluted until it provided thin but widely scattered support for 150 cities. Likewise the qualifications for the economic development administration program, which aids depressed regions, were continually broadened until about 80 per cent of the countries in the United States qualified.

In the United States a pluralistic system of government and an economy that for the most part has been at the frontier have limited the direct role of government in economic development. With the exception of antitrust and regulatory policy, industrial policies in the United States have largely concentrated on trade.

The conduct of trade policy in turn reflects the United States system of government. It is shared by the President, the Congress, and a quasi-judicial body, the International Trade Commission. The First Article of the Constitution gives Congress the power to regulate commerce with foreign nations, and Congress guards this power jealously by limiting the President's ability to negotiate tariff reductions. By successfully petitioning the International Trade Commission to prevent injury from imports or unfair trade practices, firms, trade associations, unions and groups of workers can force the President to act in a way that contradicts the overall thrust of his policies.

Over the postwar period, as foreign nations began to match United States production capabilities, American producers have experienced growing pressure from international competition. Reflecting these pressures, the types of industries seeking assistance have gradually moved up the technological spectrum—first agriculture, then textiles, then steel and automobiles and, increasingly, high-technology products such as semiconductors.

The United States industries seeking assistance have followed a two-track procedure. Some, typically the smaller ones, have obtained protection by petitioning the International Trade Commission. They have successfully argued that imports are a serious source of injury and received temporary protection in accordance with Section 201 of the Trade of 1974. Other industries have made their case on the basis of unfair trade (for example, foreign dumping or subsidies).[5] As Robert Baldwin (1984) has noted, this process does not simply rubber-stamp applications for protection; of 53 petitions received by the commission since 1975, only thirteen have resulted in higher tariffs or quotas.[6] Nor is the protection provided permanent; the commission requires industries to return after three or four years to request extensions of protection, and these have frequently been denied. Of approximately 30 industries that have received protection through safeguards since 1954, only two continue to be protected today. Thus the International Trade Commission has shown a remarkable resistance to both political and industrial pressure (witness, its negative decision on automobiles; and the fact that, with changing circumstances, it has denied protection to the very industries formerly recommended for protection).

On the other hand, larger industries have generally tried the Trade Commission route, but if unsuccessful have obtained protection by exerting political pressure directly on the President and Congress. Only five industries have been successful at this level—textiles and apparel, steel, automobiles, meat and sugar—but these industries represent about 25 per cent of all United States imports (Baldwin, 1984: 673–74). Thus the voluntary export restraints on Japanese automobiles were implemented despite the commission's rejection of the petition for import relief by the automobile industry; again, the bilateral system of quotas negotiated with European steelmakers represented a rejection of remedies suggested by the commission, and the entire arrangement for the protection of the textile industry, through first the Long-Term Cotton Arrangement and later the Multi-Fiber Agreement, bypassed the International Trade Commission altogether.

Advocates of a new industrial policy for the United States have argued that this system of conferring trade protection is highly deficient. They suggest that new, more comprehensive approaches are needed. They argue that United States policymakers, blinded by an ideological commitment to free markets, have granted protection as an exceptional and temporary response to unusual circumstances. This free-market perspective has resulted in protection that was not conditional on the implementation of specific programs designed to restore competitiveness. Inevitably, according to this view, industries fail to take the appropriate action for revitalisation, and thus trade protection becomes permanently necessary for the industry's survival. A coherent industrial policy, these observers argue, would provide easier access to government assistance but toughen the conditions on which it is granted. The current debate in the United States, therefore, surrounds this issue of conditionality.

In fact, precisely the opposite strategy has worked effectively in the United States. By not embroiling itself in the detailed negotiations of programs towards declining industries, United States policy has operated relatively successfully in facilitating adjustment in cases where protection has been administered through the International Trade Commission. The key to adjustment has been that such protection has been credibly regarded as temporary.

The difficulties of implementing detailed conditional programs towards entire industries stem from the complex nature of the required adjustment process. The introduction to this chapter contrasted the economic paradigm, which suggests that once competitiveness is lost it is rarely if ever regained, and the political paradigm, which implies that through the implementation of government policies almost any industry can be restored to competitiveness. A recent study has examined the adjustment process in sixteen United States industries that have successfully petitioned the United States International Trade Commission under Article XIX of the GATT (Lawrence and DeMasi, 1985). This examination of the actual adjustment process suggests that neither of these paradigms is generally applicable.

In the sample, there were occasions when the economic paradigm was appropriate. The problems confronting certain industries, such as those producing sheet glass or Wilton and velvet carpets, stemmed primarily from competition from a cost-effective domestically available substitute. Exit rather than modernisation was the appropriate strategy in these cases. Similarly, for trade-impacted industries making undifferentiated products in which costs alone determine sales, serious declines are inevitable when competitiveness is lost (for example, in the cases of high-carbon ferrochromium and nuts, bolts and screws). Even where revitalisation is feasible, however, it may require a change in ownership (as with television sets), a change in plant location (as in the case of bicycles), or a narrowing of market focus (as in the cases of ballbearings, footwear and stainless steel flatware). It will rarely be the case, particularly for standardised products, that simply adopting the latest technology will suffice.

Whatever innovations domestic producers can adopt, foreigners with lower labour costs will be bound to emulate. Instead, United States producers must exploit or develop the advantages conferred by proximity to the market, superior servicing, marketing, design and so on; or they may have to retreat to the production of specialised, low-volume orders. Firms in many industries have pursued such strategies, either by remaining in the particular industry but moving out of labour-intensive activities (as in the case of flatware), or by shifting to alternative activities that require similar expertise (for example, producing float rather than sheet glass). However, this will rarely be an avenue open to all firms in the industry. Jose de la Torre studied adjustment in the apparel industry and, on the basis of an extensive set of case studies, concluded in a similar vein:

> Our data show that efforts aimed at increasing or maintaining high productivity, while essential, were not sufficient conditions for successful operations. At the core of the growth company strategies was a dedication of time and resources to their external environment, that is, their marketing and their product policies. (de la Torre, 1978)

Our finding is that the International Trade Commission process has facilitated adjustment relatively successfully. It is true that many of the industries studied made repeated attempts to secure trade protection once their relief expired, but this finding should not be interpreted as a failure to adjust— quite the contrary. The majority of investigations by the commission for these repeat cases provided little evidence to support a case for protection. Indeed, adjustment had occurred, leaving a group of viable and competitive firms in the industry.

However, the successful adjustment of these industries was the result not so much of detailed government aid as of credibly temporary protection, so that firms had no alternative but to yeild to market pressures. Among twelve of the sixteen industries examined, only one—bicycles—matched the political paradigm of an industry able to restore its competitiveness by expanding employment and output and reducing import shares.[7] The more typical response was a severe reduction (or an elimination) of productive capacity down to a few firms with appropriate survival strategies.

It is ironic that adjustment has been considerable under these programs, because they have been poorly designed and their objectives have been kept vague. Protection for industries adversely affected by international competition in the United States has been justified on two grounds: first, that protection is required to prevent the 'injury' that would result from free trade; and second, that protection would facilitate the restoration of competitiveness in the future. The political pressures for providing assistance to industries stem mainly from workers in individual plants. It is natural for policymakers to expect aid to maintain *specific* jobs and plants.[8] But while 'saving jobs' is frequently the political motivation behind such actions, it is not necessarily the result.[9] This is because unlike Europe, where policies explicitly subsidise particular firms and workers, the United States relies upon the relatively blunt instrument of trade protection.

The theory of economic policy recognises that to achieve a given number of objectives, it is necessary in most cases to have at least that number of policy instruments. This suggests that only in unusual circumstances can a single policy achieve two goals. Yet in the United States, in most of the safeguard cases only a single instrument has been used (for example, a tariff, quota or orderly marketing arrangement). Protection may be intended to prevent injury to current participants and to provide time to restore competitiveness. But, if long-run modernisation requires displacement, protection that successfully induces adjustment may actually *raise* the level of injury to some existing members of the industry. On the other hand, if protection retains or attracts resources incompatible with the long-run viability of the industry, it will preclude competitiveness. Trade protection is thus an extremely imprecise method of either limiting the dislocation to existing workers and firms or inducing modernisation.

Moreover, while trade may be a source of dislocation in the industry, it is frequently not the only source. Thus dislocation may occur even if trade protection is conferred. Protection can actively increase competitive pressures for existing firms; in the television industry, for example, protection attracted new competitors for United States firms by encouraging direct foreign investment. Protection can also increase the dislocation of existing workers; in the bicycle industry, for instance, protection induced modernisation that resulted in the relocation of plants.

Trade adjustment assistance

The unique role that trade policy plays for declining industries in the United States has made possible a special adjustment program for workers who lose their jobs in industries experiencing competitive difficulties. The program has provision for training and relocation assistance, but its main focus has taken the form of supplementing unemployment benefits. Originally implemented to persuade organised labour to agree to the Kennedy Round tariff cuts, it has a mixed record of success (Aho and Bayard, 1980). From one viewpoint this program has a weak rationale: why should workers displaced as a result of one particular source of change—trade—be treated better than those displaced because of demand shifts or technical change? However, the program has been justified in a political context as compensation for the removal of protection, or as an instrument to allow the political process to voice concern without providing protection. Indeed, a third of the positive findings of the International Trade Commission resulted in trade adjustment assistance rather than protection.

A serious problem with the program has been its impact on incentives. Providing assistance as a supplement to unemployment compensation rewards only workers who *fail* to adjust. Indeed, most of the program's recipients eventually return to their original jobs. A better system would involve lump-sum grants or provide workers with a payment equal to a fixed percentage of the erosion in their earnings for a particular period—in essence, with compensation for the erosion in their specific human capital (see Lawrence, 1984:131–32).

While temporary trade protection has in general facilitated adjustment, the United States has also yielded to political pressure from several industries, which has resulted in a deviation from the conventional legalistic method of providing trade relief to an industry in trouble. The examples discussed below—the textiles and apparel industry, the steel industry, and the Chrysler bailout—highlight the risks involved in detailed government policy intervention.

Failure to adjust: textiles and apparel

The political power of the American apparel and textiles industries enabled them to circumvent the International Trade Commission and obtain trade protection that has thus far proved permanent. Because of this permanence, the system provides a classic demonstration of the pitfalls of protection towards declining industries. Even judged by its own objectives—to limit dislocation and to facilitate modernisation and competitiveness—the policies have failed. They have also proved extremely costly to United States consumers.

First, an important motive for the original imposition of protection was to aid the declining New England region. Yet the Long-Term Cotton Arrangement stimulated the development of the synthetics industry as a major new domestic competitor. Between 1961 and 1973 overall employment in the United States textiles industry increased by 13 per cent, and investment was also strong, increasing at 2.3 per cent a year. But the aggregate data mask the fact that a massive relocation occurred within the United States as firms rescued their labour costs by moving from New England to the south and west. Over the same period, textile employment in New England declined by 32 per cent while increasing by 28 per cent in the south. Thus the United States began the 1960s with one group of people who needed protection because they worked in textiles in the northeast but ended the decade with another group who needed protection because they worked in textiles in the south and west. Had these new entrants not been enticed into the industry, it could have accommodated significantly greater import penetration with no additional dislocation.

The real problem thus stems from the permanence of the Multi-Fiber Agreement. The textiles industry is characterised by a high turnover of firms and workers. In principle, if new entry could be discouraged (as it has been in sectors such as footwear that have received credible temporary protection), the industry would be capable of significant shrinkage without dislocation. But when some firms leave voluntarily, the fact that the Multi-Fiber Agreement has raised product prices creates incentives for new entry. This is a generic problem in industries with relatively low entry barriers. In these cases, the 'positive adjustment' principles of subsidies for capacity reduction are unlikely to be successful. The relative lack of success of even the Japanese in preventing new entry into this sector (through the subsidised retirement of looms) suggests that a credible declining tariff mechanism is imperative as the principle tool of adjustment (Denzau, 1983).

The steel industry: failure or success?

The poor state of the United States steel industry has tempted policymakers to pursue an explicit revitalisation program, but thus far no such policy has been implemented. The proponents of an industrial policy for steel place the blame for its decline on a myopic management's failure to invest or to modernise the large integrated United States steel mills. This popular political explanation for the United States steel industry's decline rests on a market-failure argument: inappropriate behaviour on the part of management in failing to invest, and of labour in demanding (and obtaining) wages that were too high. The solution, according to some, entails a government-led tripartite program, in which protection would be conditional on wage concessions by the unions and heavy investment by existing firms.

This view represents a classic example of the degree to which political failure may exceed (alleged) market failure. The fundamental problems facing the integrated United States steel industry make the modernisation strategy highly suspect; in fact the big United States steel firms that followed the modernisation strategy in the 1970s are those on the verge of bankruptcy today. Three factors make this approach questionable: first, as a result of lower costs of construction and raw materials abroad, the international competitiveness of the United States has been eroded; second, the growth of demand for steel is sluggish; and third, a better and cheaper technology for making steel—the mini-mill—has begun to replace the integrated steel mill.

Lawrence and Lawrence (1985) argue that the dramatic increase in relative wages in the steel industry over the 1970s was actually a response to these developments. As early as 1970, long before United States steel investments slumped and relative wages soared, the United States capital markets signalled the poor prospects for the domestic steel industry by pricing their stock at only a third of replacement costs. Ignoring this market warning, government policies have insisted on channelling more resources into the industry in the form of tax incentives and loan guarantees and providing trade relief, all in the hope of improving the competitiveness of steel. And, despite the many policies implemented over the 1970s, the United States steel industry has continued on its steady path of decline. Yet as late as 1984 the Congress passed and the President signed a bill demanding *new investments* by integrated steel as a condition for trade relief. It is the height of folly to channel resources towards sectors in which they will not earn a normal rate of return.

The Chrysler lesson

The United States government, under both President Carter and President Reagan, strayed considerably from its free-market principles by conferring loan guarantees on the Chrysler Corporation, thereby rescuing it from bankruptcy. Some suggest that this experience supports the view that an institution to perform such bailouts on a regularised basis should be part of industrial policy in the United States.

On the other hand, there is the argument that the very harsh concessions exacted from Chrysler, and from its creditors and workers, to qualify it for aid were possible only because the threat of bankruptcy was credible and the process was extremely unusual. The company had no legal claim to government aid. It was forced to convince the government that it was prepared to undertake the necessary adjustments. Eads (1981) seems correct when he argues as follows:

> A far different—and more ominous—signal would be given by the creation of a special 'revitalisation' authority with general powers to receive petitions for aid [and] work out rescue packages ... The current process certainly has been 'messy' but its very messiness helps assure that it will not be used very often.

In summary, transitory trade protection, while far from cost-effective, has in numerous cases in the United States not proved permanent and has thus been associated with significant adjustment. The success of the program has stemmed from the trade-relief mechanism, which allows the political system to voice concern for the victims of change without becoming embroiled in detailed sectoral programs with specific and precisely defined objectives. Paradoxically, the very impotence of United States industry policy instruments has made the system reasonably adaptable. The relatively superior performance of the United States in this field is thus not attributable to the superior capabilities of its political leadership; it is more directly the result of its system, which has limited the abilities of politicians to intervene effectively.

EUROPEAN INDUSTRIAL POLICIES

If the strength of the United States economy lies in its flexibility, the achievements of the European economies stem from the economic security they provide to most of their citizens. Europe's weakness, however, which has grown increasingly more apparent, arises because the policies that provide economic security also inhibit industrial adjustment. Compared with the United States, Europe gives the state a much more important role, as an agent of both economic development and redistribution.[10] Partly because of the greater latent (and even overt) cleavages in these class-ridden societies, the state is compelled to modify the distributional verdict of the market. In particular, the state has assumed obligations not simply, as in the United States, for the aggregate performance of the economy, but also for an extensive social insurance network that guarantees individuals property rights in their specific jobs.[11]

Unlike the United States, which in the postwar period has taken for granted the entrepreneurial capacities of its corporations, European economies have cast the state in a much more extensive development role. While the strategies have ranged from the highly interventionist planning processes of France to the more market-oriented social market approach of West Germany, considerable state participation in economic development has been the norm. Extensive commitments to industrial policies are thus intrinsic to European economic policy; a *laisser faire* reliance on the market would mark a radical departure from traditional practice.

European workers are much less mobile than Americans; birth and death rates of firms are much lower; real and relative wages are more rigid; and there is considerably less regional mobility. In response to economic difficulties, therefore, European workers are more likely to exert 'voice' than to leave their jobs. Despite the formation of political institutions at the level of the European Community, Europeans look to local and national political leaders for assistance. On the other hand, the European Community has tied the hands of policymakers in responding to these demands for assistance. They have, in many cases, lost the instrument of trade policy as a means of dealing with problems arising from within the Community. Thus at a national (as opposed to Community) level, policy has relied much more on direct subsidies to specific firms, workers and regions than on the indirect trade channel. As Hesselman (1983) has noted, 'the most common form of industrial policy in Europe is financial assistance in the form of tax relief, special depreciation allowances, grants and soft loans'.

In summary, it is for intrinsically political reasons that European policies differ from those in the United States. A United States government, its hands tied by free-market traditions and a lack of available instruments, can generally use trade policy to meet its domestic political responsibilities. In Europe, however, the more developed nature of governmental obligations, the less deep-rooted inhibitions on direct intervention and the constraints on trade policy make direct subsidies and nationalisation more common responses.

The discussion so far has spoken of the European approach as a whole. However, a comparison of the most interventionist—France—with the least interventionist—Germany—suggests that there are distinctive differences among the major European economies, differences that reflect historical and ideological traditions.

France

As far back as Jean Baptiste Colbert in the middle of the seventeenth century, the French state was playing a key role in economic development. Since the second world war, an elite group of civil servants, educated in special state institutions, has provided administrative continuity in the face of political instability, and managerial talent to compensate for weak entrepreneurial traditions in the private sector. The French bureaucracy has influenced resource allocation through indicative planning, reinforced by extensive control of nationalised industries, and has considerable sway over the private sector through the financial system. The relative weakness of labour and the similar educational backgrounds of civil servants and business leaders permit close collaboration between government and management. The instruments of French industrial policy have been highly selective and precisely directed. At various times, policy has focused on individual firms, projects and sectors. Unlike Germany, where most of the intervention has been generic (across the economy as a whole), French policies are highly specific.

These programs have achieved considerable success when applied to the production of goods that are heavily dependent on government purchases: military and civilian aircraft, telecommunications, nuclear power. But the achievements in market-driven products such as computers, consumer electronics and machine tools have been much less impressive. Several projects undertaken for their prestige value have been noteworthy commercial failures: the ocean liner, Le France; the Aerotrain; the supersonic aircraft, Concorde; and La Villette (a huge slaughterhouse in Paris).

Germany

Since its reconstruction after the second world war Germany has been Europe's dominant economy, with highly competitive firms and considerable domestic competition. Industrial policy has reflected a much stronger role for the private sector, facilitated (and perhaps necessitated) by the strong links between industry and the banking system. Government ownership has been fairly high in utilities, mining (coal), metals (steel and aluminium), chemicals, transportation (ships and automobiles) and nuclear energy. But in manufacturing overall, public enterprises accounted for only about 4 per cent of industrial employment and 6 per cent of industrial production in 1976 (Donges,

1980:192). In several specific areas, however, the state has intervened quite extensively.

1   In labour markets the state has established extensive training and employ-ment services; in addition, a detailed system of regulations—the code termination system—regulates relations between labour and management.

2   In specific regions, local governments—the *Länder*—engage in more exten-sive industrial policies by providing financial support and assistance to industry. The federal government has sought to attract industries to peripheral areas such as West Berlin, the area bordering East Germany, and the Saarland.

3   In declining industries government subsidies and support have been fairly extensive (particularly for steel, shipping and coalmining).

4   In high-technology industries the state has provided fairly extensive gov-ernment assistance, primarily through the Ministry of Technology.

European industrial policies since the second world war

Much has been made of the roles of different industrial policies in the per-formances of the European economies up to 1973. After 1973, however, what is most striking is the degree of convergence in the performances of these economies, with the exception of the United Kingdom.

Since the second world war the European economies have passed rapidly through several distinct phases, and the industrial policies of each period have thus reflected different concerns. The following profile typifies industrial policy in each phase.

Reconstruction

Between the second world war and 1958 the emphasis was on postwar recon-struction. In France a detailed plan called for and implemented the develop-ment of industries providing essential infrastructure, such as railways, electri-city and key intermediate inputs like coal and steel. In Germany, similar bottleneck sectors were stimulated: coal, electricity, utilities, shipbuilding, hospitals, and housing. The general need for re-establishing the coal and steel industries led to the formation of the European Coal and Steel Community in 1951, which created a common market in these industries for six European countries.

Competition (1958 to 1973)

For the major European economies, this second phase involved programs aimed at international competition (brought about for continental nations by the European Community) and, in particular, meeting the challenge posed by American multinational corporations entering the European market. Policies had two distinctive features: national-champion firms were nurtured by merger policies, government procurement and other subsidies; and technological development projects were sponsored to close the perceived technology gap between Europe and the United States.

In Britain a variety of bodies such as the National Economic Development Council and the Industrial Reorganisation Corporation aimed at improving innovation but tended to become involved in rescues. The Industrial Reorganisation Corporation promoted mergers in motor vehicles, electronics, steel, mining machinery and heavy engineering. In Germany the federal government sought to remove obstacles to the concentration of industry.[12] It also initiated projects in nuclear power, data processing, aircraft, and space and maritime research. The French responded to the American challenge by promoting national champions and new industrial organisations in glass, chemicals, non-ferrous metals and steel.

Four industries were singled out in France for *grandes programmes*—the nuclear industry, aerospace, space technologies and electronics. French policies reflected highly nationalistic sentiments. Foreign investment was heavily controlled and inhibited, while important projects aimed at avoiding dependence on foreign technology and demonstrating the superiority of French research and technologies.

Adjustment and redistribution (1973 to the present)

This period has been dominated by the need to adjust to external shocks under conditions of slow growth, to high and rising unemployment, and to increasing competition from Japan and the newly industrialising countries. The initial forms of intervention after 1973 were rescues of firms, sectoral support schemes and increases in regional aid that were assumed to be temporary responses to transitory cyclic developments. The responses gradually modified over the 1970s as fiscal constraints became much tighter and perceptions changed about the nature of the adjustment required. While the initial efforts were strongly concentrated on a few heavy industries and large firms, over time attempts were made to refocus towards encouraging new technologies, venture-capital markets and small and medium-sized firms.[13] Recently, strenuous efforts, which have not been entirely successful, have been made to terminate direct government subsidies to large firms.

The French experience differed from this typical European profile, however, because of the euphoric increase in government support for nationalised industries in the first two years of the Mitterand government (1981–83). Nonetheless, even in France efforts have recently been made to restore the profitability of nationalised firms.

The European experience since 1973 underscores the differences between industrial policies that supplement market forces during a period of expansion and those that attempt to reverse them during a period of stagnation. The response to the crises after 1973 reflected the transformation of instruments and policies that had been primarily directed to economic development towards redistribution. Both the nature of the political guarantees and the development strategies adopted before 1973 became obstacles to adjustments thereafter, including the creation of large firms as national champions, state support for industries and projects on non-commercial grounds, the vesting of property rights in particular jobs, and a social commitment to the fulfilment of rising expectations.

As long as the engine of growth keeps running, many of the constraints on flexibility in the European system are not binding. As long as productivity growth is rapid, the guarantee of rising real wages is costless. But if productivity growth declines and real wages must be reduced because of declines in the terms of trade, such guarantees inhibit adjustment. Large firms may have relatively more difficulty in reducing employment (and closing plants), but this is immaterial if no reductions are warranted.[14] Nationalised firms may potentially have access to the state's deep pockets, but this right is costless as long as they remain profitable. Marginally viable activities may require small subsidies, but these are easily disguised or sustained when government revenues are growing rapidly.

Where extensive state involvement is already present, it is much more difficult to argue the inevitability of adjustment to market forces. If the government has the direct legal and practical ability to prevent specific job loss and plant closure, it is much more difficult to resist pleas for assistance. What the government has provided, it must now take away.

Market versus political failure

Was government intervention to aid declining industries in Europe justified? Aid to troubled industries, particularly those with large capital-intensive plants, is frequently rationalised on the grounds of market failure. The arguments usually run along two lines: first, it is alleged, there are intrinsic problems with market-based decisions, which tend to systematically underestimate the long-run value of current plants and existing firms and to close them too rapidly; and second, markets fail to account for the full social costs of the dislocation created by sudden and disruptive closures and firings.

The first justification is extremely weak. Participants in capital markets have every incentive to factorise the long-run growth potential of assets and workers before reducing them.[15] There is no compelling reason to believe that government officials are better than private decisionmakers at predicting the future. Moreover, even if the state does have superior information (and it may indeed have such an advantage in reference to its own intended investment behaviour), it does not follow that it should intervene directly; rather, publicly disseminating this information is the correct response. In some cases, no doubt, markets will err in closing firms and plants that could have made a profit; but these errors must be balanced against the cost of political failures in sustaining operations that should have been closed.

The classic example of the political paradigm is provided by the behaviour of the Mitterand government in France in the first two years of its administration.[16] The explicit objective of the program was to reverse the de-industrialisation that had reduced French employment in industry by 900 000 persons between 1974 and 1981. Employment was actually increased in a number of sectors, such as steel and shipbuilding.

The nationalised industries, which were to serve as the cutting edge of this strategy, were soon in deep financial difficulties. Between 1981 and 1984, as Wright (1984) points out, the state found itself having to provide large injections of capital for a wide range of industries, including steel, chemicals, coal, textiles, toys, leather goods, machine tools, cars, furniture and electronics. The result, he notes, was that ailing and declining industries were absorbing the biggest share of state funding and more deserving industries were being starved of capital. By 1984 extensive retrenchments and reversals were required. The French example is a clear case of the folly of attempts to bring about a radical reversal of market forces. Such unrealistic efforts soon ran into fiscal constraints that have deprived industrial policymaking of another essential ingredient: a consistent long-range strategy.

The second justification—social dislocation costs that exceed private costs— has more merit. But the European experience indicates that caution is warranted in assuming that dislocation is reduced by government intervention. Nor does the European experience indicate that the adjustment is any less extensive simply because it is delayed. The wasted subsidies to production and the implicit taxes on consumers represented by such delaying subsidies must be properly accounted for.[17] Moreover, once the government became determined to restore financial viability, as in the United Kingdom, the entire labour overhang had to be eliminated much more rapidly than might have been necessary without initial government aid.

Intervention is also sometimes justified on the grounds of compensating the losers from structural change. However, such compensation should be conditional on adjustment rather than paid in the form of production subsidies to those who have failed to adjust. Income should be redistributed directly through the tax system, rather than by supporting particular forms of production. The amounts spent on preserving high-wage jobs in capital-intensive industries are paid out at the expense of consumers in the population as a whole. Given the highly capital-intensive nature of the industries generally supported, such profit-raising policies are highly regressive.

In fact, the most common reason for government involvement is often its previous involvement or the involvement of other governments. Once a government intervenes to influence a private firm's commercial decisions, its responsibility continually increases. If a government prevents the firm from laying off workers and closing plants for social reasons, or keeps the firm's profit margins low to control inflation through price controls, or insists that a firm invest in a particular region or program for the sake of prestige, it takes on implicit obligations to compensate stockholders for the consequences.

Governments are also compelled to react to foreign intervention. Political failure assumes the familiar guise of the prisoner's dilemma. If a country were certain that others would cut back their subsidies, it would have to bear less of the adjustment burden, but because it cannot be certain it sustains the subsidies. This burden stems from the nationalistic desire to maintain a complete set of economic activities rather than an adherence to the principles of efficient resource allocation.

The shipbuilding industry provides a typical example.[18] As the world economy expanded until 1973 the prospects for shipbuilding appeared favourable and, since governments considered the industry strategically important, they implemented programs to support it. The purpose of assistance to domestic firms was primarily to secure their positions in international competition. But once the industry was in trouble, programs were extended on the pretext of facilitating adjustment. Temporary support schemes have been extended and renewed and, perhaps more significantly, the provision of subsidised credit has apparently become permanent. In the early 1970s the OECD helped to negotiate a general arrangement to bring about a balanced reduction in aids to shipping. Since 1975, however, member countries have decided that such an arrangement is not practicable in the industry's present state. Thus subsidies to shipbuilding, even in free-market economies such as Germany, continue in the name of an equitable sharing of the adjustment burden.

While a market system allocates resources throughout the economy by means of decisions at the margin, the perspective of the political system is much narrower, concentrating mainly on focal points. Although the drama, and much of the attention of this chapter, have focused on the main programs of intervention, a perspective on their economy-wide impact is required. It is striking that intervention has typically been highly concentrated by firms and sectors. In Germany the chief recipients are coalmining, steel, shipbuilding and the electrical industry; in 1974 these measures amounted to as much as 29 per cent of value added for coalmining, but to only about 2.5 per cent of value added in industry overall.[19] A similar concentration is evident in France; according to the Eighth Plan Commission, government assistance in France amounted to 46 per cent of value added in agriculture, 12–20 per cent in housing, 30 per cent in nationalised companies and 2–3 per cent in other industries. Moreover, about 80 per cent of the industrial subsidies have been granted to just nine large companies.

While it is the rescue stories that grab the headlines and the attention of most government policy, the big story, the one that is going on behind the headlines, *is* dominated by market forces and macroeconomic developments. As Tables 7.1 and 7.2 demonstrate, extensive adjustment has occurred in the European economies. Industrial policies may have channelled capital towards these firms and sectors at the expense of others, but they have not been able to exert a significant impact on the overall patterns of change.

Table 7.1 Changes in employment shares in high-growth and low-growth manufacturing industries in selected countries, 1973 and 1980 (per cent)

	France[a]	West Germany[b]	United Kingdom	United States	Japan
High-growth industries[c]					
1973	31.8	39.7	30.6	30.4	32.4
1980	34.3	41.0	33.0	34.0	33.4
Percentage change in share	7.9	3.3	7.8	11.8	3.1
Percentage change in employment	−5.2	−8.2	−7.6	14.3	−5.6
Low-growth industries[d]					
1973	34.6	32.8	33.9	34.0	36.1
1980	29.1	32.8	33.9	34.0	36.1
Percentage change in share	−15.9	−9.1	−11.5	−6.8	−9.4
Percentage change in employment	−26.2	−19.2	−24.2	−4.8	−17.2

Notes: a   The 1973 low-growth data for France include iron ore and non-ferrous metal ore mining, but do not include shipbuilding. The high-growth data for both years include rubber products.
         b   German data are for 1979, not 1980.
         c   Industrial chemicals, other chemical products, plastics products, machinery, electrical machinery and professional goods.
         d   Textiles, apparel, leather, footwear, wood products, furniture, iron and steel, non-ferrous metals, metal products and shipbuilding.

Source: UN *Yearbook of Industrial Statistics* 1977, 1981

Conclusions

This chapter has drawn a contrast between the normative principles of economic theory and the actual practice of industrial policy. The challenge facing the designers of industrial policy is to achieve the best compromise between efficiency and other objectives.

The tough question for economists is, to what degree can the principles be violated and still retain their strength as guides to action? Is it possible to maintain strongly doctrinal free-market principles such as those held by the United States and West Germany, and at the same time to ignore them on numerous occasions? Or is it preferable to shift the principles towards more interventionist policies and notions such as 'workable competition' and 'positive adjustment' in the hope of channelling adjustment more closely towards market forces? Whatever political compromises these approaches involve, the recent experience of France demonstrates the costs of a headlong pursuit of the political paradigm.

This appraisal of industrial policy in the United States and Europe suggests that no simple formula is likely to hold for all countries at all times. Instead, practices must be tailored to historical and institutional contexts. With its hands tied by free-market traditions and a lack of available instruments, the American government has used trade policy as its primary instrument for aiding declining industries in the United States. Transitory protection obtained through the International Trade Commission has allowed the political system to show concern for the victims of change without implementing

Table 7.2 Selected countries: changes in employment, 1975–80, 1980–84 (per cent)

	France		Germany		United Kingdom[a]		United States		Japan	
	1975–80	1980–84	1975–80	1980–84	1975–80	1980–82	1975–80	1980–84	1975–80	1980–84
Manufacturing	−6.0	−10.0	3.0	−13.0	−10.0	−15.0	11.0	−6.0[b]	−7.0	2.0
Textiles	−16.0	−17.0	−13.0	−23.0	−20.0	−20.0	−2.0	−12.0	−14.0	−7.0
Basic metals	−14.0	−13.0	−13.0	−38.0	−21.0	−26.0	−1.0	−24.0	−14.0	−7.0
Iron and steel	−24.0	−16.0	−15.0	−44.0	−26.0	−28.0	−8.0	−31.0	−16.0	−9.0
Machinery	−8.0	−13.0	−1.0	−11.0	−8.0	−16.0	20.0	−16.0	−7.0	7.0
Electrical machinery	−4.0	−4.0	−3.0	−9.0	−8.0	−13.0	22.0	4.0	12.0	18.0
Shipbuilding and repairing	−5.0	2.0	−27.0	−21.0	−14.0	−8.0	10.0	−12.0[b]	−43.0	−14.0

Notes: a Note that data are for 1980–82, not 1980–84.
         b Data are for the first half of 1984.

Source: OECD *Indicators of Industrial Activity* (Various issues)

detailed intervention programs. This has been relatively successful in facilitating adjustment but unsuccessful in maintaining specific jobs and restoring industries as expanding international competitors. At times, however, industries with political muscle have obtained permanent quotas in the United States. The experience with these devices has been much less successful.

In Europe, direct subsidies and nationalisations have been more common responses to industrial decline. The wider use of these approaches reflects the more extensive obligations assumed by governments and the less developed inhibitions about direct government intervention that stem from the traditional role of the state as an agent of economic development. The European experience underscores the differences between industrial policies that supplement market forces during a period of expansion and those that attempt to reverse them during a period of stagnation. Many of the obligations assumed by the state before 1973 with respect to guaranteeing specific jobs and real wage growth afterwards became expensive and binding constraints. Although European countries have spent heavily on declining industries, they have been unable to avoid large increases in unemployment in several manufacturing sectors.

It is also doubtful whether delaying adjustment has made it less painful. The European experience may contain an important message for Pacific Basin countries in which the state has also assumed an important developmental role: during periods of expansion, policymakers should avoid assuming obligations towards workers and firms that will be unsustainable during periods of decline; it is crucial to incorporate the capacity for flexible responses when market forces dictate a reversal in the direction of structural change.

8 Industrial policy in Japan

MASU UEKUSA AND HIDEKI IDE

A FRAMEWORK

In a changing economic, political and social environment, Japan's industrial policy has undergone significant shifts since the second world war. But in spite of these changes, Japanese industrial policy has nearly always been divisible into four categories: policies on allocating resources among industries by protecting and supporting promising industries or adjusting declining industries; policies on industrial reorganisation, adjustment of production and investment and price stabilisation; policies on industrial infrastructure, pollution and trade friction; and policies on small and medium-sized enterprise (see Komiya et al., 1984:3–4). The first and the second have often been called 'industry-specific policies'; the third and the fourth have been referred to as 'horizontal policies' (Adams and Bollino, 1983). The former group, the industry-specific policies, are industrial policies in the narrow sense, and are what is meant here by 'Japanese industrial policies'.

Both industry-specific policies and horizontal industrial policies pertain to a series of market failures such as infant industries, economies of scale, externalities, the risks entailed in research and development, imperfect information, public goods and pollution. Moreover, both types of policies aim at enhancing allocative and technical efficiency, attaining higher economic growth, stabilising economic fluctuations and promoting technological progress. How, then, does industrial policy differ from other public policies affecting industry—i.e. antimonopoly measures and public regulation—that have the same aims as industrial policy? The principal feature of antimonopoly measures is not direct intervention in the market but indirect regulation against behaviour that distorts the market mechanism. On the other hand, public regulation of monopolies or natural oligopolies such as utilities, transportation, telecommunications and some financial sectors represents direct intervention under specific laws in corporate decisionmaking about such matters as entry and exit, production, price level and structure, and investment.

Like competition policy and public regulation, industrial policy often intervenes directly in the market and in corporate decisionmaking. But it cannot intervene as strongly as can public regulation, because an agency for im-

147

plementing industrial policy does not have the authority that belongs to direct regulation. This being so, how is industrial policy enforced?

First of all, 'policy goals' must be fitted to the international and domestic environments, and must also win the support of a wide range of the populace and interest groups. There are various organisations in Japan for gaining this support, such as the Industrial Structure Council, an advisory group of the Minister for International Trade and Industry. Then, on the basis of the policy goals, 'concrete policy objectives' are determined; for instance, the 1970s goal of forming a knowledge-intensive industrial structure led to a policy objective of promoting high-technology industries. To realise this sort of objective, a set of 'policy instruments' is selected from a range of pecuniary and non-pecuniary instruments such as fiscal, taxational, monetary and tariff or non-tariff measures, administrative guidance and the supply of information. (This constitutes a 'vision'—a term explained later.) A feature of Japanese industrial policy is its enforcement by means of these instruments rather than through special legislation (though there have been a few individual laws for promoting specific industries or adjusting declining industries). Thus it is essential to analyse Japan's industrial policy within this threefold framework of policy goals, concrete policy objectives and policy instruments.

It is well known that Japan's industrial policy has been enforced primarily by the Ministry for International Trade and Industry (MITI), as this ministry has been responsible for a wide range of sectors, including mining, most manufacturing industries, and public utilities (particularly electricity and gas). Among the manufacturing industries, the food industry is under the jurisdiction of the Ministry of Agriculture, Forestry and Fisheries; tobacco, salt, malt and liquor come under the Ministry of Finance; drugs and medicines are under the Ministry of Health and Welfare; and shipbuilding is under the Ministry of Transportation. Though conventional wisdom has it that industrial policy is directed at the manufacturing and mining sectors, the agricultural and construction sectors have also been subject to industrial policy. Public utilities, transportation, telecommunications and financing and insurance, on the other hand, have been dealt with by direct regulation rather than by industrial policy.

THE PROCESS OF FORMULATING POLICY

The main organs involved in the formulation of Japan's industrial policy are the industrial bureaus of MITI; the coordination bureau of MITI; various trade associations; advisory councils and investigative committees; business communities; and banks. (Few studies have been done, even in Japan, of the formulation of Japanese industrial policy, but Komiya et al. (1984) is helpful in understanding the process of policy formulation.) Thus government, private enterprise, labour unions and financial institutions are all represented in the process of formulating industrial policy, making it, so to speak, an 'n-person game'. Industrial policy is a product of persuasion, negotiation and frequent compromise among these players.

First, an important role is played by MITI's industrial bureaus, or so-called 'vertical divisions' (the Basic Industries Bureau, the Machinery and Information Industries Bureau, the Consumer Goods Industries Bureau and the Natural Resources and Energy Agency). Each 'vertical division' covers a particular sector of industry and is responsible for its development and adjustment; for example, the Temporary Law for Promotion of the Machine and Information Industry (1978) and the Temporary Law for Promotion of the Electronic Industry were drafted by the industrial bureaus. Plans for preferential tax treatment, tariff rates and policies for import liberalisation are originally drawn up by these bureaus and revised by the coordination bureau. The Ministry of Finance shares jurisdiction over some of these specific policy tools with MITI; in fact, industrial policy has been a product of negotiation and compromise among the ministries and agencies concerned through their respective coordination bureaus.

On the other hand, MITI's coordination bureaus or so-called 'horizontal divisions' (the International Trade Policy Bureau, the Trade Bureau, the Industrial Policy Bureau, the Industrial Location and Environment Protection Bureau and the Minister's Secretariat) handle issues common to all industries, such as business trends, the long-term direction of the economy, trade and pollution. 'Horizontal divisions' also perform an internal coordinating function within MITI; since the 1970s policy initiation has shifted from the 'vertical' industrial bureaus (oriented to industry-specific policy) towards the 'horizontal' bureaus because MITI has put heavy emphasis on coping with trade friction, environmental pollution, energy, structural adjustment in depressed industries, and development in high-technology industries.

Various attitudes of the private sector toward specific industrial policies have been voiced through the councils as well as the bureaus in charge of various industrial activities. Ministries and agencies have been authorised to set up their own councils as advisory organs, and MITI has 32 advisory committees and investigative councils. These advisory councils include representatives of industry, labour and consumer groups, scholars, journalists, former government officials and other knowledgeable individuals appointed by the minister. A well-known example is the Industrial Structure Council, which has examined MITI's views and expressed its own opinions on matters concerning Japan's industrial structure. Although its responses and recommendations have no binding effect, the council is useful in garnering support for MITI's policies from various interest groups, thereby bolstering the authority of MITI's policies.

Another important council role is to collect, exchange and disseminate information on industrial policy. Since the environment surrounding industrial policy is always complex and uncertain, it is very useful for government agencies, as well as for industry, that representatives of the various groups involved meet to discuss macroeconomic trends and inter-industrial structure, and to exchange information on new technologies, domestic and overseas market conditions and the policies of foreign governments. This Japanese system of exchanging information has been effective not only in coping promptly with new policy issues but also in reaching compromises among diverse interests and establishing consensus on what should be the primary economic goal.

Viewed as a system of information collection and dissemination, as Komiya (1975) argues, Japan's industrial policies may have been among the most important factors in Japan's high rate of industrial growth, apart from the direct or indirect economic effects of industrial policy measures. MITI has attached more importance to the information collection and dissemination system since the early 1970s, because the profound changes in the world economic environment have had a great impact on Japanese industry. MITI has also regularly published its so-called 'visions', which are outlines of likely future trends in the macroeconomy, in the industrial structure and in the main industrial sectors. They have been important guides for decisionmaking in the private sector, as well as for enforcing the concrete objectives of industrial policy.

Finally, there have been instances where a part of the business community or a group of companies possessing special access to the political parties has asked for flexible enforcement of government policies in ways that would benefit it. Recently, the ruling Liberal Democratic Party (LDP) has had increasing influence on the drafting of industrial policy, signifying the politicisation of industrial policy formulation and enforcement. It should not be overlooked, however, that the longstanding dominance of the conservative LDP has resulted in consistency in the formulation of policy.

AN HISTORICAL OVERVIEW

Industrial policy in Japan since the second world war is partly a legacy of the Meiji Era, particularly in the close relationship between government officials and business communities and in the methods of implementing various policies (for a detailed account, see Johnson, 1982). Postwar industrial policy differs from that of prewar Japan, and has continued to change over the postwar period, reflecting the transformations in the economic and political environments, both domestically and internationally. The development of Japan's economy since the war can be divided into three stages: the reconstruction period from the end of the war to the late 1950s; the period of rapid economic growth from the early 1960s to the first oil crisis; and the period since the first oil crisis. This division into stages will be useful for understanding the changes in the politico-economic environment and the concomitant shifts in the orientation of industrial policy.

1945 to 1960: reconstruction

This can be subdivided into two further periods: the Occupation years, from 1945 to 1952; and the period of reconstruction, from 1952 to 1960. During the Occupation, new institutional apparatuses for democratising the Japanese economy were established; recovery from wartime destruction was also given high priority. The economic democratisation program included farmland reform, liberalisation of labour movements and antimonopoly policy. The former two measures fuelled domestic consumption by boosting the incomes of farmers and industrial labourers. The latter—the antimonopoly policy—consisted of deconcentration measures, including the dissolution of the *zaibatsu* (prewar family-owned business conglomerates), the division of big businesses, the breaking up of cartel organisations, and the enactment of the Antimonopoly Law. These deconcentration measures represented probably the greatest use of government power in modern times to create a competitive industrial structure. They did indeed contribute to a decrease in market concentration in a large number of industries, but also to decreasing overall concentration in the Japanese economy (see Uekusa, 1978). The new, competitive market structure and the decisionmaking autonomy of managers in the companies (in contrast to the strong ties within the prewar *zaibatsu*) led to the importation of foreign technology and the creation of a large number of new industries. Thus the deconcentration measures formed the groundwork for Japan's postwar economic development.

But recovery from wartime devastation could not be wrought by the competitive market mechanism alone. The government therefore accorded special priority to certain industries, such as coalmining, electricity and steel manufacturing, and channelled government funds to them. The government also allocated imported raw materials and foreign exchange to these key industries. In order to enforce these policies—the so-called Priority Production Formula (*Keisha Seisan Hoshiki*)—the government enacted the Foreign Exchange Control Law, controlled imports of raw materials and foreign technologies by requiring special permits, and established publicly owned financial intermediaries (the Reconstruction Finance Corporation in 1947, the Japan Export–Import Bank in 1950 and the Japan Development Bank in 1951). The Priority Production Formula was the first and most powerful industrial policy in postwar Japan, in that resources were allocated among industries on a large scale, the system described above was created to enforce policy measures, and various policy tools (fiscal, monetary and international trade policy) were employed. All this was carried out under the slogan of 'solving starvation and reconstructing a production mechanism' (Marxist terminology often used during that period).

In the first half of the 1950s, a new goal—industrial rationalisation—was established. As Japan's balance of payments began to deteriorate after the Korean War, Japanese industries had to bolster their international competitiveness by lowering costs. In 1952, in order to promote investment in important industries—iron and steel, chemical fertilisers, shipbuilding, electricity, and so on—MITI enacted the Law to Promote Rationalisation, following a report submitted by the Industrial Rationalisation Council (an advisory group of MITI) in 1951. The policy tools employed for this rationalisation policy were different from those for the Priority Production Formula; the main tools were special tax treatment and low-interest loans from the government's Fiscal

Investment and Loan Fund. The tax concessions included special depreciation allowances, tax exemption for major imported products, tariff exemption for essential machinery, and exemption from property tax (for more detail, see Tsuruta, 1982).

In the latter half of the 1950s, MITI advocated a new policy of nurturing new industries and promoting promising industries. The industries targeted for government support were synthetic fibres, plastics, petroleum refining, petrochemicals, automobiles, electronics, and several machinery industries. Accordingly, MITI introduced the Five Year Production Plan for these industries, provided special tax treatment and low-interest loans, allocated foreign exchange, approved imports of foreign technology, and invested government capital (particularly in synthetic rubber). In addition, MITI erected tariff and non-tariff barriers to protect these industries from foreign competition.

In the process of modernising the steel and other established industries, nurturing promising new industries and switching from coal to oil in the 1950s, the expansion of Japan's industrial infrastructure became more urgent. The government began to increase public expenditure on land and water for industrial use, and on roads. At the same time, the government had to force the coal industry to accept an adjustment policy because of the energy revolution.

The original version of Japanese industrial policy was established through the formulation and enforcement of the priority production policy in 1946–48, the industrial rationalisation policy of the early 1950s and, in the late 1950s, the policy for promoting new industries, the infrastructure expansion policy, and the industrial adjustment policy for the coal industry. The rationalisation policy and the protective and promotive policy represented the quintessence of Japanese industrial policy, in the sense that the government targeted certain strategic industries, protected and promoted them by means of all kinds of policy tools, intervened in the decision making of private companies, and tried to form a market structure that met with MITI's approval. MITI's intervention in the market structure and its industry targeting eventually came up against the pro-competition policy of the Japan Fair Trade Commission (JFTC). As the significance of the Antimonopoly Law was not fully understood by the Japanese public at the time, the law was extensively modified in 1953 (for more detail, see Caves and Uekusa, 1976). The weakening of the law and its sluggish enforcement symbolised the growing power of MITI.

1961 to 1973: rapid growth

The 1960s was a decade of remarkable economic growth, largely because of a low capital coefficient and a very high level of capital formation, given a high savings ratio and the existence of capital opportunity in the heavy and chemical industries. The eagerness of businessmen to maintain this rapid growth made the notion of 'maximum economic growth' a virtual national policy goal. Also during this decade, Japan opened up its economy to become a full member of the OECD and other international communities. The government adopted the Foreign Exchange and International Trade Liberalisation Plan in 1960 and liberalised trade for a number of products. By 1964 the rate of liberalisation had reached 93 per cent. In that year, Japan became an Article VIII member of the IMF, and also joined the OECD. The Japanese government took the first steps toward capital liberalisation in 1967, and by 1973 the liberalisation process was almost complete. In the course of liberalisation it became another national goal to strengthen industry's international competitiveness in order to overcome the constraints imposed on economic growth by the international balance of payments.

To realise these policy goals, MITI advocated a shift toward a higher-value-added industrial structure centred on heavy and chemical industries, and also the pursuit of scale economies of production in those industries. All these measures were discussed and approved by the Industrial Structure Research Committee, which was established in 1961 and reorganised as the Industrial Structure Council in 1964. A feature of Japan's industrial policy in the 1960s was that the council became an important organisation in drawing up industrial policy, and published several reports on the future direction of industrial development.

Although various kinds of policy tools were implemented for enforcing these measures, a series of instruments for protecting domestic industries could not be confined to a few industries, given the ongoing liberalisation of international trade and capital flows. Furthermore, the policy tools became indicative and indirect. This transformation reflected not only the transition to an open economy but also a failure of MITI policy. MITI was concerned about the Japanese industries that were relatively small in scale and technologically lagged behind western developed nations in the international arena, while being excessively competitive in the domestic arena. In 1963 MITI proposed the Temporary Measures Law to Promote Certain Industries, seeking authority to promote mergers, business tie-ups, coordinative investment and other types of cooperation among firms, and to intervene in corporate decisionmaking about production, prices and investment. The bill was not enacted because its opponents argued that such a law could give MITI too much control over industry and would emasculate the Antimonopoly Law. (The Industrial Structure Research Committee, however, actually approved of laying the bill before the Diet. The bill was drawn up by a board of the committee, consisting of members who had been selected by former top government officials, and who proceeded to ignore the opinions of business and academic circles. Subsequently, this arbitrary bureaucratic decision was rejected by the National Diet. It is worth noting that the Diet thereafter became a participant in industrial policy.) After the rejection of the bill, MITI gradually shifted from direct and regulatory policy measures towards indirect and indicative ones. Thus administrative guidance (*gyosei shido*), in the form of advice, recommendation or encouragement, became a principal policy tool to influence corporate decisionmaking.

By the late 1960s and the early 1970s, rapid economic growth had created several new problems: pollution, extreme urbanisation, deserted villages and personal stress. These problems, in turn, gave rise to a growing demand for social welfare programs and better housing. In addition, the increasing international competitiveness of Japanese industry and the concomitant international-payments surplus created international trade frictions for Japan, particularly with the United States. Japan's increased dependence on imported energy also began to worry government officials and experts. These problems were carried over to the following period.

1973 to 1985: after the oil crisis

The goals of industrial policy in Japan have changed dramatically since the first oil crisis, reflecting changes in the policy environment. First, national priority has shifted from maximum economic growth towards the broader objective of comprehensive improvement of social and economic performance. Second, the relationship between the government and private enterprise has changed, in that big business that has become internationally competitive no longer shares the interests of the industrial ministries that used to intervene in strategic areas of corporate decisionmaking (Uekusa, 1984). Third, since Japan became an important actor in the world economy and subsequently became embroiled in trade frictions, Japan's actions have inevitably invited scrutiny and reaction from the United States and other nations.

Against this background, MITI decided to re-examine Japan's industrial policy. The Industrial Structure Council prepared a report in May 1971 entitled *Trade and Industrial Policies in the 1970s*, and in 1974 issued a revised version, *A Long-Term Vision on Industrial Structure*. In these 'visions' MITI announced the following: a transformation of policy goals from the pursuit of maximum economic growth to the utilisation of the potential for economic growth to improve social and economic performance; a change in policy instruments from active protection and promotion of industry to 'maximum use of the market mechanism'; the encouragement of a shift from a capital-intensive and energy-intensive industrial structure to a knowledge-intensive and energy-conservative one centred on the high-technology, fashion and information-processing industries; the promotion of energy conservation and alternative sources of energy; and the promotion of international cooperation.

Concrete policy objectives were adopted, based on these policy goals. The developments in Japanese industrial policy since the first oil crisis are shown in Table 8.1, and its principal features are summarised below.

First, MITI emphasised environmental conservation, structural adjustment in depressed industries, adjustment for trade frictions, and the promotion of research and development in high-technology industries. It is clear from the frequent use of the word 'adjustment' that industrial policy during this period became passive and negative, by contrast with the active and positive industrial policy during Japan's phase of rapid growth.

A second feature of Japan's present industrial policy is an increased emphasis on the supply of information from the government to industry about future trends in industrial structure, technological innovation and international relations. These 'visions', as they are callèd, formulated by consensus among various representatives from industry, labour, the media and certain pressure groups in a ministerial council, provide an important guide for individual firms in formulating business strategies, and could thus be considered a policy instrument. In other words, by publishing 'visions' a ministry can guide corporate behaviour in the directions it considers desirable (Wheeler et al., 1982).

Third, it should be pointed out that administrative guidance has become less effective because of the reduced kit of policy instruments and because of the change in the relations between government and private enterprise.

Finally, Japan's industrial policy since 1973 has made greater use of the market mechanism. Accordingly, reliance on protective policies for key industries has declined, and MITI and other industrial ministries have not implemented anticompetitive measures.

INDUSTRIAL POLICIES SINCE THE 1970s

Adjustment policies for depressed industries

The background to policy

Structural adjustment in declining industries has been an important issue for the Japanese economy since the first oil crisis, when for the first time since the war Japan faced the prospect of declining competitiveness in many of its key industrial sectors.

However, there were also industrial adjustment problems before the first oil crisis. The first major industrial adjustment policy was directed at the coalmining industry around 1960. In the face of the 'energy revolution' the coalmining industry declined drastically in terms of both production and employment. This process of industrial adjustment was facilitated by the 1955 Temporary Law for Rationalisation of Coal Mining, the 1959 Temporary Law for Dislocated Coal Miners, the 1961 Temporary Law for Promotion of Coal Producing Areas, and other laws.

Subsequently, in the 1970s, the numbers of employees in many industrial sectors decreased, mainly for such structural reasons as the appreciation of the yen and the emergence of the newly industrialising countries (Table 8.2). The textile industry in particular faced such problems as increased competition from some Southeast Asian countries and pressure from the United States for reduced exports. The Temporary Law for Structural Improvement of the Textile Industry in 1967 and 1974 provided various measures for rationalising and modernising this industry. It is notable that industrial adjustment in large-scale industries before the first oil crisis was limited to a few cases (mainly coal and textiles), and was undertaken with a relatively smooth trans-

Table 8.1 Japan: trends in the objectives of industrial policy, 1973–84

Year	Rank order of objectives						
	1	2	3	4	5	6	7
1973	Constructing a pollution-free society	Increasing consumption	Remodelling the Japanese archipelago	Bolstering smaller enterprises in the period of inter-nationalisation	Promoting harmony in the world economy	Advancing towards a future society	Securing a stable supply of resources and energy
1974	Stabilising prices and increasing consumption	Constructing a pollution-free society and promoting environmental conservation	Developing overall policies for smaller enterprises	Securing a stable supply of resources and energy	Adjusting industrial activity to take account of national welfare	Creating a high-level future society	Contributing to the world economy through international cooperation
1975	Stabilising prices and improving consumer life	Securing a stable supply of resources and energy	Preserving public peace and promoting measures for pollution abatement	Promoting small and medium-sized enterprises	Realising a vision of industrial structure to meet social needs	Promoting technology and realising a welfare society	Developing external economic policy
1976	Fostering economic recovery and promoting industrial policies for steady growth	Promoting small and medium-sized enterprises	Securing a stable supply of resources and energy	Devising external economic policy for steady development of the world economy	Stabilising and improving the standard of living	Securing industrial safety and promoting policies for environmental protection	Promoting technological development
1977	Developing new industrial policies under the economic slowdown	Devising external economic policy for steady development of the world economy	Improving policies for smaller enterprises	Securing a stable supply of resources and energy	Promoting technological development	Improving the standard of living	Promoting harmony of industrial activity with human life
1978	Fostering economic recovery and promoting new industrial policies	Overcoming the limitations of energy and security of resources	Contributing positively to the global community	Strengthening policies for small and medium-sized enterprises	Promoting technological development and next-leading industries	Improving the standard of living and promoting environmental policies	

Year							
1979	Devising policies to realise the MITI 'vision' for the 1980s	Establishing balanced economic relations and contributing positively to the global community		Improving policies for smaller enterprises	Promoting an overall energy policy	Promoting next-leading industries and improving policy for industrial technology	Promoting environmental policies and improving the standard of living
1980	Securing a stable supply of resources and energy	Contributing positively to world economic development	Fostering economic recovery and promoting new industrial policies	Bringing up vital smaller enterprises	Promoting balanced development and realising a higher standard of living		
1981	Establishing energy security and preparing for the post-energy society	Constructing a path towards a 'technology-based nation'	Promoting future-oriented industrial policy and technological development	Developing industrial policies to encourage creativity	Developing policies for smaller enterprises producing vitality and knowledge	Forming an attractive regional economic society and improving the quality of life	
1982	Promoting an overall energy policy	Establishing balanced economic relations and contributing positively to the global community	Revitalising and promoting technological development	Devising foreign policy for the interdependent age	Developing a policy for smaller enterprises in response to the requirements of a new age	Forming an attractive regional economic society and improving the quality of life	
1983	Revitalising industry in the medium and long terms and promoting technological development	Promoting an overall energy-and-resource policy	Contributing positively to revitalising the world economy and establishing balanced economic relations	Developing policy for smaller enterprises	Forming an attractive regional economic society and improving the quality of life		
1984	Forming the basis for creative development	Contributing to the development of the world economy and establishing balanced economic relations	Promoting energy-and-resource policy from a long-term perspective	Developing policies for smaller enterprises in a new age	Forming an attractive regional economic society and improving the quality of life		

Table 8.2   Japan: uneven growth patterns among manufacturing industries, 1965–80

Industry	Number of industries			Changes in employment (in 10 000 persons)		
	1965–70	*1970–73*	*1973–80*	*1965–70*	*1970–73*	*1973–80*
Industries with large increases in employment	63	66	37	164	72	32
Industries with large decreases in employment	40	67	100	−34	−44	−134
Industries with small changes in employment	38	8	6	46	0.4	0
Total	141	141	143	176	28	103

Note: 'Industries with large increases (decreases) in employment' denotes industries where employment increased (decreased) by more than the average for all manufacturing industries.

Source: Industrial Policy Study Group, 'Nihon no sangyo seisaku' (Industrial policy in Japan), *Nihon Keizai Shinbun* 20 October 1982

fer of economic resources into other industries because of the economy's rapid growth.

Since the late 1970s, a large number of important basic material industries have suffered from stagnation of production, as shown in Figure 8.1. These industries felt keenly the price increases for raw materials and energy that followed the first oil crisis. Moreover, they were seriously hit by the second oil crisis while they were still attempting to adjust to the first. To encourage such structurally depressed industries to scrap excess capacity and otherwise restore the balance of supply and demand, the Diet passed the Temporary Law for Stabilisation of Specified Depressed Industries (the Depressed Industry Law) in May 1978, and a new law called the Temporary Law for Structural Improvement of Specified Industries (the Structural Reform Law) was enacted in May 1983.

Adjustment policy since the late 1970s

Even after adjustment to the first oil crisis (1973–75), many industries were still beset by overcapacity and excess employment. Two structural factors were largely to blame: the costs of raw materials and energy had come to occupy 50–80 per cent of total costs in these industries; and the global economic slowdown had decreased the volume of production. In particular, the price increases for raw materials and energy led to decreased exports and increased imports, which resulted in low rates of capacity utilisation.

By enacting the Depressed Industry Law in 1978, the government began to enforce a structural adjustment assistance policy toward several depressed industries. An industry is eligible for assistance under the law if the industry has severe overcapacity; if more than half the firms in the industry are in dire financial straits in the long term (over three to five years); if more than

Figure 8.1   Japan: trends in the index of production in manufacturing
                (1975=100)

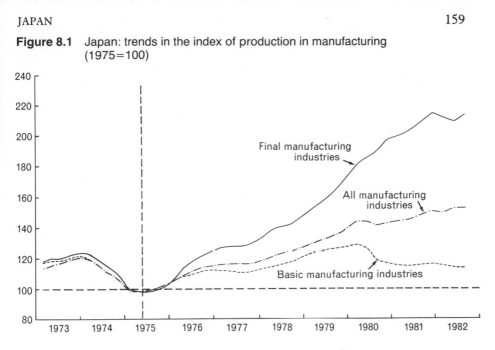

Notes: The final manufacturing industries include general machinery, electrical machinery,
          transport machinery and precision machinery. The basic manufacturing industries
          include iron and steel, non-ferrous metals, ceramics, chemicals (excluding drugs and
          medicines), pulp and paper, and wood and wood products.

Source: Toshihiko Tanabe (ed.) *Japanese Industry: 1983* Tokyo: Zaikei Shobosha (1983:7)

two-thirds of the firms in the industry sign a petition seeking designation
under the law; and if there is broad agreement in a ministerial council that
disposal of overcapacity is necessary to overcome the depressed conditions.
Although many industries (including iron and steel) were in a state of severe
overcapacity, only fourteen were designated by this law as 'structurally depressed' (see Table 8.3), including aluminium refining and synthetic fibres,
which were hurt by high energy costs; shipbuilding, which was affected by low
world demand; electric-furnace steelmaking, ferrosilicon and linerboard,
which were beset by low domestic demand; and cotton and other spinning
industries and chemical fertilisers, which were hit by increasing competition
from the newly industrialising countries.

   The Depressed Industry Law called for a number of measures for assisting
structural adjustment in these industries: the formulation of a basic stabilisation plan outlining capacity reduction, employment measures and other
conversion measures, decided through consultation with industry and union
representatives; a collective reduction of capacity among all companies in the
designated industry; the establishment of a joint credit fund for purchasing
scrapped facilities and as a guarantee of the loans from banks for the disposal
of facilities; the implementation of measures for displaced workers from designated depressed industries and the relevant depressed communities through

Table 8.3 Japan: plan for disposal of facilities in structurally depressed industries and its results

	Existence of collective action	Changes in rate of operation (1978–81) %	Targeted volume of disposal[a] kt	Targeted volume of disposal[a] %	Achieved rate of disposal[b] (1982) %	Reference column — Targeted volume of disposal under the Structural Reform Law[c] (1983–88) kt	Reference column — Targeted volume of disposal under the Structural Reform Law[c] (1983–88) %
Steelmaking by electric furnace		68–80	2850	14	95.4	3800	14
Aluminium-refining		73–59	530	32	96.7	930[c]	57
Synthetic fibres and wool							
—nylon fibre	0	79–89	74.3	20	98.1	continued	
—polyacrylonitrile wool	0	80–93	84.9	17	112.5	continued	
—polyester fibre	0	77–86	44.9	13	81.5		
—polyester wool	0	77–95	78.4	20	90.2		
—biscoase wool						44.7	15
Shipbuilding by use of a dock to build ships of over 5000 GT		51–79	3400	35	104.7		
Chemical fertilisers							
—ammonium	0	62–62	1190	26	100.0	660	20
—urea	0	50–57	1790	45	93.3	830	36
—phosphoric acid by wet process	0	58–64	190	20	91.6	130	17
—phosphoric acid by dry process						240	32
—synthetic fertiliser						810	13
Spinning mills							
—cotton spinning		70–88	67.1	56	77.9	continued	
—combed wool spinning	0	64–83	18.3	10	96.2	continued	
Ferrosilicon		55–64	10.2	21	100.0	50	14
Paper							
—linerboard	0	63–69	1150	15	94.4	continued	
—western-style paper						950	11
Petrochemicals							
—ethylene						2290	36
—polyolefine						900	22
—oxidated vinyl resin						490	24
—ethylene oxiside						201	27
Oxidated vinyl piping						116	18
Sugar-refining						1000	26

Notes: a Percentage figures are the targeted volume of disposal as a percentage of total capacity.
b The achieved rate of disposal is found by dividing the results of capacity reduction by the targeted volume of capacity reduction.
c Includes 530 kt to be disposed under the Depressed Industry Law.

Sources: MITI *Kozotukyoho no Kaisetsu* (A Commentary on the Depressed Industry Law), Tsusho Sangyo Chosakai, 1978, pp. 280–99, and *Sankoho no Kaisetsu* (A Commentary on the Structural Reform Law), Tsusho Sangyo Chosakai, 1983, p. 82; Keizaichosakenkyukai (Economic Research Committee of FTCJ), *Teiseichokeisaika no Sangyochosei to Kyososeisaku* (Industrial Adjustment and Competitive Policy under a Decelerating Economy), 1982

the National Employment Insurance Law and the specific laws for those workers; and the exemption of collective actions from the antimonopoly legislation (though the JFTC can call for alteration if there are excessively anticompetitive effects) (Uekusa, forthcoming).

It is remarkable that the law did not introduce protective measures such as import restrictions and direct government subsidies. That it did not do so reflects overseas criticism of protective measures in Japan, as well as the OECD's 1978 plug for a 'positive adjustment policy'. Industrial adjustment policy under the Depressed Industry Law, however, was not entirely limited to positive adjustment measures. MITI and the Ministry of Transportation (which has taken charge of industrial adjustment policy in the shipbuilding industry) helped to form production cartels or price-fixing agreements in the electric-furnace ironmaking, chemical fertiliser, textile, linerboard and ship-building industries, and provided low-interest financing for the aluminium-refining industry through a tariff credit system. Since these industries (except shipbuilding) were vulnerable to import competition, the collective actions (cartels for price stabilisation) did not have favourable effects. However, the capacity-disposal target was almost completely accomplished in most of the designated industries by 1982; consequently, the rate of capacity utilisation improved to some extent in these industries, except for those that were hit by the second oil crisis (see Table 8.3). In the shipbuilding industry, the targeted disposal of production facilities was completely achieved by June 1983, when the term of the Depressed Industry Law expired, and an extensive curtailment of employment proceeded quite successfully. A balance between supply and demand was thus regained, and most of the shipbuilding companies recovered from their financial straits.

After the second oil crisis, the Structural Reform Law was enacted to continue applying industrial adjustment policies in the aluminium-refining, synthetic fibre, chemical fertiliser, ferrosilicon and linerboard industries, which had been hit again by the second oil crisis, and to enforce adjustment policies in the petrochemicals, sugar-refining and western-style paper industries, which had fallen into decline after the second crisis (see Table 8.3). This law incorporates measures to revive industries through business tie-ups (for example, mergers and joint production schemes), and through specialisation of production and development of new technology, as well as through the methods of reducing capacity and adjusting employment specified in the Depressed Industry Law. In short, the 1983 law aimed at both retrenchment and the revival of declining industries. The law also stipulates that MITI, with JFTC consent, may direct collective action to scrap excess capacity and to restrict or prohibit the expansion of capacity.

It is impossible to evaluate the effects of the Structural Reform Law because it was passed only recently. However, programs carried out in accordance with the Structural Reform Law, and with the Depressed Industry Law, strongly resemble a vision because there are no compulsory measures in such programs. Apparently a consensus was reached between government and private enter-prise concerning the targeted volume of disposal, and the need for disposal of overcapacity was stressed in drafting the Basic Stabilisation Plan. If disposal of overcapacity, curtailment of employment and industrial revival through technological innovation proceed smoothly, the policy will no doubt receive widespread international attention.

The characteristics of Japan's adjustment policy

Industrial adjustment policy in Japan, especially since the late 1970s, can be characterised as follows:

1   Measures for industrial adjustment take place in an open economy, and are phased out when deemed no longer necessary.

2   The 1983 law strongly reflects the positive approach to industrial adjustment advocated by the OECD. In fact, protectionist measures such as protective tariffs or import quotas have not been adopted. Regaining competitiveness or shifting into new business areas have been private-company initiatives.

3   In general, industrial adjustment can be achieved through government policies for adjustment assistance, as well as through voluntary actions by private enterprise within declining industries. In Japan the government has formulated and implemented a positive program for structural adjustment in close cooperation with the private sector, and government policies for declining industries are believed to have contributed to successful reorganisation or retrenchment within those industries. However, it should be stressed that voluntary adjustment by private enterprise is a distinctive feature of Japanese industrial adjustment; indeed, several scholars have expressed doubts about whether the Structural Reform Law in fact succeeded in restoring declining industries (Horiuchi, 1984; Sheard, 1984; Uekusa, forthcoming).

Policies for research and development and high-technology industries

The role of government in research and development

It has already been pointed out that imports of and improvements in foreign technology were an important source of productivity growth in Japan, at least until the 1960s. The average annual growth rate of payments for imported technology, however, declined from high levels of 31 per cent in the 1950s and 21 per cent in the 1960s to 9.8 per cent in the early 1970s, and then further to 6.0 per cent in the late 1970s, showing that Japan is no longer dependent on foreign technology. Domestic research and development expenditure began to increase in the late 1960s, and has expanded rapidly since 1975. Indeed, in 1981 the national index (1975 = 100) of research and development expenditure was 143 in Japan, 133 in West Germany, 132 in France and 128 in the United

States, and in 1982 the index was 152 in Japan and 139 in the United States (*White Paper on Science and Technology*, 1984:336–45).

This rapid expansion of research and development expenditure in Japan has depended not on government spending but on private-sector outlays. Research and development expenditure funded by the government as a percentage of total research and development funds was about 30 per cent in Japan before the early 1970s (70 per cent in western countries), and has declined since then because of the faster expansion of research and development expenditure by private enterprise. At present Japanese government spending as a proportion of total research and development expenditure is the smallest among the major countries, being 23.6 per cent as compared with 46.1 per cent in the United States, 49.8 per cent in the United Kingdom, 43.5 per cent in West Germany, and 57.8 per cent in France (*White Paper on Science and Technology*, 1984). The recent rise in research and development expenditure in the private sector reflects increased competition in the development of high technology. As shown in Table 8.4, intramural expenditure on research and development as a percentage of sales is significantly higher in chemicals (especially pharmaceuticals) and electrical machinery (especially electronic equipment).

The statistics do not show the high intensity of research and development for all high-technology industries because of the broad (and perhaps traditional) industry classification. According to some newspaper accounts, research and development expenditures by large companies that have entered or are entering high-technology industries have been exceeding their investments in new plant and equipment. These research and development activities have generated high-quality integrated circuits, microcomputers, industrial robots, various information media, medicines, new industrial materials, and so on.

Thus the private sector has played a more important role than the government in Japan's research and development activities. But although its role is limited the government has had some effect in promoting research and development, like governments in other advanced countries. Significant policy measures to support research and development in Japan have been favourable tax treatment for incremental research and development expenditures and subsidies for selected research projects. Japanese government support for the latter can be divided into two types: the first is that in which the government bears the entire cost of a project; in the second, the government assists a private-sector project through a conditional loan. Current research and development projects that are entirely financed by the government include the new energies research and development program (sunshine project); large-scale industrial technologies research and development (big projects); the next-generation industrial base technologies research and development program (including the development of new materials, biotechnology and new functional devices); and the program for development of the so-called fifth-generation computers. Examples of government conditional loans to private-sector research and development efforts include the subsidy program for research and development on important technologies, the subsidy program for development

Table 8.4 Japan: intramural expenditure on research and development as a percentage of sales by industry, fiscal years 1976 to 1982

	1976	1977	1978	1979	1980	1981	1982
All industries	1.42	1.48	1.57	1.49	1.48	1.62	1.78
Agriculture, forestry and fisheries	0.24	0.31	0.60	0.45	0.17	0.26	0.27
Mining	0.57	0.50	0.54	0.48	0.52	0.46	0.64
Construction	0.48	0.53	0.42	0.40	0.46	0.37	0.43
Manufacturing	1.64	1.70	1.82	1.71	1.73	1.91	2.15
Food	0.49	0.50	0.51	0.51	0.58	0.55	0.63
Textiles	0.66	0.56	0.77	0.82	0.77	1.09	1.13
Pulp and paper	0.47	0.46	0.49	0.42	0.41	0.43	0.52
Publishing and printing	0.46	0.41	0.36	0.27	0.26	0.21	0.39
Chemical products	2.39	2.62	2.71	2.54	2.55	2.87	3.05
—industrial chemicals	1.69	1.87	1.92	1.71	1.85	2.01	2.17
—oils and paints	2.40	2.71	2.73	2.17	2.48	2.56	2.56
—drugs and medicines	5.05	4.84	5.00	5.53	5.45	5.85	5.56
—other chemical products	2.88	3.12	3.03	2.88	2.19	3.03	3.43
Petroleum and coal products	0.18	0.23	0.27	0.18	0.30	0.18	0.20
Rubber products	2.25	1.96	2.60	2.44	2.10	2.33	2.47
Clay and stone products	1.40	1.22	1.29	1.27	1.30	1.39	1.64
Iron and steel	1.02	1.11	1.08	1.04	1.14	1.30	1.50
Non-ferrous metals	0.96	1.01	1.00	0.87	1.03	1.36	1.57
Fabricated metals	1.00	1.18	1.08	1.28	1.15	1.22	1.43
General machinery	1.79	2.01	1.93	1.85	1.90	2.10	2.34
Electrical machinery	3.66	3.61	3.74	3.55	3.71	4.06	4.52
—electrical appliances	3.49	3.49	3.59	3.19	3.35	3.80	4.17
—electrical equipment	3.80	3.71	3.89	3.91	3.94	4.21	4.72
Transport machinery	2.08	2.27	2.44	2.37	2.34	2.62	2.69
—motor vehicles	2.20	2.32	2.60	2.51	2.38	2.82	3.02
—other	1.76	2.12	1.90	1.85	2.15	1.94	1.67
Precision machinery	2.37	2.91	3.15	2.96	3.02	3.47	3.97
Other manufacturing	1.24	1.15	1.16	0.91	1.16	1.11	1.30
Transportation, communication and public utilities	0.27	0.33	0.35	0.40	0.32	0.36	0.32

Source: Prime Minister's Office, Statistics Bureau, *Report on the Survey of Research and Development, 1982* Nihon Tokei Kyokai, 1983, p. 59

of computers, and the subsidy program for development of very large-scale integrated circuits for next-generation computers.

Government subsidies for research and development have recently shifted to the development of high technologies such as electronics, new industrial materials, biotechnology and new energy sources, where sufficient technological development cannot be expected to come from private enterprise alone.

Cooperative associations for research and development

The 1961 Law on Research Cooperatives for Mining and Manufacturing Technologies was the first legal framework within which private companies could conduct joint research and development efforts in mining and manufacturing technologies. This law requires that a group of companies intending to form a cooperative research association must apply for government approval. Approval is granted automatically so long as the conditions concerning the financial base and technological capability of the planned cooperation are met and the statutory requirements satisfied. Government support for such cooperative research associations includes special depreciation allowances for machinery and equipment for joint research, as well as conditional loans.

Since the enactment of the law in 1961, 75 cooperative research associations have been formed, 55 of which are still in existence. Cooperative research is characterised as follows: most members of cooperative associations are large corporations and their research and development projects tend to concentrate on developments in high technology; a cooperative research association is formed to pursue a particular research and development theme, and is dissolved when the development is completed; and such cooperative research is organised by a group of firms spanning several industrial sectors to achieve a particular objective—it is rarely formed by a single industrial sector.

The cooperative research association for very large-scale integrates (known as the VLSI) is the best known Japanese cooperative research association. It was composed of five computer producers—Fujitsu, Hitachi, Mitsubishi Electric, NEC and Toshiba—and was active from 1976 to 1979. During this period, the government contributed 29 billion yen for the development of very large-scale integrates. The association yielded about 1000 patents, and is said to have established the foundation for Japan's success in the computer and semiconductor industry. Foreign enterprises were initially barred from access to the patents by MITI, but now the results of the project have been made available in the form of patent licensing to the public, including foreign enterprises.

The research cooperative system, however, is not effective in all cases of technology development; indeed, the success of the VLSI cooperative research association is an exception. Government-financed research is often directed to developments with a higher element of risk or a longer leadtime, or to less profitable research projects, so that the number of patents as a ratio of research and development expenditure is lower in all six research cooperatives than the industrial average (Wakasugi and Goto, 1985). Furthermore, there are several problems with the system from the standpoint of competition policy—for example, a research cooperative could function as a research and development cartel. The system is also more likely to encourage anticompetitive behaviour in the product market, though the cooperative research associations have not caused price cartels or other anticompetitive behaviour that is illegal under the Antimonopoly Law (Rokuhara, 1985).

Adjustment for international trade friction

At different stages of its economic development, Japan has been confronted with trade frictions created by exports of various groups of products—textile products late in the 1950s, textile products, steel and colour television sets from 1967 to 1972, and steel, colour television sets, automobiles and high-technology products in the second half of the 1970s. In recent years, rising exports of Japanese automobiles, colour television sets and video recorders to the European Community have also been causing friction.

To resolve these trade frictions, the Japanese government has implemented the following measures: currency adjustment; the elimination or relaxation of tariff and non-tariff barriers; and the restriction of exports and promotion of imports. Repeated multilateral trade negotiations, such as the Kennedy Round (1964–67) and the Tokyo Round (1973–79), have led to drastic reductions in customs duties and a decrease in the number of items subject to import restrictions. The tariff schedule was reduced considerably over the period from the second half of the 1960s to the first half of the 1970s (Figure 8.2). Japan's tariff-burden ratio in 1979 was 3.1 per cent, which is generally lower than the ratios for other countries. The number of items subject to residual import restrictions fell from 164 in 1968 to 27 in 1979. More recently, 'voluntary export restrictions' and 'orderly market agreements' have been in force to resolve trade frictions. Representative examples of such restraints include textiles and steel in the past and automobiles and steel today. The government has guided private industries in voluntarily restraining exports, albeit with due attention to the danger of extraterritorial application of the United States antitrust laws.

Japan's adjustment policy for trade frictions has the following positive aspects, at least from the viewpoint of industrial policy: the Japanese government has made efforts to eliminate or relax tariff and non-tariff barriers; Japan has avoided protective measures such as raising tariffs or levying emergency import quotas as ways of protecting declining industries; Japan has acted positively to maintain the GATT system; and Japan has not manipulated the yen exchange rate, at least under the floating system.

However, in view of the recent intensification of trade frictions, mainly because of the trade imbalance between the United States and Japan as well as between European countries and Japan, the Japanese government should take the following measures: abolish or further relax the restriction of imports and

Figure 8.2 Tariff burden ratios of Japan, the United States and and European Community

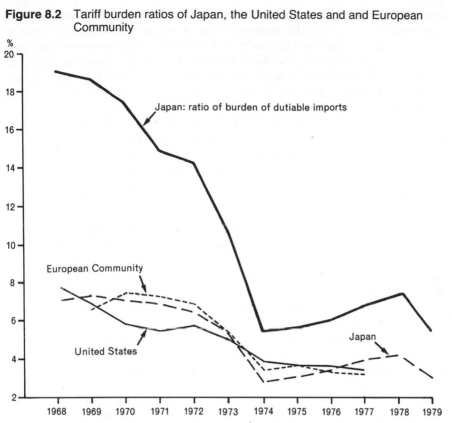

Notes: The tariff burden ratio is found by dividing tariff receipts by the total value of imports. The ratio of the burden of dutiable imports is found by dividing tariff receipts by the value of dutiable imports.

The tariff burden ratio is measured from April to March for Japan, from July to June for the United States, and from January to December for the European Community. Data for the European Community represent imports from outside the Community by the six initial participating countries.

Source: Economic Planning Agency (Japan) *The Annual Economic Report* (1982)

direct investment in the agricultural, financial and telecommunications sectors; promote direct overseas investment by Japanese companies; stimulate domestic demand; lead the exchange rate in the direction of increasing the value of the yen; and expand international cooperation in terms of technological assistance.

AN EVALUATION

Japan's industrial policy since the 1970s has differed considerably from that of the 1950s and the 1960s. Before 1970, policy goals (industrial rationalisation in the 1950s and maximum economic growth in the 1960s) received broad social support. Concrete policy objectives centred around strengthening international competitiveness through the modernisation of equipment and the pursuit of scale economies, upgrading the industrial structure, and overcoming the constraints imposed by the international balance of payments. And the ministries employed all kinds of policy tools, though by the late 1960s they were unable to effectively protect Japanese industry from foreign competition because of the liberalisation of trade and capital markets.

In those first two decades the stated goals and objectives were achieved. Nobody knows, however, the extent to which industrial policy was responsible for the attainment of these objectives, because of the difficulty of quantitative evaluation. Nevertheless, it is certain that industrial policy contributed to the modernisation of equipment, the expansion of domestic production and exports, and the stabilisation of price levels in the steel, shipbuilding and chemical fertiliser industries. On the other hand, it is also true that there were many industries, such as general machinery, electrical appliances, motor vehicles and precision machinery, that grew with little support from MITI and other ministries. Industrial policy therefore contributed only partially to the shift of the industrial structure towards heavy and chemical industries, the strengthening of international competitiveness and the resulting rapid economic growth; the private sector deserves rather more of the credit for the success of Japanese industry, a view supported by Adams and Ichimura (1983), Patrick (1983), Tresize (1983), and Wheeler et al. (1982), among others. Most essential to Japan's economic success were, first, the establishment of a competitive market structure with the dissolution of the *zaibatsu* and other deconcentration measures during the Occupation (Uekusa, 1982); second, strong domestic entrepreneurship, evidenced by efforts to improve product quality, the decision to introduce foreign technology, and entry into promising industries; third, a very high saving ratio, which permitted a high rate of capital formation; and fourth, the Japanese style of labour union (enterprise union), which has united labour with management in introducing new technologies, enhancing productivity and improving product quality. (For more detail see Uekusa, 1982 and forthcoming.)

Nor should it be overlooked that industrial policy produced some harmful effects. First, pollution, environmental damage and the excessive concentration of population and economic power in some large cities had become serious by the late 1960s, signifying that the government had not adjusted for market failures in its pursuit of rapid economic growth. Second, an administered-price problem occurred in several oligopolistic industries at that time, partly because of the promotion of a higher industrial concentration for pursuing scale economies, and the encouragement of cartels and other forms of horizontal coordination by MITI and other industrial ministries (see Uekusa, 1982 for more detail). Third, the pursuit of scale economies established a basis for phasing down production in such industries as oil refining and petrochemicals after the oil crisis. In sum, the Japanese experience in the 1950s and 1960s tells us that industrial policy had both positive and negative effects.

As noted earlier, Japan's industrial policy has altered dramatically over the past decade. The following changes are particularly notable: the decline in the protection and promotion of promising industries through a variety of government subsidies and tariff and non-tariff measures (though such industry-specific policies still exist to a lesser extent); the change in emphasis from direct market intervention towards limited intervention through maximum use of the market mechanism; the growing importance of various adjustment policies for coping with international friction, industrial decline and pollution; the promotion of research and development in new fields of technology; and the stress on supplying information. Some undesirable aspects of Japan's industrial policy yet remain: industry-specific policies for the purpose of industrial protection or promotion (such as in oil refining and agriculture); the possibility of cartelisation and other anticompetitive behaviour in the research and development cooperative associations; and the opaqueness of the process of formulating and enforcing industrial policy.

To summarise, there are three lessons to be learned from Japan's experience with industrial policy. First, MITI supplied accurate information on the direction of change in industrial structure to the heavy and chemical industries in the 1960s, to the knowledge-intensive industries in the 1970s, and to the high-technology industries in the 1980s, information that was undoubtedly useful for strategic business planning. Second, encouragement of private investment in desirable directions is preferable to direct government intervention. Third, and most important, Japan's postwar experience proves that industrial policy in itself cannot be effective in the absence of competitive markets and fair trade practices, or without skilful entrepreneurship.

PART III
INDUSTRY SECTORAL STUDIES

9 Structural adjustments in the textile and clothing industries

P.J. LLOYD

As a group, the textile and clothing industries in the developed countries (the 'developed market economies', as they are described by the United Nations) have exhibited several well-marked long-term trends.

1 Output declined for this group of countries over the period 1973–82 by 1.5 per cent a year for both the textiles subgroup and the clothing subgroup separately (GATT, 1984b:Table 2.1).

2 Employment declined for this group of countries over the period 1973–82 by 4.5 per cent a year for the textiles subgroup and 3 per cent a year for the clothing subgroup (GATT, 1984b:Table 2.2).

3 Net trade (exports minus imports) aggregated across all commodities and all countries except Australia and New Zealand (for which the 1983 data are not available) also declined over this period. In 1973 the excess of imports over exports was just over US$2 billion; it had climbed to US$14.4 billion by 1983, when these countries had a net surplus of US$3 billion in textiles trade and an import deficit of US$17.4 billion in clothing trade.

4 Export volumes have declined and import volumes have increased. The dollar value of exports of textiles and clothing by these countries declined in 1983 for the third consecutive year (GATT, 1984a:Table A.10).

5 While there is no index of real consumption and use of all textile and clothing commodities, consumer expenditure on clothing increased by an estimated annual average of 2.5 per cent in real terms between 1973 and 1982 (GATT, 1984b:Table 2.9). However, the share of consumer expenditure on clothing has declined in all developed countries (GATT, 1984b:Appendix Table A.4).

6 Gross fixed investment in these industries declined in constant prices during the 1970s (OECD, 1983b:Table 29).

These trends are not, of course, independent of each other. The first two relate to production and the others to factors which, in a complex, interdepen-

172

dent way that is not fully understood, determine the trends in employment and output.

In terms of their qualitative characteristics these trends are remarkably consistent among regions. For example, output and employment have declined in North America, the European Community and other Western European countries, Japan and Australasia, and imports have increased in all areas. Other manufacturing industries have also experienced declines in output and employment in recent years; indeed, the phenomenon has become generally known as 'de-industrialisation'. It is necessary, therefore, to place these changes within the context of changes in other manufacturing-sector activities. The shares of the textile and clothing industries in the total manufacturing output, employment and gross fixed capital formation of these countries have all declined steadily since the early 1960s or before (see OECD, 1983b: Table 5 and Chart VIII). In particular, the decline in the share of manufacturing employment accounted for by the textile and clothing industries has been continuous and dramatic in all developed countries, with the exceptions of Spain and Greece.

These trends portray a group of economic activities that have been secularly declining in the developed economies. However, the picture is not one of complete gloom. In particular, the trends have been rather different in textiles than in clothing.

Moreover, there have been substantial changes in the distribution of output and employment among the subsectors of these industries in all countries. At plant level there have been important technological changes. In textile production, the yarn-spinning process has been improved with such features as open-end spinning and improved synthetic yarns, the invention of shuttleless looms has reduced some weaving costs, and operating speeds in knitting have substantially increased. These changes have made some technologies obsolete and have tended to increase the advantages of larger scale and longer production runs. Automated and, more recently, computerised and robotised methods of cutting, stitching and sewing have been introduced into clothing operations. At product level, the clothing and household textile industries are among the areas of final consumer demand most subject to annual changes in fashion and design and, as a consequence, the derived demand for textiles, fabrics and yarns is also changing continually. Collectively, these sources of structural change have forced a shrinkage of many individual plants and an extensive reorganisation of others, and have led producer and union groups in all countries to seek various forms of government assistance in order to cope with them. Finally, there is evidence that the rates of increase in technological change and imports and the rate of decrease in employment are accelerating (OECD, 1983b).

This chapter examines some general aspects of the responses to these changes. It begins with an overview of trade in textile and clothing products by the Pacific Basin countries, and goes on to examine in somewhat more detail the industry groups in Australia and New Zealand as case studies of structural change. It then discusses the effectiveness of government policies in achieving declared government objectives, and finally explains the political economy behind the choice of ineffective instruments.

THE PACIFIC BASIN COUNTRIES

As a starting point, Table 9.1 presents export and import statistics for textiles and clothing in selected countries. Two features of the pattern of trade are immediately apparent. First, there is in all countries significant simultaneous exporting and importing of textiles and clothing—that is, significant intra-industry trade. Second, and following from the first, there are important differences among countries in the structure of this trade in terms of whether a country is a net exporter or a net importer, and in terms of the export–import composition of textile products relative to that of clothing products. Most developed countries are net importers of textiles and clothing as a group, and most developing countries are net exporters. The developed countries of the Pacific Basin, with the exception of Japan, are all net importers and have experienced substantial increases in net imports. In the developing countries of the Pacific Basin, especially the Asian newly industrialising countries, there has been a rapid growth of net exports and this product group has played an important part in the growth of manufactured exports from these countries. However, most of them are net importers of the textile subgroup and large net exporters of clothing; for example, Hong Kong, the Philippines and Indonesia. Singapore is exceptional in that it is a substantial net importer of textiles and clothing combined.

This discussion of these trade patterns will concentrate on the industrial or developed countries of the Pacific Basin, since this chapter is concerned with problems of structural adjustment in this group of major importing countries. The group comprises Australia, Canada, Japan, New Zealand and the United States. For all textile and clothing trade combined, Japan was a net exporter in 1983. Japan's excess of exports over imports for this group was US$3 billion, compared with deficits of US$2.2 billion for the European Community and US$1.5 billion for the United States. Moreover, Japan's net surplus has increased in recent years, whereas most other developed countries have experienced rising net deficits in these commodities.

A country can be classified as a net exporter or importer of textiles and clothing considered individually. Thus a two-way classification of the trade pattern of a country can be constructed. There are four possible patterns—net exporter of both textiles and clothing, net exporter of textiles but net importer of clothing, net exporter of clothing but net importer of textiles, or net importer of both textiles and clothing.

Of the five Pacific Basin developed countries, none is a net exporter of both textiles and clothing. Japan is a net exporter of textiles and a net importer of clothing products. Australia, Canada and the United States are all net importers of both textiles and clothing. New Zealand is a net exporter of clothing and a net importer of textiles.

These distinctions are incomplete. Textile fabrics are made up from man-made yarns or natural fibres (principally cotton, wool and silk), or from mixtures of manmade and natural fibres. Historically, and to a significant extent at present, the greater relative importance of the textile subsector of production in the United States arises from the comparative advantage the United States derives from being a cheap source of cotton fibre. On the other hand, in Japan, as in the United Kingdom and other European countries, the textile industry is historically based on imported natural fibres, though more recently it has been based on efficient domestic production of manmade fibres. Moreover, it is difficult to separate some of the processing activities for natural fibres from other textile-manufacturing activities; in Australia, for example, wool-scouring and top-making are important components of textile production. Hence it is desirable to consider trade and production of fibres along with that of textiles and clothing.

If the trade of an individual country in fibres, textiles and clothing is considered, the country can be classified as a net exporter or importer of each of these three product groups. Hence a three-way classification of the trade patterns of countries is possible. There are now eight possible patterns: two pure patterns—net exporter or net importer of all three groups of products—and six mixed net exporter–importer patterns.

These patterns can be quantified using measures of intra-industry and inter-industry trade. Let 1 denote fibres, 2 textiles and 3 clothing, and X_i and M_i respectively denote a country's exports and imports of commodity group i for i = 1,2,3. Total trade in textiles and clothing products is then $\sum_i (X_i + M_i)$. Net exports, $|X_i - M_i|$, for each group can then be expressed as a percentage of total trade. In this way the total trade is broken down into two components, inter-industry trade and intra-industry trade:

$$\frac{\sum_i |X_i - M_i|}{\sum_i (X_i + M_i)} + \frac{\sum_i [(X_i + M_i) - |X_i - M_i|]}{\sum_i (X_i + M_i)} = 1$$

The second component provides the Grubel–Lloyd Index of intra-industry trade (Grubel and Lloyd, 1974). Inter- and intra-industry trade in each group, and in total as a percentage of all trade in these commodity groups, are demonstrated in Figure 9.1, which reproduces these percentages for Australia, Canada, Japan, New Zealand and the United States. Exports as a percentage of total trade are measured above the axis and imports are measured similarly below. The dotted areas represent the net inter-industry trade. The column for all three groups combined ('total') thus provides a breakdown of total trade into intra- and inter-industry trade.

Note first that in Japan and the United States intra-industry trade, the non-dotted area in the 'total' column, is more important than inter-industry trade. The qualitative patterns noted above may also be verified. The countries have been arranged into three sets, since these countries display three of the eight possible patterns: Canada is a net importer of all three categories;

Table 9.1 Trade in textiles and clothing in selected countries, 1973, 1981–83 (billion US dollars)

	Textiles			
	1973	*1981*	*1982*	*1983*
Exports				
European Community (10)	11.16	21.02	19.83	19.64
Belgium–Luxembourg	1.69	3.00	2.72	2.80
France	1.69	2.89	2.68	2.59
West Germany	3.04	5.54	5.48	5.38
Greece	0.13	0.47	0.42	0.43
Italy	1.53	4.08	4.01	4.19
Netherlands	1.29	1.88	1.78	1.70
United Kingdom	1.45	2.36	2.02	1.88
Finland	0.07	0.17	0.17	0.15
Norway	0.06	0.10	0.09	0.08
Sweden	0.19	0.37	0.34	0.34
Austria	0.45	1.07	1.02	0.89
Switzerland	0.64	1.39	1.37	1.37
United States	1.22	3.61	2.77	2.36
Canada[a]	0.15	0.33	0.29	0.26
Japan	2.45	5.85	5.09	5.33
Australia[a]	0.04	0.14	0.15	—
New Zealand	0.01	0.10	0.09	—
Czechoslovakia[a]	0.21	0.41	0.50	—
Hungary	0.15	0.24	0.23	—
Poland[a]	0.17	0.39	—	—
Romania[a]	0.06	—	—	—
USSR[a]	0.14	0.13	0.13	—
Portugal	0.33	0.54	0.56	—
Spain	0.17	0.70	0.60	—
Turkey	0.10	0.57	0.77	—
Yugoslavia	0.14	0.53	0.48	—
Israel	0.05	0.12	0.11	—
Egypt	0.17	0.21	0.17	—
Morocco	0.04	0.12	0.02	—
Tunisia	0.01	0.05	—	—
Hong Kong	0.46	0.94	0.83	0.97
India	0.69	—	—	—
South Korea	0.44	2.45	—	—
Pakistan	0.44	0.98	0.93	1.31
Singapore	0.14	0.34	0.34	0.38
Sri Lanka	—	0.01	0.01	—
Thailand	0.09	0.35	0.35	—
Indonesia	0.00	0.04	0.04	—
Philippines	0.02	0.07	0.06	—
Argentina	0.02	0.03	0.04	—
Brazil	0.23	0.67	0.52	0.65
Colombia	0.05	0.11	0.09	—
Mexico	0.13	—	—	—

	Clothing				Total		
1973	1981	1982	1983	1973	1981	1982	1983
4.96	12.96	12.67	12.64	16.12	33.98	32.50	32.28
0.57	0.82	0.75	0.75	2.26	3.82	3.47	3.55
1.04	1.94	1.82	1.74	2.73	4.83	4.50	4.33
0.91	2.52	2.52	2.56	3.95	8.06	8.00	7.94
0.05	0.40	0.47	0.54	0.18	0.87	0.89	0.97
1.30	4.32	4.41	4.53	2.83	8.40	8.42	8.72
0.41	0.72	0.69	0.67	1.70	2.60	2.47	2.37
0.44	1.70	1.47	1.31	1.89	4.06	3.49	3.19
0.21	0.78	0.65	0.50	0.28	0.95	0.82	0.65
0.03	0.06	0.06	0.05	0.09	0.16	0.15	0.13
0.14	0.25	0.21	0.21	0.33	0.62	0.55	0.55
0.16	0.55	0.55	0.54	0.61	1.62	1.57	1.43
0.12	0.32	0.30	0.29	0.76	1.71	1.67	1.66
0.29	1.26	0.99	0.88	1.51	4.87	3.76	3.24
0.12	0.23	0.21	0.19	0.27	0.56	0.50	0.45
0.37	0.58	0.55	0.66	2.82	6.43	5.64	5.99
0.02	0.02	0.01	—	0.06	0.16	0.16	—
0.00	0.04	0.04	—	0.03	0.14	0.13	—
0.18	0.43	0.44	—	0.39	0.84	0.94	—
0.20	0.32	0.31	—	0.35	0.56	0.54	—
0.28	0.51	—	—	0.45	0.90	—	—
0.25	(0.71)	(0.60)	—	0.31	—	—	—
0.03	0.03	0.02	—	0.17	0.16	0.15	—
0.20	0.58	0.65	—	0.53	1.12	1.21	—
0.13	0.30	0.30	—	0.30	1.00	0.90	—
0.05	0.31	0.40	—	0.15	0.88	1.17	—
0.15	0.66	0.61	—	0.29	1.19	1.09	—
0.09	0.24	0.23	—	0.14	0.36	0.34	—
0.03	0.02	0.02	—	0.20	0.23	0.19	—
0.02	0.13	0.14	—	0.06	0.25	0.26	—
0.00	0.33	—	—	0.01	0.38	—	—
1.39	5.01	4.73	4.68	1.85	5.95	5.56	5.65
0.10	—	—	—	0.79	—	—	—
0.75	3.86	—	—	1.19	6.31	—	—
0.02	0.14	0.14	0.23	0.46	1.12	1.07	1.54
0.13	0.47	0.46	0.48	0.27	0.81	0.80	0.86
—	0.15	0.17	—	—	0.16	0.18	—
0.03	0.34	0.37	—	0.12	0.69	0.72	—
0.00	0.10	0.12	—	0.00	0.14	0.16	—
0.01	0.35	0.31	—	0.03	0.42	0.37	—
0.03	0.06	0.04	—	0.05	0.09	0.08	—
0.09	0.13	0.10	0.11	0.32	0.80	0.62	0.76
0.02	0.12	0.14	—	0.07	0.23	0.23	—
0.07	—	—	—	0.20	—	—	—

continued

Table 9.1 *(continued)* Trade in textiles and clothing in selected countries, 1973, 1981−83 (billion US dollars)

	Textiles			
	1973	*1981*	*1982*	*1983*
Imports				
European Community (10)	9.14	19.08	18.28	18.06
Belgium−Luxembourg	1.01	1.84	1.75	1.72
France	1.40	3.40	3.43	3.16
West Germany	2.74	5.29	4.81	4.94
Greece	0.09	0.34	0.31	0.30
Italy	0.91	2.01	2.11	1.97
Netherlands	1.10	1.71	1.61	1.58
United Kingdom	1.26	3.50	3.34	3.47
Finland	0.26	0.53	0.51	0.46
Norway	0.23	0.40	0.36	0.32
Sweden	0.51	0.76	0.71	0.67
Austria	0.48	0.98	0.94	0.90
Switzerland	0.50	0.92	0.86	0.85
United States	1.58[a]	3.07	2.85	3.27
Canada[a]	0.78	1.41	1.13	1.40
Japan	1.13	1.63	1.60	1.49
Australia[a]	0.62	1.15	1.11	—
New Zealand	0.20	0.33	0.36	—
Czechoslovakia[a]	0.09	0.12	0.15	—
Hungary	0.12	0.32	0.27	—
Poland[a]	0.15	0.19	· —	—
Romania[a]	0.06	—	—	—
USSR[a]	0.63	1.98	2.00	—
Portugal	0.11	0.25	0.25	—
Spain	0.18	0.29	0.31	—
Turkey	0.03	0.08	0.10	—
Yugoslavia	0.19	0.37	0.32	—
Israel	0.07	0.19	0.21	—
Egypt	0.03	0.12	0.11	—
Morocco	0.06	0.12	0.12	—
Tunisia	0.04	0.25	—	—
Hong Kong	0.94	3.43	2.97	3.26
India	0.01	—	—	—
South Korea	0.30	0.49	—	—
Pakistan	0.03	0.18	0.18	0.16
Singapore	0.42	0.88	0.88	0.96
Sri Lanka	—	0.15	0.14	—
Thailand	0.10	0.21	0.20	—
Indonesia	0.17	0.25	0.20	—
Philippines	0.05	0.16	0.15	—
Argentina	0.02	0.20	0.08	—
Brazil	0.07	0.07	0.07	—
Colombia	0.01	0.06	0.05	—
Mexico	0.04	—	—	—

Note: a Imports fob

Source: GATT (1984a)

Clothing				Total			
1973	1981	1982	1983	1973	1981	1982	1983
5.81	17.98	17.03	16.38	14.95	37.06	35.31	34.44
0.56	1.57	1.44	1.37	1.57	3.41	3.19	3.09
0.59	2.46	2.60	2.45	1.99	5.86	6.03	5.61
2.54	7.18	6.71	6.73	5.20	12.47	11.52	11.67
0.01	0.05	0.06	0.06	0.10	0.39	0.37	0.36
0.19	0.75	0.68	0.63	1.10	2.76	2.79	2.60
0.86	2.32	2.13	1.97	1.96	4.03	3.74	3.55
0.82	2.87	2.62	2.42	2.08	6.37	5.96	5.89
0.06	0.20	0.21	0.20	0.32	0.73	0.72	0.66
0.20	0.66	0.66	0.60	0.43	1.06	1.02	0.92
0.40	1.15	1.08	0.94	0.91	1.91	1.79	1.61
0.20	0.77	0.78	0.83	0.68	1.75	1.72	1.73
0.50	1.39	1.39	1.39	1.00	2.31	2.25	2.24
2.17[a]	8.12	8.79	10.42	3.75[a]	11.19	11.64	13.69
0.33	0.84	0.84	1.03	1.11	2.25	1.97	2.43
0.57	1.80	1.83	1.50	1.70	3.43	3.43	2.99
0.11	0.42	0.42	—	0.73	1.57	1.53	—
0.01	0.02	0.03	—	0.21	0.35	0.39	—
0.10	0.12	0.13	—	0.19	0.24	0.28	—
0.03	0.13	0.13	—	0.15	0.45	0.40	—
0.05	0.12	—	—	0.20	0.31	—	—
0.01	—	—	—	0.07	—	—	—
1.06	2.64	2.68	—	1.69	4.62	4.68	—
0.03	0.02	0.03	—	0.14	0.27	0.28	—
0.04	0.15	0.14	—	0.22	0.44	0.45	—
0.00	0.00	0.00	—	0.03	0.08	0.10	—
0.02	0.02	0.02	—	0.21	0.39	0.34	—
0.01	0.02	0.04	—	0.08	0.21	0.25	—
0.00	0.01	0.01	—	0.03	0.13	0.12	—
0.00	0.00	0.00	—	0.06	0.12	0.12	—
0.00	0.07	—	—	0.04	0.32	—	—
0.12	0.93	1.06	1.17	1.06	4.36	4.03	4.43
0.00	—	—	—	0.01	—	—	—
0.01	0.01	—	—	0.31	0.50	—	—
0.00	0.00	0.00	0.00	0.03	0.18	0.18	0.16
0.04	0.21	0.27	0.30	0.46	1.09	1.15	1.26
—	0.00	0.00	—	—	0.15	0.14	—
0.00	0.00	0.01	—	0.10	0.21	0.21	—
0.00	0.01	0.00	—	0.17	0.26	0.20	—
0.00	0.00	0.01	—	0.05	0.16	0.16	—
0.00	0.17	0.03	—	0.02	0.37	0.11	—
0.01	0.01	0.01	—	0.08	0.08	0.08	—
0.00	0.02	0.01	—	0.01	0.08	0.06	—
0.06	—	—	—	0.10	—	—	—

Figure 9.1   Textile and clothing trade flows in the advanced Pacific Basin
               countries, 1982

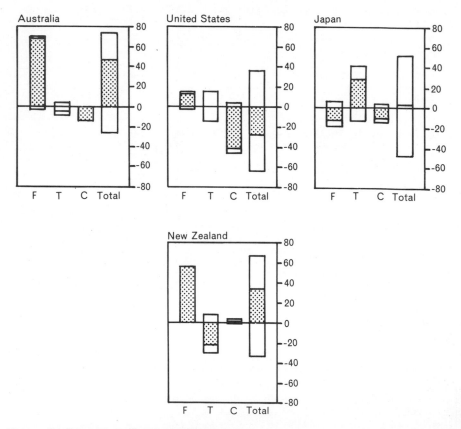

Notes: F—fibres; T—textiles; C—clothing.
          Positive quantities represent exports; negative quantities represent imports. All figures
          are expressed as a percentage of total trade (exports plus imports) in fibres, textiles
          and clothing in 1973 or 1979 in each country. The shaded part within the block
          represents the trade balance in that product.

Australia, Japan and the United States are net exporters of one group and net importers of two; and New Zealand is a net exporter of two groups (fibres and clothing).

A fourth category of products could be added, textile machinery. Textile and clothing industry machines are essential industry-specific inputs, and net trade in textile machinery may be an important determinant of a country's specialisation in textile and clothing products. Japan is the only net exporter of textile machinery. Historically, its efficient production of textile machinery has been an important determinant of the size and pattern of its specialisation in textile and clothing products. More recently, the development by Japan of the latest technology (computerised and robotised machinery and yarns with improved qualities) has enabled it to retain some segments of the textile and clothing markets and to be a large-scale exporter of this machinery (see Yamazawa, 1980; 1983). At the other end of the pattern, Australia, Canada and New Zealand all export negligible quantities of textile machinery. Their reliance on imports for most of this machinery does not increase their comparative disadvantage in textile and clothing products generally, since the countries that have been increasing their shares of the world textile and clothing markets rapidly, such as Taiwan and Hong Kong, also buy most of their machinery on competitive world markets. However, the slow rate of acquisition of this machinery by the developed countries due to the low rate of capital formation in the industry has left them with old-vintage technologies.

These flows should be disaggregated, since there is considerable specialisation within these groups in all countries. Table 9.2 gives some data at the 4-digit level of the ISIC for the years 1970 to 1980.[1] These trade data should also be linked with production data, since the ultimate concern with structural adjustment lies mostly with changes in production.

Traditionally the manufacture of final products from textile materials is divided into four stages. First there is the production of natural and manmade fibres. The second and third stages are spinning and weaving or knitting. The final stage is the production of end-products; clothing and other household items such as carpets and curtains, and other made-up articles. Figure 9.2 reproduces a simplified chart showing the main flows (OECD, 1983b:19). (For an example of a more detailed flow chart for Australia, see Textile and Apparel Industry Advisory Council, 1980:16.) Some of the production processes do not involve spinning and weaving (for example, the manufacture of carpets), whereas articles made from woven fabrics involve all four main stages. These stages may be separated geographically within or across national borders. Furthermore, the individual stages, and to some extent the production of individual items at each stage, use materials, capital and labour in widely different proportions.

The textile and clothing industries are still commonly thought of as labour-intensive. Globally this is no longer true of the textile industry, though it is still true in all countries of the clothing industry. In its survey of the industries the OECD (1983b:84) noted that 'the textile industry has by now reached the average capital intensity for manufacturing as a whole'. However, there is

Table 9.2 Clothing and textiles: market-penetration data for industrialised advanced economies

ISIC	1970	1971	1972	1973	1974	1975	1976	1977	1978	1979	1980
Production (US$'000)											
3211	37 205 024	39 657 808	46 552 064	57 833 168	59 832 656	56 508 160	64 396 080	69 700 784	77 977 008	86 782 592	93 265 168
3212	6 384 502	6 910 597	8 075 809	9 282 334	9 606 740	10 119 914	11 089 075	12 264 600	14 089 912	15 485 946	16 380 449
3213	13 332 934	14 709 474	17 694 128	20 542 592	21 005 120	21 552 736	22 474 096	24 566 880	28 382 816	31 712 896	34 109 888
3214	4 438 057	5 043 848	6 155 961	7 543 446	7 707 921	7 560 858	8 332 430	9 193 927	10 740 820	11 492 089	12 217 280
3215	633 885	672 601	770 694	989 620	1 311 722	1 183 569	1 070 629	1 273 163	1 521 117	1 647 803	1 793 455
3219	4 219 746	4 469 994	5 103 198	5 999 970	6 538 604	6 280 166	6 933 250	7 475 827	8 437 022	9 355 619	9 984 115
3220	33 751 440	36 079 408	42 341 424	49 099 792	51 347 152	54 394 960	57 712 992	62 652 400	71 886 944	79 495 648	85 087 456
Imports (US$'000)											
3211	5 443 880	6 214 988	7 801 145	11 144 780	12 193 301	11 116 512	13 523 896	14 554 709	18 052 672	22 389 200	22 731 072
3212	326 907	340 911	430 619	579 851	715 163	657 426	768 480	902 670	1 117 922	1 357 931	1 619 750
3213	649 320	862 426	851 589	963 832	1 001 740	1 036 440	1 104 552	1 139 955	1 383 214	1 786 606	1 871 016
3214	659 641	814 482	1 008 206	1 415 764	1 590 345	1 569 835	1 841 604	2 052 438	2 650 951	3 270 109	3 683 834
3215	97 483	108 187	128 233	189 211	432 315	314 503	233 948	275 080	329 123	439 377	474 440
3219	428 894	484 340	554 067	757 950	855 512	812 470	926 381	1 058 649	1 277 607	1 610 282	1 767 310
3220	4 089 143	5 076 336	6 731 282	8 967 251	10 853 037	12 245 630	15 267 486	17 079 504	21 620 928	26 533 744	29 707 552
Exports (US$'000)											
3211	6 778 569	7 573 926	8 759 482	11 968 699	14 210 543	13 105 584	14 922 576	16 403 706	18 932 224	22 839 040	24 836 304
3212	407 340	446 629	533 451	658 185	842 806	886 598	959 334	1 146 017	1 307 749	1 502 866	1 681 396
3213	877 678	1 126 323	1 162 031	1 341 773	1 474 088	1 495 453	1 505 258	1 516 216	1 699 907	2 156 949	2 391 088
3214	528 691	620 719	775 787	1 122 315	1 301 341	1 279 952	1 495 043	1 748 255	2 139 323	2 457 189	2 900 482
3215	99 728	108 991	121 679	160 070	264 646	230 425	194 120	209 906	219 420	252 461	300 188
3219	536 574	621 070	761 159	1 108 279	1 280 476	1 227 777	1 350 870	1 473 731	1 851 374	2 275 985	2 462 768
3220	3 177 347	3 628 219	4 469 971	5 377 681	6 161 153	6 925 022	7 790 052	9 289 750	11 073 132	13 552 968	15 242 559
Market-penetration ratio											
3211	15.176	16.227	17.110	19.549	21.090	20.390	21.467	21.450	23.415	25.933	24.935
3212	5.185	5.009	5.400	6.299	7.544	6.646	7.051	7.508	8.042	8.851	9.925
3213	4.954	5.970	4.898	4.779	4.878	4.913	5.004	4.712	4.928	5.700	5.570
3214	14.437	15.550	15.781	18.065	19.886	19.996	21.219	21.608	23.558	26.575	28.335
3215	15.433	16.104	16.498	18.572	29.222	24.810	21.067	20.553	20.181	23.947	24.111
3219	10.430	11.177	11.316	13.415	13.993	13.853	14.232	14.993	16.247	18.530	19.026
3220	11.796	13.526	15.091	17.019	19.366	20.506	23.419	24.246	26.227	28.692	29.841

Source: ASEAN–Australia Project and Australia–Japan Centre Data Bank, Australian National University

Figure 9.2   The process of manufacturing textile products

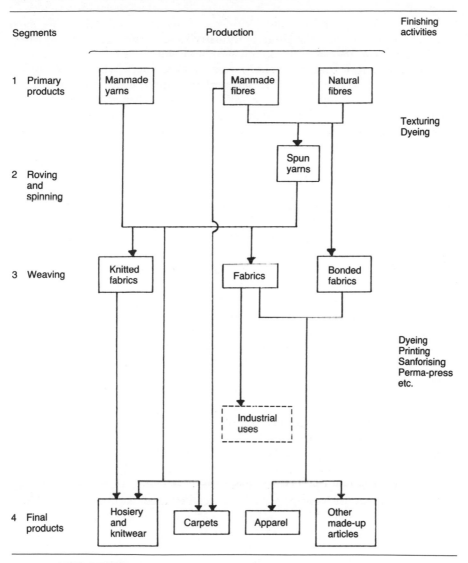

Source: OECD (1983b)

considerable variation among developed countries in the relative capital intensities of their textile industries because of the international differences in
product composition and in capital vintages of machinery. On the other hand
the OECD showed that 'the clothing industry's capital intensity is everywhere
much lower than that of textiles, and within clothing, cutting and patterning
can be *one hundred* times as capital intensive as sewing' (OECD, 1983b:85).
Hence there are many possible patterns of specialisation by each country in
narrowly defined product groups at different stages. Efficient production or
comparative advantage must be defined at a disaggregated level.

It is customary to examine the relationships between trade flows on the one
hand and domestic production on the other in terms of changes in import
shares. For example, the World Bank has prepared comprehensive tapes on
'import penetration' for these and other industries. Table 9.2 reports the
calculation of the import-penetration shares at the 4-digit level of the ISIC for
clothing and textile activities over the period from 1970 to 1980, using data
from the Data Bank of the Research School of Pacific Studies at the Australian
National University. (In the ISIC classification the 4-digit groups do not
correspond very closely to the stages described earlier; for example, 3211
combines spinning and weaving and finishing of textiles.) The shares reported
are shares of apparent consumption/use (the shares of imports in total production plus imports minus exports).

For the industrialised advanced economies (as they are described by the
World Bank) as a group, the trend in these import-penetration shares is
upward for all seven of the 4-digit groups. For the individual Pacific Basin
industrialised advanced economies the trends are upward in a majority of
commodity groups for all countries except Japan, though some other trends
are not significant and a few are negative. (Import-penetration data for these
years are available from the author for the major advanced economies of the
Pacific Basin—Australia, Canada, Japan and the United States.) For Canada
and Australia the two downward trends relate to the groups 'manufacture of
carpets and rugs' and 'manufacture of textiles nes' (a collection of floor
coverings and other items mainly for use by industries outside the textile and
clothing group). For the United States the downward trends relate to the
groups 'spinning, weaving and finishing textiles' and 'knitting mills'. However, in other textile groups, and particularly in the clothing group (3220),
the trend is upward. These results show the diversity of experience within
these countries.

The interpretation of these trends as indicators of market-share performance
is controversial. Apart from data problems and the omission of inventory
accumulation and decumulation and year-to-year variability, there are a number of conceptual difficulties (see GATT, 1984a:Appendix IV; OECD,
1983b:53). Import-share data ignore all exports. Increasing intra-industry specialisation would result in both increasing imports and increasing exports for a
given level of production. Exports have been increasing in all industrialised
advanced economies at least at current prices. Similarly, these shares ignore
the fact that many imports include a domestic content, chiefly because of

Table 9.3 Net textile and clothing exports as a percentage of apparent consumption (all advanced industrialised economies)

ISIC code	1970	1982
3211	+3.7	+2.3
3212	+1.3	+0.4
3213	+1.7	+1.6
3214	−2.9	−6.1
3215	+0.3	−8.9
3219	+2.6	+7.5
3220	−2.6	−14.5

Source: Calculated from Table 9.2

domestic equity participation in overseas assembly operations and the use by overseas suppliers of materials produced domestically at an early stage. As most imports, from the developing countries in particular, were initially of low quality but have improved in quality and unit price in recent years, these calculations based on current price flows understate the import-quantity penetration at any point in time, while they overstate the quantity growth over time. Furthermore, a rise in the import-penetration ratios of some groups covering low-cost foreign materials may be necessary to sustain the international competitiveness of later-stage domestic activities. All these problems derive from the aggregation of flows across all stages of production. Finally, the share changes also reflect increases or decreases in the levels of protection for domestic producers.

The use of *net* imports (exports) in place of gross imports overcomes problems arising from exporting and intra-industry specialisation, though it does not overcome problems due to intra-group aggregation and price effects. Table 9.3 reports net exports as a percentage of total apparent consumption of the industrialised advanced countries as a group from 1970 to 1980. (Similar calculations can be made for the individual countries and all years reported in Table 9.2.) For all seven 4-digit groups the trends are downward; net exports decrease or net imports increase as percentages of total apparent consumption, or a net-export situation has been converted to a net-import situation. However, in 1980 these countries were still net exporters in four of the seven groups. The net-import situation for all groups together and the switch from net exports to net imports is mainly due to the large increase in imports of clothing (group 3220).

Several attempts have been made to apportion the decline in aggregate employment in these industries into the contributions 'due to' rising import shares and those 'due to' changes in consumption, exports, and labour employed per unit of output. These are based on various accounting identities. (See OECD [1983b:97] for references relating to the textile and clothing industries.)

These studies have shown that the percentage of the decline due to rising imports is quite small in the import-competing industries, including textiles and clothing, and is swamped by the effect of increases in labour productivity.

However, it is now well known that these decompositions cannot be interpreted as cause and effect because changes in the labour coefficient, imports, exports and consumption are all interdependent (see Martin and Evans, 1981; OECD, 1983b:78–83). For example, an actual or threatened increase in imports may cause an increase in labour productivity because the least competitive lines of production are abandoned, or because old, low-productivity equipment is scrapped, or because innovations are introduced. The bias may be large, and it may be either positive or negative (Martin and Evans, 1981). The question of the relative importance of rising import shares can only be resolved by a fully specified and estimated model of the industries, but none exists for any country to the author's knowledge. It might be said that the textile and clothing industries have been frequently described but seldom analysed.[2]

STRUCTURAL CHANGE IN AUSTRALIA AND IN NEW ZEALAND

This section presents some observations on change and structural adjustment in the textile and clothing industries of Australia and New Zealand. It concentrates on the Australian experience, ending with some comments on the parallels in the New Zealand industries.

It was noted earlier that the Australian industries are net importers of both textiles and clothing, but at the same time Australia is a large net exporter of textile fibres, chiefly wool. The Australian wool industry has not provided a basis for a substantial textile and clothing industry specialising in materials derived from wool fibres. This is partly because Australian wool is long-staple (unlike New Zealand wool), whose end-uses in clothing are in areas where Australia is a high-cost producer, and partly because the Australian climate, while eminently suitable for growing these wools, limits the home demand for woollen clothing. Moreover, the share of woollen fibres in the global textile-fibre markets has steadily declined. Australia's clothing industry is larger in terms of value added (at domestic prices)[3] and output than its textile industry, in contrast to the situation in most developed countries. Exports constitute less than 5 per cent of domestic turnover for all sections of the industries except wool-scouring and top-making.

Australian producers in this industry have several cost disadvantages. Man-made fibres are high in cost because of domestic protection of the chemicals and fibremaking industries. Australia is also a high-wage country; in 1982 the average direct labour costs per hour of labour were A$12.73 (approximately US$13 at the average 1982 exchange rate). Moreover, production runs are generally small.

To analyse specialisation and the problems of structural adjustment in the Australian industry, it is first necessary to consider the factor intensities in the industry. In Australia both the textile and the clothing industries are relatively more labour-intensive than the rest of the manufacturing sector (IAC, 1984:Appendix D; Lloyd, 1984). As Lloyd notes, the distinguishing characteristic of the industry is the materials-intensive, multi-stage nature of its production processes. The labour component of total unit costs varies between 15 per cent and 40 per cent of total costs in the industries on average. The Australian input–output tables show that 62 per cent of all intermediate purchases by textile and clothing producers were of materials from other producers in the textile and clothing group, whereas for most industries the intermediate inputs are much more widely dispersed. The tables also show that 70 per cent of total sales by the group were to other users within the group. Thus the industry group exhibits relatively weak vertical linkages with other industries, both upstream and downstream. This somewhat unusual dominance of intra-group intermediate-input flows implies that the degree of competitiveness of higher stage downstream operations is largely dependent upon the costs of materials. This in turn depends upon both the efficiency of the local industry and its level of protection at lower stages.

The recent economic history of the textiles and clothing industries in Australia has in broad terms followed the pattern for developed economies as a group. Over the period from 1971–72 to 1981–82, real output (as measured by gross product at constant prices) dropped by an average of 0.4 per cent a year and employment declined by an average of 4.4 per cent a year (Textile, Clothing and Footwear Industry Council, 1984:Attachment 19). Dutiable imports as a percentage of the domestic market (domestic production plus imports minus exports) have tended to rise since 1970, though they fluctuate substantially from year to year and have fallen from 1981 to 1982–83, the most recent year for which comparable production and trade data are available. (The percentage of domestic market turnover accounted for by dutiable imports is, in Australia at least, a more reliable indicator of market-share trends than the percentage of total imports because non-dutiable imports are almost all non-competitive intermediate imports.) Investment has followed a downward trend for all segments of these industries and is extremely variable from year to year (IAC, 1984:Appendix E). However, in contrast to the position in the developed economies as a group, the export volume of textiles and clothing has increased because of a substantial expansion in the textile industry (Textile, Clothing and Footwear Industry Council, 1984), but net imports have also increased rapidly in real terms.

The Australian Industries Assistance Commission has measured trends in the competitiveness of the Australian textile and clothing industries in terms of the changes in the prices of Australian-produced goods relative to the changes in the prices of similar goods produced overseas, adjusted for movements in the exchange rate. The findings show clearly that between 1968 and 1983 Australian prices increased relative to prices in China, Italy, Korea, Taiwan and the United States. It is no coincidence that these are the countries from which most Australian imports of textiles and clothing are now sourced, and the obvious conclusion is that the Australian industry has become less competitive. Moreover, Australia has become less competitive relative to other developed countries (IAC, 1984:14–16).

Lloyd (1984) has attempted a decomposition of employment change in the industry using a method that is a variant of the overseas studies discussed in the previous section. Over the period 1968–69 to 1978–79 the trend level of employment declined by 44.1 per cent in the textiles industry and 40.6 per cent in the clothing industry.[4] In the case of textiles, the increase in imports accounted, statistically speaking, for 35 per cent of the reduction in employment, while the increase in consumption by itself accounted for an increase in employment equivalent to 45 per cent of the actual decrease in employment. Similarly, in the clothing industry the increase in imports accounted for 145 per cent of the decrease in employment while the change in consumption accounted for an increase in employment equal to 140 per cent of the actual decrease. These changes cannot be interpreted as independent causes of the changes in employment. In this case there is the obvious possibility that the decrease in relative prices led to an increase in consumption of the final products of the industry as these were substituted for non-textile products. The decrease in labour inputs per unit of output accounted for 106 per cent of the decrease in total employment in the textile industry and 96 per cent in the clothing industry. Thus, 'for employment, the long-term problem is one of substitution of capital for labour rather than the substitution of imported supplies for domestic supplies' (Lloyd, 1984). Any explanation of the rapid downward employment trend in these industries must include an explanation of the rapid downward trend in the demand for labour per unit of output.

To explain properly the decrease in employment in this group of industries, it would be necessary to estimate a model of the demand and supply of labour incorporating the principal features of structural change in the group. Regrettably, this cannot be done in Australia at the moment because of the absence of reliable data series for the aggregate capital stock and the total absence of any data series for the vintages of capital stocks in the group. All that can be done is to identify the main features and speculate on their relative importance. In this process it is useful to contemplate the derived demand function for labour and the factors that may have shifted it.

The principal facts to be explained are the decrease in both the total demand for labour and the demand for labour per unit of output. The main events are the approximate constancy of output (due to offsetting of the decline in competitiveness and the increasing rates of assistance), the increase in the relative price of labour, and the occurrence of capital-embodied technological change. Successive Australian governments have responded to the secular decline in competitiveness by steadily increasing assistance to the industries. The main form of assistance was the spread of quotas after 1974 in terms of commodity coverage, country coverage and duration. As a consequence the average level and the dispersion of effective rates of protection in the industries have increased. Average effective rates rose dramatically in 1974 and continued to rise until 1981–82, the most recent year for which estimates are available.[5] In 1981–82 the average effective rate of assistance to the textile industry was 74 per cent, and that for the clothing industry was 213 per cent (IAC, 1984:Table 11). There was a wage explosion in the industry after 1974, partly associated with an acceleration in the rate of increase in wages in the economy as a whole, and partly due to the introduction of wage parity for female wage earners after the 1972 equal pay decision. For the four years 1973–74 to 1977–78 the average industry wage rose by 20–25 per cent a year, which was considerably higher than the rise for the economy as a whole. Finally, the rate of capital-embodied change cannot be measured, but there has been a substantial increase in capital intensification because of the introduction of new technologies and the scrapping of older machines (see Lloyd, 1984). It has been claimed that Australia uses the newest technologies in some areas: 'It has the highest ratio of open ended spinners to spindles installed of any country in the world and ranks fourth behind the FRG, France and the USA in the introduction of shuttleless looms' (Textile, Clothing and Footwear Industry Council 1984:15).

In order to analyse the implications of these trends for employment in these industries, a tentative decision must be made about whether the labour market is in a state of equilibrium. It is arguable that the labour markets in these industries, at least in the recent history of Australia, have not cleared because of excessive and downwardly rigid real wages. Recently there has been much controversy about the number of 'outworkers' employed by contractors. These workers are omitted from all official figures issued by the Australian Bureau of Statistics. (If their number has increased, or even decreased less rapidly than the number of recorded wage employees, the official statistics have overstated the rate of decline in employment in these industries.) For the industries in question, estimates ranging from 5000 to 30 000 outworkers have recently been made, compared to the current recorded employment figure of around 90 000. Union officials contend that these outworkers make up clothing articles at a quarter or a fifth of the labour cost of unionised labour. In this context, the willingness of large numbers of workers to perform the same tasks at a fraction of the award wages is evidence that the market is not being cleared. Award wages in Australia are determined by the Federal and State Arbitration Commissions according to the movements of nominal wages in the industry relative to those in other industries and to the consumer price index, and on the basis of other criteria that conflict with the setting of wages at market-clearing levels.

Accepting for the moment that there is an oversupply of workers, the discussion can now focus on the derived demand for labour function. The increase in the relative price of labour and the embodied technological change have reduced the demand for labour, whereas the increase in assistance alone would have increased output and the demand for labour. Since the aggregate output has been roughly constant, the compensated (constant-output) demand function can be used. The decrease in the demand for labour in total and per unit of output can be explained by the increase in wage costs and the embodied technological change. However, these are not independent events. Most technologies in the textile and clothing industries seem to approximate those of the putty-clay vintage capital model. Hence an increase in the relative price of labour inputs does not lead to a substantial substitution of capital for labour in the short run, given the vintages of the machines, but capital is substituted for labour in the longer term through the introduction of new capital-embodied labour-saving technologies. Moreover, had real wages not increased as rapidly as they did, the effect of a higher output combined with lower wages would also have slowed down the rate of decrease of employment.

In short, assistance measures implemented by the government succeeded in maintaining output in this industry group in the face of declining competitiveness but failed to maintain employment. There is a strong prima facie case that the regulated wage system in Australia aggravated the problems of labour displacement and unemployment in these industries.

In New Zealand the structure of the industry and the recent trends seem to parallel those of the Australian industry in most respects, though there is a lack of comparable and up-to-date statistics. The clothing subsector accounts for more than half the employment but less than half the value added (at domestic prices). The New Zealand industry has declined in relative importance but, in contrast with the experience of most developed economies, real output increased by roughly 1 per cent a year between 1956 and 1976 and imports fell in real terms between 1963 and 1978. Exports increased steadily in current prices between 1976 and 1981 and probably increased in real terms, though no constant price data were available to the author. In recent years New Zealand has become a net exporter of clothing. Full-time employment declined by less than 1 per cent a year between 1970 and 1982. (All statistics are calculated from Brook, 1983.) Thus, rather than declining in absolute size (as has happened in most other developed economies), the industry in New Zealand has stagnated.

There are two obvious hypotheses that might explain the relatively favourable performance of this group of industries in New Zealand. First, New Zealand had the fourth lowest per capita income among the industrial market countries in 1984 (World Bank, 1984b). Since hourly labour costs are positively and significantly correlated with per capita incomes (OECD, 1983b:Chart IX), New Zealand may have a comparative advantage, or at least a smaller comparative disadvantage, in the labour-intensive segments of the industries. In addition, New Zealand affords a lower level of protection to the lower stages of production. The alternative hypothesis is that, since most of the import-competing segments of these industries were protected by import licensing throughout the 1970s and 1980s, it is possible that these quantitative restrictions were administered to retard more substantially the rate of growth of imports. Unfortunately, it is not possible to be certain about the explanation in the absence of any data series relating to capital intensities, competitiveness and effective rates of protection over this period.

One other feature of the New Zealand experience is noteworthy. As in Australia, intervention by the government has been designed mainly to provide relief from increased import competition rather than to promote more rapid structural adjustment, and the main instrument of assistance has been import quotas. In February 1980 the government announced a Textile Industry Development Plan that provided for some trade liberalisation, but since much of this related to lower stage yarns and fabrics, the effects on the average levels of protection for the whole industry group are uncertain.

THE EFFECTIVENESS OF GOVERNMENT POLICIES

In the presence of exogenous sources of change in supply and demand, profit-maximising producers in a country will respond by changing their input and output mixtures. They may make adjustments at a number of margins, which will improve their competitiveness; they may shift towards higher quality and higher priced articles, adopt cost-reducing technologies, close or relocate plants, and merge with other companies. Typically, many activities are vertically integrated within big firms, some of which are manufacturers and wholesalers and retailers. Firms such as Sears Roebuck in the United States and Marks and Spencer in the United Kingdom run multinational operations, providing designers and materials to clothing firms in other countries and deciding which activities will be carried out in different countries.

Two responses in particular have been credited with the revitalisation of parts of the textile and clothing industries in countries such as West Germany and Japan. These are the movement upmarket of product lines and the introduction of more capital-intensive, automated methods of production (see OECD, 1983b; Yamazawa, 1983). The important question here is whether the market provides the incentives for producers to adjust most effectively, or whether there is a case for government intervention.

While governments may intervene in an attempt to facilitate structural changes by subsidising labour retraining, plant scrapping and other changes, there is a general assumption that unregulated and unassisted markets are desirable because they provide more correct information about future prices to both producers and consumers.[6] (For some general discussion of the limitations of structural adjustment policies, see Bhagwati, 1982; Lloyd, 1983; OECD, 1983a.) In Japan, for example, adjustment assistance was introduced in order to encourage private firms to respond to external changes. The principal measures have been the subsidised scrapping scheme and the rationalisation and modernisation programs, especially for small and medium-sized firms. Yet at least one commentator concludes that these policies have been ineffective:

> Both measures ... have tended to discourage voluntary unsubsidized scrapping and to prolong the survival of inefficient firms ... Structural changes in the Japanese textile industry observed over the last two decades are attributed not so much to structural adjustment assistance by the government as to the continuance of competitive pressure. (Yamazawa, 1983:38–39)

In Australia there has been no government plan to improve productivity by scrapping obsolete plant, or by plant conversions or mergers. The only industry-specific measures taken have been the measures included in the

Productivity Improvement Program, which was set up in 1977. Under this program Industry Program Groups have been created to improve productivity through management training, product rationalisation and various other means. However, the program carries no budget for direct grants. In New Zealand the Textile Industry Development Plan, which began in July 1980, did produce a movement towards lower and more uniform levels of nominal protection in the industry by amending the complex structure of tariffs, import-licensing quotas and bounties, but it provided little in the way of positive structural adjustment measures, apart perhaps from a 40 per cent investment allowance. The United States government has similarly avoided comprehensive structural adjustment schemes.

However, governments in all developed countries have intervened in the textile and clothing industries on a systematic scale. The predominant strategy has been to increase levels of protection from import competition rather than to promote structural change. Most of this restriction has come from quantitative limitations that were initially declared to be temporary. For developed countries, bilateral trade restrictions have been permitted under the Multi-Fiber Agreements (MFA I, II and III), and Australia and New Zealand have operated multilateral non-discriminatory import quotas outside these agreements.

To evaluate these interventions the objectives of the government policies must first be considered. Typically, the governments of most developed countries have declared their support for preventing large losses in employment in these industries and maintaining an 'efficient' industry. For example, when announcing the current seven-year plan for these industries the Australian government saw this plan as '... safeguarding employment and ... [encouraging] further improvements in the efficiency of the industry, reductions in costs and responsiveness to changing consumer needs' (Joint Statement, 1980). If production is to be truly efficient, it must be internationally competitive, and large sections of the textile and clothing industries in developed countries are far from being internationally competitive. The two objectives of maintaining employment and achieving international competitiveness will therefore frequently conflict. It seems clear that the paramount objective in many countries has been to maintain output, and particularly employment, or at least to slow down their rates of decline. In other words, protection of these industries has been intended primarily as job protection.

How effective have government policies been in achieving this objective? A basic criticism of the increased protection of textile and clothing manufacturers is that it has failed to prevent rapid reductions in the labour employed in these industries, though of course the level of employment and the real wages of workers who have remained in the industries would have been lower, in the short run at least, had these increases in protection not been granted. There are a number of reasons for this failure.

For the first time, as far as I am aware, a general argument has recently been put forward that trade policies are likely to be *'inefficacious'* because consumers and producers will find a number of ways to reduce their impact (Baldwin,

1982). A trade tax or quota may be legally avoided, in part or completely, by shifting to a substitute product, or by changing the quality mixture, or by changing to another country source if the instrument is discriminatory among countries (as are voluntary restraints and preferences for developing countries). Since the production processes in this industry group include a number of stages, the introduction of a new barrier to trade at a single stage provides an incentive for importers and producers to shift imports to stages that are now relatively less protected. For example, the application of a tariff or quota to a processed item (say a category of clothing) may produce a smaller-than-expected domestic price increase because the item may be imported in a less processed form (say as fabrics) and processed domestically. Thus an increase in value added at one stage of production may result in a decrease at an earlier stage; or, if the tariff or quota is introduced at an earlier stage of production, there may be a decrease in value added at a later stage. With multi-stage processes the effects of intervention at one stage on upstream and downstream stages may be complex and difficult to predict. All the effects described have been observed in the textiles and clothing trade. (Lloyd [1984] discusses untoward effects of this kind in Australia.)

One instance of inefficacy has been identified in the textiles and clothing industries in Australia, namely, the effects of a quota that covers a heterogeneous group of products (Gibbs and Konovalov, 1984; IAC, 1980). A quota may be fixed in terms of the (maximum) aggregate quantity or aggregate value that may be imported for the group. Government administrators have preferred volume-based quotas to value-based quotas, partly for administrative simplicity and partly to avoid potential problems arising from transfer pricing under a value-based regime of quotas. When a quota volume entitlement is aggregated over quantities, an importer maximises his profit by equalising among the different products imported the difference between the cost of importing and the price realisable on the domestic markets. A volume quota is thus equivalent to a set of uniform specific tariffs on the products in the group (Falvey, 1979). Within a category the ad valorem equivalent tariffs are higher for lower priced units. When a quota is introduced or the size of an existing quota is reduced, other things being equal, the composition of imports shifts within the quota category towards the higher priced products. This has the effect of encouraging the domestic industry to increase production of its lower priced items—the very items in which it is least competitive. However, if the objective of the intervention were to restrain the *quantity* of imports, the best form of intervention would be a uniform set of specific tariffs, not uniform ad valorem tariffs or an equivalent tendering system (Anderson, 1985; Corden and Falvey, 1985; Gibbs and Konovalov, 1984).

It must be asked whether it is sensible to specify a 'non-economic objective' of government policy in terms of the quantity of imports. The immediate objective of government policy has been to protect employment, so that, instead of being defined in terms of the quantity of imports, the 'non-economic' objective might be specified in terms of the quantity of employment. It can then be shown that, under certain conditions, the most efficient instrument is a set of uniform wage subsidies to all employees in the industry.[7] To achieve an employment objective, wage subsidies are preferable to assistance in the form of protection from import competition because they reduce the deadweight loss to consumers.[8] These losses must have been substantial when protection was increased in many developed countries because of the high increase in nominal rates of protection. In Australia, for example, assistance to the industry through tariffs, quotas and other instruments is equivalent (for consumers) to a consumption tax of around 80 per cent (IAC, 1984:Figure 7), a situation that probably applies in most other developed countries.

While a policy of protecting employment in the industry by subsidising wages would represent an improvement over protecting import-competing output, it is subject to two powerful objections. First, one of the principal causes of the decrease in employment in these industries, in Australia at least, is the downward inflexibility of real wages because of labour-market monopolies and government regulation. Even if labour is industry-specific, it will remain employed in the face of a decrease in the output price as along as real wages are downwardly flexible and the value of the marginal product remains positive. Improved downward wage flexibility might of itself substantially improve the job prospects of workers in industries such as clothing and textiles where the demand for labour is falling.

There is another objection to the employment objective. Surely the maintenance of employment in subsectors of industries must be accepted as a short-term expedient only, not as a true objective of government policy. If a government has a long-term objective of providing employment for members of the labour force, that objective must apply to all members of the labour force and must be specified in terms of the general desirability of employment, not necessarily of retaining employment in the current job. From this perspective, quotas that restrict import competition diminish the incentives for producers to reduce costs and become more competitive in the long term.

The reliance in most developed countries over the past ten years or so on protection from import competition as the primary instrument of assistance to the textile and clothing industries represents an example of policies that are *ineffective* in Mundell's sense (that is, they are not closely tailored to the objective). These forms of intervention do not perform well in achieving the employment objective of government policy (they are inefficacious), and they impose heavy costs on other income groups in the economy.

THE POLITICAL ECONOMY OF SELECTING INEFFICIENT POLICIES

There is an apparent paradox in the choice by governments of policy instruments that are not effective, and in some cases not efficacious. This paradox might be explained by two factors.

First, there has probably been a lack of understanding of the real objectives of governments and a failure to recognise the ineffectiveness of chosen instruments. Studies should be promoted to measure the costs and benefits of chosen instruments against those of alternative and more effective instruments.

The paradox might also be explained by a model of the political process determining the choice of instrument. Several models have been developed to explain why governments give permanent protection to particular industries, and these models can be adapted to explain the protection of declining industries. The specific-factor model of international trade analyses the effects of an exogenous shock on an industry in an open economy. Take, for example, a fall in the exogenous price of an importable commodity. This represents an improvement in the commodity terms of trade and a potential welfare gain for the economy. Let this commodity be the labour-intensive commodity to model the increased import penetration in the textile and clothing industries. The fall in this price induces producers to lower the output of this commodity. In the new equilibrium the rents received by the specific factors in the industry will have fallen. Moreover, the fall in rents is proportionately greater than the fall in the domestic price of the output, and this fall is greater the more labour-intensive the production process (Ruffin and Jones, 1977). Since there is some specificity on the part of both labour and capital factors, it is not difficult to see how a vigorous coalition of producer interests will emerge to lobby for the prevention or deceleration of the structural changes that would otherwise occur, and how this producer coalition will dominate the anti-protection consumer lobby. In domestic political processes the interests of overseas suppliers are completely unrepresented, and international organisations such as GATT and UNCTAD have not been able to prevent outcomes that have negative sums for the world economy as a whole.

10 The United States automobile industry: a case study of a de facto industrial policy

LAWRENCE J. WHITE

Industrial policy continues to be a widely debated topic (Johnson, 1984; Magaziner and Reich, 1982; Reich, 1983a, b, 1985; Schultze, 1983). No public consensus has been achieved within the United States, and no formal governmental measures have been taken. Yet, as some authors have argued, the sum of all governmental actions and policies affecting an industry could be considered a de facto industrial policy (e.g. Reich, 1983a).

This chapter will examine one such de facto industrial policy: the United States government's policies towards the American motor vehicle industry during the past six years. This study should prove instructive for two reasons: first, the motor vehicle industry is a sizeable industry; in 1984 it accounted for direct domestic employment of about 866 000 individuals, for direct and indirect employment (that is, including the industry's input–output relationships) of about three times that number, and for 4.3 per cent of gross national product (Automotive News, 1985; MVMA, 1984). Second (and related to the first point), the industry has been the subject of a comparatively large number of recent governmental actions.[1]

Further, the lessons should have wider applications, since domestic motor vehicle industries figure prominently in the economies of a number of Pacific Basin countries. Though those industries range from fully mature (as in Japan) to young and growing (with an outward orientation, as in Korea, or an inward orientation, as in Southeast Asia), an analysis of the strengths and weaknesses of a major producing country's policies should be useful for students of those industries. This chapter begins with a description of the background to the problems experienced by the United States motor vehicle industry. Government actions in response to these problems are then reviewed and assessed, and some concluding comments are offered.

BACKGROUND

The 1970s—at least until 1978—were largely prosperous years for the United States motor vehicle industry. Table 10.1 provides the relevant data on sales, production and profitability.[2] Automobile imports were rising, but domestic

196

producers were coping reasonably well. The 1973 oil shock produced some temporary dislocations, but by the late 1970s the industry and clearly adjusted. With the real price of petrol down to almost its late 1960s level, the demand for large cars, vans and pickup trucks—areas where domestic producers faced less competition from abroad and appeared to enjoy greater profits per unit— was booming. In 1978, because of the constraints imposed by federally deman- ded fuel-economy standards, Ford began to ration large V-8 engine cars among its dealers. In late 1978, dealers' supplies of domestic cars on hand were relatively low—always a sign of demand pressing on supply—while inventories of imported cars were starting to pile up.

At the same time, domestic producers were hedging their strategies some- what: General Motors had introduced the subcompact Chevrolet Chevette in 1975, and its first generation of smaller front-wheel cars (the X-cars) was ready for introduction in the spring of 1979. Ford's Pinto model was well estab- lished, and the subcompact Ford Escort and Mercury Lynx were planned for introduction in 1980. And Chrysler had introduced the subcompact front- wheel-drive Dodge Omni and Plymouth Horizon in the fall of 1977 and had its front-wheel-drive K-cars planned for 1980.

Then, in the early spring of 1979, the Iranian crisis precipitated the second oil shock, causing the retail price of petrol to virtually double in the space of less than six months, and the roof fell in on domestic motor vehicle manufac- turers. The demand for large cars, vans and pickup trucks dropped precipi- tously and car buyers began to look for smaller, more fuel-efficient vehicles. To some extent they did turn towards the smaller American-made vehicles. But Ford was hobbled by the allegation that the Pinto model had a dangerous tendency to burst into flames if struck from the rear; ironically, the alleged design flaw had been corrected in 1979, but the public seemed not to care and stopped buying the model. And Chrysler was handicapped by a supply arrangement with Volkswagen that limited the number of engines that Chrys- ler could buy for its Omni and Horizon models. (The decision to buy from Volkswagen rather than to produce the engines inhouse had been made in the wake of Chrysler's financial problems in the mid-1970s.)

More importantly, consumers turned towards vehicles produced by smaller manufacturers—especially Japanese manufacturers—who had been designing vehicles for their domestic markets (where petrol had always been priced relatively higher than in the United States and where, accordingly, buyers tended to demand more fuel-efficient vehicles), and who could offer prices and qualities that United States consumers found attractive. Imports grew substan- tially, relative to domestic sales: in 1979 imports exceeded 20 per cent of total sales for the first time in history; in 1980 they would exceed 25 per cent.

Chrysler was the first to show the strain. The company had a postwar history of management and periodic financial problems (White, 1971; 1982a), and had lost money in 1978. By the late spring of 1979 it was in serious financial difficulties and was appealing to the legislative and executive branches of the United States government for assistance. Chrysler eventually lost US$1.1 billion in 1979, setting a record for the largest loss in American

Table 10.1 Recent annual data for the United States motor vehicle industry

	Automobile sales				Truck sales				Production		Motor vehicle industry[a]		
	Domestic ('000)	Imports ('000)	Total ('000)	Imports as share of total (%)	Domestic ('000)	Imports ('000)	Total ('000)	Imports as share of total (%)	Automobiles ('000)	Trucks ('000)	Employment ('000)	Profits (US$b)	Investment[b] (US$b)
1970	7 116	1 288	8 403	15.3	1 746	73	1 819	4.0	6 550	1 773	799	1.2	3.0
1971	8 676	1 566	10 242	15.3	2 012	85	2 096	4.1	8 558	2 088	848	5.0	2.4
1972	9 322	1 622	10 943	14.8	2 486	143	2 629	5.4	8 828	2 483	875	5.9	3.0
1973	9 670	1 777	11 447	15.5	2 916	233	3 148	7.4	9 667	3 014	976	5.7	3.8
1974	7 449	1 403	8 852	15.8	2 512	176	2 688	6.6	7 310	2 747	908	0.1	4.3
1975	7 050	1 577	8 627	18.3	2 249	229	2 478	9.3	6 741	2 270	792	1.9	3.4
1976	8 607	1 493	10 100	14.8	2 944	237	3 181	7.5	8 538	3 000	881	7.2	3.6
1977	9 104	2 071	11 176	18.5	3 352	323	3 675	8.8	9 294	3 489	947	9.4	5.8
1978	9 308	2 000	11 308	17.7	3 773	336	4 109	8.2	9 153	3 723	1 005	8.9	7.2
1979	8 316	3 328	10 644	21.9	3 009	470	3 479	13.5	8 418	3 046	990	4.7	8.3
1980	6 578	2 397	8 975	26.7	2 001	487	2 487	19.6	6 417	1 634	789	-3.8	9.1
1981	6 206	2 326	8 533	27.3	1 809	451	2 266	20.0	6 280	1 690	789	0.3	10.1
1982	5 757	2 222	7 978	27.9	2 146	414	2 560	16.2	4 974	1 912	705	0.8	7.9
1983	6 795	2 386	9 181	26.0	2 658	471	3 129	15.1	7 112	2 424	772	7.4	7.2
1984	7 952	2 442	10 393	23.5	3 475	618	4 093	15.1	7 778	3 146	886	10.9	11.0

Notes: a Includes manufacturers of parts
b Expenditure on new plant and equipment

Source: Automotive News 1985

corporate history. In response to fears of a Chrysler bankruptcy, Congress in late 1979 authorised a loan guarantee of US$1.5 billion.[3]

By late 1979 the United States economy was simultaneously experiencing a quickening of inflation and a slide into another recession, depressing the demand for domestic motor vehicles yet further. The 1980-model cars, introduced in the fall of 1979, had to meet tighter exhaust-emission standards mandated by the Clean Air Act Amendment of 1977, and the 1981 models would have to meet yet more stringent standards, requiring expensive exhaust sensors and microprocessors on most models to maximise the trade-offs between an engine's fuel economy and its exhaust pollutants.

By 1980 there was a general recognition that the domestic motor vehicle industry was in crisis. Multiple government reports were issued and congressional hearings held.[4] Sales and production were in decline. All the major motor vehicle manufacturers reported losses. Chrysler beat its record of the previous year, losing US$1.7 billion, and apparently averted bankruptcy by only a narrow margin. For General Motors, it was the first loss since the early 1920s. And the future looked bleaker still. There was a general recognition that at prevailing exchange rates Japanese motor vehicle manufacturers could produce and land cars at costs substantially below those of domestic producers for comparable vehicles. (Trucks were less of a problem, primarily because they carried an import duty of 25 per cent—a legacy of a trade dispute with West Germany in the 1960s, in which the United States retaliated with higher tariffs on trucks when West Germany restricted imports of frozen chickens from the United States—whereas automobiles carried duties of less than 3 per cent.[5])

The sources of the domestic industry's problems were many and varied. First, despite their hedging, the domestic manufacturers' main product offerings were not geared to the higher petrol prices of 1979. Given the long leadtimes required to develop new vehicles (four to five years, under the best of circumstances) the industry was going to need a few years to adjust to its new environment in any event.

Second, the industry and allowed its labour costs to grow in a manner that could not be sustained. Collective bargaining patterns had developed in the twenty years following the second world war, when the industry was relatively unconstrained by import competition (Katz, 1985; MacDonald, 1963). The industry, dominated by three large producers, enjoyed profits that (measured as rates of return on equity) were well above the average for all manufacturing. And, as has apparently been true for other concentrated industries as well, organised labour was able to appropriate some of the rents (Freeman and Medoff, 1984:ch.12; Salinger, 1984; *but* see also Clark, 1984).

This pattern continued through the 1970s. As can be seen from Table 10.2, the differential between wages and labour costs for motor vehicles and those for all manufacturing widened during this decade. If the products of overseas manufacturers had not become an alternative for many consumers, this wage and labour cost pattern might have been viable. But with the labour costs of

Table 10.2 Labour compensation in the United States motor vehicle industry

	Average hourly earnings (US$)			Total hourly compensation (US$)		
	Motor vehicle industry (1)	All manufacturing (2)	(1) as percentage of (2)	Motor vehicle industry (3)	All manufacturing (4)	(3) as percentage of (4)
1970	4.42	3.35	132	—	—	135
1971	4.95	3.57	139	—	—	—
1972	5.35	3.82	140	—	—	—
1973	5.70	4.09	139	—	—	—
1974	6.23	4.42	141	—	—	—
1975	6.82	4.83	141	9.44	6.35	149
1976	7.45	5.22	143	10.27	6.93	148
1977	8.22	5.68	145	11.45	7.59	151
1978	8.98	6.17	146	12.67	8.30	153
1979	9.74	6.70	145	13.68	9.07	151
1980	10.80	7.27	149	16.29	9.89	165
1981	12.29	7.99	154	17.28	10.95	158
1982	13.01	8.49	153	18.66	11.68	160
1983	13.36	8.83	151	19.02	12.31	155

Sources: Crandall (1984); Munger (1985); US Bureau of Labor Statistics *Employment and Earnings* (various issues)

Japanese producers at only 50–70 per cent of those in the United States (at prevailing exchange rates) the pattern was not sustainable.

Third, industry management may have become slack, though this is difficult to document rigorously. It is clear that management (and engineers) in the 1970s were much more preoccupied with regulatory matters—especially emission control and safety regulation—than had previously been the case. In any event, the quality of the vehicles produced does seem to have diminished. *Consumer Reports*, for example, in its testing of vehicles, continually complained about the quality of American vehicles, and its readers' comments and repair records supported these complaints. 'Fit and finish' became a sore spot with American producers and their customers. By contrast, Japanese producers acquired a strong reputation for high quality and high marks on 'fit and finish'.

Fourth, Japanese vehicle producers had clearly acquired (at prevailing exchange rates) a substantial cost advantage in producing small, fuel-efficient vehicles. Estimates of their advantage varied, but $1500 per car (landed in the United States) was a frequently cited figure.[6] That advantage was a compound of lower wages, lower steel costs (United States vehicle producers were certainly not helped by the protection that had been given to United States steel producers), good management, and physically compact arrangements that permitted low inventories.[7]

Finally, the industry was unlucky enough to be faced with problems of product mixture and heightened import competition at just the time when the United States economy was entering a severe recession and the demand for vehicles was slackening.

Table 10.3   United States motor vehicle industry: average annual percentage increases in output per labour hour and in prices

	1957–78	1970–78
Output per labour hour		
—motor vehicle industry	3.5	3.7
—all manufacturing	2.7	2.3
—all private business	2.4	1.5
	1955–79	1970–79
Consumer price index		
—new cars	1.7	4.9
—durable goods	2.7	6.1
—overall index	3.8	7.1

Note: All rates of increase are the slope coefficients of ordinary-least-squares regressions of the logarithms of the relevant variables on time.

Source: Lawrence J. White 'The Automobile Industry' in Richard R. Nelson (ed.) *Government and Technical Progress: A Cross Industry Analysis* New York: Pergamon, 1982, pp. 422, 424.

It is worth pointing out that by comparative standards within the United States the domestic vehicle manufacturers' record on manufacturing productivity improvements was quite good. As can be seen in Table 10.3, the average annual rate of labour productivity increase—even for the 1970s—was well above the average for all manufacturing. A similarly favourable story is told by the record on price increases, as measured by the components of the consumer price index.[8] Thus the industry's performance in absolute terms was quite respectable. But, given the circumstances it faced, that performance was not good enough.

GOVERNMENT ACTIONS

The principal actions of the United States government to assist domestic vehicle manufacturers over the past six years fall into four categories.[9]

Import restraints

As losses and unemployment mounted in the motor vehicle industry in 1980 and early 1981, protectionist sentiment mounted also (Winham and Kabashima, 1982). Earlier in the 1970s the United Automobile Workers had switched from a free-trade to a protectionist stance. Now the principal manufacturers, who had generally been anti-protectionist, joined the United Automobile Workers in asking for protection. The arguments for protection were a mixture of the traditional infant-industry argument that has surrounded most American industries' pleas for protection—'give us time to invest, and we will make ourselves more efficient'—and the argument that unemployment in the motor vehicle industry had high social and tax costs. Congress seemed increasingly receptive to these arguments, and numerous proposals for import restraints and/or domestic-content restrictions were advanced.

In the spring of 1981 the Reagan Administration—professing free-market principles and arguing that it was only trying to forestall even more restrictive legislation by Congress[10]—pressured the Japanese government into 'voluntarily' restricting exports of automobiles to the United States.[11] The Voluntary Restraint Agreement, as it was subsequently labelled, limited the importation of Japanese-produced vehicles into the United States to 1.68 million for the period 1 April 1981 to 31 March 1982; also, an extra 82 500 cars were allowed to be imported into Puerto Rico, and 70 000 vans were allowed to be imported into the United States. These limits were repeated for the two subsequent twelve-month periods. For 1 April 1984 to 31 March 1985, these figures were raised to 1.85 million, 90 850, and 77 080, respectively. The agreement expired at the end of March 1985 and has not been renewed. The Japanese government announced, however, that it would limit Japanese car exports to 2.3 million units a year, so as to prevent a surge of exports that might reignite protectionist sentiment.

The Chrysler bailout

In December 1979 Congress authorised a loan guarantee of US$1.5 billion for the faltering Chrysler Corporation. The formal arrangements for the loan were made in early 1980 (Stewart, 1983:ch.5) and Chrysler promptly made use of them, eventually drawing on US$1.2 billion of the guaranteed loans. By 1982 Chrysler had turned the corner and earned a small profit, and by the end of 1983 the corporation had repaid the guaranteed loans.

Antitrust

In 1982 General Motors and Toyota announced the formation of a joint venture to assemble automobiles (based on a Toyota design) at the General Motors assembly plant in Fremont, California. The Federal Trade Commission assessed the possible anticompetitive implications of the joint venture and concluded in December 1983 that the venture did not violate the antitrust laws. Chrysler brought a private antitrust suit to try to challenge the decision, but that suit was settled by the parties out of court. The first car produced by the joint venture emerged from the Fremont plant in December 1984.

Also, in 1981 the Federal Trade Commission terminated a major investigation of the automobile industry that had been conducted over the previous five years. And in 1982 the US Department of Justice modified an earlier consent decree (the 'smog decree') that had been entered in 1969 and that restricted collective action by motor vehicle manufacturers with respect to the development of pollution-control devices.[12] The modification eased the restrictions somewhat.

Regulation

In April 1981 the Reagan Administration announced a package of proposed regulatory modifications that would ease the burden of regulation on the motor vehicle industry.[13] However, some of the proposals were never converted into action: the focus here will be on those that did have an eventual impact on the industry.[14]

In the safety area, the National Highway Traffic Safety Administration in 1981 first granted a delay and then withdrew the requirement that passive restraints (airbags or automatic seatbelts) be provided in all cars; the requirement had been scheduled to take effect for the 1982-model year for large cars, the 1983-model year for middle-sized cars, and the 1984-model year for small cars. In 1982 the DC Circuit Court of Appeals overturned the administration's relaxation, and in 1983 the Supreme Court upheld the DC Circuit, ordering the administration to develop a new passive-restraint rule. In 1984 the National Highway Traffic Safety Administration announced a new rule, requiring the installation of passive restraints in all vehicles by 1989 (unless States representing two-thirds of the United States population had enacted laws making the use of existing seatbelts compulsory by that date). In effect, the companies obtained a delay of at least five to seven years in the requirement to install passive restraints (see Tolchin, 1984).

Also in the safety area, the National Highway Traffic Safety Administration in 1982 lowered the standard for crash resistance of bumpers from 5 miles per hour to 2.5 miles per hour.

In the area of fuel economy, the Traffic Safety Administration in 1984 eased the fuel-economy standards for light-duty trucks. And in 1985 it eased the fuel-economy standards for the 1986-model year for automobiles from a corporate-fleet average of 27.5 miles per gallon to an average of 26 miles per gallon.

In the area of air-pollution-emission standards, the Environmental Protection Agency in 1982 eased the exhaust-emission standards that applied to heavy-duty trucks, and the following year the agency eased particulate standards for automobiles and light-duty trucks.[15] No action was taken, however, on the expensive emission requirements applying to gasoline-powered automobiles (White, 1982b).

AN ASSESSMENT OF THE ACTIONS

This section will offer some 'horseback' judgments about the worth of the government actions just described. The primary standard that will be used is the familiar one of 'market failure': that government intervention is best justified when monopoly or oligopoly threatens, when serious externalities are present, when 'public goods' are involved, when serious informational asymmetries are present, or when important (by some definition) income-distribution considerations are at stake (Bator, 1958).[16]

Table 10.4   Facilities of Japanese motor vehicle manufacturers in the United States

Company	Site	Production date
Honda	Marysville, Ohio	November 1982
Nissan	Smyrna, Tennessee	June 1983 (trucks) March 1985 (cars)
Toyota (1)	Fremont, California	December 1984
Toyota (2)	(to be determined)	1988
Mazda	Flatrock, Michigan	Fall 1987
Mitsubishi	(to be determined)	1988

Sources: New York Times 21 April 1985, #4, p. 5; Wall Street Journal 24 July 1985, p. 25

The Voluntary Restraint Agreement

The basic consequences of the Voluntary Restraint Agreement for automobiles
are clear. Imports were effectively restricted, and prices for imported and
domestically produced vehicles were maintained at higher levels than otherwise would have been the case. Also, as many had predicted, Japanese manufacturers upgraded the mixture of vehicles that they sent to the United States
(Feenstra, 1985; Gomez-Ibanez et al., 1983). And all the principal Japanese
manufacturers have established some manufacturing facilities in the United
States, or have plans to do so. Table 10.4 summarises the pattern of these
Japanese investments.

A quantitative measure of the effects on car prices, quantities and direct
employment requires estimates of the requisite elasticities. Table 10.5 provides
a summary of the consequences, as estimated in four recent studies: Crandall
(1984); Gomez-Ibanez et al. (1983); Tarr and Morke (1984); and the US
International Trade Commission (1985). In all cases, the effects are measured
for a single year only. As can be seen, the estimates of the effects vary widely,
but even the smallest estimates show sizeable consequences for the United
States economy. The cost to the economy per job protected in the motor
vehicle industry has been high indeed.

At the same time, the domestic companies have undertaken substantial
investments and made considerable efforts to upgrade their manufacturing
processes and reduce their costs (US International Trade Commission, 1985).
(See Table 10.1 for the relevant figures on new plant and equipment expenditures.)

Was the Voluntary Restraint Agreement worthwhile? The basic case for
unrestricted trade as the best way for a society to allocate its resources is a
familiar one and will not be repeated here. The 'perfection' assumptions of the
pure model underlying the argument will never be met in practice, and one
should always be mindful of the cautions of Lipsey and Lancaster (1956–57)
concerning 'second-best'. Nevertheless, the case is a powerful one and carries a
strong presumption of validity.

The arguments in favour of the agreement are not strong. For an infant-

Table 10.5 Studies of the consequences of the Voluntary Restraint Agreement

	Gomez-Ibanez et al. (1983)	Tarr and Morke (1984)	Crandall (1984)	United States International Trade Commission (1985)	
Year of effect	1981	1981	1983	1983	1984
Average effect on all new car prices	+0.9%	+1.4%	+5.5%	+5.5%	+8.5%
Effect on domestic sales of automobiles	+0.5%	+2.0%	+7.0%	+5.3%	+7.8%
Effect on domestic employment in the automobile industry	+6500	+4600	+26 200	+25 600	+44 100
Cost to consumers	$566 million	$1109 million	$4300 million	$4680 million	$8516 million
Cost to economy	$272 million	$994 million	$2400 million	$1841 million	$3427 million
Cost per job created in the automobile industry	$42 000	$216 000	$92 000	$72 000	$78 000

industry argument to be valid, there must be some market failure (for example, learning or educational externalities) that prevents the relevant parties from reaping the fruits of their own investments in improved facilities (or whatever it is that the 'infant' will do so as to achieve the efficiencies that will eventually permit the termination of protection). In essence, the infant industry is saying, 'Our industry's customers should be taxed so as to provide us with the funds for the needed investments'. But if the investments are worthwhile the appropriate source of funding is the capital market, unless a serious externality or other market failure is present. None comes readily to mind for the Voluntary Restraint Agreement for automobiles.[17]

Further, in a system of floating exchange rates any net job creation or job protection arising from import restraints is likely to be largely illusory. Specific jobs in the specific import-threatened industry may be created or protected, but only at the price of the loss of a similar number of jobs in export industries that fail to expand or that contract because of the appreciation in the exchange rate caused by the restriction in imports. If the import restrictions reduce or eliminate the hardship costs, adjustment costs and tax costs in the protected sector (for example, through unemployment and welfare payments), they can do so only by increasing those costs in the export sector. The former costs may be more readily identifiable than the latter, but the latter costs are nevertheless real. These principles are surely applicable to the Voluntary Restraint Agreement.

Finally, even on income-distribution grounds the agreement fails. As noted above, motor industry workers have traditionally earned wages that are well above those for all of manufacturing (which, in turn, are above the average wages paid across the remainder of the economy). Buyers of automobiles—many of them with lower incomes—are thus being asked to pay higher prices so as to preserve the jobs of relatively well-paid automobile workers.[18] An office worker interviewed by the *New York Times* (1 September 1985, p. 36) may have provided the best description of this phenomenon (albeit with some hyperbole): '... the only people who can afford to buy American-made cars ... are the Americans who make them.'

What would have happened in the absence of the Voluntary Restraint Agreement (and in the absence of protectionist measures generally)? The domestic companies would have been less profitable over the four-year period, but would probably have pursued a pattern of investment similar to that which actually occurred. Chrysler might have had a harder time, but the United Automobile Workers surely would have been more conciliatory in its wage policies. And the United States motor vehicle industry might have been more vigorous in opposing protection for steel and other inputs. (Even before the Voluntary Restraint Agreement the motor vehicle industry was noticeably quiet on the subject of protection for its inputs, and it continues to be so.)

Two other consequences of the agreement should be mentioned. First, it encouraged the use by European countries of similar import restraints on vehicles. And, second, it provided Japan's Ministry of International Trade and Industry with added power and influence over the Japanese vehicle industry.[19]

In sum, the best that can be said about the Voluntary Restraint Agreement is that it expired after four years.

The Chrysler bailout

In 1980 Chrysler was teetering on the edge of bankrupcy; today it is a thriving, prosperous company. In that sense, the loan guarantee program was a success. But deeper questions must be asked.

What would have happened in the absence of the loan guarantees? First, Chrysler might not have gone bankrupt. One other motor vehicle manufacturer, International Harvester, came close to bankruptcy in 1983 but, through arrangements with its creditors, managed to avoid being plunged into the abyss. Perhaps the same could have been arranged for Chrysler.

Second, even if bankruptcy had occurred, it need not have meant the demise of the company. Many companies have gone into bankruptcy, continued to operate, and emerged as viable companies, albeit with some losses to stockholders and creditors. It is true that a company selling durable goods to consumers, who might worry about the continuation of spare parts supplies and service facilities and about owning 'orphan' vehicles, would face a difficult task in convincing them of its long-run viability. But the scrapping of the company after a bankruptcy was not a foregone conclusion.

Third, even if the company had disappeared, many of its resources (and workers) would have been absorbed by the expanded operations of the remaining domestic producers. With the disappearance of one of the three principal domestic producers, the likelihood of oligopolistic behaviour might have increased. But, ironically, the product strategy that Chrysler developed during the loan guarantee period called for the abandonment of the production of large cars (except the Imperial). Consequently, Chrysler has focused on producing small and middle-sized cars, but this is the area where the competition from overseas producers is the strongest. Accordingly, Chrysler's continued presence as a producer may not have made much difference in the effective competition over the various segments of the automobile market (although Chrysler is a likely potential entrant into the large-car segment).

Finally, even if it was successful on its own terms, the intervention established a precedent (following that set by the rescue of Lockheed a decade earlier) that may be used to support bailouts of worthwhile ventures in the future. The incentives and consequent behaviour created by the precedent may be quite costly.[20]

Antitrust

The crucial action here was the Federal Trade Commission's approval of the General Motors–Toyota joint venture. It is not clear how much the commission's decision was affected by the automobile industry's weakened state. The majority of the commission might well have favoured the joint venture even in the context of a healthy industry.

The claimed social benefits of the joint venture lie in the ability of General Motors to learn about the efficiencies of Japanese management through the joint operation of the Fremont facility. But it is far from clear that these benefits are large compared with what General Motors could learn through extensive contacts, or even joint ventures, with the two smaller Japanese companies, Isuzu and Suzuki, in which General Motors has minority ownership.[21] At the same time, the joint venture raises the possibilities of diminished product and price competition and the exchange of sensitive planning and price information between the first and fourth largest sellers in a concentrated market with high entry barriers.

In sum, the efficiency gains do not seem to be very great; the competitive dangers seem to be greater. The decision of the Federal Trade Commission may well have been a mistake.

Regulation

Here again, it is difficult to judge how much the regulatory actions were motivated by the weakened state of the industry, since the Reagan Administration was generally committed to regulatory modification anyway. The industry's weakened state, though, probably hastened the process.

For the most part the regulatory actions were sensible, representing cost-effective modifications of earlier regulations (see White, 1981; 1982b). The most controversial decision was the suspension of the passive-restraint requirement. Here there are some uncertainties as to the costs and effectiveness of the measures and whether drivers, if forced to acquire more safety devices than they would buy voluntarily, would take offsetting actions such as driving more recklessly (Peltzman, 1975). But an important aspect of the dispute is a philosophical question: should the government interfere with safety decisions when the primary bearers of the risks and costs are the decisionmakers—the drivers—themselves?[22] (It should be remembered that seatbelts have been a standard fitting in new cars since 1966, so the public is quite familiar with them; and, since 1974, another standard fitting has been a reminder buzzer that sounds briefly if the seatbelts are not fastened when the ignition is turned on. Yet only 10–15 per cent of drivers choose to use their seatbelts.) To this author, freedom of personal choice should be the guiding principle in such situations.[23]

In sum, the regulatory modifications have been sensible.

CONCLUSION

As this chapter is being written, the United States motor vehicle industry is enjoying a phase of substantial prosperity. Sales, though not at their record levels, have rebounded from the low point of 1982. At the same time, the companies have pared their costs substantially, and profits (at least in nominal terms) are at all-time highs. Also, the companies are buying their way into high-technology areas: General Motors has purchased the Electronic Data Systems Corporation and the Hughes Aircraft Company; Chrysler has bought the Gulfstream Aerospace Corporation; and Ford may well either make a similar purchase or expand its own capabilities. These purchases seem to be aimed at diversification for its own sake, and also at improving the companies' technological capabilities (with hoped-for benefits for their manufacturing operations).

Has the de facto industrial policy of the United States government towards the motor vehicle industry therefore been a success? A successful industry policy must be able to pick winners and encourage them in a way that private markets would somehow fail to do, and/or it must help to accommodate the adjustments necessary for declining industries. It is clear that the policies towards the United States motor vehicle industry have not been designed to accommodate change and adjustment; rather, they have been designed to protect, revive and strengthen the industry. But is the industry a long-run winner? And even if it is, did it need the special help it was given? The answers to both questions are far from clear.

In the first place, at current exchange rates Japanese manufacturers still have a substantial cost advantage. (And, so long as the United States persists with fiscal policies that generate relatively low domestic rates of net saving, those exchange rates are likely to persist.) Domestic manufacturers still face high labour costs relative to those for all United States manufacturing and for Japanese vehicle manufacturers (Crandall, 1984; Munger, 1985), and it is unclear whether substitution of capital for labour and/or improved managerial practices (or improved work rules) can offset this wage structure. The industry, even with the Voluntary Restraint Agreement ended, has not been exposed to the full competitive force of an unshackled Japanese automobile industry, since the Japanese government, fearing a revival of United States protectionism, continues to restrain Japanese manufacturers. Further, United States truck production continues to benefit from a 25 per cent protective tariff wall. And it appears that Korean manufacturers, either alone or in conjunction with other manufacturers, may soon test the United States market.[24] (American manufacturers are forming alliances with Korean companies, so the effect of this entry may be felt less on domestic profits than on domestic employment.) Thus the true long-run competitive position and equilibrium size of the domestic industry in an unrestrained environment have yet to be determined.

Second, many of the industry's investments and efforts at cost reduction would probably have occurred anyway. The special externalities or market failures necessary to justify government intervention do not seem to have been present. The allocational costs have been high. And the precedents may come back to haunt future policymakers in even less worthy contexts.

Overall, then, with the exception of the regulatory changes, the de facto industrial policy of the United States with respect to the automobile industry has been costly; it may not have been necessary; and it may not have picked a winner. This author is not prepared to characterise it as a success.

One final point should be discussed with respect to a specific part of the de facto industrial policy—the Voluntary Restraint Agreement. Like most import quotas, the agreement allowed the scarcity rents to remain with overseas exporters, greatly magnifying the welfare loss to the United States economy. In the language of the geometry of welfare losses, though the deadweight-loss triangles of departures from competitive conditions are usually quite small, the Voluntary Restraint Agreement expanded them into much larger rectangles from the United States perspective.

There is an important political economy puzzle here. The voting public would surely remove from office any elected official who endorsed a policy of imposing tariffs on imports *and automatically sending the tariff revenues to the overseas exporters*. But this, of course, is exactly the effect of the Voluntary Restraint Agreement and other import quotas. Why does the United States political system persist in favouring quotas and 'orderly marketing arrangements' over tariffs? Is it purely administrative convenience and the preference for certainty with respect to quantity effects? Is it a consequence of the GATT's emphasis on tariffs? Is it a political economy compromise between the United States and its trading partners—'In return for letting us protect our industries, we will let you capture the scarcity rents on the restricted imports'? Are there other explanations?

Since import quotas will surely continue to play a role in American de facto industrial policy for other sectors, this topic bears further exploration.

11 Changing comparative advantage and trade and adjustment policies in the steel industry

CHONG HYUN NAM

Industries in the advanced industrialised countries rarely seem to adjust smoothly to changing comparative advantage. Their loss of comparative advantage in the textile, footwear and colour television industries, for example, was not accepted quietly. Trade suits were filed; orderly marketing arrangements or voluntary export restraint agreements were signed; and antidumping measures or countervailing duties were applied on a number of occasions. The steel industry was no exception. Faced with deteriorating international competitiveness and declining domestic demand since the late 1960s, many of the advanced industrialised economies have resorted to a range of import restrictions and other measures to support the industry and avoid a sudden rise in unemployment.

As far as the steel industry in developing countries is concerned, government intervention has also been the rule rather than the exception. But the motives for intervention have differed. For one thing, the steel industry has long been considered of vital strategic importance in an economy contemplating economic growth through industrialisation, since it is a principal supplier of inputs to a wide range of steel-intensive industries, and itself constitutes a significant manufacturing industry.

For another, the traditional steel-intensive industries, such as shipbuilding, metal fabrication and even the automobile industry, have been relocating internationally from the advanced industrial countries to some of the advanced developing countries. For these reasons many developing countries, particularly the advanced ones, have attempted to establish and promote the steel industry through various trade and industrial policies, often much earlier than would have been suggested by considerations of comparative advantage based on their factor endowments.

The steel industry seems, therefore, to offer valuable insights into the development of trade and industrial policies, particularly in relation to structural adjustment in both the advanced industrialised countries and the advanced developing countries in the face of shifts in comparative advantage. Government policies in these two groups of countries differ markedly as a result. Whereas policies in the industrialised countries aim to support and restructure a declining industry, governments in the advanced developing countries—

211

motivated by dynamic considerations of comparative advantage—have embarked on programs of 'picking winners', in which steel has figured prominently.

This chapter examines the main trends in international production and consumption of steel, and explains the migration of the industry from the advanced industrialised countries to the advanced developing countries. It begins with a background survey of trends in production, consumption and trade, principally since 1970. Then the factors underlying these trends are analysed with reference to the theory of changing comparative advantage. Finally, the more important issues raised by the international relocation of the industry are examined.

Two points should be stressed at the outset. First, the main emphasis is on steel manufacturing rather than steel-using activities. Much of what is referred to as the steel industry in developing countries is in fact the steel-using sector rather than primary steel-manufacturing capacity. Second, in examining the rise of the advanced developing economies as steel producers the main focus is on South Korea, although similar observations apply to several other newly emerging producers of steel.

GLOBAL TRENDS IN STEEL CONSUMPTION, PRODUCTION AND TRADE

Consumption

The principal cause of difficulties in the world steel industry since the 1970s has been the fall in demand. In particular, the collapse of the market in late 1974 and the continued stagnation over subsequent years precipitated the steel crisis in the advanced industrialised countries. Steel is a derived demand, determined by the growth of steel-intensive industries such as shipbuilding, automobiles, consumer durables and the construction industry. Structural changes in the steel-consuming industries of the advanced industrialised economies are reflected in trends in steel consumption. For instance, the United States and the European Community experienced a boom in steel-intensive industries in the 1950s and 1960s, but by the late 1960s the growth in steel consumption was already slowing down. In Japan, however, the average annual growth in steel demand was 13 per cent between 1964 and 1973, and it was not until 1974 that the growth in steel demand fell below that of GNP.

Global steel consumption increased by 17 per cent between 1970 and 1980, but absolute levels of steel consumption declined in the United States by 9.5 per cent and in the European Community by 15.8 per cent,[1] while in Japan over the same period there was a slight rise of 5 per cent (Table 11.1). Thus the sum of steel consumed by these regions—the United States, the European Community and Japan—decreased by 28 million tonnes, from 318 million tonnes in 1970 to 290 million tonnes in 1980, resulting in a decline of their

Table 11.1 Steel consumption trends in advanced industrial countries

	Consumption of crude steel (Mt)			Consumption of steel per capita (kg)			Steel intensity (kg/1975US$)	
	1970	1980	1982	1970	1980	1982	1970	1980
Japan	69.9	73.4	63.7	670	629	538	0.176	0.116
United States	127.6	115.6	84.3	623	519	636	0.121	0.080
European Community (7)	120.4	101.4	90.6	504	401	337	0.106	0.065
West Germany	45.0	33.8	31.0	669	549	436	0.107	0.067
France	23.8	20.6	17.5	458	385	318	0.083	0.052
United Kingdom	23.8	13.2	14.9	461	236	254	0.120	0.053
World	589.1	714.8	641.5	162	161	138	—	—
Japan plus United States plus European Community (7) as percentage of world total	54.0	40.6	37.2					

Sources: Korea Iron and Steel Association Iron and Steel Statistics Yearbook (various issues); C.H. Nam and Associates Development Patterns of the Steel Industry: An International Comparative Study Economic Development Institute, Korea University, 1983 p. 9

combined share in global steel consumption from 55 per cent to 41 per cent over the decade. It is worth noting that this change in steel consumption took place despite the growth of real GNP by 61 per cent in Japan, 36 per cent in the United States and 69 per cent in the European Community over this period, suggesting that economic growth was accompanied by substantial structural changes that reduced the 'steel intensity' in these countries.[2] The estimates of steel intensity for these countries, in fact, clearly showed a decreasing trend—from 0.176 to 0.116 in Japan, from 0.121 to 0.08 in the United States and from 0.106 to 0.065 in the European Community between 1970 and 1980.

On the other hand, the developing countries have experienced much faster growth in steel consumption than the world average. For example, between 1970 and 1978 global steel consumption increased by 22 per cent. But whereas consumption in developing countries more than doubled, in the advanced industrialised countries it fell by 2 per cent (IISI, 1980:17). The increase in the steel consumption of some advanced developing countries is even more astounding. Steel consumption in Korea, Taiwan and Mexico increased by 355 per cent, 534 per cent and 205 per cent respectively from 1970 to 1981 (Table 11.2). The growth of steel consumption far exceeded that of GNP in all three countries, resulting in sharp rises in steel intensities from 0.125 to 0.245 in Korea, from 0.09 to 0.238 in Taiwan, and from 0.064 to 0.107 in Mexico over this period. This implies that all these advanced developing countries experienced very rapid structural change towards more steel-intensive industries during the 1970–81 period. This trend is likely to continue for some time, as per capita steel consumption in these countries was still less than half that in the industrialised countries in 1981.

Table 11.2 Steel consumption trends in advanced developing countries

	Consumption of crude steel (kt)		Steel consumption per capita (kg)		Steel intensity (kg/1975US$)	
	1970	1981	1970	1981	1970	1981
Korea	1 643	7 482	51	193	0.125	0.245
Taiwan	982	6 221	67	343	0.090	0.238
Mexico	3 863	16 780	76	148	0.064	0.107

Source: C.H. Nam and Associates *Development Patterns of the Steel Industry: An International Comparative Study* Economic Development Institute, Korea University, 1983, p. 18

Production

The world steel industry grew steadily from 1950 to 1974, with production increasing at 6 per cent a year and reaching 704 million tonnes in 1974 (Table 11.3). Since then, however, the industry has declined: world steel production in 1983 was only 663 million tonnes, 6 per cent less than that of 1974, despite

Table 11.3   Crude steel production by major producing countries (million tonnes)

	1950	1974	1983
European Community (7)	—	155.0	108.5
United Kingdom	16.6	22.3	15.0
West Germany	12.1	53.2	35.7
France	8.7	27.0	17.6
United States	87.8	132.2	75.6
Japan	4.8	117.1	97.2
Korea	—	2.3	11.9
Taiwan	—	0.6	5.0
Mexico	—	5.1	6.8
Brazil	—	7.5	14.7
World	189.6	703.5	662.7

Source: Korea Iron and Steel Association *Iron & Steel Statistics Yearbook* (various issues)

a brief recovery in 1979. The decline has resulted in very low rates of capacity utilisation in the principal steel-producing countries—in 1983 about 50 per cent in the United States and the European Community, and only slightly above 60 per cent even in Japan (Korea Iron and Steel Association, 1984:235).

As well as considerable fluctuations in world steel output, there has been a continuous shift in the location of steel capacity since the second world war. For instance, the United Kingdom produced 8.8 per cent of the world's steel in 1950, but only 2.2 per cent in 1983. More importantly, United States production has declined from 46.3 per cent of world output in 1950 to 11.4 per cent in 1983.

Over this period several important new steel producers have emerged. Of the newcomers Japan exhibited the most rapid growth, from 2.6 per cent of world production in 1950 to 14.7 per cent in 1983. In 1980 its crude steel production of 111.4 million tonnes surpassed the United States figure (102 million tonnes) for the first time. Japan's production has not grown since 1973, however, when it reached a peak of 119.3 million tonnes; in fact, it fell to 97.2 million tonnes in 1983. During the 1970s it has been the newer steel-producing countries that have experienced the most rapid growth in output. The share of developing countries, which accounted for 7 per cent of production in 1970, grew rapidly to reach 13 per cent in 1978.[3] In particular, some of the advanced developing countries—including South Korea, Taiwan, Mexico and Brazil—turned in impressive growth performances during the 1970s. The sum of steel produced by these four countries was only 13.7 million tonnes in 1973, but by 1983 it had reached 38.4 million tonnes, increasing their combined share in world production from less than 2 per cent in 1973 to nearly 6 per cent in 1983. Of these four countries, Brazil became a net steel-exporting country in 1978 and South Korea in 1979. This suggests how the location of steel production is likely to shift in the future.

Table 11.4 Structure and growth of world steel trade

	1950		1970		1980		Average annual growth rates	
	Production (Mt)	Share in total trade (%)	Production (Mt)	Share in total trade (%)	Production (Mt)	Share in total trade (%)	1950–80 (%)	1970–80 (%)
Exports								
European Community (9)	8.4	65.9	18.9	31.8	29.0	29.6	4.2	4.4
North America	2.8	21.9	8.1	13.6	7.3	7.4	3.2	–9.9
Japan	0.5	4.3	17.6	29.5	29.7	30.3	14.2	5.4
East Europe and Russia	0.6	5.0	6.6	11.1	8.0	8.2	8.8	1.9
Others	0.4	2.9	8.3	14.1	24.0	24.5	14.6	11.2
World total	12.8	100.0	59.6	100.0	98.0	100.0	7.0	5.1
Imports								
European Community (9)	0.4	2.9	8.9	14.9	10.9	11.1	12.0	2.0
United States	1.1	8.7	11.8	19.9	13.7	14.0	8.7	1.5*
East Europe and Russia	0.3	2.1	3.6	6.0	7.9	8.1	11.9	8.2
Latin America	2.1	16.8	3.4	5.6	8.0	8.1	4.5	8.9
Africa and the Middle East	2.2	17.3	6.2	10.5	14.9	15.2	6.6	9.2
Asia and the Far East	1.9	14.6	8.6	14.4	22.2	22.6	8.6	9.9
Others	4.8	37.5	17.1	25.6	20.4	20.8	4.9	1.8
World total	12.8	100.0	59.6	100.0	98.0	100.0	7.0	5.1
World crude steel production	189.6		596.4		716.0		4.5	1.8

Note: These data exclude intra-European-Community and intra-Comecon trade.

Source: International Iron and Steel Institute Steel Statistical Yearbook 1981

Trade

World trade in steel products grew much faster than world steel production between 1950 and 1980 (Table 11.4). World trade in steel grew from 12.8 million tonnes in 1950 to 98 million tonnes in 1980, an average annual growth rate of 7 per cent. By contrast, world production grew at an average annual rate of 4.5 per cent for the same period. Even in the 1970s world trade in steel showed an annual growth rate of over 5 per cent, despite the considerable slowing down in production growth, which averaged only 1.8 per cent a year.

Table 11.4 shows the structure and growth of world steel trade, in which the changing pattern of steel trade is clearly demonstrated. In particular, there was a rapid decline in the shares of the United States and the European Community and a dramatic rise in the relative importance of Japan and other countries in world steel exports. For instance, during the period 1950 to 1980, the share of the European Community in total exports declined from 65.9 per cent to 29.6 per cent, and the share of North American exports decreased from 21.9 per cent to 7.4 per cent. In contrast, the share of Japan in world exports rose from 4.3 per cent in 1950 to over 30 per cent in 1980. The combined share of others, mostly western nations outside the European Community and developing countries, also showed a dramatic increase, from 2.9 per cent to 24.5 per cent for the same period. It is notable, however, that the shares of Japan and the European Community in world trade remained almost unchanged during the 1970s, but that the aggregate share of the others continued to grow, from 14.1 per cent to 24.5 per cent. This is largely a reflection of the fact that a growing percentage of world exports comes from western nations outside the European Community and from the advanced developing economies, including South Korea, Brazil and others.

Table 11.4 also shows the changing pattern of world steel imports over the same period. The most dramatic change that occurred in the period was, of course, the shift of the United States from the status of a major steel exporter to that of the single largest steel-importing country; the United States supplied 22 per cent of world exports of steel products in 1950, but was absorbing nearly 20 per cent of world steel imports by 1970. The developing countries, however, are still substantial net importers of steel products, though a small number of advanced developing countries are now emerging as net exporters. Among others, the countries in Asia and the Far East have had the fastest growing markets, increasing their combined import share from 14.4 per cent to 22.6 per cent during the 1970s. In 1980 Asia and the Far East, together with Latin America, Africa and the Middle East, accounted for more than 45 per cent of world steel imports. On the other hand, the aggregate import share of the United States and the European Community in world trade declined from 35 per cent to 25 per cent during the 1970s, reflecting primarily the general recession of steel markets in the advanced industrial countries, but also partly the effects of import controls, which were applied in a somewhat heavy-handed manner by these countries during that period.

CHANGING COMPARATIVE ADVANTAGE IN STEEL PRODUCTION

It has been shown that the decline of the steel industry in the advanced industrialised countries was the result of two main factors. The first of these, on the demand side, was the general economic slowdown in the 1970s, combined with substitution effects in important steel-using industries such as automobiles. The second was the international relocation of the industry and the emergence of several advanced developing economies as significant producers of steel. This section focuses on the second of these factors. Its purpose is to explore the determinants of comparative advantage in steel production in order to understand why the industry has begun to relocate from the industrialised to the developing countries.

What are the principal determinants of comparative advantage in steel manufacturing? According to the theory of factor proportions, steel is traditionally regarded as a (physical) capital-intensive industry, and its location in the advanced industrial countries has usually been explained in terms of the abundance of such capital in those countries. But such an explanation requires qualification. For one thing, physical-capital intensity of itself cannot, in the presence of open capital markets, be the principal factor, since capital is an internationally mobile factor of production. Moreover, during the 1970s the United States—the most 'capital-rich' country in the world—became a major steel importer, and some other industrialised economies also showed signs of becoming net importers of steel during this time. On the other hand, Japan became a major steel exporter at a time when it could appropriately have been classified as an advanced developing economy. More recently, Korea and some other developing countries have become net steel exporters. These trends are illustrated in Table 11.5, which computes net exports as a percentage of domestic supply for several countries over time.

An explanation of the location of the industry solely in terms of capital intensity is inadequate for another reason—that steel is generally not among the most capital-intensive industries. This is shown in Table 11.6, which presents alternative measures of factor intensity in steel manufacturing. Measure A represents a ratio of the value added per labour employed by the steel industry to that of the manufacturing-sector average, whereas measure B represents a ratio of the share of labour compensation in value added in the steel industry to that of the manufacturing-sector average. (Of course, neither of these is an unambiguous measure of capital intensity. For example, the differential structure of protection affects the usefulness of measure A as an indicator of capital intensity; similarly, measure B incorporates the costs of both skilled labour [that is, human-capital intensity] and unskilled labour. But taken together the two measures constitute useful general indicators.) Thus the steel industry can be classified as a relatively capital-intensive industry if measure A is greater than one, or if measure B is less than one. According to these measures, the steel industry tends to be relatively capital-

Table 11.5   Trade indexes in the steel industry (per cent)

	Average 1967−71	1976	1981
United States	−9.2	−9.6	−16.0
Japan	24.4	42.6	42.8
United Kingdom	10.7	−2.0	3.9
West Germany	11.0	9.2	15.2
France	5.8	−1.2	12.5
Korea	−58.6	−5.7	28.7

Note: The trade index equals (exports minus imports) divided by (domestic production plus imports)

Source: C.H. Nam and Associates *Development Patterns of the Steel Industry: An International Comparative Study* Economic
Development Institute, Korea University, 1983, p. 127

Table 11.6   Factor intensities in steel production

	1972			1978		
	Per capita GNP (US$)	A^a	B^b	Per capita GNP (US$)	A^a	B^b
United States	5678	1.03	1.21	9858	1.01	1.24
Japan	2841	1.46	0.96	8383	1.59	0.88
United Kingdom	2859	0.91	1.23	5652	0.85	1.36
West Germany	4207	1.07	1.00	10504	0.93	1.05
France	3788	—	0.69	8932	—	0.94
Korea	306	1.50	0.95	1279	1.74	0.85

Notes: a A = (value added per labour employed in the steel industry) divided by (value added per labour employed in the
manufacturing sector)
b B = (the share of labour compensation in value added for the steel industry) divided by (the share of labour
compensation in value added for the manufacturing sector)

Source: C.H. Nam and Associates *Development Patterns of the Steel Industry: An International Comparative Study* Economic
Development Institute, Korea University, 1983, p. 128

intensive in Japan, France, and Korea, whereas the reverse holds true in the
United States and the United Kingdom, and the position is indeterminate in
West Germany. In fact Crandall (1981:33) claims that the steel industry is even
more labour-intensive than the apparel and electronics industries on the basis
of measure B as calculated for the United States. But in addition to the
qualification mentioned above, it is likely that the labour intensities estimated
in Table 11.6 for the United States and the United Kingdom are substantial
overstatements because intervention by strong labour unions in the United
States and by government employment policies in the United Kingdom could
have distorted wage rates and employment in their steel industries.

For all these reasons, an explanation of the location of steel production in
terms of the traditional two-input factor proportions theory is unsatisfactory.
It is necessary as well to incorporate the effects of relative production costs
in steel manufacturing and the impact of other factors not easily captured
in the traditional factor-intensity theory, notably the age of capital stock
and intensities of scale. These issues are examined in the following two
subsections.

Trends in production costs

Accurate and detailed data on the costs of steel production for various countries are very difficult to obtain. Even if the relevant data are available, it is still difficult to make them internationally comparable because of differences in product mixture, quality of labour, degree of government intervention, and so on. However, the economics of the international steel trade have recently been intensively investigated by various institutions and individuals and a few useful estimates have become available. These include Marcus (1982), Mueller (1978, 1982), and the US Federal Trade Commission (1977), among others.

Table 11.7 presents a summary of inter-country cost comparisons made by Mueller (1978, 1982) for some of the main factors entering into the production of steel, such as energy, raw materials and labour. These data indicate that the inter-country differences in the costs of energy and raw materials have been almost eliminated over the period 1960–80, except perhaps for the United States. In fact, in 1960 the United States enjoyed an absolute cost advantage for energy and raw materials over both the European Community and Japan, but this advantage had disappeared by 1980 as falling costs of ocean transport increasingly favoured countries with plants located on the seaboard. By 1977 nearly 90 per cent of Japanese steel was being produced by seaboard-located plants, whereas only 18 per cent of United States steel was so produced. This,

Table 11.7 Trends in variable costs of steel production

| | Variable costs (US$/t) | | | |
	Energy	Raw materials (iron ore and scraps)	Labour	Total
1960				
United States	19.8 (18)	22.0 (20)	68.3 (62)	110.1 (100)
Japan	22.0 (22)	47.4 (48)	29.8 (30)	99.2 (100)
European Community (6)	22.5 (30)	26.5 (36)	25.4 (34)	74.4 (100)
1970				
United States	24.3 (18)	27.6 (21)	81.6 (61)	133.5 (100)
Japan	23.1 (29)	33.1 (41)	24.3 (30)	80.5 (100)
European Community (6)	24.3 (29)	23.1 (28)	36.4 (43)	83.8 (100)
1976				
United States	65.0 (25)	57.3 (22)	141.1 (53)	263.4 (100)
Japan	67.2 (39)	48.6 (29)	55.1 (32)	170.9 (100)
European Community (6)	77.2 (34)	48.5 (22)	100.3 (44)	226.0 (100)
1980–82				
United States	79.4 (19)	113.5 (27)	228.2 (54)	421.1 (100)
Japan	70.5 (29)	99.2 (40)	77.2 (31)	246.9 (100)
European Community (6)	68.3 (22)	110.2 (35)	137.8 (43)	316.3 (100)
Brazil	71.6 (31)	104.7 (45)	57.3 (24)	233.6 (100)
Korea	72.8 (36)	99.2 (50)	28.7 (14)	200.7 (100)

Note: The costs per net ton in Mueller's work were converted to costs per tonne using a conversion factor of 1 tonne = 1.1023 net tons.
Figures in parentheses represent percentages of total costs.

Source: Mueller (1978:3; 1982:47)

Table 11.8 Steel production costs: Japan and Korea (US$/tonne)

	Raw materials	Labour	Depreciation	Interest	Other costs	Total
1979						
Korea	177.6 (51)	21.3 (6)	58.9 (17)	36.3 (10)	56.8 (16)	349.9 (100)
Japan	189.9 (56)	70.5 (21)	27.2 (8)	27.9 (8)	24.5 (7)	339.2 (100)
Korea *minus* Japan	–11.5	–49.2	31.7	8.4	32.3	–9.3
1981						
Korea	213.8 (54)	–9.8 (5)	38.0 (19)	45.5 (12)	75.8 (19)	392.9 (100)
Japan	241.3 (56)	98.4 (23)	33.6 (8)	30.2 (7)	27.3 (6)	430.8 (100)
Korea *minus* Japan	–27.5	–78.6	4.4	15.3	48.5	–37.9

Note: Costs are estimated on the basis of production of ordinary carbon steel. Figures in parentheses represent percentages of total costs.

Source: C.-H. Nam and Associates *Development Patterns of the Steel Industry: An International Comparative Study* Economic Development Institute, Korea University, 1983, p. 156

however, does not constitute a major factor in inter-country cost differences. In 1980–82 Japan had a cost advantage over the United States of more than US$150 per tonne in labour alone, whereas its corresponding cost advantage in energy and raw materials was only US$25. It is therefore very clear that labour cost is an important factor in determining international cost differences in steel production. By 1970 Japan had become the most efficient major steel producer in the world in terms of labour cost, but its labour-cost edge was being seriously challenged by some of the advanced developing countries by 1980; for example, in 1980–82 the labour cost per tonne of steel produced in Korea was less than half that in Japan.

In order to make a better comparison between steel production costs in industrialised and developing economies, an attempt was made to estimate the relative production costs of steel for Japan and Korea, and the results are given in Table 11.8. The table clearly shows that Korea has an advantage over Japan, in terms of not only labour cost but also overall production costs, at least for ordinary carbon steel production. Similar patterns may be detected for other advanced developing countries.

Factors influencing production costs

International differences in the costs of steel production can be traced, in general, to two sources—differences in factor productivities and differences in factor prices. In the case of the steel industry, it is well known that the productivity levels of steel production factors are largely governed by the scale of production,[4] as well as by a variety of technologies that are mostly embodied in the physical plants. Consequently, newer and larger plants are generally more efficient than old plants. Table 11.9 gives some statistics on technology factors in steel production for the principal steel-producing countries. As expected, Japan and newcomers like Korea seem to be more favourably placed in terms of the age and scale of their plants. Japan is also very advanced in the adoption of continuous casting methods, resulting in a higher recovery rate as well as lower energy consumption.

These technology factors are also illustrated by the differences in labour productivity between countries (Table 11.10). Assuming a capacity utilisation rate of 90 per cent, labour productivity in Japan exceeds labour productivity in the other industrialised economies and Korea by 20–30 per cent. It should also be noted that labour productivity is greatly affected by the rate of capacity utilisation in the steel industry of each country.

The most important of the factor prices is wage rates, since the prices of other factors are not likely to vary internationally to the same extent. Hourly employment costs seem to differ widely, even among the industrialised economies (Table 11.10); in 1980, for example, they were about US$19 in the United States but only about US$10 in Japan and the United Kingdom and US$15 in West Germany and France. However, the greatest anomaly is in the Korean hourly wage; at US$2 it is only one-tenth that of the United States and

Table 11.9 Steel-technology factors in major producing countries

	Percentage of facilities ten years old or more		Scale: average of ten largest plants (Mt)	Ratio of continuous casting (1981; %)	Energy consumption (1978; million BTU)	Recovery rate (1978)
	Coke-oven	Cold-rolling				
United States	84	89	5.0	21.1	30.0	72
Japan	32	66	9.6	70.7	20.4	85
European Community	67	83	7.2		25.0	77
West Germany				53.6		
France				51.3		
United Kingdom				31.8		
Korea	0	0	8.5[a]	44.3	21.4	85.5[b]

Notes:
a The figure for Korea is based on one plant only.
b The figure for Korea is the author's estimate for 1981.

Sources: International Iron and Steel Institute *Steel Statistical Yearbook* 1981; Korea Iron and Steel Association *Iron & Steel Statistics Yearbook* (various issues); Mueller (1982)

Table 11.10 Labour productivity and costs in the steel industry, 1980

	Man-hours per tonne of production (mhs/t)		Hourly labour costs (US$/hr)	Labour cost per tonne of production (US$/t)	
	Current capacity utilisation rate	90% capacity utilisation rate		Current capacity utilisation rate	90% capacity utilisation rate
United States	9.6	9.0	19.1	183.4	171.9
Japan	9.2	7.4	10.2	93.7	75.5
West Germany	11.0	8.8	14.9	164.1	131.1
France	11.2	10.1	15.4	172.0	155.5
United Kingdom	41.2	10.0	10.0	410.1	123.0
Korea[a]	10.4		1.6	16.6	

Note: a The data for Korea are estimated by the author

Source: Marcus (1982)

one-fifth that of Japan, even though Korean labour productivity is already very close to that of the advanced industrialised countries. Furthermore, it is possible that hourly employment costs have been greatly distorted in some industrialised economies by the intervention of strong labour unions or by government policy. For instance, in 1981 hourly wage costs in the United States steel industry exceeded those for the manufacturing sector as a whole by almost 80 per cent, although the corresponding proportions were only 30 per cent in Japan and 21 per cent in the European Community (Mueller, 1982:29).

To sum up, a number of factors appear to be contributing to the progressive relocation of the steel industry in the advanced developing countries. One of these is that wages are significantly lower in these countries than in the advanced industrialised countries, a factor which, although very difficult to quantify, certainly confers a competitive edge on the developing countries at the margin. A second factor, equally difficult to quantify but perhaps more important, is the age of plant and equipment. Technological advances in steel production have been so extensive that newer equipment is substantially more efficient. The traditional steel producers—the United States and the European Community—saddled with a large stock of old equipment (see Table 11.9), have been unable to compete with the new producers—Japan in the 1960s and the advanced developing countries in the 1970s. The new technology embodied in the latest equipment may be one of the most important factors explaining international cost differences. Over and above this technological advantage, producers in some countries—notably Japan in the 1960s and more recently Korea—have been assisted by government subsidies, particularly through the capital market.

TRADE AND ADJUSTMENT POLICIES IN THE PRINCIPAL STEEL-PRODUCING COUNTRIES

One of the distinguishing features of the steel industry is extensive government intervention, in both developed and developing countries. The motivation for and nature of intervention, however, appear to have been widely different.

In developing countries, steel policy has generally been geared to promote investment in the steel industry or to expand national steel-producing capacity, initially aiming at self-sufficiency. This policy may be explained by the fact that steel is often viewed as a strategic industry since it supplies a major input to a wide range of steel-consuming industries. Thus adequate and assured availability of steel at stable prices has been considered a kind of prerequisite for industrialisation, and governments have not hesitated to provide the incentives necessary to induce investment in the industry. The construction of steel plants, however, requires large amounts of capital, often in excess of the capacity of the private sector in developing countries, particularly where capital markets are distorted. It is not surprising, therefore, that in nearly all developing countries, including the advanced ones, integrated steel plants have been introduced as state-owned or publicly controlled firms.[5] These firms

Table 11.11   Capacity utilisation rates in the steel industry in major producing countries (per cent)

	1966	1971	1975	1980	1982
United States	68.3	64.5	76.2	72.8	48.4
Japan	81.4	73.4	67.3	70.2	63.0
United Kingdom	96.5	79.7	73.0	40.3	54.4
West Germany	84.8	69.7	64.3	64.0	53.0
France	91.0	84.0	64.0	71.3	62.0
Korea	—	—	88.8	91.7	89.7

Source: Korea Iron and Steel Association *Iron & Steel Statistics Yearbook* (various issues)

initially aim at import substitution, but they can begin to export as soon as they attain international competitiveness. Some advanced developing countries, such as Korea and Taiwan, have already been successful in doing so. Both in Korea and Taiwan integrated steel plants were introduced as state-financed firms during the 1970s: the Pohang Iron and Steel Corporation of Korea completed its first phase of construction in 1973, and the China Steel Corporation did so in 1978. Since then both companies have grown exceptionally rapidly; in 1983 the Pohang Corporation produced more than 8.4 million tonnes of steel and the China Steel Corporation more than 3.4 million tonnes. One of the factors behind the success of these firms is that their management has been largely left to professionals, so that the separation between management and ownership has been firmly established. The contrary is often cited for less successful cases in many other developing countries, such as Mexico.

In contrast, recent steel policy in the advanced industrialised economies has been mostly concerned with falling demand as well as deteriorating international competitiveness. The fall in demand reflects, of course, the general worldwide recession, but also, and more importantly, long-term structural changes in the patterns of steel consumption in these countries. These changes in demand have resulted in persistent excess capacity in the advanced industrialised countries since the late 1960s (Table 11.11). As noted in the previous section, the loss in international competitiveness of the advanced industrialised economies basically reflects the shifts in comparative advantage in steel production.

These problems became particularly acute after the 1974 downturn in world markets. However, the need to adjust to such changes became apparent as early as the 1960s in some advanced industrialised countries as international frictions in the steel trade became more intense, particularly after the rapid growth of Japan and the relative decline of the United States as steel producers.[6]

In response to the sharp increase in imports in 1968, the United States negotiated voluntary export restraint agreements with Japanese and European exporters of steel to the United States. This move was initially intended to provide a temporary breathing space so that the United States steel industry could invest and thus improve its international competitiveness. The results suggest, however, that the reduction of import competition was used more as a way of improving profits than as an opportunity to restructure the industry.[7] According to estimates by Takacs (1975), the 1968 voluntary export restraints had the effect of raising United States steel prices by more than 10 per cent, but Crandall (1981:105–7) asserts that they would have increased capacity utilisation in the United States steel industry by less than 3 percentage points. In any case, the voluntary export restraints marked a sharp turnaround in the hitherto relatively free trade in steel products. In Europe, also, voluntary export restraints were negotiated with Japanese exporters, and imports from Eastern Europe were controlled by quotas.

In 1973 there was a rapid rise in world demand for steel, and the 1968 voluntary export restraints were phased out. But the unprecedented boom of 1973 was followed by a deep recession, beginning in late 1974 with the first oil crisis. Initially it was believed that the downturn was cyclical. But as the recession persisted through to 1977, steel producers and policymakers began to realise that they were confronted with more of a long-term structural crisis. Thus, the post-1974 world steel crisis resulted in increased government intervention, particularly in the advanced industrialised economies. First of all, public ownership or control of the steel industry increased significantly during the 1970s. The United Kingdom had already nationalised its steel industry in 1967, and large segments of the Italian, Belgian and French steel industries became publicly owned or controlled during the 1970s. In 1981 France finally nationalised its two largest steel producers, Usinor and Sacilor. Indeed, among the main advanced industrialised steel producers, the United States, Japan and West Germany are now perhaps the only countries whose steel industries remain under private control.

As steel market conditions continued to deteriorate, United States steel producers began to file petitions for antidumping or countervailing duty actions under the 1974 Trade Act, claiming that unfair competition from imports was the principal cause of injury to the United States steel industry, and also started to press hard for government help in the form of tighter import controls. The government's answer to this claim was the so-called 'Solomon Report (1978)', produced in December 1977, which laid out a comprehensive program for the ailing steel industry. The main objectives of the Solomon Report were to help the industry to compete fairly, and to ease the burden of adjustment to changing market forces for both industry and labour. The main instrument employed in this program was the trigger-price mechanism, which was a kind of compromise between efforts to avert bankruptcies of domestic firms and at the same time avoid serious damage to United States trade relations with Japan and the European Community. The trigger-price mechanism was an acceptable proposition to Europe and Japan, too, because it was seen as greatly preferable to the alternative approach of relying on antidumping investigations, which would have substantially increased uncertainties for European and Japanese exporters.

The 1978 trigger prices were based on Japanese unit costs of production plus freight from Japan. According to Crandall's (1981:108–115) price model, the average price increase due to the trigger-price mechanism was estimated to be 10.3 per cent and the market share of imports was expected to fall from 18 per cent to 11 per cent. In fact, however, import prices rose by 30 per cent and the market share of imports fell from 18 per cent to 15 per cent between 1977 to 1979, implying that the decline in the value of the dollar and general inflation had a much more powerful influence than the trigger-price mechanism. The market share of imports began to rise again in 1980.

As import penetration continued in the early 1980s, despite the trigger-price mechanism, United States steel producers again began to file antidumping suits against imports, mainly from the European Community, and the Commerce Department had to suspend the trigger-price mechanism in early 1982. But before the International Trade Commission reached a final ruling, the European Community agreed with the United States to limit its exports voluntarily until 1985 if the United States would abandon countervailing and antidumping actions. However, there has already been a relative shift in the pattern of United States imports, with Japanese and European exports slowly being replaced by exports from newly emerging steel producers. For instance, between 1976 and 1983 the combined share of Japan and the European Community in total United States imports declined from 68 per cent to 51 per cent, whereas the aggregate share of the newly emerging steel producers rose from 13 per cent to 26 per cent.[8]

Furthermore, the import penetration ratio reached over 20 per cent of apparent domestic consumption in 1983 and over 25 per cent in 1984. In response to this trend, the Bethlehem Steel Company and United Steelworkers filed a petition in early 1984 under Section 201 (the escape clause) of the 1974 Trade Act to limit the import share of the market to less than 15 per cent, and the International Trade Commission recommended a relief program to limit import penetration to a maximum of 18.5 per cent, thereby admitting material injury to the United States steel industry from the sudden rise in imports. The United States government has already concluded voluntary export restraint agreements with most steel-exporting countries in an attempt to limit import ratios to less than 20 per cent on average for the next five years.

In Europe, even long before the steel crisis, the steel industry was greatly affected by the formation of the European Coal and Steel Community after the Treaty of Paris in 1951. This organisation was certainly instrumental in expanding trade within the European Community, but it fell short of presenting a competitive market edge as if under one regime. Governments of the member countries were still allowed considerable autonomy in controlling their national steel industries with respect to investment financing, pricing, distribution, and so on. The European steel industry has therefore experienced a sort of oligopolistic equilibrium within the Coal and Steel Community, with the steel industries in member countries diverging in structure and performance. Apparently this was one of the reasons why the European Community's steel industry adjusted relatively slowly in the 1960s and entered the 1970s with a large segment of inefficient capacity. The slow pace of structural adjustment during the 1960s meant that the European Community's steel industry was particularly hard hit by the collapse of the steel market in 1974. Soon after the steel crisis began in late 1974, there were signs of ruinous competition within the European Community, and the prospect of massive bankruptcies and increased unemployment in areas that were heavily dependent on the steel industry. This led to a series of anticrisis measures by the Commission of the European Community. The commission has extensive powers of intervention granted by the European Coal and Steel Community under the Treaty of Paris, including powers to control prices, to establish production quotas, and even to levy taxes or penalties on countries or firms.

The commission first introduced voluntary measures in an attempt to stabilise the European steel market in 1975 (EC Commission, 1975), providing delivery guidelines first by country and then by firm.[9] As the market continued to deteriorate throughout 1977, however, the commission produced the first phase of the so-called 'Davignon Plan' in 1977, with the aim of reducing ruinous competition within the European Community and helping to ease the burden of structural adjustment for its steel industry. The main instruments used were mandatory minimum prices for trade within the European Community as an internal measure, and the basic price system for imports from outside the European Community, along with bilateral price and volume negotiations with the principal exporters, as external measures (EC Commission, 1977). The plan therefore amounted to an attempt to establish a sort of recession cartel through an institutional channel of the European Community. But it was not very successful because it lacked the power to use production quotas, which were necessary to support the minimum price system. Thus, as soon as the world steel market collapsed again in 1980, the EC Commission declared a 'manifest crisis', which was the precondition for establishing production quotas (Article 58 of the European Coal and Steel Community). The commission also tried to ensure that real adjustment took place by using the powers granted by the Treaty of Paris, because it was convinced by then that the problem was of a more long-term, structural nature. A comprehensive program, the second phase of the 'Davignon Plan', was therefore formulated by the commission in 1980. The program included such measures as compulsory production quotas by country and by firm; investment licensing on projects financed by governments or public funds; agreements incorporated in the Aid Code of 1981 to limit the abuse of subsidies by member countries;[10] and tighter import controls requiring exporters, given a global quota, to diversify in products and regions, and even to space out exports over time.[11] As well, the commission can restructure assistance through the European Investment Bank under Article 54 of the European Coal and Steel Community, and reconvert assistance through Article 56 for unemployment compensation, retraining and so on.

The second phase of the Davignon Plan was therefore an attempt to combine immediate anticrisis measures with longer term restructuring strategies. It was also a step towards the setting up of an improved recession cartel because it was equipped with production quotas. Experience suggests, however, that the continued use of short-term anti-crisis measures could considerably erode or adversely affect the long-term objective of structural adjustment.

Table 11.12 Non-tariff barriers in industrial countries by product category, 1983 (own imports coverage ratio; all exporters; per cent)

Industrial country market	All products	All except fuels	Fuels	Agriculture	Manufacturing	Textiles	Footwear	Iron and steel	Electrical machinery	Vehicles	Rest of manufacturing
European Community	22.3	21.1	24.4	36.4	18.7	52.0	9.5	52.6	13.4	45.3	10.3
Belgium–Luxembourg	26.0	33.9	10.0	55.9	33.6	38.3	12.3	47.4	19.5	54.3	30.6
Denmark	11.7	15.9	0.0	28.5	13.2	46.5	13.6	49.9	6.7	35.0	5.4
France	57.1	28.1	91.0	37.8	27.4	48.4	6.6	73.9	41.7	42.9	19.4
West Germany	12.4	18.3	0.0	22.3	18.5	57.0	9.7	53.5	6.8	52.0	6.6
Greece	13.4	23.2	0.0	46.4	20.4	21.8	22.8	54.5	13.5	65.5	8.5
Ireland	13.4	15.0	0.0	24.8	13.8	31.7	8.8	23.0	0.5	65.8	6.6
Italy	6.9	14.6	0.0	39.9	9.3	37.2	0.2	48.6	7.1	10.2	2.6
Netherlands	25.5	28.0	22.0	51.9	17.8	57.3	12.0	35.5	4.0	49.7	10.7
United Kingdom	14.3	17.5	0.0	34.9	14.8	59.6	12.2	42.1	12.7	44.3	6.7
Australia	34.1	24.1	98.0	36.1	23.6	30.9	50.0	55.6	48.7	0.7	21.6
Austria	4.9	6.0	1.0	41.7	2.4	2.2	0.1	0.0	0.0	2.9	3.0
Finland	34.9	9.2	94.0	31.5	6.7	31.0	68.8	43.9	0.0	0.0	0.4
Japan	11.9	16.9	7.0	42.9	7.7	11.8	34.1	0.0	0.0	0.0	7.7
Norway	5.7	5.8	5.0	24.2	4.1	42.9	5.4	0.1	0.0	0.2	0.4
Switzerland	32.2	23.6	94.0	73.4	17.6	57.4	0.0	3.9	28.1	1.1	14.6
United States	43.0	17.3	100.0	24.2	17.1	57.0	11.5	37.7	5.2	34.2	6.1
All sixteen markets	27.1	18.6	43.0	36.1	16.1	44.8	12.6	35.4	10.0	30.4	8.8

Source: J. Nogués, A. Olechowski and L.A. Winters 'The Extent of Non-tariff Barriers in Industrial Countries' World Bank Development Research Department Discussion Paper No. 115, Washington, DC, 1985

One of the common features of the steel policies adopted in both the United States and the European Community for the past ten years or so is that they have increasingly relied on restrictive trade policies to meet their objectives. As a result, iron and steel products, which enjoyed relatively free trade during the 1950s and early 1960s, have become increasingly subject to non-tariff barriers, next only to textiles in world trade in manufactures today. As can be seen from Table 11.12, 35.4 per cent of iron and steel imports in the sixteen advanced industrialised countries were subject to non-tariff barriers in 1983, whereas the proportion for the manufacturing sector as a whole was only 16.1 per cent.

In Japan, government intervention in the steel industry began in the 1950s when the Ministry of International Trade and Industry developed its rationalisation plan for the so-called basic industries, including electricity, coal, steel and shipping. The principal instrument employed was a system of preferential loans. However, the rationalisation efforts have largely shifted from government to the industry since the early 1960s. Also, the need for public intervention was greatly reduced as Nippon Steel increasingly assumed a leadership role in price determination, wage negotiations and so on. But the government often intervenes to make recommendations on various activities, including investment decisions. Indeed, this informal style of intervention by the government may have been much more effective than the formal intervention in many other advanced industrialised countries, given the well known degree of cooperation between the government and the business community in Japan.

The Japanese steel industry was also affected by the 1974 market downturn. But it entered the recession in a much better position than its competitors, in terms of production efficiency as well as financial strength. It was its financial strength that enabled the Japanese steel industry to continue investing in energy conservation and automation despite the recession. The increases in export prices due to the trigger-price mechanism and the basic-price system also enabled the industry to remain profitable, even though it was operating at only around 70 per cent or less of capacity. Evidently the industry also continued its efforts to develop new products with higher value added and to diversify into other industries. More recently, however, there have been indications that the Japanese edge has been dulled somewhat as some of the advanced developing countries have emerged as efficient producers of ordinary carbon steel products. In 1983 Japan's imports of ordinary carbon steel amounted to more than 3 million tonnes, of which two-thirds were supplied by Korea and Taiwan.

CONCLUSION

Historically the steel industry has been of strategic importance, mainly because it supplies a vital input to a wide range of steel-consuming industries. Indeed, the need for assured availability of steel at stable prices was a major factor in the decisions of many developing countries to establish national steel industries, perhaps even earlier than their factor endowments would have warranted. This argument, however, has lost much of its power, largely because of the free trade in steel products that has developed since the second world war. If there are problems with the international steel trade, they have more to do with excess capacities, dumping or subsidies than with shortages, monopolistic pricing or international cartels. In any case, there are many other intermediate goods that are as important as steel, or more important, in any modern industrial economy.

On the other hand, the main problems faced by the steel industries of most advanced industrialised economies since the 1970s can be traced to the need to adjust to falling demand and deteriorating international competitiveness. The fall in demand and the loss in international competitiveness were, of course, accelerated by the general worldwide recession. But basically they reflected long-term trends of shifts in the pattern of steel consumption and movements in comparative advantage, and they therefore presented a long-term restructuring problem for the steel industry in the advanced industrialised countries.

In general, restructuring involves rationalisation of production facilities by merging and modernising existing plants; by diversifying into higher-value-added products; by constructing new plants incorporating the best available technologies; or by moving out of the steel industry altogether. Most of these activities, however, can and should be carried out by the industry or the firms themselves. If there is any rationale for government intervention, it probably has to do with fostering an environment in which the steel industry can adjust to changing market forces smoothly and with the least disruption for the owners of capital and labour. Thus it might be suggested that government policies should be directed to providing reconversion assistance for those affected by plant closures, to facilitate restructuring.

Nonetheless, for many years steel producers in the advanced industrialised countries have claimed that unfair import competition has been the root of the problems that have undercut their attempts to restructure the steel industry. The most popular form of government intervention in these countries has been a trade policy to limit imports. This response may be understandable, especially as a short-term measure, but these restrictions have been in existence for more than ten years. Moreover, they are now stronger. When the trigger-price mechanism and the basic-price system did not achieve the original purpose, antidumping or countervailing actions were started, and finally bilateral voluntary export restraints on a global basis were sought by the United States and the European Community.

Thus, in assessing the steel policies of the advanced industrialised economies, attention must be paid to the effect of these essentially short-term trade policies on long-term structural changes in both industrialised and developing countries. Presumably the continued use of import restrictions has contributed to the increased profitability of the steel industry by raising prices as well as capacity utilisation rates, but only at the price of wasted resources and massive income transfer, delayed structural adjustment and an accelerated decline in the steel-intensive industries, many of which were already in trouble.

In the future, growth in world steel capacity is likely to occur predominantly in developing countries, particularly the advanced developing economies, due to rapidly rising domestic demand, improving international competitiveness and the age profile of their equipment.

12 Industrial policy for petrochemicals in selected Pacific Basin countries

AI TEE KOH

It is difficult to give a precise definition of the term 'petrochemicals'. According to John Wong,

> the category of chemicals called petrochemicals is understood differently in different countries. A narrow version of the industry is to confine it to the first-line raw materials and monomers; but a broader definition would include polymers and plastics, manmade fibers, fertilizers, pharmaceuticals and in fact, hundreds of other chemicals. Such a broader definition clearly brings the 'petrochemical industry' to overlap with the 'chemical industry'. (Wong, 1985:14)

Another commentator describes petrochemicals as 'chemicals directly derived from petroleum sources' (Menon, 1966:1). A more specific definition refers to the petrochemicals industry as

> ... the organic chemical industry which uses hydrogen carbon contained in petroleum or natural gas as its raw material. Ethylene, propylene, benzene, xylene, etc. are separated to produce intermediate products from which polyethylene, vinyl chloride, polypropylene, acrylonitrile, caprolactam and other derivatives are produced. At final stage, they are processed into plastic products, rubber products, textiles, etc.[1] (IDE, 1982b)

Figure 12.1 reproduces a flow chart showing the derivations of the end-products of the industry from raw materials through intermediate products. In general, the feedstocks on which petrochemicals are based take the forms of natural and associated gases, liquid naphtha, and solid petroleum products like petroleum coke and petroleum wax. Natural gas comprises mainly methane, ethane, propane, butane, pentane and hexane. It is found either associated with crude oil or non-associated. In its associated form it occurs as a solution gas, either dissolved in the oil or lying above the oil as a gas cap. The production of associated gases, therefore, is linked with the production of crude oil.

Given the diversity in the definitions of petrochemicals, this discussion of industrial policy for petrochemicals will highlight such differences where they

Figure 12.1 Flow chart for petrochemicals

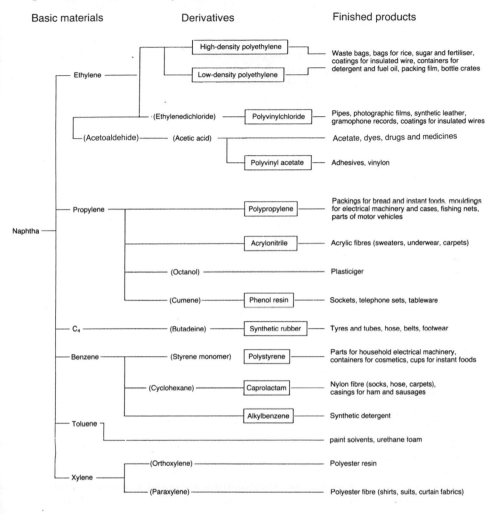

Basic materials   Derivatives   Finished products

arise and make appropriate provisions for cross-country comparisons or the like.

The first section provides an overview of the world petrochemicals industry in terms of certain salient characteristics and development features. This is followed by some discussion of industrial policy for petrochemicals in the main production centres of the United States, Europe and Japan. The next section examines in greater detail and as case studies industrial policy for petrochemicals in Japan, Singapore and the Philippines, and finally some concluding remarks are offered.

THE WORLD PETROCHEMICALS INDUSTRY

Some characteristics

According to a UNIDO report, the petrochemicals industry accounts for some 25 per cent of the chemical industry's turnover and provides the basic inputs for all organic chemicals. The main users of petrochemicals are the packaging, building, construction, textile and transportation industries, which on average absorb two-thirds of a country's consumption of petrochemicals (UNIDO, 1983:314).

The output of the petrochemicals industry is accounted for mainly by four industrial branches: industrial chemicals (ISIC 351); other chemical products (ISIC 352); rubber products (ISIC 355); and plastic products (ISIC 356). In 1979 these four branches accounted for 13.9 per cent of total manufacturing value added in the developed market economies and the developing countries (UNIDO, 1983:Table III.5). The developed market economies continue to account for the major share of world output of these four branches, although their shares have declined over time (UNIDO, 1983:Table III.7). Conversely, the shares of the developing countries have increased.

Plastics alone account for approximately half the final products of the industry, followed by synthetic fibres (25 per cent), with the rest shared by synthetic rubbers, paints, detergents, and so forth (IDE, 1982b:235). The development of the petrochemicals industry is therefore highly correlated with that of the plastics industry. The five main plastics are high-density polyethylene, low-density polyethylene, polyvinyl chloride, polystyrene and polypropylene.

The growth of international trade in chemicals has roughly paralleled that of international trade in general. It represented 7.7 per cent of the value of trade in 1980, a slight rise from the 1973 figure of 7.3 per cent. Between 1973 and 1980 chemicals trade fluctuated between 7.2 per cent and 8.0 per cent of world trade. Over the same period it averaged 10.3 per cent of exports from the developed market economies, while its shares of exports from the centrally planned economies and the non-oil-exporting developing countries were 5.0 per cent and 3.0 per cent respectively. No group of countries displayed any marked trend, nor was any trend observable in the shares of individual countries. During this period, the developed market economies accounted for a virtually stable 86 per cent of all chemicals exports. The corresponding share for the centrally planned economies was just over 6 per cent, and that for the non-oil-exporting developing countries was 5 per cent (UNIDO, 1983:314–15).

Development: past, present and future

Until the second world war the chemicals industry based on petroleum was known only in the United States, where the industry was then in its infant stage. It was immediately after the war that the growth of the petrochemicals industry became spectacular. By 1964 more than 3000 chemicals were being produced from petroleum sources. During this period, in the United States alone, more than 75 per cent of the organic chemicals produced belonged to the petrochemicals group. In Western Europe the production of petrochemicals accelerated from only 3000 tonnes in 1944 to nearly 2 million tonnes in 1964 (Menon, 1966:1).

The 1960s saw extremely rapid growth in the chemicals industry and its petrochemicals adjuncts. This was particularly true of the developed market economies, where chemicals was consistently the fastest growing branch of industry from the late 1950s to the later 1960s, recording growth rates nearly twice those of manufacturing overall (UNIDO, 1981:113). This was the outgrowth of two forces. On the supply side, technological innovations in products such as high-density polyethylene opened up new uses for plastic, which was increasingly used to substitute for wood, metal, glass, paper and other materials. Polypropylene replaced hessian, rope and twine in the production of sacking and related products. The growth of production led to exploitation of economies of scale and cost reductions, thus further facilitating the development of the industry. In a span of twenty years (1955–75) the annual world output of plastics grew from 5 million tonnes to 40 million tonnes. On the demand side, the relatively high and stable GDP growth rates being enjoyed across the world over the same period raised worldwide demand for many consumer durables (for example, cars and household appliances) whose production increasingly employed plastics. The growth in real incomes also fuelled the demand for new and more health-related chemical products such as pharmaceuticals.

This scenario was not sustained in the late 1960s and 1970s, which witnessed a substantial deceleration in the demand for chemical products for the following reasons. First, the growth of real GDP in the developed market economies slackened considerably, depressing the growth rate of overall demand for chemicals-using products. Second, the oil price shocks of 1973–74 and 1979–80 raised the costs of oil-derived products and hence encouraged the search for more energy-conserving modes of production and less energy-intensive product mixtures.

In the belief that the demand for petrochemicals products would continue to outstrip industrial output generally, planners reacted only slowly to the deceleration in demand that had become evident by the 1970s. The advent of the world recession in the late 1970s and early 1980s thus created serious problems of overcapacity in the industry, particularly in Europe and to some extent in Japan. Base chemicals and the five main plastics were particularly hard hit in Western Europe, where ethylene and polypropylene producers are carrying overcapacities of 29 per cent and 30 per cent respectively (UNIDO, 1983:322).[2]

The problems of excess capacity for existing firms in the industry have been exacerbated by the emergence in the 1980s of new supply sources that are threatening to depress further an already soft market. The foremost of these is the planned growth in production of petrochemicals in certain OPEC countries, particularly Saudi Arabia. According to UNIDO,

> the interest in petrochemical production follows from OPEC's enhanced oil refining plans since 1973. The adjustment of oil prices in that year, with its attendant increments to government revenues, helped concretize a long-standing intention to invest more heavily in processing oil, rather than merely exporting it in crude form. (UNIDO, 1983:317)

The ability to supply oil and gas inputs at extremely low cost to their petrochemical plants appears to be an important motivating force for the OPEC interest in petrochemicals.[3] Despite initial higher capital costs for the OPEC projects, the UNIDO report is of the opinion that there is substantial scope for competitive pricing by new OPEC producers vis-à-vis existing ones. The estimate is that by the late 1980s petrochemical plants in Saudi Arabia alone will be able to meet world needs as follows: methanol, 8.5 per cent; ethylene glycol, 7.2 per cent; ethanol, 7.0 per cent; and ethylene, polyethylene, styrene and urea, 1.0–2.5 per cent. By 1990 this region could be supplying around 10 per cent of Europe's base chemical needs (*Arabia*, December 1981, p. 76).

Another factor in the supply equation is Canada, which promises to become an important new source of traded petrochemicals in the 1980s. This has been the result of the imposition of price controls on natural gas in Canada on the one hand, and the United States trend towards decontrol of energy prices on the other. The outcome of these developments is a substantial relocation of American investment into petrochemicals in Canada, where production costs are lower than at home. It is estimated that between 1982 and 1986, some US$6.5–8.0 billion will have been invested, mostly in Alberta, in petrochemicals capacity. As a result, Canadian plants are expected to double, to 6 per cent, their share of world petrochemicals output by the late 1980s (UNIDO, 1983:321–22).[4]

In spite of these problems, the prospects for the world petrochemicals industry are not all that gloomy. There is widespread agreement within the industry that the demand for petrochemicals will continue to grow, albeit more slowly than in the boom period of the 1960s (UNIDO, 1983:323, Table XI.3). One reason for this optimism, in the case of plastics at least, is that demand for plastics in the automobile industry is forecast to grow considerably in the 1980s. Continuing their search for weight reduction, automobile manufacturers are expected to reduce by 26 per cent the average amount of steel used in each vehicle between 1980 and 1985, and to increase the amount of plastic used by 37 per cent.[5] Further penetration of the automobile industry could occur if such parts as wings were moulded from plastic. The substitutions now considered feasible could roughly double the weight of plastic used in a car. Another area with growth potential is the production of food containers, especially in view of the high energy costs of making containers from glass and tin.

The foregoing discussion suggests two prospective scenarios. On the international trade front, the high likelihood of penetration of Canadian exports into the United States market will probably induce American exporters to push hard for new export markets, particularly in Europe. This, together with the increasing penetration of Middle Eastern chemicals into Europe, will mean an erosion of the dominant position of European chemicals producers as net exporters. Second, the anatomy of the petrochemicals industry is expected to undergo increasing transformation as a result of firms' reactions to the problems facing the industry. One notable feature has been the move by many existing firms to scale down their production of bulk petrochemicals in order to move downstream and concentrate on speciality items (such as resins, solvents, lubricant additives, oil-field chemicals and synthetic elastomers) as well as pharmaceutical products (UNIDO, 1983:324). Since these are items that are high in value added, require sophisticated marketing and advertising skills and are intensive in research and development, such emphasis tends to characterise petrochemicals producers in the developed countries. In sum, the late 1980s are likely to witness a gradual shift in the centres of bulk petrochemicals production away from the older centres of Europe, the United States and Japan towards the oil-rich countries of the Middle East. Established producers in the developed countries are likely to restructure and refine their output towards products such as speciality chemicals and pharmaceuticals where they have a greater comparative advantage.

INDUSTRIAL POLICY IN THE MAIN PRODUCTION CENTRES

The problems and opportunities facing producers of chemicals and petrochemicals cannot be fully understood without relating them to actions taken by government policymakers. This section looks briefly at some broad aspects of industrial policy in the main petrochemicals production centres of the United States and Europe. (Japanese industrial policy is examined in a later section.)

According to UNIDO, the history of government involvement in the petrochemicals industry in the United States is quite different from its history in Europe and Japan. In the postwar period,

> an extremely complex set of laws governing oil taxation came into force, which led to a proliferation of small-scale oil refineries as well as—until very recently—very competitive and profitable oil and gas-based chemical operations . . . The November 1974 Entitlements Programme allowed for the subsidization of imported oil and the award of certain benefits to small refiners: those with secured access to United States price-controlled oil had to compensate those without. (UNIDO, 1983:332)

A major consequence of this policy was rapid growth in the petrochemicals exports of American firms. The industry's trade surplus grew consistently throughout the 1970s, reaching US$10 billion in 1979. Export sales eventually accounted for between 11 per cent (in the cases of ethylene and butadeine) and

33 per cent (for polyxylene) of total output. Imports of these products, by contrast, accounted for under 2 per cent of total demand. The same study reports on the European petrochemicals industry as follows:

> By mid-1982, European petrochemical producers were estimated to be losing $200 million a month, and several of them requested the Industry Commissioner of the EEC to sanction open discussions on closures. The Treaty of Rome's anti-cartel rule prohibits collusion among firms on such matters as price or capacity, so what was needed was a dispensation to begin talks. So far, only outline talks have been undertaken, with different companies' representatives urging one another to desist from dumping. (UNIDO, 1983:330)

Suggestions had also been made by the largely state-owned French and Italian industries to set up a Europe-wide cartel, similar in certain respects to the one established for the steel industry, in order to coordinate redundancies. However, the UNIDO report takes the view that it is unlikely that any action will be taken on the matter until the European Council of Chemical Manufacturers' Federations has reached a decision on whether market forces alone should be allowed to trim the industry. In any event, European subsidiaries of American-owned petrochemicals and plastics firms would not be allowed to participate in this proposed 'crisis cartel' because of United States antitrust legislation.

CASE STUDIES

Japan

Basic features

In terms of relative importance, the Japanese petrochemicals industry contributed about 10 per cent of the 1980 world ethylene output of 54 million tonnes. This share is equal to that of the USSR and East Europe combined, but considerably lower than the North American and Western European shares of one-third each (IDE, 1982b:Table 10.1). Although the share of the less developed regions is increasing gradually, it is still very low, even in terms of the prediction for 1985. In terms of world plastics materials production, the Japanese share in 1980 increased slightly to 12.5 per cent (IDE, 1982b:Table 10.2). The rankings of North America and Western Europe were reversed and the share of the USSR and East Europe increased, thus reducing the share of the less developed countries.

The dynamics of demand and supply over the two decades from 1960 to 1980 are shown in Table 12.1. As is evident from the table, substantial investments in the petrochemicals and plastics industries in Japan were concentrated in the latter half of the 1960s. Trends in consumption per capita in general paralleled those of production. Towards the late 1970s Japan's trade surplus in plastics had been eroded because imports had increased and there

Table 12.1 Japan: demand, supply and per capita consumption of plastics, 1960–80

	1960	1965	1970	1975	1980	Average annual rate of increase (%)	
						1960–70	1970–80
Production (kt)	554	1601	5127	5167	7518	24.9	3.9
Exports (kt)	51	250	1029	1259	1112	35.9	0.1
Imports (kt)	41	23	52	78	294	2.4	18.9
Domestic consumption (kt)	544	1373	4080	3986	6700	22.3	5.1
Population (million)	93	98	104	110	117	1.1	1.2
Per capita consumption (kg)	5.8	14.0	39.1	35.9	57.2	20.8	3.9

Source: IDE (1982b)

had been no rise in exports, which held steady at 1.1 million tonnes. Export growth trailed that of imports by a substantial margin in the 1970s, a completely different scenario from the 1960s, when exports grew at an extremely strong annual rate of 36 per cent, compared to a meagre 2 per cent for imports.

Table 12.2 shows the relative position of plastics materials and products industries in the manufacturing sector in Japan vis-à-vis other Asian countries. In general, in terms of value added, employment, exports and number of establishments, the plastics materials and products industries occupy a share of less than 3.5 per cent in the overall manufacturing sector. This is also true for most other Asian countries, with the exception of Taiwan and Hong Kong, where the shares can rise to 9–11 per cent.

Problems

The Japanese petrochemicals industry is suffering at present from structural depression, with substantial losses because of the rapid price hike of petroleum, which accounts for some 70 per cent of the total production cost. This is compounded by faltering domestic demand arising not only from the depression of the entire market but also from the trend towards deriving energy from coal instead of petroleum and from the drop in consumption owing to the energy-saving efforts of the energy-intensive iron and steel and cement industries. These effects are particularly severe for the petroleum refinery sector, which operates upstream of the petrochemicals industry.

The outcome has been a serious underutilisation of capacity as well as a loss of competitive edge, particularly to Middle East countries, the United States and Canada, which are blessed with indigenous feedstock. United States petrochemicals, for instance, started penetrating the Japanese market in 1979, and at the same time began to erode Japan's share of the Southeast Asian markets, which had been Japan's largest export markets (IDE, 1982b:225).[6]

Table 12.2 Positions of the plastics materials and plastics products industries in the Asian manufacturing industries

	Japan 1978	Korea 1978	Taiwan 1977	Hong Kong 1978	Singapore 1979	Philippines 1977	Thailand 1978	Malaysia 1974	Indonesia 1978
Number of establishments									
1 Plastics materials	244	445	—	41	—	17	7	—	10
2 Plastics products	25 481	623	5 068	4 515	188	234	460	173	218
3 Manufacturing	744 897	29 864	93 169	41 240	3 137	74 641		4 696	7 955
1/3 (per cent)	0.03	1.5		0.9		0.02			0.1
2/3 (per cent)	3.4	2.1	5.4	10.9	6.0	0.3		3.7	2.7
Value added (million US$)									
4 Plastics materials	5 085	269		15		—			0.2
5 Plastics products	8 476	224	280	362	63	31	48	20	27
6 Manufacturing	293 414	16 927	8 744	4 178	2 991	1 705	3 412	1 149	2 281
4/6 (per cent)	1.7	1.6		0.4		—			—
5/6 (per cent)	2.9	1.3	3.2	8.7	2.1	1.8	1.4	1.7	1.2
Number of employees ('000)									
7 Plastics materials	89	24	9	0.3	—	2.7	2.6		0.3
8 Plastics products	336	32	158	87	8.6	19.3	34	8	15.2
9 Manufacturing	10 931	2 112	1 764	817	271.4	778.0	1 327	261	821.1
7/9 (per cent)	0.8	1.1		—		0.3			2.0
8/9 (per cent)	3.1	1.5	9.5	10.6	3.2	2.5	2.6	3.2	1.9
Exports, 1978 (million US$)									
10 Plastics materials	1 313	32	79	35	52	8.8	5.7	6.0	0.1
11 Plastics products	149	60	354	139	17	4.1	9.9	7.9	0.3
12 Manufacturing	84 874	10 956	10 925	10 127	4 309	680.0	868.0	897.0	203.0
10/12 (per cent)	1.5	0.3	0.7	0.3	1.2	1.3	0.7	0.7	—
11/12 (per cent)	0.2	0.5	3.2	1.4	0.4	0.6	1.1	0.9	—

Notes: Plastics materials—ISIC 3511; SITC 581. Plastics products—ISIC 356; SITC 893.

Sources: IDE, CAM country reports; UN *Yearbook of Industrial Statistics* 1979, *Yearbook of International Trade Statistics* 1979

Industrial policy

Since its inception in the mid-1950s, Japan's industrial policy for the petrochemicals industry has undergone severe changes in response to internal and
external developments. Since the goals of industrial policy in the 1960s were to
encourage rapid economic growth through special emphasis on promoting high
income elasticity and high-productivity activities, the petrochemicals industry
was actively encouraged through various fiscal and tax measures. On top of
this, external factors in the shape of a strong demand for petrochemicals and
cheap petroleum feedstock further boosted the industry. The Petroleum Act,
which favoured setting up indigenous refining capacity through restricting
naphtha imports, was originally intended to promote the petrochemicals industry by supplying it with domestically generated feedstock.

With the reversal in the industry's fortunes since the mid-1970s, policy
actions to reduce excess capacity in bulk products have been similar to those
that created the original excess. In the 1960s the Ministry of International
Trade and Industry assisted firms with tax concessions and subsidies, and
ethylene output grew at an average annual rate of 30 per cent between 1965
and 1970. In view of the current situation, where some 30 per cent of the
country's 6.2 million tonnes of ethylene capacity is surplus to needs, MITI is
providing a framework for firms to restructure. Measures towards this end
include the following:

1 Encouraging higher expenditure on research and development, with
   a view towards moving into more technology-intensive downstream
   products (such as speciality chemicals and pharmaceuticals) and away
   from production of bulk petrochemicals, in which Japan is suffering from
   comparative disadvantage because of higher feedstock costs. The latter
   problem is less important for downstream products, which are less energy-
   intensive.

2 Arranging mergers to cut costs and realise economies of scale.

3 Promoting overseas joint ventures, particularly with a view to securing a
   cheaper and more stable supply of feedstock.[7]

4 Pursuing a 'scrap and build' policy whereby old capacity is replaced by
   more modern and efficient capacity of similar size.

By and large, industrial policy for petrochemicals in Japan can be described
as oriented towards positive adjustment, in that it recognises and moves along
with economic change—in this case, the loss of comparative advantage in
feedstock-intensive upstream activities and the need to move downstream or
relocate elsewhere where such advantage can be maintained. Since this is a
move in the right direction, it is only a matter of time until Japan's restructuring efforts bear fruit.[8]

Singapore

Background

The petrochemicals industry in Singapore has an extremely short history; it started operating in February 1984.[9] The S$2 billion project reflects in part the government's policy shift to diversify the manufacturing base away from overdependence on the embattled oil-refining sector towards downstream operations. It is also in line with the government's emphasis since the early 1970s on moving out of labour-intensive operations towards more capital- and technology-intensive activities. The petrochemicals industry, with its characteristics of scale economies, high capital investment, dependence on sophisticated technology and low labour intensity, appears to fit this criterion.

However, between the conception of the complex more than ten years ago and its establishment in 1984, teams of officials were continually flying between Singapore and Tokyo to thrash out countless knotty problems. One of these, which cropped up after the project was almost mechanically complete, was the falling prices of petrochemicals. Both sides argued long over the wisdom of starting up the complex in the face of poor market prospects. Eventually the decision went in favour of going ahead with the project instead of waiting for market conditions to improve. The rationale for this was to allow the complex to establish its name earlier (*Straits Times* 10 March 1985).

The project comprises an upstream plant and four downstream plants. The former is operated by the Petrochemical Corporation of Singapore, while the downstream plants are run by the Polyolefin Company, Phillips Petroleum Singapore Chemicals, Denka Singapore and Ethylene Glycols Singapore.[10] Three of the downstream plants started operations in February–March 1984, and Ethylene Glycols commenced activity a year later, in March 1985.[11]

Performance and challenges

Since it started up in February 1984, the industry in Singapore has suffered losses. The Petrochemical Corporation of Singapore alone has lost S$30 million, although this loss is nowhere near as high as expected. According to Dr Han Cheng Fong, the corporation's deputy managing director, it was 'a good first year, considering high initial start-up costs, costly feedstocks in the early part of last year and the fact that the main cracker was only operating at 67 per cent capacity because one of the downstream plants was still being built' (*Business Times* 9 March 1985). Denka Singapore was also hard hit, with the lowest utilisation rate (65 per cent) among the three operational downstream plants. Phillips Petroleum and the Polyolefin Company performed much better in terms of capacity utilisation (Table 12.3). The sales performance of the whole complex would have been better had it not been affected by a fire at Polyolefin in April 1984, which necessitated a 40-day shutdown in October for maintenance.

On top of problems associated with the general worldwide slowdown in the

Table 12.3 Design capacity and sales revenue of Singapore's petrochemicals complex, 1984–85

	1984		1985	
	Percentage of design capacity	Sales revenue (million S$)	Expected percentage of design capacity	Expected sales revenue (million S$)
Petrochemical Corporation of Singapore	67	318	87	435
Polyolefin Company	93	245	100	300
Phillips Petroleum	90	82	109[a]	120
Denka Singapore	65	5.5	95	20
Ethylene Glycols[b]	—	—	100	75

Notes: a This figure is technically possible because the company installed equipment intended for a larger design plant.
b Ethylene Glycols began operation in 1985.

Source: *Business Times* 8 March 1985

demand for petrochemicals, the most immediate challenge to the Singapore petrochemicals industry on the supply side is the impending competition from new Saudi petrochemicals that came on stream in early 1985. At the time of writing the Saudis have not yet started exporting to Southeast Asia, but the psychological impact was already being felt by the end of 1984, when prices, particularly of low-density polyethylene, started tumbling by as much as US$50 a tonne. The basic fear is the pricing of Saudi chemicals below prevailing market prices, a move that is feasible in view of the almost zero-cost natural-gas feedstock on which Saudi chemicals are based. Already the Saudis are pitching their low-density polyethylene in Europe at US$500 a tonne, exactly US$50 cheaper than the price charged by Singapore's Polyolefin Company. The latter's fear is that customers who make plastic bags out of low-density polyethylene film may convert their plants to use the Saudi product instead if it is US$50 a tonne cheaper.[12]

Another big worry is the protectionist barriers that the United States and Europe might put up against Saudi products. If these two big markets close their doors, the Saudis' alternative outlet is the Far East. This will cut into the markets that the Singapore complex is selling to—ASEAN, Hong Kong, China and Japan. Recourse to the domestic market is not viable because its size is limited. Furthermore, there is the possible influx of cheap ethane-based Canadian petrochemicals, with China as their main target. Again, such a development will undermine Singapore's market share there.

Closer to home, recent sentiments expressed by Thailand and Malaysia in favour of setting up their own petrochemicals industries are another source of great concern. In March 1984 the Thai National Petrochemical Corporation started looking for an international engineering consultant to direct feasibility studies for their project, which is designed with the domestic market in mind.

The corporation plans to use natural-gas fractions produced by the Petro-leum Authority of Thailand's gas separation plant (*Straits Times* 23 March 1984).[13]

The desire for self-sufficiency also prevails in Malaysia, which seems to be reviving plans for its own plant. At a joint Malaysia–Japan Economic Associa-tions Forum on 6 March 1984, Malaysia made a bid for Japanese participa-tion in the project.[14] On the assumption that it takes at least five years to build a petrochemicals plant from scratch, the Thai and Malaysian plans, should they materialise, would pose a long-term threat to the Singapore plant.

Industrial policy measures

Policy measures relating to the petrochemicals industry may be conveniently divided into those that initiated and helped get the project on its feet and those that represent responses or adjustments to the challenges posed by external developments.

It seems reasonable to say that the most important support given to the industry is in terms of the government's own degree of involvement—a 30–50 per cent stake in the petrochemicals companies. The companies also enjoy pioneer status, industrial land at concessional rates, and other fiscal and financial incentives. These measures are by no means peculiar to Singapore. Other countries starting on petrochemicals for the first time (such as Japan and Korea) had previously adopted fairly similar measures.

In an attempt to meet the challenges, government authorities have also embarked on a host of measures to cut costs, search aggressively for new markets and upgrade and diversify existing operations, as well as venturing into new areas of development.

One cost-cutting measure has been to extend the search for cheaper feed-stocks of liquefied petroleum gas beyond Indonesia and the local oil refineries to Burma and China. In March 1985, officials of the Petrochemical Corpora-tion of Singapore indicated that Burma could start supplying liquefied pet-roleum gas by the end of the year. China has become a promising source since it began sending more crude oil to Singapore for refining. The corporation hopes to deal directly with China on a barter basis, whereby Singapore will supply petrochemicals in exchange for Chinese feedstock.

Another (short-term) strategy to stay afloat has been the recent tendency among local oil refiners to buy more discounted crude oil on the spot market instead of purchasing on long-term contracts. The resultant lower cost of crude oil benefits the petrochemicals industry in terms of lower feedstock costs. This strategy, however, is viable only for as long as the global oil situation remains weak and while there is rampant price undercutting between OPEC and non-OPEC oil producers.

Yet another cost-cutting measure, as outlined by Dr Han Cheng Fong (the deputy managing director of the Petrochemical Corporation of Singapore), is the replacement of the fairly sizeable expatriate staff on the complex by local personnel as soon as they are ready to take over. Dr Han has acknowledged·.

that keeping expatriate staff in Singapore is expensive (*Straits Times* 9 March 1985).

A continual and relentless reach is being seriously pursued for new markets as far away as the United States, taking into consideration freight costs. Even Japan is under closer scrutiny to see where certain Singapore-manufactured products that have not reached their maximum quotas can further penetrate an already tough market.

Meanwhile, plans are being made to improve the performance of the existing complex. Inhouse studies have been under way since early in 1985 to examine the feasibility of adding a new plant to the complex to absorb and process the surplus petrochemicals that are now exported at low prices. Processing them further in Singapore would enhance their value added.[15]

As part of a wider diversification drive to cushion the manufacturing sector from overdependence on the oil industry, including petrochemicals, one of the recent moves in the government's restructuring effort has been to encourage the development of pharmaceuticals and speciality chemicals, which have been the prime movers of the chemical industry in recent years. The speciality chemicals industry, although small, has been identified by the Economic Development Board for priority development, as its knowledge-intensive and very high value-added aspects fit in well with the government's restructuring efforts.[16]

These efforts have met with a fair degree of success. Thus late 1982 saw the setting up of some pharmaceuticals projects, the chief of which is the S$120 million Glaxochem plant to produce ulcer medication. In 1983 expansion activities were conducted for some existing speciality chemicals projects such as Nalco Southeast Asia, Ferro Southeast Asia and Agfa-Gavaert, a division of Bayer. More significantly, 1984 witnessed the establishment of two leading manufacturers of speciality chemicals, Lubrizol and Hunt Chemicals (*Business Times* 12 December 1984).[17]

Yet another diversification strategy and recent policy move to counter the threat of competition from the establishment of refining and petrochemicals facilities in neighbouring countries is the Economic Development Board's recent intention to promote Singapore as a centre for oil trading, a move interpreted by many as a reflection of the government's strategy of steering Singapore away from its traditional role as a major refining centre and developing it into an important oil-trading centre. This was very obvious from the request made early in 1985 to Japan by the Minister for Trade and Industry, Dr Richard Hu, to help to develop Singapore into a leading oil-trading centre (*Business Times* 27 February 1985).

Reflecting this interest, the Economic Development Board, along with the Trade Development Board, recently co-sponsored an international conference on 'Oil Trading Activities and Opportunities' in Singapore. Discussion focused on oil-trading patterns in the Asian-Pacific region, the role of Singapore as a centre for oil trading, and the development of oil futures.

In more practical terms, the government has gone ahead to support the five major oil companies' strategy of shifting from refining to trading by setting

up two independent oil-storage terminals operated by Van Ommeren and
Paktank, both of Holland. The Van Ommeren terminal was set up in 1983,
while Paktank started operations in March 1985. There is government
participation in both ventures.

Prospects

The outlook for the future is one of cautious optimism. With possibly some
older plants being mothballed in Japan and Europe and no new plants being
built in the near future (the next five years) in this region, the sentiment
among Singapore's petrochemicals producers is that the Singapore complex
will have no difficulty in selling its products, even if it has to face stiff price
competition from Saudi Arabia. In Dr Han's view, 'Demand is there. The
impact of the Saudi plants is more on prices'. This optimism is reflected in the
companies' sales projections for 1985. All of them projected sales increases,
one of them by a factor of as much as four (see Table 12.3).

The Philippines

Definition and brief history

The petrochemicals and plastics industry in the Philippines is classified as a
chemicals-based industry and consists of three subgroups: industrial chemicals; other chemical products; and plastics products. The first two of these deal
with the manufacture of synthetic resins, while the third is involved in trans-
forming resins into final plastic forms like sheet tubing and containers. The
output of plastics products manufacturers can be classified into consumer
goods, industrial and electrical parts, agricultural pipes and sewers, and other
civil-works applications.

The plastics industry in the Philippines originated in 1948 with plastics
products manufacturers who were mainly engaged in the commercial fabrication of plastic novelties. The early and middle 1950s saw the introduction of
injection- and compression-moulded household wares, and a diversification
into other processing fields using primarily imported raw materials. The latter
were replaced by locally produced raw materials in 1965 with the establishment of the country's first synthetic resin (polyvinyl chloride) production plant
in Iligan City, Mindanao, by the Mabuhay Rubber Corporation (now the
Mabuhay Vinyl Corporation). Since then, more local resin- and plastics-
manufacturing plants have been set up to meet increasing domestic demand as
well as in response to the development of new technologies that have opened
up new uses for plastics. With the proposed establishment of the country's
first petrochemicals complex, from which resin manufacturers will be able to
get their raw materials, the industry is projected to grow even more.

Industrial policy: goals, instruments and effects

The goal of the postwar Philippines economy was to modernise and upgrade the economic structure through industrialisation. Throughout the 1950s and 1960s the prime strategy adopted had been import substitution based on a protective system that favoured the domestic production of final consumer goods. Industrial policy focused on large-scale capital- and import-intensive enterprises located in or around Manila and catering to domestic urban markets (see Krueger, 1978).

A shift in industrial policy took place in the 1970s towards greater emphasis on attracting investment into the industrial sector, redirecting import-replacing activities and giving impetus to export industries. This was achieved through the Investment Incentives Act of 1967 and the Export Incentives Act of 1970 (to be examined later), among other measures. But export promotion during this period was not accompanied by any liberalisation of imports. The permitted import levels of restricted commodities continued to be dictated very much by considerations of the country's capacity to import and the need, as perceived by the authorities, to promote certain industries.

The task of formulating and implementing industrial policy in the Philippines rests with the Ministry of Trade and Industry and the Board of Investment. The ministry is the primary policymaking, planning, programming, coordinating and administrative entity of the government, and is charged with developing, promoting and expanding domestic and international trade. The board formulates plans and programs to encourage projects that can bring long-term benefits to the economy in the forms of foreign-exchange savings or earnings; increased export opportunities; progressive increases in domestic content; fuller use of existing facilities; and development of management methods, technical expertise and marketing strategies. Its package of incentives aims to encourage projects that will disperse industries among the rural areas, generate employment opportunities, promote labour-intensive manufactured goods for export, develop small and medium-scale industries, and increase the use of indigenous raw materials.

The basic industrial chemicals, synthetic resins and plastic products industries are among a group of industries (such as textiles, cement, basic metal products and electrical and electronic products) that are considered by the Board of Investment as preferred areas for investment, and have therefore been included in the board's Investment Priorities Plan.[18] A producer enterprise registered with the board is entitled to:

Protection of patent and other proprietary rights
Exemption from capital-gains tax
Deduction of organisational and pre-operating expenses
Accelerated depreciation
Carryover of net operating losses
Tax exemption on imported capital equipment

Tax credit on domestic capital equipment
Tax credit for withholding tax on interest
Incentives for necessary and major infrastructure and public facilities
Employment of foreign nationals
Deduction from expansion reinvestment
Protection against dumping
Protection from government competition
Deduction of labour-training expenses

If the registered enterprise is export-oriented, it is entitled to additional incentives in the forms of:

Tax credits
Reduced income tax
Exemption from sales tax
Exemption from export tax and import fees
Tax-free importation of capital equipment

These incentives seemed to have some success in promoting the petrochemicals industry in the 1970s. In terms of contribution to value added within manufacturing, the industry's share rose from 7.9 per cent in 1970 to a high 15.6 per cent in 1977 but eased to around 10 per cent in 1978–80 (IDE, 1982a:Table 10.1). In terms of exports, its share of manufactured exports rose from 0.2 per cent to 1.0 per cent between 1970 and 1980, while its share of total exports increased from zero to 0.4 per cent over the same period (IDE, 1982a:Table 10.2) However, import dependence as measured by its share of total as well as manufactured imports was fairly stable, and much higher than its export contribution in the 1970s. There is considerable scope for improvement as far as the objective of developing the petrochemicals industry into an important earner of foreign exchange is concerned. The results of a survey conducted jointly by SGV and the Institute of Developing Economies in 1981 showed that stiff price competition in the international market has made exports substantially less profitable than domestic sales, particularly for primary producers. The survey cites economies of scale, more cost-efficient production, and the use of more advanced and sophisticated production techniques as the underlying reasons for the lower prices of foreign competitors, and underscores the need for producers in the Philippines to move in that direction (IDE, 1982a:62).

SUMMARY AND CONCLUSIONS

The world petrochemicals industry is undergoing a transition phase in terms of having to adjust to both a slowdown in demand and considerable excess capacity in many established firms in the traditional production centres in Europe, Japan and the United States. The emergence of cost-competitive production in the oil-rich areas of the Middle East suggests the probability of a shift in the international division of labour, whereby countries with indigenous feedstock are likely to dominate the production of bulk petrochemicals, with established producers in the developed countries moving further downstream towards more research-and-development-intensive products or forming joint ventures with oil-rich producers in bulk production of petrochemicals. Japan is a good example of the latter countries in view of its loss of comparative advantage in bulk petrochemicals. Energy-deficient countries (such as Singapore) who have only recently started producing petrochemicals have a tough road ahead in terms of price competition, and will need to find ways of cushioning themselves from the vagaries of a soft market for oil and petrochemicals. Serious cost-benefit analyses will have to be conducted for others (such as Malaysia, Thailand, the Philippines and Indonesia) who intend to set up petrochemical facilities in the near future, in terms of export prospects, the cheaper alternative of importing, and so forth. Such caution seems especially warranted for energy-deficient countries (such as the Philippines) where there are also debt and other problems to contend with.

PART IV
THE REGIONAL ASPECTS OF INDUSTRIAL POLICIES

13 Industrial cooperation in ASEAN

R.B. SUHARTONO

THE ASSOCIATION OF SOUTH-EAST ASIAN NATIONS

ASEAN (the Association of South-East Asian Nations) has been in existence for nearly two decades.[1] Though ASEAN was established as an association for regional cooperation, it began to adopt measures towards economic cooperation only in 1976, after nearly a decade had passed since its formation. Since then it has given greater emphasis to regional economic cooperation, particularly in trade and industrial development.

The Declaration of ASEAN Concord, signed by the ASEAN heads of state in Denpasar on 24 February 1976, provides that member states shall take cooperative action in their national and regional development programs, using as far as possible the resources available within the ASEAN region to broaden the complementarity of their economies. The program of action adopted as a framework for ASEAN cooperation in the economic field includes cooperation on basic commodities, particularly food and energy; industrial cooperation; cooperation in trade; a joint approach to international commodity problems and other world economic problems; and machinery for economic cooperation. Meetings of the ASEAN economic ministers were to be held regularly or as deemed necessary in order to formulate recommendations for the strengthening of ASEAN economic cooperation; to review the coordination and implementation of agreed ASEAN programs and projects on economic cooperation; to exchange views and consult on national development plans and policies as a step towards harmonising regional development; and to perform other such relevant functions.

At the ASEAN Summit Meeting in Bali in 1976, the first package of industrial projects was identified, to be known later as the ASEAN Industrial Projects—urea projects for Indonesia and Malaysia, superphosphates for the Philippines, diesel engines for Singapore, and soda ash for Thailand. The second ASEAN economic ministers' meeting (Kuala Lumpur, 8–9 March 1976) agreed to the establishment of these projects. In the light of the increasing emphasis on economic cooperation, the foreign ministers subsequently signed the Agreement on ASEAN Preferential Trading Arrangements in Manila on 24 February 1977.

The desire to intensify cooperation in the field of industry led to the signing of the Basic Agreement on ASEAN Industrial Projects in Kuala Lumpur on

6 March 1980. The purposes of the agreement were twofold: first, to cooperate in establishing large-scale ASEAN industrial projects, particularly to meet regional requirements for essential products; and second, to give priority to projects that use the resources available in the member countries, and that contribute to increased food production and foreign-exchange earnings or save foreign exchange and create employment. Although the provisions of the agreement initially applied to the first five ASEAN Industrial Projects mentioned earlier, they will also apply to subsequent sets of projects unless the ASEAN economic ministers decide otherwise.

Meanwhile, the private sector was also active in promoting industrial cooperation; the suggestions advanced by the ASEAN Chamber of Commerce and Industry, as well as the confidence it demonstrated in the viability of ASEAN industrial complementation and ASEAN industrial joint ventures, led to the conclusion of the Basic Agreement on ASEAN Industrial Complementation (signed in Manila on 18 June 1981) and the Basic Agreement on ASEAN Industrial Joint Ventures (signed in Jakarta on 7 November 1983). These agreements provide guidelines and an institutional framework within which the ASEAN governmental machinery and the private sector through the Chamber of Commerce and Industry may collaborate to pursue industrial complementation and industrial joint ventures, and increased industrial production for the region as a whole.

During the first decade of ASEAN's existence, and even since then, there have been voices that, while admitting the indisputable cohesiveness of ASEAN as a political force, have criticised the sluggish progress and lack of tangible results in economic fields. In so far as these criticisms have been based on misconceptions of the purpose of ASEAN (such as that ASEAN was intended as an instrument for complete economic integration), they may be considered irrelevant and brushed off. Similarly, if it is suggested that regional or joint projects have been too few, it must be borne in mind that the political will for the pursuit of economic cooperation in general and industrial cooperation in particular, as well as the establishment of the proper machinery for giving concrete expression to this pursuit, has been crystallised and consolidated only since the Summit Meeting of 1976.

Nevertheless, it is perhaps pertinent to ask why ASEAN has opted for economic cooperation rather than striving towards economic integration, in contrast to other regional groupings of developing countries.[2] In discussing industrial cooperation in ASEAN this question is of particular relevance, since obviously the kinds of industrial cooperation that emerge will in large measure be defined by the economic framework for cooperation adopted.

THE FRAMEWORK FOR INDUSTRIAL COOPERATION: ECONOMIC COOPERATION, NOT INTEGRATION

Economic cooperation is distinct from economic integration not only in its institutional setting but also in its function—both qualitatively and quantitatively. Cooperation can be a loose arrangement, not requiring a formal institutional framework, while integration depends on it. Economic cooperation includes various measures designed to harmonise economic policies and lessen discrimination; the process leading towards economic integration entails the unification of economic policies and the suppression of discrimination. More importantly, economic integration implies that policies and measures are subordinated to a general strategy of market integration through liberalisation of trade; within a framework of economic cooperation, the integration of specific markets is a means that can be applied only very selectively.[3]

As explained earlier, the ASEAN declaration established a framework for cooperation; in none of the official documents is there any suggestion that ASEAN should aim at economic integration.

There is no ascertainable explanation of why ASEAN has not chosen economic integration; the nearest to an authoritative discussion of the question is to be found in the report of a United Nations team commissioned in 1970 by the governments of the ASEAN countries (UN, 1974).

To achieve the overall objectives of economic cooperation, as broadly defined in the ASEAN Declaration, the UN team considered it necessary not only to identify opportunities for cooperation but to develop a set of techniques and policy instruments that would enable the individual ASEAN countries to take collective action within a comprehensive, coherent and agreed framework.

It has been suggested that

> the idea of trade liberalization as a technique of co-operation in trade and industry was conceived as far back as 1970 when the ASEAN Governments commissioned a United Nations team to study the possibilities for closer co-operation ... Complete removal of tariffs and non-tariff barriers would have offered the quickest way of expanding the ASEAN market, but this met with objections from some member countries for fear of possible adverse effects on their domestic economies. (Ooi Guat Tin, 1981:1)

This interpretation is not borne out by the report itself. The UN team believed that 'there will not as yet [in the ASEAN context] be a preparedness to accept very close and complete integration in the form of a complete free trade area, a customs union or a common market'. It assumed instead, in the light of the many economic and political forces working in favour of cooperation, that

> there will be a welcome for a limited trade liberalization scheme, covering a number of carefully selected commodities and a limited scheme for co-operation in the development of new industrial projects, supplemented by a number of other co-operative measures of a more direct character in the monetary and financial fields, in the provision of agricultural services, in shipping, in tourist facilities and in other similar forms. (UN, 1974:50)[4]

Accordingly, the team worked out three principal and general techniques of cooperation in trade and industry: selective liberalisation of trade; industrial complementarity agreements; and the so-called 'package-deal' technique.

Selective liberalisation of trade

Cooperation through selective liberalisation of trade was designed to increase efficiency and secure a more economic use of resources in both the short and the long terms by boosting trade among the ASEAN countries and permitting increased specialisation in activities in line with comparative advantage. Given the circumstances of ASEAN, a step-by-step approach was considered appropriate, with a policy of progressive advancement towards the long-run goal of a limited free-trade area.

Selective liberalisation of trade was to be negotiated item by item, and applied progressively on a wider scale in a series of annual or biennial negotiations designed to enable the ASEAN countries to develop a balanced trade among themselves in the products in which they had individual advantage, and to benefit by increasing specialisation and exchange. It was recommended that the technique be applied principally in those industries where production was in the hands of numerous small or medium-scale enterprises in which capacity was underutilised and opportunity existed for profitable intra-ASEAN exchange. Each country was to prepare a list of selected products for which it would like the other ASEAN countries to grant it concessions, and a list of commodities for which, in return for such concessions, it would itself be prepared to offer concessions. Among the commodities for which such trade liberalisation might first be negotiated were a number of products now imported by some ASEAN countries from sources outside ASEAN but manufactured by others, possibly including certain types of textiles, clothing and footwear, certain chemicals and pharmaceuticals, certain types of preserved and packaged foods, and certain types of household equipment and other consumer durables.

Industrial complementarity agreements

The purpose of industrial complementarity agreements was to expand trade and industrial cooperation, at the level of the individual industry or small group of related industries, through negotiations. The negotiations were to be conducted by representatives of manufacturers in different countries, with the aim of preparing an agreement covering that industry for government approval. Proposals might include measures for the encouragement of specialisation and the exchange of products or components through unidirectional preferences, the reduction or abolition of intra-regional tariffs, the removal of quantitative restrictions, the establishment of joint ventures, and the sharing of markets.

Through complementarity agreements, those engaged in private enterprises in individual industries (or small groups of related industries) in the different ASEAN countries were to be encouraged to work out together a scheme for specialisation by different countries in the various products of the industry concerned and the exchange of those products between them. Such agreements might cover not only existing products but new ones, and might involve proposals for assistance in the form of tariffs or other incentives.

It was recommended that the technique be applied principally in those industries where relatively few larger enterprises were making a number of products or components that could more efficiently be produced in larger quantities with greater internal specialisation of the enterprises. Thus greater efficiency and a reduction of costs could be achieved through regional cooperation within the industry and through the adoption of a framework treaty or enabling agreement within which all the issues that had been shown by experience elsewhere to be necessary could be negotiated.

It was also recommended that the first discussions that might lead to complementarity agreements be initiated in five to ten industries; these might be selected from a list of some sixteen sectors in which the opportunities for successful agreements were believed, largely on the evidence of responses to a questionnaire, to be greatest. Among others, the list included domestic appliances, rubber products, motor vehicles, agricultural machinery, pharmaceuticals, electrical equipment, building materials, processed food-stuffs, leather products, clothing and textile products.

Package-deal agreements

The third recommended technique took the form of an agreement to allocate among the ASEAN countries certain large-scale industrial projects for a specified and limited period, and to create the conditions, including unidirectional trade liberalisation measures, that would enable them to serve the whole or a large part of the ASEAN market. The suggestion for setting up a number of relatively large-scale industries, in effect directed at collective import substitution, was considered a practicable way of industrialising without loss of efficiency.

The package-deal agreements were to be negotiated among the governments of the ASEAN countries to establish new, large-scale projects, mainly in industries that had not hitherto been introduced into the region, and to allocate them for a limited period to particular ASEAN countries, together with agreements to provide for the products involved the tariffs or other forms of assistance necessary to make them viable. The technique was to be applied principally to industries that could be efficiently established only if, through cooperation, access by a single large enterprise to the markets of all or almost all ASEAN countries could be assured.

On the basis of initial pre-feasibility studies, a number of projects were to be provisionally accepted and allocated. Thereafter there were to be detailed feasibility studies of each project in relation to a possible location in the country to which it was to be allocated. For the initial package deal, consideration was to be given to thirteen projects for which the UN team had prepared pre-feasibility studies. They comprised projects designed to meet the estimated gaps between forecast demand and planned production (if any) for the following products: nitrogenous and phosphatic fertilisers; caprolactam, dimethyl terephthalate and ethylene glycol, as representing essential basic inputs for the developing manmade-fibre industries; sheet glass and newsprint, as intermediate products for which there were growing demands in the region; steel ingots, as representing the basic input for the steel-rolling and steel-fabricating industries that were developing to meet regional demands from the construction, shipbuilding and other metal-based industries; sealed compressors, as an example of a variety of mass-produced manufactured components at present imported for inclusion in electrical products made in the region; and small diesel engines and typewriters, as representing light-engineering products, both of them requiring a considerably larger scale of production than the demand of any one industrial ASEAN country could justify.

THE ASEAN APPROACH TO INDUSTRIAL COOPERATION

As ASEAN economic cooperation gained momentum after the Bali Summit in 1976, it substantially followed the approach recommended by the United Nations team. The cornerstone of the various industrial cooperation schemes has been the ASEAN system of Preferential Trading Arrangements (Sadli, 1983).

ASEAN Preferential Trading Arrangements

It has often been noted that the five ASEAN member states hold divergent views on the desirable method and pace of liberalising trade. The Philippines and Singapore have been said to be strongly in favour of across-the-board trade liberalisation, while Indonesia and Malaysia have inclined to a cautious, step-by-step approach.[5] Given the existing disparities in tariff rates, however, the item-by-item approach recommended by the United Nations team appeared to promise more success in the ASEAN context (Ariff, 1975:158–59).

While negotiations on preferential trading arrangements as stipulated in the Declaration of ASEAN Concord were going on, Singapore, the Philippines and Thailand proceeded with preferential bilateral and trilateral trading arrangements.[6] Later these arrangements were apparently superseded by the Agreement on ASEAN Preferential Trading Arrangements, which established preferential trading arrangements among the member states with the object of expanding ASEAN trade. Under these arrangements, the ASEAN governments have agreed to extend trade preferences to each other; to implement concessions on products originating from all member countries, agreed upon among them through negotiations; and to cooperate through mutual assistance in respect of basic commodities, provision of market support for the products of the ASEAN industrial projects, expansion of intra-ASEAN trade, and an increase in the use of the raw materials available in the member countries.

Table 13.1   Status of margins of preference extended by ASEAN member countries (at 1 April 1985)

	Number of items	Preferences expressed in percentage terms						
		20	25	30	40[a]	50[a]	60–100	Binding
Indonesia	2 670	958	937	587	86	43	—	2
Malaysia	2 234	974	33	506	124	33	486	—
Philippines	3 415	2 003	260	1 109	5	26	—	2
Singapore	2 450[b]	1	—	130	13	11	14	2 280
Thailand	1 823	521	62	1 030	151	49	—	10
Total	12 592	4 457	1 292	3 362	379	162	500	2 294

Notes: a The eighteenth meeting of the Committee on Trade and Tourism agreed that items with margins of preference of 33⅓ per cent, 35 per cent and 45 per cent should be rounded to margins of preference of 40 per cent or 50 per cent. The seventeenth meeting of the ASEAN economic ministers has endorsed this decision.
   b This figure includes a batch of more than US$10 million implemented on 1 April 1985.

Source: Committee on Trade and Tourism Interim Technical Secretariat

Tariff preferences

Initially, the margins of preference were to be negotiated product by product; whether the concessions were reached multilaterally or bilaterally, they were to be extended to all member states on an ASEAN most-favoured-nation basis.[7] More recently, these preferences have also been negotiated across the board.

At first 71 preferences were identified (21 negotiated and 50 based on voluntary offers). The list became effective on 1 January 1978, with preferential rates ranging from 10 per cent to 30 per cent of existing rates.[8] Progress accelerated dramatically in 1979, when the ASEAN economic ministers agreed to expand the number of preferences exchanged, to make deeper tariff cuts, and to automatically include small items under the preferential trading arrangements.[9] Within three years the number of preferences that had been implemented increased from 71 to 5588, and there are now around 12 600; the status at 1 April 1985 is indicated in Table 13.1.

One attempt (Ooi Guat Tin, 1981) to estimate the effects of tariff preferences on intra-ASEAN trade, however, seems to indicate that the progress achieved in terms of the number of items given preference was accompanied by low, if not negligible, trade expansion.[10] At the same time, the values of member countries' exports under the preferential trading arrangements, relative to the values of their total exports, seem very small—not exceeding US$50 million.

In addition to negotiated tariff preferences, the ASEAN governments have agreed to provide mutual support through long-term contracts, purchase-finance support and preference in government procurement.

Long-term quantity contracts

The member countries have agreed to undertake long-term supply contracts for selected products—generally three to five years, depending on the products and their quantities and subject to annual review—giving priority supply in times of worldwide shortage. Contract prices were to be negotiated, providing lower and upper ceilings.

A number of such agreements have been concluded. An emergency sharing scheme for crude oil and oil products was drawn up in 1977. For Thailand's rice exports, Singapore, Malaysia and Indonesia have been given priority over non-ASEAN countries. Singapore and Thailand have concluded a bilateral long-term agreement for the preferential supply and purchase of maize. Recently, Indonesia signed an agreement with the Philippines to export 100–150 kt of ammonia annually, in exchange for around 440 kt of phosphoric acid over five years (60–80 kt for the first year, increasing to 100–150 kt for the fifth year).

Purchase-finance support

For selected products of ASEAN domestic origin, purchase-finance support at preferential rates may be applied to exports to, or imports from, the member states. The Committee on Finance and Banking and the ASEAN Banking Council of the private sector have already discussed the possibility of setting up an ASEAN export–import bank.

Preference in government procurement

In respect of procurement by government entities, pre-tender notices for international tenders should be sent by one member state to the others. A preferential margin of 2.5 per cent (but not to exceed US$40 000) per tender from untied loans is to be offered and applied on the basis of the lowest evaluated and acceptable tender.

The preferential trading arrangements were also to be applied to basic commodities (particularly rice and crude oil), to products of the ASEAN industrial projects, and to products for the expansion of intra-ASEAN trade, subject to certain requirements on the rules of origin and to certain escape clauses. The latter allow for the suspension of preferences in certain situations: if imports eligible for preferential trading arrangements threaten to cause serious injury to trade; if there is an overriding balance-of-payments problem; if there is a need to limit exports in order to ensure sufficient domestic supply; and if other members do not fulfil their obligations. Preferences are to be accorded product by product taking into account existing levels of tariffs in the respective countries. Special preferential trading arrangements with respect to the ASEAN Industrial Projects are embodied in Supplementary Agreements. The products of the ASEAN Industrial Complementation Projects will qualify for Preferential Trading Arrangements.

The Committee on Trade and Tourism was established by the third meeting of ASEAN economic ministers in January 1977 to conduct trade negotiations as well as to review and supervise the implementation of the agreement. The committee is assisted by a technical body, the Trade Preferences Negotiating Group.

The ASEAN Industrial Projects scheme

The package of ASEAN Industrial Projects, which provides for the establishment of large-scale industrial plants, particularly to meet regional requirements for essential commodities, was the first important initiative for industrial cooperation in ASEAN. The decision at the 1976 summit to allocate the first package (two industrial urea projects for Indonesia and Malaysia, diesel engines for Singapore, superphosphate for the Philippines, and soda ash for Thailand), subject to feasibility studies, was a bold and significant one, even though it soon attracted criticisms that foreshadowed later difficulties.[11]

The package-deal approach aimed at giving each country at least one Industrial Project. Following the initial allocation of an Industrial Project to a member country, similar new national projects were to be established after consultation with member states.[12] The output was to be marketed within ASEAN and accorded trade preferences under ASEAN preferential trading arrangements, but allowing a portion to be exported.

The equity structure of an ASEAN Industrial Project is such that the host country holds 60 per cent of the total equity, the balance to be shared by the other member countries. But there was provision for the private sector, whether ASEAN or non-ASEAN, to participate. Majority ownership was envisaged to be held by state agencies acting as ASEAN shareholders.[13] Indeed, since the minimum government share in the equity is only one-third, private interests could theoretically hold a maximum equity of 67 per cent.

Selling prices throughout the life of a project were to be calculated in US dollars. The products of the Industrial Projects were to be sold at world prices, between floor and ceiling prices based on minimum and maximum project rates of return, using free-on-board selling price. The actual selling price was to be determined by the company operating an Industrial Project, based on the prevailing world market prices generally applicable in the ASEAN region.

By May 1985, of the five projects, only the ASEAN fertiliser project in Indonesia was in operation: P.T. ASEAN Aceh Fertilizer was officially inaugurated by the President of Indonesia on 18 January 1984. According to the Joint Venture Agreement the total investment for the project was estimated at US$313 million, funded initially on an equity-to-loan ratio of approximately 30:70. The initial equity structure of the company and the respective share allocations are shown in Table 13.2.

In its first year of operation (1984) the project yielded a dividend of around US$10 million. The first export shipments were made in December to Malaysia, amounting to 20 kt (out of an order of 100 kt), and to Japan, amounting to 4 kt (out of an order of 8 kt). In the first six months of operation, production reached 88 per cent of the installed capacity, while projected capacity utilisation was 75 per cent.

The Malaysian project, ASEAN Bintulu Fertilizer Sdn. Bhd., was in the construction stage and was expected to be completed six months behind schedule. The government of Thailand had decided to liquidate the ASEAN Soda Ash Co. Ltd and had not proposed any new project.

Table 13.2 Share allocations in the ASEAN urea project in Indonesia

	Share in percentage terms	Capital in US$'000		
		Authorised	Issued	Paid up
Indonesia	60	56 340	11 280	1 128
Malaysia	13	12 210	2 440	244
Philippines	13	12 210	2 440	244
Singapore	1	930	180	18
Thailand	13	12 210	2 440	244
Total	100	93 900	18 780	1 878

Note: In its first year of operation (1984), P.T. ASEAN Aceh Fertilizer yielded a dividend amounting to around US$10 million.

The construction of the ASEAN Copper Fabrication Project in the Philippines, involving an investment cost of US$280 million, was still in preparation. Invitation-to-bid documents had been released to approved bidders. The Singapore ASEAN Hepatitis B Vaccine Project was also still in the preparatory stages; the Supplementary Agreement for this project was approved by the ASEAN economic ministers meeting on 9 May 1984.

The ASEAN Industrial Complementation scheme

Like the ASEAN Industrial Projects, the ASEAN Industrial Complementation scheme is a package deal. There are, however, some differences. First, while governments play the main role in an Industrial Project, the initiative under the Industrial Complementation scheme lies with the private sector: the identification of products for inclusion in the package is to originate from the ASEAN Chamber of Commerce and Industry.[14] Second, the package in the Industrial Projects scheme consists of industrial projects that need not have inter-industry linkages, whereas the Industrial Complementation projects make up a package in a particular branch of industry. Third, while all the signatory countries participate in the Industrial Projects scheme, in the Industrial Complementation scheme any four countries are involved; accordingly, while in the former case each signatory country shall have at least one project, in the latter any one country may choose to have none. Finally, Article 3 of the agreement stipulates that the Industrial Complementation products in a package must, whenever feasible, be equitably allocated to the participating countries, an issue that does not arise in an Industrial Project.

Coverage

A product of the Industrial Complementation scheme is an industrial product manufactured or to be manufactured in a member country; the product is allocated to that particular country as its participation in an Industrial Complementation package, where the latter consists of organised complementary trade exchanges of specified processed or manufactured products. The ASEAN Chamber of Commerce and Industry identifies products for inclusion in any Industrial Complementation package. The product should be of internationally accepted quality and relatively competitive in price, and continuity of supply should be assured.

Qualification for preferences

The ninth meeting of the ASEAN economic ministers agreed upon the following three principles. First, industrial complementation should be organised by allocating products to specific member countries for a limited period—two years in the case of ongoing projects or four years from the date of approval in the case of new projects. Second, any preferences granted within the framework of the ASEAN preferential trading arrangements for any product by a particular country are to be extended on an ASEAN most-favoured-nation basis to similar products produced in other ASEAN member countries, in accordance with the basic principles of the preferential arrangements. Third, member countries may grant additional preferences, such as recognition of local content on a country basis and mandatory sourcing; such additional preferences should be negotiated separately between the countries concerned.

An existing product in an ASEAN Industrial Complementation package enjoys exclusivity privileges for a period of two years, a new product for three years. During the period of exclusivity, special preferences outside the preferential trading arrangements can be granted, such as mandatory sourcing and recognition of local content, to be applicable only to specific countries.[15]

The Committee on Industry, Minerals and Energy evaluates the proposals for Industrial Complementation packages, and recommends to the ASEAN economic ministers the allocation of products in the package to participating countries. After the ministers' approval of the allocation, the participating countries are to negotiate preferences within the preferential trading scheme, as well as other special preferences within a set negotiating period (a maximum of six months for existing products and one year for new ones). Upon successful completion of the negotiation the Committee on Industry, Minerals and Energy will recommend to the ASEAN economic ministers the final approval of the package with any necessary modifications, including arrangements for trade preferences.

The ASEAN Industrial Complementation scheme, which is intended to be undertaken by the private sector, presents an opportunity for foreign investment with equity capital up to 49 per cent. Thus far it appears to have attracted interest only in the motor vehicles industry; there have been proposals from manufacturers of cars and motorcycles on brand-to-brand complementation.

The first meeting of the ASEAN Economic Ministers on Industry endorsed the proposal of the Committee on Industry, Minerals and Energy to recommend for the ministers' approval the following products as the first package for automotive complementation:

Indonesia —diesel engines (80–135 hp)
Malaysia   —spokes, nipples, drive chains for motorcycles, and timing
           chains for motor vehicles
Philippines—Ford body panels for passenger cars
Singapore —universal joints
Thailand   —body panels for motor vehicles of 1 tonne and above

Some existing products were also endorsed for the approval of the ASEAN economic ministers, to be selected and agreed upon from the indicative offer list of components, in order to arrive at a more practical, realistic and balanced implementation of the first package.[16] The meeting also agreed on the nomination of the following new products to be considered for inclusion in the second package:

Indonesia —steering systems
Malaysia   —headlights for motor vehicles
Philippines—heavy-duty rear axles for commercial vehicles
Singapore —fuel-injection pumps
Thailand   —carburettors

Subsequently the ASEAN economic ministers approved the first and second packages of automotive-component manufacturing under the industrial complementation scheme.

Before the first meeting of the ASEAN Economic Ministers on Industry (29–30 September 1980), the third meeting of the ASEAN Experts Group on Automotive Industry (22–23 September) recommended to the Committee on Industry, Minerals and Energy the creation of an Automotive Preferences Negotiating Group to negotiate directly for tariff and other special preferences as a package. Consultations about trade preferences began in January 1981 at the eighth meeting of the Trade Preferences Negotiating Group of the Committee on Trade and Tourism.

The ASEAN Industrial Joint Venture scheme

The third and newest plan for ASEAN industrial cooperation is the ASEAN Industrial Joint Venture scheme. Like industrial complementation, the joint-venture scheme was initiated primarily as a private-sector endeavour, in the shared belief that the private sector has an important role to play in the development of the region. Certain differences, however, may be discerned.

First, while the Industrial Complementation scheme was established to pursue industrial complementation through organised complementary trade exchanges, the joint-venture scheme aims at industrial joint ventures through the consolidation of markets among ASEAN countries, Second, while there must be at least four participating countries in an Industrial Complementation package, a minimum of two ASEAN countries may participate in a joint-venture package. Third, while non-ASEAN interests may hold a 49 per cent equity under both schemes, in the joint-venture scheme there is provision for a higher share if certain conditions are met.

A country participating in an ASEAN Industrial Joint Venture is an ASEAN member state that has indicated its intention to participate by providing tariff preference to a particular ASEAN joint-venture product included in the final list approved by the ASEAN economic ministers where the list carries with it the commitment to extend a minimum 50 per cent margin of tariff preference. Investors in a joint venture are free to site their projects in any of the participating countries. An ASEAN member country that has not indicated its intention to participate by providing tariff preference for a particular joint-venture product is a non-participating country with respect to that product. Non-participating countries automatically waive tariff preferences.

Exclusivity privileges will be granted by the participating countries for three years if there is only one approved project for a new Industrial Joint Venture product. During the period of exclusivity the participating countries cannot set up production facilities other than the approved project for the product in question unless 75 per cent of the non-joint-venture production is for export to non-ASEAN countries.

OVERVIEW

As has been repeatedly emphasised, ASEAN's objective is not the economic integration of its members. In earlier regional groupings of developing countries, industrial cooperation was expected to occur as a result of economic integration: in ASEAN, industrial cooperation is viewed simply as a special case of economic cooperation. But economic cooperation in ASEAN does not seem to have been clearly defined, in terms of either form or objective. From one perspective this may have produced a somewhat hazy notion of economic cooperation, but in another way it has the advantage of considerable flexibility, and suits the ASEAN preference for a cautious and step-by-step approach. Economic cooperation has become an idea to pursue, to nurture, to develop; to be approached pragmatically as warranted by the progress that could be achieved. The Declaration of ASEAN Concord adopted a program of action as a framework for economic cooperation, rather than taking economic cooperation as a rationale for action.

At first there may have been two forces at work in ASEAN for giving concrete expression to the concept of economic cooperation: some were pushing for market integration through a general liberalisation of trade; others favoured joint production through the integration of specific markets. ASEAN did not fully embrace or fully reject either approach, but accommodated both; and in the process it bypassed the traditionally thorny and intractable problems of sharing the costs and burdens of cooperation. It has nurtured consensus rather than floundering in the confrontation of national interests that in other cases had fuelled the forces of disintegration.

ASEAN has recognised the merit of market integration, but it has not gone all out for a general liberalisation of trade; rather, it has chosen selective integration of its markets through preferential trading arrangements. Again, it has accepted the value of integrating production but has not gone all the way towards comprehensive planning for regional industries; rather, it began with the identification of a package of industrial projects whose implementation was contingent on their mutual economic feasibility without any one of them being made to depend on the others. The selective integration of production makes way for the development of joint endeavours, as well as inter-industry linkages and complementarities; these, in turn, are supported by selective integration of markets through preferential trading arrangements. The role of governments in undertaking industrial cooperation has been recognised as important, but the private sector is given ample opportunities to participate.

In the process, mechanisms and structures have developed for effecting industrial cooperation, formalised in basic and supplementary agreements. During the deliberations leading to these various agreements, certain factors become evident. First, the political will for effecting industrial cooperation has without question been present, although its realisation has naturally posed painstaking and complicated technical and economic problems, including the scope and feasibility of projects, the formulation of pricing policy, the yardsticks to be applied, and many more. Second, the availability of finance does not guarantee success; in any event, its non-availability does not appear to have constituted a significant constraint. Third, in addition to differences among the ASEAN countries with respect to their stages of economic and industrial development, there are different legal systems and practices, different economic policies, different investment incentives, and so on. Fourth, and perhaps most important, all the member countries have continued to strive to solve problems through consensus. The Agreement on ASEAN Preferential Trading Arrangements, and the Basic as well as Supplementary Agreements on ASEAN Industrial Projects, ASEAN Industrial Complementation and ASEAN Industrial Joint Ventures, may all be considered manifestations of the attempt to develop a common and harmonious framework for realising industrial cooperation.

In terms of the number of industrial projects that have been implemented or are in the pipeline, the effort to achieve industrial cooperation may not yet seem very impressive. But numbers may not be all that important, and even if the numbers seem too few by any specific yardstick, this may reflect fundamental problems, rather than any inadequacy in the framework of industrial cooperation that has been adopted. If so, these problems must be examined before the present framework is hastily changed.

14 China's economic development and policy

MU YANG

Economic policy plays a role in every country's economic development. Its influence is especially important in the People's Republic of China, which has been a centrally planned socialist economy for a long time. In order to accelerate the process of socialist modernisation, since 1978 China has been assessing the lessons of the past on economic development and adopting policies of economic readjustment, structural reform and an open door to the rest of the world. Its aim is to find a new pathway towards economic development, achieving better results at a more realistic pace and with greater benefit to its people.

THE HISTORY OF CHINA'S ECONOMIC DEVELOPMENT

Since the People's Republic of China was founded in 1949, China's national economic and social development have proceeded with considerable success.

An independent and relatively complete national economic system has been created through large–scale economic construction. China's total capital investment in construction (state-run enterprises only) from 1950 to 1983 was RmbY897 billion. More than 3800 large and medium-sized projects were completed, with the amount of new fixed assets totalling RmbY644 billion. Thus a relatively firm material and technological foundation has been laid for increasing social productivity, changing the distribution of production and improving the living standards of the population. From 1949 to 1983, total fixed assets in industrial construction increased by a factor of 43.5 while capacities in the coal, electricity, iron and steel and textile industries multiplied several times. Simultaneously, China broadened its industrial base with new industries such as automobiles, tractors, aircraft, electronics, petrochemicals and defence equipment, and a batch of new industrial bases emerged in the interior. The value of the gross industrial output of the inland area in relation to that of the whole country reached 40.5 per cent in 1983, compared with 30.6 per cent in 1952.[1]

In the fields of agriculture and irrigation, 170 000 km of new embankments and 80 000 new reservoirs have been built, increasing flood control, and the effective irrigation area has expanded to 670 million mu.[2] The agricultural

269

machinery industry has been developed from nothing, and now has a total capacity of over 200 million horsepower.

In transportation, operating railway length has reached over 50 000 km, from 21 800 km in 1949, and trains are running in every province except Tibet. Some lines are double-tracked and electric lines have also been introduced, thus raising transportation capacity. Automotive transportation is available in all except two of China's more than 2000 countries. Waterways, civil aviation and pipeline transportation have also made great progress.

Alongside this economic development, the scientific and technical sectors have been expanding steadily. In 1983 natural-science and technical personnel working in state-owned units totalled 6.85 million, 15.1 times more than the 1952 figure. In the past 30 years many significant scientific and technological results have been achieved. The success of the 'milky way' computer and communications satellites mark China's latest attainments in science and technology.

In terms of social development, the material and cultural lives of people in both urban and rural areas have gradually improved and food and clothing problems have been virtually solved. The consumption level of the Chinese people has risen, especially in recent years; per capita consumption in 1983 was 1.5 times higher than it had been in 1952. The government has adopted a series of policies designed to raise living standards. From 1979 to 1983, living expenditure per capita by staff and workers in urban areas showed an average annual growth rate of 7.4 per cent in real terms, while per capita income increased by 18.3 per cent. Prices have been generally stable. From 1951 to 1983, the general price index increased by 55.6 per cent at an average annual rate of 1.35 per cent. Because of gradually increased incomes and stable prices, people's basic living conditions have improved. A small surplus has also been produced.

At the end of 1983 savings deposits in urban and rurual areas totalled RmbY89.3 billion, 103 times more than they had been in 1952. At the same time medical services and health have improved and a widespread interest in sporting activities has developed. These factors have contributed in raising the average lifespan in China to 67.9 years, compared with a life expectancy of around 50 years in the early 1950s. By the end of 1983 the numbers of students in primary schools, high schools and universities were 5.6, 36.9 and 10.3 times more, respectively, than they had been in 1949. Adult education is entering a golden age, with more than 26.3 per cent of China's staff and workers participating in technological or cultural studies.[3] The people's cultural level has generally improved. The world has witnessed China's achievements in economic and social development, as the World Bank's Mission to China pointed out in its March 1982 report, *China: Socialist Economic Development*.

The economic history of the People's Republic of China can be divided into four stages.

The first period, 1949–56, was a time of postwar economic recovery, during which China carried out large-scale socialist construction and reform. The economy grew rapidly with good economic results. The balance among the principal economic sectors was reasonably satisfactory. Markets were prosperous, prices were stable, and living standards improved remarkably.

The second period, 1956–66, saw the launching of the 'Great Leap Forward', which blindly sought rapid economic expansion, and economic development suffered severed setbacks. However, through readjustment in the early 1960s the economy recovered quickly and achieved some success. For example, industrial fixed assets increased by a factor of three. New industries such as petrochemicals and electronics emerged, and the oil industry became self-sufficient. Large-scale capital construction in agriculture was accomplished. With the building of new factories in inland areas, the distribution of industry in China became more rational.

The third period, 1966–76, is known as the 'Great Cultural Revolution'; during this time China's economic system and its planning for economic development became confused and the economy suffered heavy losses. However, thanks to the efforts of the Chinese people China still managed to achieve success in some areas. For example, grain production grew steadily, and some important railway lines as well as the Nanjing bridge over the Yangtze river were completed. A number of large, advanced industrial complexes went into production. The hydrogen bomb experiments continued and the launching and recovery of satellites succeeded.

In the fourth period, beginning in October 1976, China's economic construction entered a new historical phase. This step forward was confirmed by the strategic decision of the Third Plenary Session of the 11th Central Committee of the Chinese Communist Party in December 1978: that priority should be given to socialist modernisation. China's economic organisation gradually entered a time of stable development. Agriculture broke its long stagnation and entered a prosperous new phase. The industrial structure was readjusted, and economic results improved in consequence. The balance among the main sectors of the national economy is now more satisfactory. Prosperity is evident in both urban and rural markets, a situation rarely observed before. The quality of life has risen, with rapid improvements in the standards of education, science, culture, health and sport. At the same time reform of the economic system has been launched, and some achievement and experiences have been gained.

The fluctuations in China's economic development through these four periods are clearly observable, with economic policy playing a decisive role in the changes.

CHINA'S ECONOMIC POLICY SINCE 1949

The Third Plenary Session in December 1978 forms a natural boundary dividing the history of economic development in the People's Republic of China into two phases.

Lessons and experience from 1949 to 1978

There were some very important achievements in Chinese economic development during this period, but there were also many serious failures. The Great Leap Forward, which started in 1958, led to serious economic imbalance, and within five years China was forced to make readjustments. To make matters worse the Cultural Revolution, which began in 1966 and was entirely misconceived, lasted a whole decade, and led to the most severe economic setback since liberation. After the purge of the Gang of Four, various unrealistic and overambitious slogans and targets were promulgated, but served only to add to the difficulties of economic development. The official explanation stated that the chief target of China's economic development was to achieve socialist industrialisation centred on heavy industry and strive to surpass the developed capitalist economies. Efforts were made to alleviate the worst aspects of poverty, but the need to meet the continually increasing expectations of the population was not given enough attention. Thus there were failures of economic policy.

The first problem was that economic development was too rapid; in the blind quest for increased productivity and competitiveness, economic proportion and the long-term economic consequences were neglected. For example, during the second five-year plan (1958–62), under the banner of 'catching up with the US and surpassing Britain', a target of doubling iron and steel output within one year was set. The result was the exact opposite of what the 'Great Leap Forward' was aiming for; over the whole period of the second five-year plan, national income declined at an average annual rate of 3 per cent.

The second problem was with industrial structure; there was a one-sided emphasis on heavy industry, which had an unfavourable impact on the development of agriculture, light industry and other sectors of the national economy. In 1949 the respective shares of agriculture, light industry and heavy industry in the national economy were 70 per cent, 22.1 per cent and 7.9 per cent; by 1978 these proportions had swung round to 27.8 per cent, 31.1 per cent and 41.1 per cent. Agriculture reached its lowest point, 21.8 per cent, in 1960, while heavy industry's share climbed to 52.1 per cent. Meanwhile the proportion of the population engaged in agriculture has always been over 80 per cent. The preponderance of heavy industry led to an imbalance in the economic structure. Heavy industry also had a tendency towards self-service, causing it to fail to serve agriculture, light industry and technological innovation in the national economy.

The third problem was related to the accumulation and expenditure of funds. For quick realisation of heavy-industry-oriented industrialisation a policy of high accumulation of funds was adopted, which prevented the gradual raising of consumption levels. During the first five-year plan (1953–57) the average annual accumulation rate was 24 per cent. It climbed to 30–40 per cent in the 'Great Leap Forward', and stayed at over 30 per cent throughout the 1970s. After the purge of the Gang of Four in 1978, it climbed to 36.5 per cent. This was beyond the limits that the state or the people could afford.

The fourth problem was connected with development strategy. There was an extensive development strategy consisting of new, expanding construction projects, but the potential of existing plants was neglected and older, more backward facilities were not renovated. As a result, many of China's existing enterprises, facilities and technology remained at 1950s and 1960s levels.

The fifth problem was to do with production relations and management systems. The unrealistic raising of the level of nationalisation, as in the transition of collective systems to state-run systems, amounted to a denial of the positive role of a private economy in urban areas. In 1952 there were 8.83 million people in the private sector in urban areas; by 1957 the number had fallen to 1.0 million, and in 1975 there were only 0.24 million. The state-run sector was dominated by a highly centralised administration and management in which market mechanisms were ignored and played no part. As a result, economic activities were overcontrolled, leading to a deterioration of the economy.

Finally, in the area of foreign economic relations, there was the problem of adopting a closed-door policy with the object of long-term self-reliance. This policy saw foreign trade merely as a means of exchanging a few necessary commodities with foreign countries. In the 1950s China's share in world trade was 1.43 per cent, but it declined to only 0.78 per cent in the 1970s, which was a poor performance for a big country with a population of over one billion.

Economic policy since 1978

Since 1978 there has been a strategic shift in China's economic policy, leading to policies of readjustment, economic reform and rapprochement with the world—the so-called 'open-door policy'.

Economic readjustment

The target is to reform and rationalise the economic structure, which means changing from a heavy-industry-oriented strategy to a consumer-oriented strategy in order to build up a balanced economic structure with the production of consumer goods as its target. Readjustment in recent years has put emphasis on two fields.

The first aim is to strengthen the agricultural sector in order to promote the development of light industry and the further development of heavy industry. From 1979 to 1983 the gross value of agricultural output grew at an average annual rate of 7.9 per cent, and by 1984 this rate had risen to 14.5 per cent, which was much higher than the average annual growth rate of 3.2 per cent from 1953 to 1978. The development of agriculture provides industry with raw materials, markets, funds and labour. At the same time, China adopted a series of policies to speed up the development of light industry and compel heavy industry to serve the development of agriculture and light industry. The gross value of light industrial output grew at an average annual rate of 11.2 per cent from 1979 to 1983, and the growth rate in 1984 was 12.9 per cent. At first heavy industry declined with the introduction of a readjustment policy in 1980 and 1981. But it recovered quickly; the annual growth rates of heavy industry output in 1982, 1983 and 1984 were 9.8 per cent, 12.4 per cent and 14.2 per cent.

The second aim is to change the proportions between accumulation of funds and consumption. The share of accumulation in national income was reduced to 28.5 per cent in the early readjustment period, compared with 36.5 per cent in 1978. It has recovered a little since 1982, and the figure for 1984 was around 31 per cent. This large reduction in capital construction was achieved through rising incomes, especially in the rural sector. The increase in consumption demand stimulated production, while the expansion of production created the conditions necessary for further improvement of the people's living standards.

Reforming the economic system

The objective is to reform China's highly centralised system, which operates mainly through bureaucratic forms of administration. Thus it tends to act as a check on positive action by both enterprises and individuals, and has proved unable to meet the continually increasing demands of the population.

Economic reform began in the rural areas. Since 1979 China has practised a system of family responsibility for production, with peasant families subcontracting land as a unit from the production brigade. This system clarifies the allocation of responsibility, rights and benefits among the state, the collectives and individuals, giving incentive to the rural population and promoting the development of the agricultural economy. By the end of 1982, 92 per cent of all production teams had adopted the responsibility system.

China has also gradually experimented with expanding the discretion of enterprises in urban areas by converting its capital construction investment, which previously came directly from the state budget, into a form of bank loan. Moreover, construction-project investment, which used to be interest-free, now has to pay interest. In 1984, encouraged by the evident success of these moves, China introduced a new system for all state-run enterprises, requiring them to pay tax rather than deliver all profits. China has also decided to reform the construction industry and planning system, and to further develop multi-economic activity and management methods.

All these initiatives have led to a very active situation in urban China. The decision on the reform of the economic system, taken at the Third Plenary Session of the 12th Central Committee of the Chinese Communist Party, set up basic principles and gave a clear direction for economic reform. China's reform is now entering a new period, with the urban areas as its priority.

The purpose of structural reform in the urban areas is to increase the capacity and productivity of enterprises. Within the framework of the state plan, enterprises will have the right to choose flexible management measures; to arrange production, purchasing and marketing; to own and allocate capital; to hire, promote and discharge staff and workers; to decide the prices of their products within a permissible range; and so on. In order to bring this about, it is necessary to rationalise the pricing system, but because any price change will affect both the national economy and the lives of individuals, great care must be take at every point. There are three principles to be observed. First, price relations among all products must be regulated; some prices will increase, while others will decrease. Second, processing industries must make efforts to use inputs more efficiently so as to prevent the prices of consumer goods from rising when the prices of raw materials increase. Third, when the prices of agricultural products go up, the government will have to provide subsidies or increase wages and salaries to maintain standards of living. At present the prices of consumer goods sold by these urban enterprises are fluctuating freely but the prices of some raw materials are still fixed under the state plan. Some Chinese economists have called this the two-track system of price reform.

The open-door policy

Since 1978 China has steadfastly implemented an open-door policy in order to supplement the weaker aspects of its economy, to employ both domestic and foreign resources, and to develop both domestic and foreign markets. After some experimentation, the pace of the open-door policy is quickening. China developed the Shenzhen, Zhuhai, Shanton and Xinamen special economic zones in the late 1970s and opened up fourteen coastal cities in 1984. These cities have been given wider discretion in the development of foreign investment projects. They are striving to revitalise old enterprises by introducing advanced foreign technology and offering favourable investment conditions to foreigners. The scope of the open-door policy has gradually widened from single items to a whole system, corresponding to economic reform in urban areas. During recent years China has offered foreign investors a number of favourable conditions, and has begun to allow some foreign joint ventures to sell their products on China's domestic market. In 1984 the value of China's two-way trade reached RmbY120.1 billion, an increase from the 1983 level of 39.7 per cent in nominal terms and 19.6 per cent in real terms. This is higher than the growth rates of gross value of industrial and agricultural output and of national income. China approved 741 joint ventures in 1984, more than the total figure for the preceding five years. Foreign funds already in use reached US$2.66 billion, a 35.7 per cent increase over the 1983 figure. Of this, US$1.32 billion was in the form of various loans, 25.7 per cent higher than in 1983, and US$1.34 billion was in the form of direct foreign investment, a 47.3 per cent increase over the 1983 level. The number of contracted technology-transfer projects rose to 1000, more than it had been in 1983. The number of contracted construction and labour service projects with foreign countries reached 585 with a total value of US$1.68 billion, an increase of 82.6 per cent from the 1983 level. Of this, completed plant was worth US$0.55 billion, a 22 per cent increase over the figure for 1983.

Thanks to economic readjustment, reform and the open-door policy, a new economic situation has emerged in China with continuous, stable and balanced development. The gross value of industrial and agricultural output in 1984 was more than RmbY1000 billion, an increase of 14.2 per cent over the 1983 value, following an average annual growth rate of 7.9 per cent between 1979 and 1983. National income and state financial revenue each increased by 12 per cent, and the state finance situation is continually improving. Average consumption per person in both urban and rural areas rose from RmbY175 in 1978 to RmbY288 in 1983 and RmbY320 in 1984. This represents an average annual growth rate of 7.3 per cent in real terms, much higher than the rate of 2.2 per cent between 1953 and 1978. Good economic circulation has begun to emerge.

Nevertheless, there are still urgent problems to be solved. First, there is still some evidence of a blind quest for rapid economic growth for its own sake, despite the most important historical lesson in China's economic development: that it should never again blindly seek rapid high growth. Although the situation has improved in recent years, some sectors are still seeking an unrealistic level of power and attempting to match pace with each other, without considering social demand and supply, demand on the market, the limits of both material and financial ability and the balance of finance, credit and national and foreign exchange. If these tendencies are not corrected soon, they will lead to an excess of bureacratic red tape and to various dishonest practices, putting pressure on every aspect of the economy and handicapping the process of economic reform. Too high a speed of development cannot be sustained over a long period, and shortages in energy, infrastructure and raw materials will undermine the stability of China's economy. The experience of Eastern European countries suggests that it is very important to choose an appropriate growth rate, to reduce construction investment and avoid sharp increases in wages and bonuses from the very beginning. The purpose is to provide enough funds for economic reform and to guarantee a better environment for reform. In 1984, the gross value of China's industrial output was 14 per cent higher than it had been in 1983, and in the first quarter of 1985 it increased by over 20 per cent from the 1984 level. On the one hand, this shows that China's economic situation is improving, but it is also a reminder that control must be maintained and economic overactivity reduced.

The second problem is that consumption funds are increasing too quickly. In 1984 China's average wage was 19 per cent higher than it had been in 1983, with an increase of 38 per cent in the fourth quarter of the year. People expected their living standards to rise rapidly after the launching of the economic reform program and the adoption of the open-door policy, but the correct psychological handling of such expectations is very important. Although China's economy has performed well in recent years, China is still a very poor country with an average national income per person of only slightly over RmbY500. Living standards can be raised only by hard work and by revitalising the state economy. Rapid economic development that ignores increasing consumption demands is not the answer, nor is raising wages and incomes without taking account of the realities of production.

Third, the scale of bank-loan and fixed-assets investment is too large.

China's bank credit increased quickly in 1984; the total value of various kinds of loans rose by 28.9 per cent from the 1983 level, and almost half of this increase took place in December. Soaring credit resulted in too many construction projects, a tight supply of building materials and a poor result in terms of completed projects, with the share of completed projects in total capital construction declining to 48 per cent in 1984 from 53.2 per cent in 1983. Building completion rates declined to 49 per cent from 52.3 per cent, and the fixed-assets completion rate also declined.

The fourth problem stemmed from China's lack of experience of macroeconomic control in the attempt to revitalise enterprises. Reform was not launched simultaneously at all main points in the economic system, but step by step. For example, in reforming the planning system measures have been taken to gradually reduce both the range and the extent of compulsory planning; and in reforming the price system a combination of 'adjustment' and 'freeing' has been employed. This kind of approach allows reforms to be introduced smoothly and without a shock to the social system, so that people will accept them more easily. But on the other hand it will lead to the existence of dual systems for quite a while, and the two systems will certainly conflict. In addition, the old system of economic control, which relied on an administrative style of management, has been dismantled and the new mechanism of planned commodity control has not yet been built up. All these factors make the macroeconomic management of China's economy more difficult. How to revitalise the economy and at the same time strengthen macroeconomic control and harmony is a problem that remains to be solved in China's economic development. University and business personnel in China are confronting these problems and trying to devise effective solutions.

COOPERATION BETWEEN CHINA AND THE ASIAN–PACIFIC REGION

Since the implementation of the open-door policy to the outside world by the Chinese government, economic and technological cooperation between China and countries all over the world has been making great headway. The total value of China's two-way trade in 1979 was US$29.3 billion; by 1984 the figure had reached US$49.7 billion (US$53.5 billion according to the customs statistics). From 1979 (when the Law of the People's Republic of China on Chinese–Foreign Joint Ventures was promulgated) to the end of 1984, agreements signed by China using foreign capital reached a total value of US$28 billion; they included 931 joint ventures, 2212 contractual joint ventures, 74 enterprises with solely foreign investment, 31 oceanic petroleum exploration and development projects, and 1371 compensatory trade contracts. The growth of import–export activities and the progress in the use of foreign capital have played an active role in making up the deficits of domestic funds and raw and semi-finished materials, and also in importing advanced technology and equipment. The improvement of China's economic situation in recent years is mainly due to the adoption of the open-door policy and the policy of structural reform.

The importance of the Asian–Pacific Region to China

The Asian–Pacific region has always occupied an extremely important place in China's foreign trade. The figures for recent years show that import and export trade with Asian countries (mostly in East and South Asia) accounted for about 40 per cent and 67 per cent respectively of the total volume of China's import and export trade, making Asia the most important trading partner in the world for China. If Latin America, North America and Oceania are added, the proportions of import and export trade are 71 per cent and 79.5 per cent (1983 figures).

In the items of technology imported by China, the Asian–Pacific region has played an important role. In the past three years 653 contracts have been examined and approved by the Ministry of Foreign Economic Relations and Trade, with a total value of US$1.87 billion and covering 21 countries and regions; imports from Japan and the United States accounted for the biggest proportion, with West Germany ranking third. Items imported into China from these three countries accounted for 67 per cent of the total volume of imports and 77 per cent of their total value.

According to the statistics, in June 1984 more than 370 foreign enterprises in China were from nineteen countries and regions: 286 from Hong Kong, 23 from the United States, seventeen from Japan, six from the Philippines, four from Thailand, and the remainder from Australia, New Zealand, Singapore, and so on. All in all, businessmen in the Asian–Pacific region account for most foreign enterprise in China.

It is not accidental that the Asian–Pacific region occupies such an important place in China's economic and technological cooperation with other countries. In the first place, China is itself a Pacific country, with a continental coastline of more than 18 000 km, so that it is convenient for China to develop trade and economic and technological cooperation with Asian and Pacific countries through sea transport. Since the adoption of the open-door policy, China has taken four important steps; one is that the provinces of Guangdong and Fujian can apply special policies in their foreign economic activities; the second is the operation of four special economic zones, Shenzhen, Zhuhai, Shantou and Xiamen; the third is the opening up of fourteen coastal cities; and the fourth is the opening up of the Changjiang and Zhujiang Deltas and the triangular region in Southern Fujian. All the areas covered by these four steps are located along the Pacific coastline.

Second, the countries of the Asian–Pacific region, especially those in South and Southeast Asia, are geographically close to China, with fairly similar consumption behaviours and cultural heritages, as well as traditions of relatively close economic relations.

In the third place, the countries of the Asian–Pacific region are at different stages of development; there are developed countries with advanced technologies, there are newly industrialising countries with rapid economic growth, and there are a number of countries that are still in the preliminary stages of economic development. These different levels of development create a broad prospect for extensive economic and technological cooperation. The potential for economic and technological cooperation between the countries of the Asian–Pacific region and China is fairly great, and such cooperation has been making considerable headway in recent years, but it is still far from adequate in terms of China's modernisation target.

The role of exports in overseas cooperation

At present the crux of further development in China's overseas economic and technological cooperation is the extension of exports. Generally speaking, the development of China's overseas economic and technological cooperation has been fairly rapid in recent years. In the past few months, however, exports have been showing a tendency to decline. According to preliminary statistics, the volume of exports from January to May in 1985 showed a slight decrease from the volume for the corresponding period of the previous year, while the volume of imports has increased with the trade deficit. If this tendency cannot be controlled quite soon, it will be detrimental to China's efforts towards further development of overall foreign economic and technological cooperation.

First, exports are the most important source of China's foreign-exchange income, more than 80 per cent of foreign exchange at present coming from merchandise exports, and the proportion of foreign-exchange income not pertaining to trade is quite small. This sort of income structure is not likely to change in the immediate future. The drop in exports will lead to a reduction in foreign-exchange income, thus affecting the use of foreign exchange to import technology and equipment.

Second, in order to surmount the difficulties arising from the shortage of domestic funds, it would be advisable for China to encourage as much foreign investment as possible, yet the scope for attracting foreign investment cannot be extended at will. In general, foreign-exchange expenditure used to repay foreign investment, together with the interest for the current year, accounts for only about 20 per cent of China's total foreign-exchange income. Any reduction in foreign-exhange income will affect China's scope for using foreign investment.

Third, the experience of other countries suggests that there is a very close relationship between exports and the process of modernisation. From 1955 to 1979, the volume of Japan's exports increased more than fiftyfold, while the value of gross national output rose only fifteenfold in the same period; clearly the pace of export growth far exceeded the growth rate in the value of gross national output. Moreover, a corollary of Japan's immense trade surplus was that imports of technology accelerated greatly. It is important for China to heed the lesson of such experience: that the growth of exports should outpace the increase in the value of gross national output.

There are many different views on the reason for the slowdown in China's export growth. In the author's opinion, the main cause is the present excessive increase in investment in fixed assets, which has resulted in too drastic a rate of development. The value of China's gross industrial output from January to July of 1985 was 23.0 per cent higher than the value in the corresponding period of the previous year, a rate of progress rarely witnessed in recent years. One result of this extremely rapid growth is an increasingly serious shortage of materials and equipment; consequently, prices on the domestic market have risen and the potential profits from export contracts are lower than those from domestic trade. Another result is that, because of the insufficiency of energy and raw and semi-finished materials as well as the inadequacy of transport facilities, the input requirements for producing export commodities can hardly be satisfied in full.

The second reason is that the increase in China's exports over recent years has been mainly due to policy improvements rather than to technological progress and higher product quality. Hence no further improvement in China's export performance can be expected unless the existing export structure, in which energy, light industrial products and farm and sideline produce are dominant, can be broadened. However, there is still fairly ample potential to improve the quality of existing export commodities through technological progress.

The third reason is that China is still in the early stages of implementing the open-door policy. China lacks the necessary experience and knowledge, and is not familiar with the market conditions of other countries or the particular requirements of customers. For a certain period any reversal of China's trade deficit with some developed countries will not be possible; for example, in 1984 its trade deficit with Japan reached US$2 billion. In particular, some developed countries still use import quotas, thus restricting imports from the developing countries; for example, the discussion in the United States in 1985 about the implementation of legislation concerning textile products and the clothing trade represents a new offensive by the trade protectionists. In recent years, China has been importing airplanes, equipment, instruments, wheat and various other items from the United States, with the import volume increasing by 37 per cent in 1984, and China's exports of textile products and clothing to the United States represented 38 per cent of its total exports. If there should be a serious curtailment of China's exports of textile products and clothing to the United States, China's foreign-exchange income for this component of exports would also be seriously reduced, which would be bound to affect imports from the United States.

A determined effort to overcome and change the factors that are bringing about the decrease of China's export growth is the key to expediting China's economic and technological cooperation with other countries, especially the countries of the Asian–Pacific region.

Measures to increase exports

First, the rate of China's economic development must be properly controlled. As the Hungarian economist Tanos Kornai (1980) points out, there is an economic phenomenon of 'over-heating' in the use of resources in the socialist countries; a little carelessness in the formulation of policy can give rise to excessive investment and too great a speed of development. As long as the structural reform of China's economy remains incomplete, control of the scale and the rate of development of capital construction must remain an important task in the state's macroeconomic policy. The proper course is appropriate shrinkage of credit and strict procedures for examining and approving new construction or the extension of present construction; the scale of construction increase should be kept within reasonable bounds, and the requirements should not be continually increased. The domestic market for most products will then become a buyer's market as early as possible, and enterprises will be forced to extend their exports and search for outlets in the international market.

Second, alongside the enhancing of macroeconomic control and the popularising and implementation of the import–export agency system, the level of foreign exchange retained by enterprises must be expanded and foreign-exchange control gradually relaxed. Exporting firms should have the right to use their own foreign-exchange income and to really benefit by it; this would stimulate the initiative of firms to produce commodities for export and to change the existing situation, in which the export trade is less profitable than domestic marketing. In the case of products that have the potential to bring in foreign exchange, yet incur 'false losses' at present because of the domestic pricing and taxation systems, such measures as subsidies and exemption from taxation or other special tax treatment could be adopted to help enterprises to enlarge their export sectors.

Third, imports of technology must first of all serve to develop exports. In arranging import projects, the first consideration should be the requirements of factories producing export commodities, and conversely imports of advanced foreign technology should have priority in the development of export commodities. China's present export structure is rather backward. Primary products accounted for as much as 43 per cent of the total volume of exports in 1983, while chemical products and transport and mechanical equipment accounted only for 11.1 per cent, lagging far behind some of the newly industrialising countries of the Asian–Pacific region. By importing technology and thus raising the standard of processing and improving product quality, China will be able to change its backward export structure and increase its foreign-exchange income from exports. At the same time, the import emphasis should be in such areas as the transfer of specialised technologies, cooperative production arrangements and technical and consultancy services, so as to improve the economic effectiveness of the import structure.

Fourth, China should strive to increase its mutual understanding with countries in the Asian-Pacific region and throughout the world in order to open up more opportunities for economic and technological cooperation. In recent years, a number of countries in the Asian–Pacific region have been giving China much help in this respect; for example, in 1983 the Australian Department of Trade worked out its 'Action Program on China', which implemented measures to expedite the development of economic and trade relations between Australia and China, especially in the field of imports from China to Australia. The 'Study and Discussion Conventions on Australian Trade' held in Beijing, Tianjin and Shanghai in 1984 and in Nanjin, Shanghai and Guangzhou in 1985 have helped Chinese enterprises to understand the Australian market. These initiatives will be beneficial to China's export trade and to economic and technological cooperation between the two countries, and in the final analysis will benefit both China and Australia.

CONCLUDING REMARKS

It is true that China's exports are competing with exports from other countries. But such competition is to the benefit of consumers in those countries, and can also promote shifts in the industrial structure of advanced countries. China is still a backward country with a low level of consumption. Its export commodities are not competitive enough compared with those of other countries, and do not constitute a big threat to commodity exports from relatively advanced countries. Trade balance is one of the fundamental conditions for economic development and expansion of imports. Some of the advanced countries are already helping to raise China's imports, and China sincerely wants to cooperate with Pacific countries in these areas.

In summary, the Asian–Pacific region already occupies a relatively important position in China's present programs of economic and technological cooperation with other countries. Nevertheless, the key to further development of these cooperative activities is the enhancement of the export potential of Chinese products; this in turn requires the adoption of a series of measures by China and the understanding as well as the assistance of the countries in the Asian–Pacific region.

PART V
CONCLUSION

15 Summary of chapters and discussion

DAVID HUGHES, JAMES JORDAN,
FRANCES McCALL, HIROMICHI MUTOH,
SUEO SEKIGUCHI, KOTARO SUZUMURA
AND IPPEI YAMAZAWA

James Jordan and Frances McCall prepared a transcript of the discussion at the conference, from which the editors wrote an initial summary of proceedings. David Hughes was responsible for the final draft of this chapter, including the summaries of the papers and the integration of their main themes with the discussion.

The development of an analytical framework for the study of industrial policy was the starting point for discussion of the conference papers that form this volume. Indeed, as Gregory (chapter 1) points out, the relationship between economic theory and the political practice of industrial policy was a theme throughout the discussion. In the end this fundamental issue was perhaps less than totally resolved, reflecting widely varying conceptions of the role and conduct of industrial policy.

THE CONCEPTUAL FRAMEWORK

Okuno and Suzumura (chapter 2) provided some useful general observations on industrial policy in their opening paper, including a definition which some participants found a convenient focus for discussion: the enhancement of economic welfare in the presence of market failures. They also stressed that institutional factors can be both obstructions to the development of a universal theory and considerations in any decision about the efficacy of industrial policy. Given their definition, the body of the paper logically concentrated on three market-failure arguments for the presence of government industrial policy: positive externalities associated with the development of a new industry; the extraction of foreign-monopoly rents; and the regulation of 'excessive competition' in an oligopolistic industry.

The prepared responses by Paul Krugman and Peter Lloyd emphasised the need for caution in examining the causes for these three arguments.

Krugman argued that the analysis of external economies must provide the basis for assigning a crucial role to industrial policy, if there is such a basis. However, external economies leave no 'paper trail' of market transactions by which their importance can be measured. While it is plausible that new

285

industries are a sector where external economies are likely to be important, this notion should be qualified since the extent of externalities also depends on other characteristics of a given industry. For example, microelectronics is hardly a new industry, but the productivity of its intellectual terrain keeps it innovative; the liquid-fructose industry in the United States is new, but has never been strongly innovative; and finally, the aircraft industry is innovative, but is not a great generator of externalities because the benefits of innovation can be appropriated by a few large firms.

With regard to the extraction of foreign-monopoly rent, Lloyd stated that nothing in the argument for a production subsidy depends on the monopolist being foreign-owned, and that the best remedy is appropriate antimonopoly action. On this point, Krugman noted that profit-shifting policies work only as long as there are profits to shift, and that most economists believe that economic profits (that is, profits above a normal return) are not very large. Nevertheless, Okuno said in reply, the consumer-surplus gains from erecting entry barriers may still be large, and these entry barriers are even more important in modern, large-scale industries with substantial scale economies.

On the third argument examined by Okuno and Suzumura—the special Japanese concern about excessive competition—Lloyd observed that for internationally tradable goods, far fewer industries are oligopolistic in a global sense than appear to be so from the perspective of a single nation. If the problems are due to an international oligopoly it is doubtful whether national governments acting alone can do much to correct the excess capacity. Bela Balassa expressed doubts about the realism of the conjectures embodied in the Cournot model and about the assumption of homogeneous output used in the analysis. Suzumura replied that, with regard to these conjectures, the results do hold more generally and that excessive competition does occur with homogeneous products in Japan because of the government's use of the share principle in giving priority to firms. The homogeneous products model was not therefore chosen just by chance.

Having examined the specifics of Okuno and Suzumura's paper, discussion swung, on the first of many occasions at this conference, to the legitimate scope of industrial policy, involving the question of how economic and political analyses are to be treated and related.

Wontack Hong argued that industrial policy in economically mature countries encompasses distortions that have nothing to do with market failures. Where a legacy of distortions has been handed down and cannot be removed, second-best policies may be preferred. In such a case, an unrestricted competitive functioning of the market mechanism may not be the ideal policy. Obviously this argument is not limited, as Hong suggested, to a mature economy like Japan, but may also apply to economies regarded as in their infancy or decline, to use Okuno and Suzumura's categorisation.

In Caves' paper (chapter 3), the arguments for industrial policy are seen as very often the same as the traditional arguments for intervention in international trade. He dismisses some of these as of dubious worth before considering those problems of resource allocation that he considers may form a valid basis for intervention: externalities in research and proprietary knowledge; international oligopoly and the scope for strategic behaviour; and failures in the adjustment process and related information problems.

To a certain extent, therefore, Caves' concerns overlap the three arguments for industrial policy examined by Okuno and Suzumura. The differences between the United States and Japanese economies may be reflected in the different emphases of the two papers: failures in the adjustment process by the United States; regulation of 'excessive competition' by Japan.

Having dealt with problems of resource allocation, discussion focused more on the latter part of Caves' contribution—on the political economy of industrial policy, and on industrial and trade policies and international relations.

Like Okuno and Suzumura, Caves stressed institutional factors, but with an eye to their incorporation in analysis rather than as an obstruction to it. 'The framework for analysing industrial policy should include the political economy surrounding it', he said, and he referred to various models of rational individuals making economically sensible political decisions that might provide the beginnings of such a framework.

But their application may miss an important observed fact—'that industrial policy in the United States and Europe has a manifest tendency to support the losers rather than aid the winners among industries facing international competition'. This is because the political process balances perceived equities among various political claimants. Interest groups are rewarded in proportion to their perceived income shortfalls. 'The conventional vote-maximising model of political behaviour implies that a government will enact any measure that a majority of voters perceive to provide benefits to themselves in excess of the cost to them in taxation. Such a model is consistent with helping losers if a taste for a collective good is assumed—that is, the sense that fellow-citizens are being treated fairly in the light of their reasonable expectations.'

Michihiro Ohyama noted that in Japan, too, industrial policy is biased towards losers, but took exception to the logic of explaining this in terms of maximising utility. Taken with the assumption that equity of treatment within the national coalition is a substantial public good, this amounted to assuming a large part of the conclusion and therefore should not be accepted too readily.

McFetridge noted that there are Canadian proponents of activist industrial policy who believe it is possible to orient policy towards winners, and they cite Japan as evidence of this. Ryuhei Wakasugi, in the discussion of Nam's examination of the steel industry reported later in this chapter, points to Korea's policy of 'picking winners' in its third and fourth five-year industrial rationalisation programs. High priority was given to steel, much as it was in Japan in the 1950s and early 1960s.

He also questioned whether there is, as Caves had proposed, a concept of justice supporting a pay-off for losers. There exist competing explanations— for example, industrial policy can be viewed as insurance against change or modelled from the perspective of Olson's institutional sclerosis backed up by lobby groups against change.

Caves perceived equality as a public good, providing pressure towards equality through aiding losers and taxing winners. His reply that McFetridge's notion of insurance against change could be integrated with his own treatment of equity therefore seems reasonable.

In the final part of his paper Caves examined some of the effects of industrial policy on international trade—specifically, positive and negative externalities where one nation must suffer a decrease in welfare to improve the welfare of another nation or the world as a whole.

Ohyama pointed out that when discussing international policy coordination Caves considered only symmetric spillovers. But asymmetric spillovers may also be important, especially between advanced industrialised countries and less developed industrialising countries with regard to the relocation of industries. Nobuyoshi Namiki argued that the central problem is one of international industrial transformation: the developing countries want to increase their industrial capacity, whereas the developed countries need breathing space to convert their declining industries. Since it is difficult to make these two requirements compatible, difficulties have arisen in international trade. Namiki thought that the market-failure terminology was unduly restrictive for explaining the cause of the difficulties, since political, social and historical aspects are at the root of the problem. Ohyama also noted that Caves made no mention of the increasing returns to scale in modern industries, which are often cited as a major reason for international coordination in research and development and for international sharing of important industries, usually with learning-curve effects.

Frank Holmes returned the discussion to the definition of industrial policy. Okuno and Suzumura and Caves had provided one approach: policy designed to change the sectoral allocation of resources. Others, he said, would adopt a broader definition, encompassing policies aimed at promoting exports and employment, encouraging decentralisation (or regional dispersal), decreasing foreign control, providing industrial infrastructure, and supporting small businesses.

This is not just a matter of semantics. As Holmes noted, the implication of accepting changes in the sectoral allocation of resources as the definition of industrial policy is that the merits of particular policies are judged by the criteria of improving the efficiency of allocation. Presumably the second definition, which sees industrial policy as a tool for achieving broad government policy, economic, political and social, would have different and more complex criteria for measuring success.

The implications for a nation of accepting the broader definition and acting upon it was the substance of Holmes' description of 50 years of New Zealand industrial policy. Holmes reported that successive governments had intervened extensively in the industrial process in New Zealand since 1935. As a result a complex web had gradually developed of ad hoc intervention instruments with multiple objectives. The performance of the economy was relatively disappointing, and it had become apparent that the industrial policies themselves were partly responsible. Especially when it was found increasingly necessary for the government to subsidise primary industries in which New Zealand was thought to have a strong comparative advantage, it became obvious that new approaches were needed. The policies were also failing to achieve other important purposes at which they were aimed. They did not seem to be sustaining employment very well, even in the protected sectors; they did not overcome the overseas-exchange bottleneck; they seemed to aggravate inflation of costs and prices; they did not reduce regional disparities; the benefits did not seem to go to those whom the government was most anxious to help in terms of social justice. These considerations had led the Labour Party elected in 1984 to depart radically from these approaches to industrial policy, thus showing that public debate and changing circumstances can alter even deeply entrenched attitudes, policies and practices.

The problems of ad hoc policy were no doubt in Hugh Patrick's mind when he suggested that there is a distinction between industrial policies and industrial policy, on the basis that the latter requires a coherent aspect. In the session on country studies, in particular, the lessons of history and the complex issue of policy versus policies was given a good airing from a number of national perspectives.

COUNTRY STUDIES

English and McFetridge's paper (chapter 4) describing the Canadian experience of industrial policy highlights two distinctive features of the Canadian economy (which are common also to Australia): a heavy dependence on exports of resource-based products, and a federal system. In their history of Canadian industrial policy, English and McFetridge point to two major concerns in the 1960s that seemed to flow directly from being a resource-rich federal nation: the high levels of foreign ownership both in high-risk resource sectors and in the protected manufacturing sector, and the cost to outlying provinces of maintaining secondary manufacturing in central Canada (Ontario and Quebec). But, as they note, 'during the middle and late 1970s, the main focus of debate seemed to shift somewhat towards a contest between those who stressed trade liberalisation as a cornerstone for public policy and those who stressed the need for direct government intervention in support of Canadian technology and management so as to encourage Canadian exports of specialised processed and manufactured products'. The role of trade policy and a longer term structural policy on technological innovation are therefore the major concerns of their paper.

They conclude that 'for a medium-sized economy such as Canada's the centrepiece of industrial policy is trade policy'. Trade liberalisation, they contend, has contributed to a more efficient manufacturing sector, and, in particular, 'the evidence is that even more dramatic gains can be obtained by moving towards more comprehensive free trade with the United States'. As for technological change, they see strong theoretical and practical objections to engineering comparative advantage, and suggest international cooperation to counter competing government subsidies to research and development.

A detailed comparison of Australian and Canadian experiences of industrial policy would be a useful exercise given the many similarities between the two economies. Peter Forsyth highlighted two of the main differences. First, while Canada is close to its main export market, Australia is distant from *all* its markets. Second, Australia, in spite of having a smaller market, has in most industries more firms and plants, operating at lower scale and higher cost than Canadian enterprises. It is possible to argue that this is due to Australia's higher protection, which creates rents that attract new firms to an industry. Thus Australia has more and smaller firms all producing at high cost. One implication of low-scale production is that the cost of protection can be very high, a problem only dimly perceived in policy discussions. If anything, the workings of policy in Australia have exacerbated the problem in some industries. In the motor vehicle industry there were already too many producers (four) in 1970, but protection was increased and there are now five producers. Recently the scale problem has been recognised, and the latest policy calls for a reduction in numbers of producers.

On the more general issue of policy, Forsyth said that if governments do not wish to remove all protection immediately and are seeking a policy whereby to ease the adjustment process, it should be asked whether the policy will lower the cost of change. It is necessary to examine which way the incentives work; do they induce factors to move or to stay? It is difficult for governments to give a credible commitment to make protection temporary, so that firms spend the rents they gain from 'temporary' protection on lobbying for that protection to continue. Rather more insidiously, they play a game with the government by making further investments.

Ambiguities in industrial policy arising from the tendency of governments to say one thing but do another can also be very costly. A potential investor finds it difficult to know the general thrust of policy. Potential investors in industries that require protection to survive are dissuaded because they are uncertain whether such protection will be forthcoming. Potential investors in industries that can survive in an economy with low protection and a low real exchange rate are dissuaded. Thus there may be a bias in the direction of investment towards those industries where the comparative advantage is very clear, or towards non-traded industries. Thus, overall, industry policy may either promote or hinder efficiency, but whatever its direction, the ambiguity of policy may be costly.

The closest and most important of Canada's trading partners is the United States, and the relationship with that country was not unnaturally the main focus of the discussion arising out of the paper by English and McFetridge.

Ariff made the point that if Canada is more dependent on the United States than the other way around, and if the economic links between Canada and the United States are stronger than those between the Canadian provinces, it is possible that a Canada–United States bilateral free-trade arrangement would impose serious constraints on Canada's industrial development, by strengthening the present complementary structure so that Canada would remain a source of raw materials for United States industries and a market for United States manufactures.

Kiyoshi Kojima asked why Canada wants a wider free-trade arrangement with the United States alone. Why not include Japan? Lawrence White was astounded at the estimates (5–10 per cent of GNP) of the potential gain for Canada from free trade with the United States, and urged Canadian policymakers to be careful in drawing conclusions from the results of the Automotive Pact, since it had yielded gains in economies of scale that he does not believe will be found in other industries. Balassa thought that trade diversion should be discussed in this context, as it might be to the detriment of Pacific countries if a United States–Canada free-trade area did eventuate.

Ariff and Hill's examination of the ASEAN 'big four' was simplified by the similarity of the industrial policy objectives pursued in each. And '[a]part from the Philippines, where the immediate problem is to overcome the present serious financial crisis, the principal issues concern the impending second round of import substitution and the continued growth of manufactured exports'. The relative successes in manufacturing performance will depend largely on the policies chosen.

Discussion focused mainly on this question of import substitution versus export promotion, there being general agreement with Ariff and Hill that this was at the heart of the economic planning debate for the next ten years.

Somsak Tambunlertchai outlined the following examples of the obstacles confronting export promotion in Thailand. It is difficult to adjust the tax and tariff structure, which discriminates against export industries because import duty is an important source of government revenue. Also there is a chronic trade-deficit problem, and reductions of import tariffs on final goods may result in an upsurge of imports. Increasing export incentives by other means is obstructed by the threat of retaliatory countervailing duties. In addition, the international environment facing the ASEAN countries in the 1980s is quite different from that of the previous two decades. There is increasing protectionism among developed countries, and competition in promoting labour-intensive exports is very intense among developing countries. If a country like Thailand is to continue its policy of promoting manufactured exports, export products other than traditional goods such as textiles and footwear will have to be found. This is by no means an easy task, given the competition from the Asian newly industrialising countries and less industrialised countries like China and Sri Lanka, who are all pursuing similar policies.

Thus alternative strategies, more inward-looking than export promotion, have to be considered. For example, promotion of small-scale industries may be justified because they are in general more labour-intensive, more geographically dispersed and use locally produced inputs more intensively than large-scale industries.

Although the promotion of small enterprises is a declared objective in Thailand, very little has actually been done in this area. The present system still discriminates against small businesses. Again, budgetary constraints are evident here: while tax and duty exemptions for large enterprises involve substantial forgone revenue, they do not involve any large expenditures, whereas assistance for small enterprises tends to involve manpower and money. Nor can the lobbying power of large enterprises be ignored. This was a concrete example of industrial policy being lost or overturned by more immediate policies.

M. Hadi Soesastro agreed with the authors' conclusion that ASEAN manufacturing is at a crossroads, particularly since a second round of import substitution is being mooted. A comparative analysis of these ASEAN countries is instructive in that it could shed some light on the effects of market size on industrial strategy for industries in which economies of scale are important. He cited a study of Indonesia's industrial sector by UNIDO, which suggested the merit of a selective approach of blending import substitution with a labour-intensive strategy. The argument was that certain capital-intensive industries provide a stronger basis for longer term development and technological deepening, which would minimise the need for longer term protection. Soesastro also pointed out that the second round of import substitution in ASEAN will be different from the first in many respects, and agreed with Ariff and Hill that if it were not for the emerging financial difficulties the four big ASEAN countries would have gone further in promoting heavy industries. In view of this inherent tendency towards heavy, capital-intensive industrialisation, there is a need for countervailing measures such as convincing political leaders of the real cost of that tendency, and 'getting prices right' by correcting 'overvalued' exchange rates and eliminating other distortions in the wage–rental ratio. There is also a need, he said, for a bureaucracy with the ability to design a package of selective and specific market-facilitating measures; this, indeed, had been the basis of Japan's successful industrial policy.

Lawrence Krause also took up the issue of choosing between import substitution and export promotion, arguing that the choice must depend on the expected growth in international markets. Since the United States is trying to correct its trade imbalance, another round of import substitution is the more likely outcome. But posing the alternatives this way is too constraining. As Tambunlertchai seemed to suggest, an inward-oriented development policy does not have to be import-substituting. Many other things are important for welfare and employment and go down the growth road without following the import-substitution track—housing, for example. These considerations, and not just export promotion, are part of the reason for Korea's economic growth.

Seeing industrial policy as an all-or-nothing choice between two diametrically opposed approaches may itself be part of the problem. Annibal Villela commented that 30 years of observing the process of alternating between import substitution and export promotion in Brazil suggest that much more attention should be paid to evaluating proposed policies. Brazil's experience has shown too much Latin enthusiasm and too little analysis.

Some discussants were concerned about the exclusive focus on market failure, which seemed an incomplete explanation of, and guide to, industrial policy. This was especially true for less developed countries, said Kojima, where lack of markets, not market failure, was the chief justification for industrial policy.

Sekiguchi took this point a step further, arguing that there is a case for industrial policy beyond the failure or absence of markets. In particular, he referred to the well-established theory that there is a take-off for sustained growth when governments induce resource reallocation towards growth-oriented sectors. For example, suppose there are two sectors, one exhibiting increasing returns to scale, and the other with constant returns to scale. Suppose further that the terms of trade for the first sector are independent of the country's production but that the country has large world markets for the second sector (for example, rubber in Malaysia), and assume sticky capital allocation. Here a strong case exists for government policies that redirect resources into the sector with increasing returns to scale. In practice, the use of taxes and subsidies for this purpose is an important aspect of industrial policy in many developing countries. Of course, Sekiguchi added, an incorrect assessment by a government may result in a misallocation of resources and a worsening in economic performance, a point which other participants would no doubt emphasise.

The contribution by Liang and Liang (chapter 6) on the industrial policy of a newly industrialising country (Taiwan) provided a useful comparison with the ASEAN countries. Taiwan's industrial expansion until the late 1950s was inward-oriented, based on a strategy of multiple exchange rates and strict import controls. Poor growth prospects induced a series of government reforms between 1958 and 1961. A conscious, export-led industrialisation drive based on following Taiwan's comparative advantage resulted.

The role of industrial policy in this may be regarded as relatively narrow: helping to remove structural rigidities, facilitating the restructuring of industry, and promoting the flow of resources to the most productive areas. The industry and trade sectors have been dynamic; government policies have been correspondingly flexible.

To draw out fully the lessons of Taiwan's experience it is instructive to compare it with Korea. In many ways they are similar economies and societies, but important differences have occurred, with marked effects on their patterns of development. In contrast to Korea, Taiwan has had very high levels of domestic savings, has become a net creditor nation, and has followed a path of industrialisation founded on small and medium-sized independent businesses.

Toshio Watanabe drew these points together to provide two pictures of macroeconomic management. Korea stressed heavy and chemical industries; the trade balance deteriorated; and investment has continued to exceed domestic savings. The Korean economy therefore faced the pressure of excess demand and ensuing price increases, which in turn dampened domestic savings and stimulated equipment investment. In contrast, Taiwan's emphasis on export-oriented industrialisation kept a lid on inflation while improving the trade balance. Moreover, Taiwan's household savings ratio grew remarkably, through the increase in labour's relative share of income. Some of these points were expanded by discussants.

Hong concentrated on the discrepancy between domestic savings and investment in Taiwan. In 1984, saving as a share of GNP was 34 per cent while the share of domestic investment was only 21 per cent, generating a huge export surplus. The surplus savings have been accumulated in foreign assets whose rates of return are believed to have been much lower than those to domestic investment. Indeed, it would be extremely difficult for Taiwan to find investment projects overseas that are more profitable than those in its own economy. If Taiwan has to search for investment projects abroad, the obvious conclusion is that something has gone wrong with the basic Taiwanese economic system. The most likely cause of the problem is that Taiwan's backward and undeveloped financial regime has failed to function as an efficient intermediary between savers and investors. What may be needed is a fundamental reform of the financial system.

Krugman said that something peculiar seemed to be happening, since there has been a huge swing in Taiwan's export surplus as a percentage of GNP, which has its counterpart in a collapse in investment spending. He thought this looked like capital flight; but since there are effective restrictions on capital transactions by individuals, the curious situation obtains of the central bank accumulating foreign assets, that is, acting as the agent of capital flight. Lawrence added that there seemed to be a chronic inability to adjust the exchange rate, and that if the US dollar weakens considerably over the next five years, maintaining a fixed peg will exacerbate Taiwan's weird situation even further.

Hong made the further point that whatever the attractions of small and medium-sized enterprises, scale economies do exist in some industrial activities. So, over a quarter of a century of rapid growth, a substantial number of big enterprises ought to have emerged. That they have not done so must be due to structural defects in the economy that hinder the exploitation of scale economies. It cannot be simply attributed to the allegedly staunch individualism of the Chinese people that contrasts with the supposed group-thinking mentality of the Japanese and the Koreans. In reply, the Liangs said that the reason for the lack of large enterprises is that the government stresses liquidity and accordingly limits credit extension by banks to business. Businesses therefore find it difficult to obtain capital once they become larger, and this results in a fragmented corporate structure. This was not, however, a point to belabour. Economies of scale are not so important in electronics, a skill-intensive area which Hong had also observed as a targeted industry for Taiwan. Indeed, smaller entrepreneurial firms are probably a necessary part of any 'Silicon Valley'-style development.

Despite some cautionary remarks from discussants, Taiwan was generally perceived as a success. Balassa clearly associated this success with a consistent policy based on export promotion. The resultant large export surplus had given Taiwan a choice between reducing protection or revaluing its exchange rate. Both he and the Liangs thought the former a better policy. As a contrast to Taiwan, Balassa cited the Philippines from 1970 to 1982, where import-oriented policies were associated with very poor economic performance. Following Villela's earlier comments, he noted how outward-looking policy in Brazil in the mid-1960s had been replaced by inward-looking policy in the 1970s, resulting in growth but a large increase in debt.

The Liangs, in answer to a question from Hill, were not sure why Taiwan had had an easy transition from import-substitution to export-promotion policy. An educated and hard-working population, talent from the mainland and United States aid all may have played a part, but well-administered, flexible government policy in response to the dynamics of comparative advantage may also have been significant.

Taken together, these various comments highlight the difficulties of accounting for different rates of economic growth, and especially of deciding the importance to be attached to social and political factors. The lessons for other countries, such as the ASEAN nations, may not be so easily applied, and, as noted by discussants on the ASEAN 'big four', competition from more developed countries such as Taiwan may represent a problem. Good timing is, in part at least, a matter of good luck.

Lawrence, in his paper (chapter 7), followed Okuno and Suzumura's definition of industrial policy as all policies designed to affect the allocation of resources. Economics provides a framework for this, in identifying a variety of market failures and suggesting guidelines to how intervention should take place. These principles hardly match the realities of the conduct of policy: a case of policy versus policies or, as he puts it, of the efficient allocation of resources so as to maximise economic welfare versus diverse political objectives.

'These observations suggest that no positive analysis of industrial policies can ignore political considerations,' argues Lawrence. His approach is to look at the impact of historical traditions, economic positions and political institutions on industrial policy in the United States and Europe, and then to judge their efficacy. The message for Lawrence is that industrial policies that supplement market forces may do some good, or at least not much harm; if they try to reverse market behaviour, they will be costly and perhaps counterproductive.

Namiki proposed that we should consider industrial policy as policy that governments adopt either to introduce new industries or to revitalise industries which seem to lag behind their competitors abroad. This is not inconsistent with Lawrence's advice that policy should follow the market, but it does seem to conflict with Lawrence's clear distinction between economic efficiency (or policy) and other, political objectives (policies). For Namiki, industrial policy is a historical phenomenon, and to prove the usefulness of his perspective he provided examples of industrial policy in developed countries ranging from France just after the Revolution (1789) to the first cases of industry-revitalisation policy in Britain in the 1920s and 1930s. Needless to say, in the future Japan may face the necessity of introducing a second round of industrial policy to revitalise and remodernise its industrial structure. As other participants had said in discussion of the paper by Liang and Liang, the success of such industrial policy depends quite strongly on a nation's value system.

More specifically, Namiki questioned Lawrence's stress on the temporariness of United States import restrictions in view of the existence of the Multi-Fiber Agreement, the international cartel in the shipbuilding industry, and the de facto continuation of import restrictions on steel and also on motor cars. He argued that there was a return to free trade in television sets for the simple reason that many foreign companies had already established themselves in the United States through direct investment, so that import restrictions just meant giving profits to foreign companies which then repatriated the profits, aggravating the balance-of-payments position. He conjectured that the case of video recorders will proceed in the same way but that the steel and car industries cannot because of their economic importance. Lawrence agreed that in the television industry protection induced investment, which facilitated adjustment. He stated that multinationals have increasingly been the best friend of the liberal trading system, and that it is crucial to facilitate this process of inter-market penetration.

Balassa cited a number of examples to show that while there has been some increase in protection in the United States, this has only partially compensated for the overvaluation of the dollar, but that the corresponding undervaluation of European currencies has not been accompanied by reductions in protection. Rather, the Common Market countries have become increasingly protectionist. He therefore questioned Lawrence's conclusion that the United States had used trade policy to meet domestic policy responsibilities. Europe had tended to do this *and* to use direct subsidies and nationalisation, a conclusion Lawrence said he had not intended to dispute. Balassa claimed, however, that there was a trend in Western Europe, especially in the United Kingdom and Italy, towards increased reliance on market forces and so a de-emphasis on industrial policy.

With regard to conditionality of adjustment assistance, Sekiguchi said that workers need incentives to try to find new jobs; the Japanese government provided detailed measures in this regard. In reply, Lawrence thought that a tariff that is preset to decline and is credibly temporary was all that was needed. He was very sceptical of a government's ability to program the direction of change.

In response to Uekusa's enquiry about the role of industrial policy at the State level in the United States, Lawrence said that the States are becoming increasingly involved, especially since locational decisions are sensitive within a specific region. While the nation would be better served by taking a larger view, he thought that the issue was of little importance overall, particularly since the States themselves are up against fiscal constraints.

The compass of Japanese industrial policy, examined by Uekusa and Ide in chapter 8, is often divided into 'industry-specific policies' and 'horizontal industrial policies'. 'Industry-specific policies' are concerned with allocating resources among industries through protecting and promoting promising industries and adjusting declining industries, and thus with industrial reorganisation, the adjustment of production and investment, and price stabilisation. 'Horizontal industrial policies' cover providing industrial infrastructure, dealing with pollution and trade friction, and promoting the development of small and medium-sized enterprises. The former are industrial policies in the narrow sense and constituted the focus of Uekusa and Ide's paper, though both types of policy pertain to a series of market failures. The authors provided a description of the process of policy formulation in Japan, and a history and evaluation of Japanese industry policy.

Japan is often cited as a success story for industrial policy, and it is looked to for lessons by less developed and developed countries alike. Uekusa and Ide's overview of Japan's postwar policy and practice suggested that, although there have been some negative effects, the stated goals of industrial policy have generally been achieved. This may seem prima facie evidence for its efficacy, but then it is impossible to say whether similar or indeed better results could have been achieved under different (including less interventionist) industrial policy. This cautionary note was endorsed by other participants, and draws one to conclude, with Uekusa and Ide, that 'industrial policy in itself cannot be effective in the absence of competitive markets and fair trade practices, or without skilful entrepreneurship'.

But Uekusa and Ide did accept that industrial policy has played its part in Japanese economic growth, especially during the postwar period, when recovery 'could not be wrought by the competitive market mechanism alone'. Hugh Patrick was rather less sanguine about this. For him, the dominant reason for Japan's economic success has been vigorous, competitive, entrepreneurial private business operating in a conducive and supportive environment engendered in part by the government, including its industrial policy. The great contribution of the Ministry of International Trade and Industry was to induce new entry into capital-intensive large-scale sectors and to force competition to international price levels. Japanese industrial policy today, he added, is largely defensive, with the biggest share of government resources going to agricultural producers and small businesses, all for income redistribution and vote-buying. Certainly this is neither growth-inducing nor helpful for structured adjustment. A second area of policy is geared towards smoothing the adjustment process for declining manufacturing industries, mainly through reducing inefficient excess capacity. Mergers or an orderly sharing of capacity cuts are preferred to the normal individualistic process of bankruptcy. Success in this area has been limited to shipbuilding; notable failures include textiles. There is also a third policy element that supports potential high-technology winners, mainly through support for research and development. There are probably also hidden agenda in high-technology policy, namely to keep security and strategic options open.

The main lesson for the United States that Patrick drew out is on structural adjustment, where the Japanese approach may be preferable to the ad hoc import restrictions used so far in the United States to protect the automobile, steel and textile industries. Here policymakers may be forced to accept second-best policy given the political clout of these industries.

Peter Drysdale drew from the paper a taxonomy of industrial policy analysis—policy goals, concrete policy objectives and policy instruments—which emphasises that industrial policy instruments are targeted towards a social purpose defined in a political process. This relationship between political choice and economic policy has been, he added, a recurring if unresolved theme.

For Drysdale, there is an important message in the literature of political economy—namely, that the elevation of irrational policy choices or the pursuit of private interest into public goods in policy debate does not detract from the sensible idea that different politics will at different times define different social and policy goals as the targets of industrial policy instruments. He thought an examination of the Japanese case suggested that national and private energies had been more or less successfully mobilised towards such goals. This was done first in the course of reconstruction and recovery (a period of heavy regulation and intervention in Japan, as well as in other countries); then it was done in the course of heavy industrialisation and rapid economic growth (which was a period of progressive liberalisation of trade, investment and technology policy); and it is now being done during the process of adjustment in a mature economy (a period in which adjustment of distressed industries and support for high-technology industry have been taken up as prominent policy goals).

Drysdale emphasised the message in the Uekusa and Ide paper that the process of heavy industrialisation and rapid growth involves a significant retreat from industrial regulation. Moreover, there was more than a hint in the paper that, as regulatory controls are released or significantly modified, so-called 'administrative guidance' rapidly becomes a less effective policy instrument, as would be expected.

Drysdale also commented on the evidence that adjustment assistance policies are relatively unimportant in facilitating the phasing out of declining industries; he agreed with Uekusa and Ide that the evidence suggests that cross-subsidisation and mutual assistance within Japanese corporate groups (*keiretsu*) have ultimately been much more important in the successful closure of aluminium, cement-making and petrochemicals capacity. It is salutary to remember that the aluminium industry was never competitive in Japan (even in the era of cheap energy), and survived only through organising substantial protection for itself. The enterprise groups themselves eventually took the important initiatives and bore the brunt of the cost of closing down a large part of the industry. In textiles, coal and aluminium the discipline of the market had its way, mainly because, in the case of textiles there was no protection for export sales, and for coal and aluminium the manufacturers of final products would no longer bear the costs.

Lawrence took up this topic with the remark that he was mystified by the discussion of depressed industries and the temporary laws of 1978, as it is said that the laws were not accompanied by import protection but that the appearance of cartels became a problem. He then posed a few questions. In the case of a standardised product without import protection, how can a cartel be formed? Given that the United States chemicals companies have access to very cheap feedstock through regulations in the natural gas area, how does the Japanese chemicals industry manage without import protection in some form or other? What were the informal import barriers that must have existed? He also remarked that if such barriers did exist the Japanese program was incompatible with the OECD guidelines. Uekusa responded only that there were free imports of chemicals. Both Drysdale and McFetridge wondered what actually went on in regard to the regulation of direct foreign investment and technology imports, Drysdale asking whether Japanese experience suggests that a judicious control over foreign-entry and technology-import policy can be effectively directed towards capturing foreign technology rents.

Other participants raised a number of issues that they thought might warrant further attention. Yamazawa noted the importance attached to the industrial-relations system in explaining Japan's economic success, and wondered whether the role of the Japanese labour unions, in comparison with say the United States unions, was an important factor. White thought the role of high savings in determining growth needed to be more fully explored. He added that in a growth economy industrial policy usually works reasonably well; the real test of industrial policy comes when growth tails off. Akrasanee thought there was a conspicuous absence of discussion on the promotion of manufactured exports as part of industrial policy.

INDUSTRY STUDIES

Certain industries figure more prominently than others in the debate on industrial policy. Basic heavy industries such as steel, chemicals and aluminium, and major manufactures like motor vehicles, electronics and textiles, clothing and footwear are vital concerns for economists and government policymakers. This is reflected in the papers and discussions of the first two sessions of this conference.

To put the matter simply, for developing countries basic input industries like steel are often seen as strategic parts of an industrialisation program and, together with lower and mid-range technology manufacturing, are generally at the heart of both import-substituting and export-oriented industrial policies. For the developed countries, on the other hand, they are often crisis points in the economy, with large-scale employers facing increasing competition from overseas.

The four industry sectoral studies presented in the third session reflected these differing perspectives. Lloyd's paper on textiles and clothing (chapter 9) and White's paper on automobiles (chapter 10) considered the responses of developed nations to structural adjustment in major industries. Nam on iron and steel (chapter 11) and Koh on petrochemicals (chapter 12) took a broader look at the changing nature of world trade in these industries, and examined the different effects on, and the industrial policies of, developed, advanced developing and less developed nations.

These papers highlighted some of the points made earlier: the need to consider differing national perspectives in analysing industrial policy, including the observation that a country's stage of economic development influences policy; the importance of understanding a nation's social and political structure; the significance of changes in comparative advantage; and the close connection between industrial and trade policies. They provide a useful extension, therefore, to the papers and discussions from the second session.

The textile and clothing industries have declined in all the developed economies except Spain and Greece. Lloyd gave an overview of trade in these products by the five advanced Pacific Basin nations before considering Australia and New Zealand in more detail. He then briefly discussed why government structural adjustment policies have been ineffective in achieving declared government objectives. Two reasons were advanced: one was simply a lack of understanding, suggesting the need for more studies to measure the costs and benefits of policy instruments; the other was the political process determining the choice of policy instruments. Several models have been developed to explain government policymaking; for example, the specificity of labour and capital factors may give rise to a vigorous coalition of interests to lobby for the deceleration of structural change.

C.H. Liang recognised that the textile and clothing industries are facing adjustment problems that they cannot surmount on their own, and, like Lloyd, he questioned the appropriateness of the measures taken by governments. Further studies on the impact of government policies compared with their intended effects would be of great interest, particularly to the developing countries that are now trying to modernise their textile and clothing industries.

Yamazawa extended Lloyd's analysis of intra-industry trade, asserting that large multinational firms dominate the production of inputs (especially synthetic fibres) and the marketing of final products, leaving the middle-stream processes of spinning and weaving to smaller firms. Because these giant companies pursue global strategies and respond to the adjustment processes of numerous countries simultaneously, they probably do not have much impact on the textile-trade policies of the developed countries. Instead, intra-firm trade creates a constituency in opposition to the government's import-restriction policies.

Following the same line of thought, Krause suggested that Lloyd develop a political model of protection. In the United States, for example, Congress, the lobbying industry and the bureaucracy all have an interest in protection but not in limiting imports. Congressmen aim only to satisfy their constituents; lobbyists for their part, would lose customers if imports were cut off. This line of analysis explains the numerous exceptions to the Multi-Fiber Agreement, for example.

Yamazawa also questioned Lloyd's blanket assertion that the governments of all developed countries have increased import restrictions at the expense of structural adjustment. In Japan's policy mixture, domestic adjustment assistance features more prominently than restriction of imports. This lower reliance on import restriction is due in part to Japan's emergence in the 1960s as a major exporter of textiles, and in part to its chronic surplus with many of its trading partners. Meanwhile the Japanese government has been providing adjustment assistance for domestic producers. But in the final analysis it has been the private sector's efforts to introduce automation, develop new products and improve standard products that have contributed most to the revitalisation of the Japanese textile and clothing industries. These efforts, in turn, were a response to severe competition, both within the domestic market and from the tightening of export markets.

However, Balassa referred to statistics showing that Japan's imports of textiles and clothing from the developing countries increased by only 50 per cent between 1973 and 1983, while Europe's imports increased by a factor of three and America's by a factor of five over the same period. Japan in particular might have been expected to increase imports of textiles and clothing from the less developed countries more rapidly, since Japan's factor-endowment structure has become more like those of other developed countries. Meanwhile, Japan's increase in imports from developed countries grew by a factor of 3.4 over the same period, suggesting that Japanese consumers prefer high-quality goods. Japan may have few overt import restrictions, but it is clear that it is limiting in some way its imports from less developed countries. Tambunlertchai pointed out that Thailand's products do not sell well in Japan, not only for quality reasons but also because Thai producers lack the close ties with Japanese wholesalers that Taiwanese and Korean firms have. Lloyd replied that caution should be exercised in using import-share statistics, since they include both competitive and uncompetitive imports.

English disagreed with Lloyd's application of the concept of materials intensity, arguing that its significance is not for the location of production and marketing, but rather for the interrelationship between the clothing and textiles industries. In Canada, for example, the textiles industry is capital-intensive but favours protection nevertheless, first because it is an established industry that does not care for outside competition, and second because it is heavily dependent on the more labour-intensive domestic clothing industry. This is not to say, however, that the two sectors are never at loggerheads about the protection of the other.

In Australia and Japan the social and political climates are relatively favourable to broad industrial policy, but in the United States its legitimacy is still a widely debated topic. This may explain why, as White maintains in chapter 10, the American government has taken no formal measures in this direction. Nevertheless, White regards the sum of all governmental actions and policies affecting an industry as de facto industrial policy. In his paper the United States government's policies towards the American motor vehicle industry from 1979 to 1985 are examined as one such de facto industrial policy.

Hiromichi Mutoh noted two additional effects of the Voluntary Restraint Agreement that White could profitably have investigated: first, bilateral agreements have proliferated as a result of the United States–Japan agreement, extending now to Japan–West Germany, Japan–Benelux, and Japan–Canada; second, since the Ministry of International Trade and Industry played a crucial role in apportioning export market shares to each of the domestic car makers, its power over the Japanese car industry has been strengthened.

Mutoh also suggested a re-examination of the assumptions underlying the various empirical studies of the impact of the Voluntary Restraints Agreement. The International Trade Commission study, for example, assumes a price elasticity of minus 2.0 in American demand for Japanese cars, but a recent study by Tsurumi shows that the elasticity fluctuated significantly over the 1970s. It might then be useful to compare the situation under the Voluntary Restraint Agreement with a hypothetical free-competition case. In response,

White stated that all four studies of the agreement that he had cited led to the same conclusion, namely, that it involved high costs in exchange for few jobs saved.

Patrick noted that, although the agreement was at first thought to be a good idea, it has lost its lustre. It is not as easily removed as was once thought; many of the scarcity rents accrue to the competitors (Japan); its cost to American consumers is significant; and it has kept alive marginal producers in Japan who otherwise would have left the scene. From the United States standpoint, then, the agreement seems to favour Japan. Patrick also pointed out, however, that American producers might regain competitiveness if they used cheaper overseas components. Japan's benefit from using relatively lower cost sources may therefore be only temporary.

Forsyth agreed with White and Patrick that the Voluntary Restraint Agreement transfers scarcity rents from the United States to Japan, but suggested that the agreement reflects the 'horse-trading' situation between the United States and Japan, in which each recognises the other's scope for retaliation.

The effect of product differentiation on the process of adjustment was particularly emphasised by Caves. In the automobile industry (unlike steel, for instance), different countries have differentiated products, so that a change in the pattern of trade restrictions leads to a shift in the prices of the various products. Automobile makers in the United States reacted to their worsening comparative advantage by raising the price–cost margin on their principal product lines, leaving consumers worse off and creating cost margins that are inconsistent with the competitive world prices.

English drew attention to the perspectives offered by branch plant economies of the sort practised by Canada and Australia (some might call these arrested adolescent economies) and by the developing economies.

A lesson from Canada's experience is that when protection is combined with product differentiation and foreign investment, achieving internationally competitive production is not easy. An interventionist industrial policy may solve the problem only partially if it does not incorporate a commitment to eliminate or reduce production.

Developing countries face similar difficulties, but there are no solutions that do not involve a commitment by the international companies in these countries to rationalise their productive activities. Even if a rationalisation policy were adopted, it would benefit the developing countries only if the remaining rival firms were subject to some threat of competition from other producers.

Narongchai Akrasanee also was interested in the lessons for developing countries, especially Southeast Asia, arguing that an extension of White's analysis to that region might have been more suitable to the main theme of the conference. As he saw it, Southeast Asian countries have two basic options with regard to structural adjustment in the automobile industry. First, as typified by Malaysia's policy choice, they can adopt an import-substitution strategy and impose local-content requirements. Alternatively, they can pursue an export-oriented strategy, as Thailand is considering doing. The Philippines and Indonesia have opted for compromise strategies that incorporate local-content provisions with export promotion.

White responded by pointing to the dismal history of the automobile industry in Latin America. The developing countries in Southeast Asia, he said, would pay a similarly high price for trying to foster a domestic automobile industry.

It has already been noted that the steel industry occupies a prominent position in the industrial policies of a number of countries. Nam emphasised this special consideration given to steel in his paper (chapter 11). Developing countries often attempt to establish a domestic steel industry much earlier than would have been suggested by an assessment of national factor endowments because steel is a vital input for a wide range of manufacturing industries. The governments of advanced industrialised countries, even though faced with deteriorating international competitiveness and declining domestic demand over the past twenty years, have resorted to various protectionist measures to avert a collapse of their steel industries. The steel industry is thus a useful case study for examining structural adjustment, in both the advanced industrialised countries and the advanced developing countries, in the face of shifts in comparative advantage.

Nam's prediction for the world steel industry is that the most dynamic growth will take place in the advanced developing countries because of their rapidly rising domestic demand and improving international competitiveness. Korea, in particular, is in an advantageous position as an emerging steel exporter because of its dynamic domestic economy and its low relative costs of steel production. Any attempts by the advanced industrialised countries to forestall the emergence of steel exporters in the developing countries would snowball, necessitating the protection of the industrialised countries' steel-intensive industries as well.

That rapid structural change is not occurring is indicative of the political sensitivity of the steel industry, and provides a very clear example of the need to include political considerations in any practical analysis of industrial policy. It also highlights the opposing interests at work in different countries at different stages of development.

Wakasugi characterised industrial policy towards the steel industry simply as 'picking winners' in advanced developing countries and 'picking losers' in advanced industrialised countries. Even in Japan, which has placed greater stress on readjustment than have the other industrialised economies, none of the adjustment programs has been completed within the specified time. The developing countries, on the other hand, force the industrialised countries to adjust or flounder by pouring resources into their domestic steel industries. But, Wakasugi emphasised, both picking losers and picking winners distort international trade.

Some of the discussants were pessimistic about how far structural adjustment would proceed. Patrick thought a de facto cartelisation of the world steel industry was a possibility. Krugman agreed, citing the United States–Japan agreement as a probable model. Nam, in reply, noted the difficulties for an international cartel in reaching consensus among producers.

The case of Japan was given a further dimension by Namiki, who took exception to the twofold categorisation of winners and losers; he argued that there are no declining industries in Japan—rather, older industries are revitalised.

Ohyama felt that Nam dismissed the factor-proportions theory too lightly, since world trade is still shaped by internationally immobile factors such as land and labour. Nam countered that once technology is embedded in a plant there is little substitution between labour and capital, so that latecomers have a decisive advantage. Patrick concurred, pointing out that the Japanese steel industry's success was partly attributable to the new technologies it adopted in the 1950s and 1960s. By contrast, it was difficult for the older plants in the United States and Europe to take advantage of the new technologies. The existing, small-scale plants were handicapped when the Japanese plants came on stream. Hill made the same point in comparing the different factor intensities for the steel industries of the United Kingdom and Korea.

Krugman, however, was not convinced by these arguments. It is true that no greenfield plants were built in the United States during the 1950s and 1960s, and that existing plants are therefore outmoded. But the reason for this was not American error; greenfield plants would not have earned a competitive rate of return. Even in Japan in the late 1960s, the rate of return to the steel industry was less than half that to the manufacturing industry as a whole.

A number of people doubted whether the low cost of labour in the advanced developing countries would make much difference in the long run. Hill pointed out that steel production technology has been moving rapidly in the direction of physical-capital intensity, capital being a relatively mobile factor in the Pacific Basin. Ariff added that if technology and capital are mobile (and the steel industry is intensive in both) countries with raw materials, such as Brazil, would have a long-term advantage. Nam may therefore be too optimistic about the future of Korean steel.

English agreed with both Hill and Ariff, stressing that substantial protection of the transportation industry favours countries endowed with raw materials rather than countries with low labour costs (which are likely to rise in the long run).

Nam replied that while it is difficult to project the steel industry's course in the long run, lower labour costs are a clear source of comparative advantage, at least in the short run. The current shares of labour costs in total steel production costs are 35 per cent in the United States, 20 per cent in Japan, and only 5–6 per cent in Korea; Korea's cost advantage is obvious.

Several participants pointed to the long-term growth potential for steel in countries close to iron-ore sources, such as Brazil. Similarly, Koh in her paper on petrochemicals (chapter 12) saw proximity to raw materials as the principal determinant of success in that industry. She pictured the world petrochemicals industry as undergoing a period of transition. Weaker demand for petrochemicals and associated products has resulted in excess capacity in traditional centres of production in Japan, the United States and Europe. At the same time the emergence of cost-competitive production in the oil-rich areas of the Middle East suggests the likelihood of a shift in the international division of labour; countries with indigenous feedstock will probably come to dominate the production of bulk petrochemicals, with the established producers in the developed countries moving further downstream towards more research-and-development-intensive products or forming joint ventures with the oil-rich producers.

Koh's more detailed studies of three countries—Japan, Singapore and the Philippines—support this broad analysis of the world industry. Japan is a good example of the developed countries, given its loss of comparative advantage in bulk petrochemicals. Energy-deficient countries like Singapore who have only recently entered the petrochemicals industry have a rough road ahead in terms of price competition, and need to cushion themselves from the vagaries of a soft petrochemicals market.

Serious cost–benefit analyses must be conducted for countries such as Malaysia, Thailand, the Philippines and Indonesia who intend to set up petrochemicals facilities in the near future. Full consideration should be given to the export prospects, and to the possibility of importing more cheaply from the Middle East. Caution is especially warranted for energy-deficient countries such as the Philippines who are simultaneously saddled with debt and other problems.

Miyohei Shinohara was also pessimistic about Japan's petrochemicals industry. After the oil crises and the tightening of the market for petrochemicals, Japan should now proceed with adjustment policies, but little improvement is likely in the short term.

Raul Fabella remarked that if a technologically advanced country like Japan is retreating from petrochemicals, it would be suicidal for oil-deficient developing countries to join the fray. But the criticisms of economists had not stopped the Philippine government from going ahead with large-scale plans to develop a domestic petrochemicals industry. Misguided nationalism, said Fabella, lures the governments of less developed countries into hopeless ventures.

Opinions on the future of Singapore's petrochemicals industry were a little more mixed. Although Koh had predicted a hard road ahead, Singapore's comparatively high real growth in petrochemicals was a cause for at least some optimism. Shinohara was less hopeful, pointing out that even if Singapore can keep down the price of its petrochemicals, the fact that Singapore is a small economy and a price taker on the world market means that the benefits of cost-cutting technological progress will flow overseas, rather than be captured by the domestic economy. Koh agreed, but John Wong added an optimistic word, emphasising that Singapore's neighbours are still net importers of petrochemicals, and that the demand for petrochemicals is sure to rise. In response to Wong, Patrick said that geographic proximity should be of little importance if transport costs are low.

Siow-Yue Chia compared Singapore's petrochemicals industry to its oil-refining industry. Because of changes in the external environment, Singapore's comparative advantage has become disadvantage in both industries. But unlike Singapore's oil-refining industry, which was largely built by foreign direct investment, its petrochemicals industry is heavily subsidised by the government. The petrochemicals industry, Chia surmised, would therefore be politically more difficult to mothball, even though it is cheaper to import petrochemicals from oil-rich countries. Hill commented that petrochemicals in Singapore should serve as a useful test case of a government's ability to pick winners and losers, since Singapore is generally regarded as a strong government that is free from bondage to interest groups.

As a final point on the future of the petrochemicals industry in the Middle East, Patrick thought its comparative advantage would be considerable if flare gas does indeed have close to zero opportunity cost, and if it is abundant in the Middle East. Krause took some exception to this, arguing that the opportunity cost of flare gas approaches zero only at huge production levels. Under present circumstances, said Krause, there are important opportunity costs even for OPEC countries. Koh did not have statistics on the real cost of flare gas, but she believed it to be quite low.

Koh was uncertain about the extent to which ASEAN wanted Singapore to play a regional role in petrochemicals, although in her paper she had emphasised the desire of ASEAN nations to develop their own petrochemicals industry, a move regarded by participants as fraught with danger.

In concluding the discussion of industry sectoral studies, Tsuruhiko Nambu provided a different perspective on the relationship between the economic theory and the political practice of industrial policy by describing the role of government in the development of Japan's high-technology industries (Nambu, 1986). He outlined a model of bureaucratic decisionmaking in which industrial policy is effective only when the supply of and demand for government market intervention coincide. The supply side involves intra- and inter-ministerial competition for the provision of market intervention; the demand-side represents business response to intervention, which would be favourable only if profits arising from the government action exceeded costs. This analysis provided a framework for understanding the role of Japan's Ministry of International Trade and Industry in the development of high-technology industries. Nambu concluded that the ministry's success relies on providing subtle signals to business rather than on direct intervention or subsidy, such signalling being a particularly important part of the Japanese socioeconomic system.

Nambu's model and his appraisal of Japanese bureaucratic success drew comments from a number of participants. Krause thought Nambu's theoretical framework could be strengthened by stressing certain universal aspects of bureaucratic politics, such as the tendency of bureaucrats to serve their own ends along with those of society. Nambu replied that the Japanese and United States bureaucracies were markedly different; in particular, the incentive structure of the Japanese bureaucracy tends to subordinate self-interest to the public interest.

Chia, while he agreed that the Japanese bureaucracy had been fairly effective in guiding economic growth, noted some instances of bureaucratic error and inability to pick winners. For example, MITI had initially opposed the establishment of a modern steel industry in postwar Japan, on the grounds that Japan could not compete against the United States. Again, Sony had to postpone its efforts to import transistor technology from the United States because the Japanese bureaucracy did not believe that the company would be able to make good use of the technology.

Eduardo Lora thought more consideration should be given to the connection between the model of individual behaviour and the successful actions of the bureaucracy as a whole which Nambu had identified. And Paul Krugman noted that Nambu had attempted to explain why MITI intervenes in the market without first describing how it promotes high-technology industries and to what effect.

As a final point arising from this discussion, both Chia and Holmes questioned the applicability of the Japanese model of industrial policy to other Pacific countries. Chia thought the developing countries of Asia and the Pacific lacked both the bargaining leverage to import technology and the financial resources to plough back into research and development. Holmes pointed out that in New Zealand the bureaucracy is reluctant to become involved in policies of protection and promotion.

REGIONAL ASPECTS

The nature of ASEAN industrial cooperation was the subject of R.B. Suhartono's paper (chapter 13), the first of two papers presented, in the fourth session of the conference, on regional aspects of industrial policy. Suhartono's paper may be regarded as an extension of a theme developed throughout this conference: accommodating both economic and political perspectives in the analysis of industrial policy. The final paper, by Mu Yang (chapter 14), explored this theme for the rather different but increasingly important case of the People's Republic of China.

Suhartono regards ASEAN as distinct from earlier regional groupings of developing countries, in that it has not adopted the economic integration of its member countries as a primary objective. Rather, it has taken a cautious, step-by-step approach to economic cooperation, leaving the final goal unspecified. The general objective of economic cooperation has given ASEAN the flexibility to adapt to shifting national interests in a changing international environment. He argues that the theory of economic integration has little relevance for developing countries. A look at historical examples indicates that attempts to transplant the theory to developing countries have produced undesirable results.

Instead of embracing trade liberalisation as a means of achieving market integration, ASEAN opted for selective integration of markets through preferential trading arrangements. Selective integration encourages the development of joint ventures and inter-industry linkages, paving the way for greater participation by the private sector.

On both the governmental and the private-sector levels, the process of selective integration has resulted in the institutionalising of certain practices and forms of interaction. There is evidence for an emerging framework for industrial cooperation in the Agreement on the ASEAN Preferential Trading Arrangement, the Basic and Supplementary Agreements on Industrial Projects, the ASEAN Industrial Complementation scheme, and the ASEAN Industrial Joint Ventures.

Cooperative industrial projects that have been undertaken or are being considered are still few in number, but this may reflect basic structural problems such as conflicts of national interest rather than any flaw in ASEAN's framework of industrial cooperation in itself. If this is the case, these problems need to be examined instead of being assumed away as many integrationists are wont to do. Given the circumstances, ASEAN's modest approach seems preferable to the more ambitious alternatives, however appealing they may sound.

Suhartono's presentation to the conference included a lengthy discussion of integration theory, which, English thought, placed too much stress on economies of scale; it may reflect the integration literature, but it is defective and should be corrected. While Lee generally agreed with Suhartono's scepticism about the relevance of the theory of economic integration when applied to developing countries, he could not follow how Suhartono reached his conclusion that economic cooperation is preferable to economic integration; some of the arguments against economic integration apply equally to economic cooperation, so that the irrelevance of economic integration does not necessarily imply the appropriateness of economic cooperation.

Akrasanee and Soesastro thought Suhartono spent too much time apologising for the slowness of ASEAN's progress towards greater cooperation, whereas he should have been criticising ASEAN for stalling. Most ASEAN countries, they said, want to continue in the general direction of cooperation but are unwilling to take the next step—sharing their markets. Both felt that market sharing would be desirable, and Akrasanee suggested that if ASEAN is still unable to share markets in a way that satisfies all its members, it should implement programs to enhance the feasibility of market sharing. Such moves should include establishing consistent trading regulations, customs procedures, industrial policies, development strategies and decisionmaking mechanisms within ASEAN. Akrasanee was aware that a subregional scheme of preference is a form of market distortion, and is thus welfare-reducing. But he was faced with a dilemma: the economic principles of free trade are often at odds with the realities of cartelisation, discrimination and local vested interests. He thought a subregional preference system would help ASEAN to compete in the world of imperfect competition.

Krause remarked that although ASEAN's achievements in economic planning have been negligible, it has nevertheless succeeded in creating networks within the business community, sharing resources, and operating as a pressure group in the outside world. Patrick supported this third point, pointing to ASEAN's success in obtaining foreign aid from the United States and Japan. English had also been impressed by the business networks within ASEAN, but cautioned that they may begin to unravel if the ASEAN governments do not demonstrate to the private sector that they take cooperation seriously. Krause stressed the related point that ASEAN support is important for the Philippines during its present problems. When the Philippines eventually pulls through, he said, the ASEAN countries will be in a position to establish even stronger ties with the new government in Manila. Lee added that, although ASEAN's Industrial Projects and Industrial Complementation schemes have not been tremendously successful, ASEAN Joint Ventures have had a better record of getting off the ground. Seven joint ventures have been approved to date, and two are already at the test-run stage.

Patrick recalled that in 1979, at the Tenth Pacific Trade and Development Conference in Canberra, many of these very issues had been discussed. Six years ago it was concluded that little had yet occurred in ASEAN but that something might; that conclusion probably still holds, and Suhartono might usefully refer to those studies. Lee suggested that relating ASEAN industrial cooperation to the industrial policies of its member countries might also prove useful.

English was disturbed by the implication that national industrial policies should be established first, before considering regional liberalisation. Canada's experience, he said, showed how difficult it is to implement an industrial policy without reference to outside interests and opportunities. Holmes added that New Zealand's policy of closure had led to falling per capita income, which had forced the government to reconsider trade liberalisation as a policy alternative. Consequently, New Zealand and Australia have begun to open up their markets on a bilateral basis, and will perhaps liberalise more widely in the future. Australia's willingness, as the stronger economy, to make concessions to ease the transition had been a factor in the success of this policy.

Trade liberalisation, on a slightly grander scale, was one of the policies examined by Yang (chapter 14) in his survey of economic development and policy in China since 1949. Government economic policy plays a particularly large and distinctive role in centrally planned socialist economies such as China. Nevertheless, China's economic experience may hold valuable lessons for non-socialist countries, and perhaps suggest some common features, for the successful application of industrial policy.

As Yang noted, since 1978 China has reassessed its past economic experience and adopted policies of readjustment and openness. China now aims to achieve economic development at a more realistic pace and with greater benefit to its population. China's previous economic policies certainly succeeded in a number of areas, including the development of infrastructure and improvements in standards of living. But numerous policy failures during the Great Leap Forward, the Cultural Revolution and the years following the Gang of Four left China's economy with severe imbalances and at a level of development far short of its potential.

Since 1978 China's economic policy has stressed agriculture, light industry, and heavy industry, in that order, with the aim of redressing the former overemphasis on heavy industry and capital accumulation. Second, China has decentralised many aspects of its economic planning and production in efforts to better meet the demands of the people. Stronger performance incentives at lower levels will add dynamism to the Chinese economy. Third, China has embraced an open-door policy in order to make better use of foreign resources and markets. In particular, four special economic zones and fourteen coastal cities have been granted considerable discretion in attracting foreign investment projects.

Yang concluded that China is still beset by a number of policy problems, such as the temptation to pursue too-rapid economic growth and lack of experience in macroeconomic control. But at least the course has been set in the right direction. As an Asian nation with a growing external sector, China will play a positive role in the development of Pacific trade.

Sekiguchi agreed that China seems to be on the right track but argued that, since Yang's paper focused on strategies rather than policies, it was still not clear what particular policy instruments the Chinese government would use to avoid fluctuations in the economy. Reducing direct controls may lessen the volatility arising from political succession, but there will be other sources of cyclic fluctuation that will have to be better managed; for instance, changes in state investment have been important sources of fluctuations in the past. Emphasis is now placed on investment decisions by factory leaders and provincial governments. This will certainly enhance the cost-consciousness of producers, but on the other hand business cycles will ensue, and these will have to be managed by fiscal and monetary policies. Yang replied that the Chinese government would be looking to more flexible monetary policies and to industrial policies, and repeated his earlier comment that macroeconomic management was in its infancy in China, making it difficult to go into greater detail.

Not unnaturally, many of the participants saw Chinese economic development as predicated on a continuing movement towards a market-based system. Sekiguchi was interested to know how far reforms had gone in allowing factory leaders to make decisions on production, investment and employment. Wong was also concerned that reforms continue to further decentralise economic decisionmaking. This introduced the important, long-run question of what is the appropriate balance between the planned and the market segments of the economy. Lawrence suggested that once China has decontrolled even one part of the system, it will have little choice but to decontrol the rest. And once the ball is rolling China had better proceed rapidly, because the coexistence of a deregulated and a regulated sector causes all sorts of dislocations in the economy, as well as corruption on the part of those who find ways to arbitrate between the two sectors.

Wong further noted that socialist economic reform is politically an immensely difficult process. In the short run, the cost of political, social and economic adjustment is high for all sectors. In China the problem is compounded by economic backwardness and bureaucratic resistance. The success of the reform program depends critically on the existence of a strong political will, which means strong leadership. There is a nagging uncertainty here: what will happen after Mr Deng? It is encouraging that China's recent economic reforms have not only had positive results but have also extended in such a way that more and more people have acquired a stake in the new economic system. The reform process will become self-sustaining once its gains are diffused widely enough.

Balassa agreed that macroeconomic policy reform would be difficult to carry out in China, especially because regional authorities want to expand regional economies, making it difficult for the central government to exercise fiscal or monetary restraint, a point with which Yang agreed. Balassa acknowledged China's success in reforming its agricultural sector, but stated that industrial reform would be more difficult. The problem, he said, is how to proceed simultaneously on four fronts: decentralisation, proper incentives for managers, price rationalisation, and competition. He noted that Hungary's industrial sector is still not fully restructured, despite ten years of reform.

All participants were interested in China's international trade policy, both for its potentially profound effects on the world and Pacific economies and as a part of overall economic policy. As Wong noted, although the open-door policy was initiated some years ago, it is intimately linked with the recent economic-reform packages. The open-door policy was a political decision, but one that carries economic and social consequences. The close interrelationship between the two policies is clear in that opening up the Chinese economy requires changes in China's economic structures. If the Chinese economic system remains cumbersome, with an irrational price structure, the Chinese economy will not be able to interact positively with the world economy. Hence the need for reforms and restructuring, which will, in turn, hasten the opening-up process.

Sekiguchi, Yamazawa and Akrasanee also expressed concern about China's system of administered prices. Yamazawa saw it as detrimental to the development of trade between socialist and market economies. Akrasanee pointed out that Thailand's response to the slashing of China's export prices was to ban Chinese imports such as farm machinery. The discussants stressed the need for China to adopt a market-based pricing system in order for China to engage in international trade. Yang agreed, and said that China's policy was moving in that direction.

Namiki contended that, even if China were to dispense with its administered-price system, it would be difficult for the markets of the developed countries to absorb China's output once its economy moved into full swing, Drysdale, however, was less pessimistic. He agreed that China should be sensitive to its potential impact on the world economy, and should proceed cautiously in its export drive. But, he pointed out, China's potentially huge purchases of highly processed raw materials would also open up opportunities for regional specialisation. The involvement of China in international and regional forums would be an important factor in its smooth transition to the status of a major trading nation. Lawrence, who was also concerned about the absorption problems posed by China's economic emergence, suggested that Yang might consider undertaking some further work on projections of China's impact on the world economy.

While many participants stressed, quite rightly, the unique circumstances of

Chinese economic development, the analysis of China's economic policy picked up many familiar themes from throughout this conference: for example, the importance of market forces; the roles of entrepreneurs and bureaucrats; and regional and international considerations. Like all other countries, China has to deal with the complex mesh of political, social and economic forces that determines industrial policy.

Appendix 1
ASEAN: selected industrial data

Table A1.1 ASEAN: manufacturing value added—relative and absolute shares

ISIC code		Indonesia (1) 1971	Indonesia (1) 1982	Indonesia (2) 1977	Indonesia (3) 1970s	Malaysia[a] (1) 1971	Malaysia[a] (1) 1981	Malaysia[a] (2) 1978	Philippines (1) 1971	Philippines (1) 1980	Philippines (2) 1978	Philippines (3) 1970s	Thailand (1) 1971	Thailand (1) 1982	Thailand (2) 1978	Thailand (3) 1970s
311–2	Food products	28.8	9.3	1.5	1.3	13.8	16.8	1.2	25.0	18.2	3.4	2.2	21.3	17.7	2.3	1.6
313	Beverages	1.7	1.4	0.6	0.9	3.4	3.2	1.0	7.8	5.6	2.3	1.4	8.8	6.5	4.9	2.4
314	Tobacco	23.7	13.2	9.6	1.7	6.8	3.1	3.5	7.3	6.1	2.9	1.1	9.6	5.8	6.4	2.0
321	Textiles	11.2	9.0	1.9	0.6	2.7	4.6	1.5	6.8	6.7	1.2	0.5	9.2	7.8	3.0	0.8
322	Garments	*	0.9	*	0.1	1.6	2.1	0.6	1.9	4.4	1.3	1.2	6.4	11.7	2.5	2.4
323	Leather and leather products	0.3	0.2	0.4	0.5	0.1	0.1	0.2	0.2	0.1	0.4	0.3	[0.8	[0.3	0.9	0.7
324	Footwear	0.5	0.3	1.1	1.0	*	0.4	0.4	0.3	0.3	*	*			3.6	2.3
331	Wood and wood products	1.2	6.4	1.4	1.2	9.1	7.9	3.5	4.2	4.5	1.8	1.7	2.4	2.0	1.1	1.8
332	Furniture	0.3	0.1	0.2	0.4	0.8	1.0	0.4	0.4	1.1	0.2	0.5	1.2	1.0	0.5	2.1
341	Paper and paper products	1.7	0.8	0.3	0.7	0.7	1.1	0.3	2.7	3.3	1.1	2.3	0.8	1.2	0.1	0.3
342	Printing and publishing	1.7	1.2	0.4	0.7	5.9	4.4	0.8	2.4	1.1	0.4	0.9	2.4	2.4	0.6	1.7
351	Industrial chemicals	0.7	5.5	0.9	1.3	2.2	1.8	0.4	4.5	5.2	0.6	1.5	[6.4	[7.1	*	*
352	Other chemicals	3.2	5.0	0.6	0.8	5.7	3.3	0.8	8.6	5.9	1.7	1.9			0.7	0.8
353–4	Petroleum and related products[b]	15.0	21.3	14.4	10.9	6.8	5.7	1.3	6.2	5.5	4.0	3.8	8.4	9.8	1.8	1.8
355	Rubber products	1.1	2.4	0.6	1.5	14.1	7.0	8.1	2.1	2.5	1.0	1.5	1.6	1.6	0.7	0.8
356	Plastics products	0.4	0.6	0.3	0.9	3.0	2.0	0.9	1.1	1.3	1.2	2.7	na	na	0.4	1.7
361	Pottery, china and earthenware	0.5	0.2	0.4	0.4	0.1	0.3	0.7	0.1	0.5	0.4	0.5				
362	Glass and glass products	0.4	1.0	0.6	0.5	0.4	0.7	0.6	1.8	0.9	1.1	1.6	[6.0	[6.7	1.1	1.4
369	Other non-metallic minerals products	2.1	3.6	2.0	1.8	6.2	5.1	1.4	2.8	2.8	0.7	0.8	1.2	1.2	0.9	1.2

ISIC		Indonesia (1)	(2)	(3)	Malaysia (1)	(2)	Philippines (1)	(2)	(3)	Thailand (1)	(2)	(3)
371	Iron and steel	*	1.8	*	2.8	2.1	1.8	9.4	0.8	1.1	1.4	0.2
377	Non-ferrous metals	*	*	*	0.3	20.3	0.7	0.8	0.6	1.5		0.5
381	Metal products, excluding machinery	2.0	3.6	0.5	4.2	4.0	3.1	2.2	0.3	2.4	1.5	0.3
382	Non-electrical machinery	0.3	1.4	0.1	2.5	3.6	0.9	1.4	*	1.6	1.6	0.1
383	Electrical machinery	2.1	4.3	0.3	3.0	13.9	3.8	3.9	0.2	1.2	2.2	0.1
384	Transport equipment	0.8	6.0	0.4	2.9	4.7	3.2	5.5	0.4	4.4	8.2	0.7
385	Professional and scientific equipment, etc.	*	*	*	0.4	0.6	0.1	0.2	0.5	2.6	3.7	0.7
390	Miscellaneous products	0.3	0.3	*	0.4	0.7	0.3	0.7	0.9	3.9		2.3
	Total	100.0	100.0	0.7	100.0	100.0	100.0	100.0	1.7	100.0	100.0	1.2

Notes: The column headings for each country are as follows:
(1) Value added as a percentage of total manufacturing value added.
(2) Relative specialisation in manufacturing output; defined analogously to the index of revealed comparative advantage—that is, distribution of manufacturing value added relative to that of comparable country group. The groups are:
Indonesia—large countries;
Malaysia—small countries with ample resources and industrial orientation;
Philippines—large countries;
Thailand—large countries.
(3) Relative degree of industrialisation; defined as actual manufacturing output relative to that of comparable country groups, adjusted for per capita income.
a Data for column (2) refer to West Malaysia only. Column (3) is omitted because data are not available.
b Data for columns (2) and (3) refer to ISIC 353 only. The figure for Indonesia is an estimate: see Hill (1984: 33).
*—less than 0.1.
na—not available.

Sources: Column (1): UNIDO, unpublished statistics; and Indonesia—Biro Pusat Statistik Statistik Industri 1982 (Industrial Statistics 1982) vol. 1, Jakarta, 1984; Malaysia—unpublished data, Department of Statistics (the assistance of Ms F. Rani in extracting the data is gratefully acknowledged); Philippines, National Census and Statistics Office (1983); Thailand—World Bank (1983a: 117); Columns (2) and (3): UNIDO (1982)

Table A1.2 Indonesia: effective rates of protection by major product groups, 1971–80 (per cent)

	1971	1975 (I)	1975 (II)	1980
Consumer goods[a]	na	na	137	58
Durable consumer goods	315	224	na	na
Non-durable consumer goods	19	9	na	na
Tyres and tubes	b	4315	185	3
Motor vehicles	526	718	28	33
Dairy products	na	na	41	15
Drugs and medicines	na	na	85	0
Cigarettes	556	4	246	105
Rice milling	−15	1	354	−1
Sugar refining	53	−9	−8	0
Electrical appliances	96	88	35	58
Garments	199	110	117	na
Structural clay products	90	26	20	−20
Intermediate goods[a]	62	49	81	61
Plastics	na	na	117	70
Weaving industries	b	192	135	127
Spinning industries	134	56	30	16
Cement	159	64	23	4
Pesticides and agricultural chemicals	−9	31	na	na
Capital goods[a]	13	15	8	2
Shipbuilding and repair	2	45	0	−13
Non-electrical machinery	5	18	16	15
Structural metal products	na	na	3	−1

Notes: Estimates for 1971 and 1975 (I), and 1975 (II) and 1980 are not directly comparable; see text.
     a Averages for 1975 (II) and 1980 are weighted according to production
     b Negative value added at world prices
     na—not available

Sources: 1971—M.M. Pitt 'Alternative Trade Strategies and Employment in Indonesia' in A.O. Krueger (ed.) *Trade and Employment in Developing Countries* vol. 1, Chicago: University of Chicago Press, for the NBER, 1981; 1975 (I)—World Bank, as cited in M. Pangestu and Boediono 'The Structure, Causes and Effects of Manufacturing Sector Protection in Indonesia' in C.C. Findlay and R. Garnaut (eds) *The Political Economy of Manufacturing Protection in ASEAN and Australia* Sydney: Allen & Unwin, 1985; 1975 (II) and 1980—Pangestu and Boediono

Table A1.3 Malaysia: effective rates of protection by product category, 1965–78 (per cent)

Product category	1965	1970	1978
Processed food	7	n	24
Beverages and tobacco	73	na	44
Construction materials	9	73	23
Intermediate products I	9	−19	n
Intermediate products II	25	52	42
Non-durable consumer goods	20	17	85
Consumer durables	−5	103	173
Machinery	6	64	39
Transport equipment	n	164	−5
Total manufactures	25	44	39

Notes: n—negligible
na—not available

Sources: 1965—J.H. Power 'The Structure of Protection in West Malaysia' in B. Balassa and Associates *The Structure of Protection in Developing Countries* Baltimore: Johns Hopkins University Press, for the World Bank (1971); 1970—M. Ariff 'Protection for Manufactures in Peninsular Malaysia' *Hitotsubashi Journal of Economics* 15, 2, pp. 41–53, 1975; 1978—K.H. Lee 'Malaysian Manufacturing Sector Protection' in C.C. Findlay and R. Garnaut (eds) *The Political Economy of Manufacturing Protection in ASEAN and Australia* Sydney: Allen & Unwin, 1985

Table A1.4 The Philippines: effective rates of protection by product category, 1961 to the 1980s (per cent)

	1965	1974	post-1980
Consumption goods	86	77	42
Intermediate goods	65	23	33
Inputs into construction	64	16	31
Capital goods	34	18	25
Total manufacturing[a]	51	44	36

Note: a Average tariff rates (weighted).

Sources: 1965—J.H. Power and G.P. Sicat *The Philippines: Industrialization and Trade Policies* London: Oxford University Press, for the OECD, 1971, pp. 93, 99; 1974—Tan (1979:148); post-1980—N.A. Tan 'The Structure, Causes and Effects of Manufacturing Sector Protection in the Philippines' in C.C. Findlay and R. Garnaut (eds) *The Political Economy of Manufacturing Protection in ASEAN and Australia* Sydney: Allen & Unwin, 1985

Table A1.5 Thailand: selected effective tariff rates, 1974, 1978 and 1982 (per cent)

	1974	1978	1982
Processed food			
Sugar	−86	−20	−22
Sweet condensed milk	a	34	62
Wheat flour and cereals	30	467	2949
Fruit canning	−8	na	a
Animal feeds	−1	−2	−4
Beverages and tobacco			
Beer	a	40	15
Cigarettes and tobacco	1067	−25	−7
Construction materials			
Cement	44	na	0
Intermediate products I			
Veneer and plywood[b]	a	−13	−21
Thread and yarn	39	25	67
Sheet glass and products	73	a	280
Iron and steel basic industries	38	58	59
Rope and cordage	29	−4	29
Intermediate products II			
Rubber tyres and tubes	33	25	48
Paints and varnishes	58	84	38
Chemical products, plastics and synthetics	35	76	123
Finished structural metal products	49	80	41
Other metal products	58	81	80
Consumer non-durables			
Clothing	a	243	106
Textile articles	94	62	30
Shoes	200	669	173
Drugs and medicines	60	−15	−17
Soaps and detergents	84	150	67
Consumer durables			
Motorcycle assembly and parts	36	103	15[c]
Television sets and household appliances	830	a	188
Wood furniture	189	a	1693
Machinery			
Tractor assembly	6	6	na
Wires, cables and accessories	62	76	86
Transport equipment			
Car assembly	354	a	na
Truck assembly	101	392	308[d]
Motor vehicle parts	85	55	na
All sectors			
Non-import-competing	40	52	47
Import-competing	45	78	37
Exports			
—domestic sales	−40	38[e]	43[e]
—export sales	na	−40[f]	−18[f]

Notes: a Negative value added at world market prices
b Including sawn goods
c Including bicycles
d Including passenger cars, commercial vehicles and parts
e Average rates for industries with export sales of more than 10 per cent; the rates would be negative if only export sales were included
f Average rates for industries with export sales of more than 10 per cent

Sources: 1974—N. Akrasanee *The Structure of Effective Protection in Thailand: A Study of Industry and Trade in the Early 1970s* Bangkok, 1975; 1978—D. Wisuthachinda, Custom Tariff of Thailand, unpublished paper, Bangkok, 1982; 1982—Ministry of Finance. The authors are indebted to Dr Juanjai Ajanant for assistance with the preparation of this table.

Appendix 2
Taiwan: selected industrial data

Table A2.1 Taiwan: major economic indicators, selected years

	1952	1955	1960	1965	1970	1975	1980	1984
Computation of per capita income								
Gross national product (NT$ million at 1981 prices)	145 824	188 801	261 223	410 422	654 345	995 706	1 654 875	2 150 514
Population (in thousands)	8 128	9 078	10 792	12 628	14 676	16 150	17 805	19 013
Gross national product per capita (NT$'000 at 1981 prices)	17.10	19.90	23.40	31.70	44.90	62.20	93.30	114.00
Percentage shares in gross national product (at current prices) at factor cost by industrial origin								
Primary production	38.01	34.61	35.10	29.26	19.41	16.18	10.26	8.28
Manufacturing	10.84	13.80	16.83	20.14	26.43	29.28	34.23	36.24
Social overhead[a]	8.90	9.64	9.86	11.34	12.68	14.57	15.82	14.26
Services	42.25	41.95	38.21	39.26	41.48	39.97	39.69	41.22
Percentage shares in gross national product								
Government current revenue	23.56	24.59	23.77	20.06	22.68	23.36	24.25	22.69
Government saving	5.47	5.08	4.01	2.40	3.46	7.04	7.96	5.75
Total domestic saving	15.38	14.63	17.86	20.82	25.71	26.96	32.74	34.16
Gross capital formation	15.40	13.40	20.30	22.83	25.69	30.81	34.32	21.38
Exports	8.07	8.28	11.30	18.73	29.72	39.50	52.97	57.60
Imports	14.21	12.62	18.86	21.75	29.77	42.82	54.18	45.38
Share of manufactured exports in total exports								
Manufactured exports (NT$ billion)[b]		0.14	1.69	7.78	43.60	163.53	628.08	1 096.76
Manufactured exports as a percentage of total exports	7.60		28.20	42.60	76.70	81.30	88.20	91.00

	1952–55	1955–60	1960–65	1965–70	1970–75	1975–80	1980–84	1952–84
Compound annual growth rates								
Gross national product (at 1981 prices)	9.80	6.70	9.50	9.80	8.90	10.60	7.00	8.90
Gross national product per capita (at 1981 prices)	6.00	3.30	6.30	7.20	6.90	8.50	5.20	6.20
Index of manufacturing output	16.30	11.10	13.80	20.60	12.70	15.80	8.40	14.20
Total exports (at 1981 prices)	6.00	12.10	22.10	22.80	17.20	17.10	11.40	15.90
Employment								
—total	2.00	2.20	2.20	4.00	3.80	3.50	2.80	3.00
—manufacturing	4.30	4.60	3.60	9.00	10.20	7.50	3.80	6.30
—agriculture	0.50	0.90	0.10	–0.80	–0.00	–5.30	0.20	–0.80
Real wages								
—manufacturing	5.80	–0.90	5.60	6.60	8.30	8.60	8.60	6.00
Prices								
—gross national product deflator	14.30	8.60	2.80	4.80	11.70	8.90	4.60	7.90
—wholesale price index	12.10	9.10	2.10	1.90	12.60	8.90	1.70	6.90

Notes: a Includes construction; electricity, gas and water; and transport, storage and communications
b Includes SITC categories 5–8

Sources: Council for Economic Planning and Development Taiwan Statistical Data Book; Department of Statistics, Ministry of Finance Monthly Statistics of Exports and Imports, the Republic of China; Directorate-General of Budget, Accounting and Statistics National Income of the Republic of China, Monthly Bulletin of Labour Statistics, Republic China; Overall Planning Department, Council for Economic Planning and Development Research Report No. (66) 120.119, July 1977; Research, Development and Evaluation Commission Commodity Trade Statistics of the Republic of China (SITC Revised), 1954–74 August 1976

Table A2.2 Taiwan: key indicators of financial deepening, 1961–84

	1961–65	1966–70	1971–75	1976–80	1981–84
Ratio of M1 to GDP (per cent)	12.4	15.5	20.2	23.3	25.7
Ratio of M2 to GDP (per cent)	28.5	37.8	49.8	58.4	72.0
Percentage change in wholesale price index	2.1	1.9	12.6	8.9	1.7
Interest rate on one-year deposits (per cent)	12.9	9.8	10.9	10.9	10.4
Real return on holding one-year deposits (per cent)	10.8	7.9	–1.7	2.0	8.7
M2 at 1981 constant prices (NT$ billion)	79.7	189.1	425.9	818.9	1456.1
Net assets of domestic banks as percentage of gross domestic product	33.4	42.0	54.4	78.2	74.3
Ratio of net private national saving to national income (per cent)	9.7	12.3	17.0	16.3	18.0
Government bonds outstanding as percentage of gross domestic product	1.8	4.2	2.4	1.6	2.0
Corporate bonds outstanding as percentage of gross domestic product	0.2	0.3	0.3	1.3	1.8
Market value of stocks outstanding as percentage of gross domestic product	20.0[a]	8.6	12.1	14.8	13.6

Notes: M1 and M2 are the averages of monthly figures. M1 equals net currency issued plus demand deposits adjusted plus passbook deposits; M2 equals M1 plus quasi-money. M2 at 1981 constant prices is deflated by the wholesale price index.

a This figure is for 1962–65; the stock market was established in 1962.

Sources: Directorate-General of Budget, Accounting and Statistics *Commodity Price Statistics Monthly, Taiwan District, the Republic of China*, *National Income of the Republic of China*; Economic Research Department, Central Bank of China *Financial Statistics Monthly, Taiwan District, the Republic of China*; Securities and Exchange Commission, Ministry of Finance *SFC Statistics*

Table A2.3 Taiwan: exports to and imports from the United States, Japan, the European Community and the Organization of Petroleum Exporting Countries as percentages of total exports and imports, selected years

	1952	1955	1960	1965	1970	1975	1980	1981	1982	1983	1984
United States											
Exports	3.45	4.07	11.59	21.33	38.08	34.34	34.12	36.10	39.45	45.11	48.82
Imports	46.98	47.76	38.05	31.65	23.88	27.76	23.69	22.48	24.16	22.90	22.96
Japan											
Exports	52.59	59.35	37.80	30.67	14.58	13.07	10.97	10.96	10.73	9.86	10.46
Imports	31.02	30.35	35.35	39.75	42.85	30.44	27.13	27.97	25.31	27.54	29.34
European Community[a]											
Exports	5.17	5.69	6.10	10.00	9.52	13.83	14.16	11.46	10.77	9.86	9.03
Imports	5.88	5.97	8.42	7.37	8.33	11.46	8.06	7.50	9.68	9.33	8.72
Organization of Petroleum Exporting Countries[b]											
Exports	2.59	8.13	10.98	2.22	4.52	8.59	9.52	8.82	9.18	7.21	5.10
Imports	0.03	6.97	6.40	4.14	4.79	13.98	23.61	23.40	20.79	20.39	17.80

Notes: a Belgium, Denmark, France, West Germany, Greece, Ireland, Italy, Luxembourg, the Netherlands and the United Kingdom.
b Algeria, Ecuador, Gabon, Indonesia, Iran, Iraq, Kuwait, Libya, Nigeria, Qatar, Saudi Arabia, the United Arab Emirates and Venezuela.

Source: Inspectorate-General of Customs (PRC) *The Trade of China* (various issues)

324

Table A2.4 Taiwan: average annual percentage changes in wages, labour productivity and unit labour costs in manufacturing, 1952–84

	1952–55	1955–60	1960–65	1965–70	1970–75	1975–80	1980–84	1952–84
Money wages	16.11	9.42	8.04	11.19	21.01	17.95	12.58	13.55
Consumer prices	9.90	9.52	2.39	4.36	12.20	8.67	5.25	7.34
Real wages[a]	5.65	−0.07	5.52	6.54	7.85	8.54	6.96	5.79
Labour productivity	11.51	6.26	9.89	10.37	2.73	8.25	4.13	7.41
Unit labour costs[b]	4.60	3.16	−1.85	0.82	18.28	9.70	8.45	6.14

Notes: a Money wages divided by the index of urban consumer prices
b Differences between rate of change of money wages and rate of change of labour productivity. (Labour productivity is calculated by dividing the output index by the employment index.)

Sources: Council for Economic Planning and Development *Taiwan Statistical Data Book, Adjusted Statistics of Manufacturing in Taiwan Area* (First Quarter 1952 to Fourth Quarter 1976). *Adjustment of Labor Force, Unemployment and Employment by Sectors in Taiwan Area 1952–77*; Directorate-General of Budget, Accounting and Statistics *Commodity-price Statistics Monthly, Monthly Bulletin of Labor Statistics*; Ministry of Economic Affairs *Taiwan Industrial Production Statistics Monthly*

Table A2.5 Taiwan: export values of textiles subject to quota restrictions, 1980–84 (US$'000)

	1980	1981	1982	1983	1984
Exports to United States					
Total exports	1 267 611	1 496 820	1 635 430	1 864 389	2 537 272
Exports subject to quota restrictions	1 152 820	1 373 442	1 442 418	1 708 079	2 267 392
Quota restrictions coverage (per cent)	90.0	91.8	88.2	91.6	89.4
Exports to European Community					
Total exports	500 037	459 651	450 852	424 342	404 545
Exports subject to quota restrictions	377 554	359 341	352 834	334 577	343 243
Quota restrictions coverage (per cent)	75.5	78.2	78.3	78.9	84.9
Exports to Canada					
Total exports	105 690	146 382	140 458	178 080	209 271
Exports subject to quota restrictions	100 896	131 530	116 856	148 316	185 231
Quota restrictions coverage	95.5	89.9	83.2	83.3	88.5

Source: Taiwan Textile Federation

Notes

CHAPTER 1

1   To some extent this view was rationalised by the following arguments. It was suggested that positive industrial policy is easier in a follower situation, that is, industrial policy is easier to implement in a nation that is catching up to other nations with high per capita incomes. Once a nation becomes a leader, however, industrial policy at the frontier is more difficult. This, of course, is not an argument for industrial policy per se, because the follower situation obtains in the relationship between governments and the private sector. To support a positive industrial policy the argument needs to demonstrate some market failure by the private sector. It was also suggested that governments and bureaucrats, almost by definition, cannot do better than a competitive capitalist system. In the view of most participants bureaucrats cannot 'pick winners' any better than the private sector, and indeed, there are good reasons why it is to be expected that they will do worse. Furthermore, in most democratic systems the government process cannot deal effectively with the mistakes. It is very difficult for most governments to withdraw support for an industry once it is in place. However, whether the view that the United States could not emulate Japan was based on something deeper than this—the different value structures of the societies, for example—was never explored in any great detail.

CHAPTER 2

This chapter is an outgrowth of the authors' joint research with Professor Motoshige Itoh and Mr Kazuharu Kiyono, which is turn originated from a larger joint project on Japanese industrial policy under the auspices of the Tokyo Center for Economic Research. As such, the chapter capitalises in part on Itoh et al. (1984–85) and Komiya et al. (1984). Sincere gratitude is expressed to those who have participated in these joint projects, without holding them responsible for any defects in this chapter. Thanks are also due to Professors Bela Balassa, Paul Krugman, Peter Lloyd and Hugh Patrick for their helpful comments at the conference.

1   Standard references in the study of Japanese industrial policy are Komiya (1975), Komiya et al. (1984), and Tsuruta (1982). A detailed list of other references may be found in Komiya et al. (1984:487–504).
2   This is basically the same definition as that adopted in Komiya et al. (1984). See also Komiya (1975:208).

3   Typical examples of *tangible* measures of industrial policy actually used in postwar Japan are: protective tariffs, import quotas, regulation of direct foreign investment, and other non-tariff measures for direct protection from foreign competition; direct industrial subsidies and grants; implicit industrial subsidies through preferred access to and/or preferred terms of credit, favourable tax concessions and special accelerated depreciation allowances; and entry–exit regulations through licensing and other measures. In addition there are several *intangible* measures such as organising cooperative research and development projects, collecting, exchanging and disseminating industrial information that is crucial but not acquired through purely private incentives, and administrative guidance and other advisory measures. Note, however, that the effectiveness of advisory measures, which are not clearly based on a legal foundation, quite often hinges upon the availability of other (tangible or intangible) measures that may be invoked if the advisory measures in question are not voluntarily adopted.

4   For a discussion of the theory of policy intervention in the presence of 'non-economic' objectives, the reader is referred to Bhagwati and Srinivasan (1983: ch.24). Note, however, that the distinction between 'economic' and 'non-economic' objectives is not as clear as it may seem; indeed, Bhagwati and Srinivasan (1983:246–47) exemplify in several contexts that what seems at first to be a 'non-economic' objective may in fact be regarded as an 'economic' objective from a wider perspective.

5   To cite a few salient examples from Japanese experience, the most powerful policy measures the Japanese government could use in pursuit of its postwar industrial policy were the authorisation of individual patent and know-how contracts, the screening and authorisation of joint ventures between foreign and Japanese companies, and, in some industries of 'strategic' importance like petroleum refining, shipbuilding and electric power supply, the mandatory authorisation of new producton facilities. The liberalisation of trade and direct foreign investment virtually deprived the Japanese government of these powerful policy measures.

6   The discussion later in this chapter of the regulation of 'excessive competition' will show how this may happen, and how it may bring about an inefficient use of resources.

7   This omits two quite important issues: the reorganisation or modernisation of an existing industry, with special emphasis on research and development; and adjustment assistance for ailing or declining industries. Concerning the first issue, the reader is referred to Itoh et al. (1984–85) and Kamien and Schwartz (1982); the second is discussed in Bhagwati (1982), Chaney and Thakor (1985) and Flam et al. (1983).

8   If capital markets are imperfect and firms that are willing to take the risk of making up initial losses by future profits are unable to finance their attempt to do so, there may be an apparent case for protection. What is in fact needed, however, is not provision of industrial protection by such measures as tariff and/or non-tariff barriers but complementation of the imperfect capital markets.

9   This argument is drawn essentially from Kemp (1960). It is well recognised that an appropriate tax-subsidy scheme may improve economic welfare if one industry is exerting a favourable external effect upon others. The case along Kemp's lines for protecting infant industries may be regarded as an example of this argument.

10 This argument is drawn from Negishi (1972:ch.6); see also Johnson (1970).

11 The reader is referred to Panagariya (1981) for an underlying analysis of the international trade model with Marshallian externalities.

12 A rigorous analysis of this case for industrial policy may be found in Okuno (1985).

13   The reason for such a downward shift, say, is not without ambiguity. For the present argument, readers should keep the following examples in mind: as an industry expands, inter-firm exchange of technical and other information may be facilitated, pooling of industry-specific labour may be realised, and specialisation in the production of materials and parts may become worthwhile. Interested readers will discover their own examples of Marshallian external diseconomies.

14   The alert reader will have noticed that, given p, E^* is the best attainable production point. Note, however, that PRT (X_{E^*}, Y_{E^*}) differs from p, so that the realisation of E^* would necessitate *permanent* intervention in the economy, which is very undesirable.

15   One possible reading of this famous thesis, which seems to be relevant in the present context, is as follows. In oligopolistic markets price exceeds marginal cost, since profit-maximising behaviour leads to equality between marginal cost and (perceived) marginal revenue. If, in addition, the industry allows free entry, price equals average cost. Consequently, average cost exceeds marginal cost, leaving the possibility of further reduction in average costs. If an expansion of the market (i.e., of demand) leads to an increase in the individual firm's output, this reserved potentiality of average-cost reduction will be used effectively to the extent of the expansion of demand.

16   In this context, Komiya's (1975:221) remarks are most revealing: 'Whatever the demerits of the system of industrial policies in postwar Japan, it has been a very effective means of collecting, exchanging, and propagating industrial information. Government officials, industry people, and men from governmental and private banks gather together and spend much time discussing problems of industries and exchanging information on new technologies and domestic and overseas market conditions. People at the top levels of the government, industries, and banking circles meet at councils, and junior men meet at their subcommittees or less formal meetings. Probably information related to the various industries is more abundant and easily obtainable in Japan than in most other countries. Viewed as a system of information collection and dissemination, Japan's system of industrial policies may have been among the most important factors in Japan's high rate of industrial growth, apart from the direct or indirect economic effects of individual policy measures.'

17   The analysis in this section owes much to Brander and Spencer (1981), Dixit (1979; 1981; 1984), and Krugman (1984), among others.

18   A similar analysis applies in the case where the foreign firm becomes the dominant price leader and the home firm forms a competitive fringe.

19   In postwar Japan, colour television sets, automobiles, heavy electrical equipment and large-scale computers may be cited as relevant examples of commodities for which this role of industrial policy may have been of critical importance in the infancy stage of their development.

20   The effect on the foreign country's economic welfare is ambiguous.

21   As far as the authors are aware, it was von Weizsäcker (1980a; 1980b) who first pointed out that the equilibrium number of firms may exceed the 'first-best' number of firms in terms of a numerical example. Suzumura and Kiyono (forthcoming) prove, first, that this is not simply a pathology but is a reflection of a general property of a homogeneous-output oligopoly model; and, second, that the same 'excessive competition' thesis holds true in the case of the 'second-best' optimality. A related result reached by Tandon (1984) should also be mentioned.

22   Examples of such industries are iron and steel, petroleum refining, petrochemicals, certain other chemicals, cement, paper and pulp, and sugar refining. See Komiya (1975:214), among others.

CHAPTER 3

I am indebted to various participants in the Fifteenth PAFTAD Conference for useful suggestions, especially Bela Balassa, Sir Frank Holmes, Michihiro Ohyama, and Hugh Patrick.

1   This is reminiscent of Baldwin's (1970) attempt to classify non-tariff barriers to trade, which wound up including all policies designed to affect consumption or production of the competing domestic sector's output.

2   Recent work on game theory points out that fast-growing activities need not yield profits, and can indeed produce losses if producers must make their resource commitments *ex ante* and with incomplete information about commitments by other entrants. On the other hand, a capital market that allocated risk-bearing inefficiently could underfund new ventures or expanding sectors, which would be evidenced by persistent excess rates of return to them.

3   These issues could be pursued in much greater analytical detail. For example, depending on the technology of appropriation, productivity gains for an industry may yield no rents to the factors employed there (e.g., if all producer rents are captured by the industry that supplies capital goods embodying the improvement in productivity) or no rents to any specific factors of production (e.g., if the productivity gain is an inappropriable gift of intangible knowledge and the industry is competitive, so that all welfare gains pass to consumers of its product). Thus, not only should it be generally expected that entrepreneurs will anticipate any appropriable gains that can be expected and will invest to capture them, but also it should not be assumed that the gaining industry appropriates any producer rents at all.

4   For a similar analysis, see Krugman (1983), who also considers the proposal that domestic industries should be assisted in order to combat foreign industrial targeting.

5   There is important statistical evidence (Lieberman, 1984) that learning diffuses from the firm to its industry, but whether the diffusion is international or only national remains uncertain.

6   Brander and Spencer (1981) show that, if the foreign monopolist is limit-pricing to preclude the rise of domestic competition, such a tariff is (up to a point) a free ride for the nation imposing it, since it entails no cost from the distortion of domestic consumption.

7   Of course, the absence of perfect foresight also provides grounds for intervention. For example, if expectations are static so that capital owners expect intersectoral differences in rates of return to persist, capital will be reallocated between sectors at a faster rate than is socially optimal (given the assumed existence of adjustment costs of reallocating it); see Mussa (1978).

8   Houseman (1985:ch.5) builds upon Spencer and Brander (1983) to show that there is a role for national public policy in an international declining industry. Public assistance to a national duopolist in such an industry may provide the commitment that leaves a foreign rival no option but to exit first, letting the domestic seller collect from foreign buyers some terminal monopoly rents that contribute to the national income.

9   This formulation was suggested to me by Donald McFetridge.

10 To appreciate the importance of perceived fairness as an influence on policy, at least in the United States, note that assistance to domestic industries facing import competition is heavily, although not exclusively, conditional on the subsidisation of

foreign exporters or their use of price discrimination. If the issue were simply one of preserving existing jobs or altering rates of adjustment in private markets, the basis for the intervention would not depend on the reasons for the advantage held by foreigners.

11 Devotees of rational expectations have argued that the expectation of losses would be built into the supply price of labour, so that the wage compensates workers in advance for such welfare losses. The logical force of this point is somewhat blunted by the long time-horizons of many workers' attachments to their jobs, which limit their ability to distinguish job-loss probabilities in the distant future. It is also blunted if the political process of balancing equities that has been hypothesised fails to perceive the premium for risk-bearing built into the wage.

12 Grossman and Eaton (1985) provide a normative model that draws upon risk aversion to demonstrate that free trade may not be optimal even for a small country when the terms of trade are uncertain and markets for contingent claims are incomplete.

13 An obvious exception is the use of trade taxes or subsidies to manoeuvre the profits of international oligopolies into the national income. These measures are first-best at the national level.

14 Only limited property rights exist guaranteeing countries the right to compensation for spillovers from foreign policy measures such as selected articles of the GATT.

15 The more closely correlated among countries are consumers' losses of surplus to monopoly profits and monopoly profits exacted from consumers, the more certain is it that each nation gains from a global policy of promoting competition. The fact that international oligopolies and differentiated-product industries (even without oligopoly elements) tend to undertake intra-industry trade—a central conclusion of modern theoretical research—favours just this correlation. A presumption is supported that parallel applications of pro-competitive policies in the leading producer countries will increase each country's welfare as well as bringing the international economy closer to a global optimum.

16 In this context it is worth noting that modern theoretical research acknowledges the possibility that oligopolistic rivalry in innovation by itself can cause excessive resources to be devoted to this activity (see, for example, Dasgupta and Stiglitz, 1980).

CHAPTER 4

1 By 1960 the Canadian market was five times larger in real terms than it had been in 1930, as population had doubled and per capita income was two and a half times higher.

2 For a concise review of agency practice, see Safarian (1983).

3 An example is that issued by James F. Kelleher, Minister of International Trade, 'How to Secure and Enhance Canadian Access to Export Markets'.

4 The Canadian ratio of non-defence research and development expenditure to GDP is 73 per cent of the United States ratio (see McFetridge, 1985).

5 See Tarasofsky (1984) for a description of the details of Canada's research and development subsidy programs.

6 The scheme was called the Scientific Research Tax Credit Scheme, and is described in Department of Finance (1983) and McFetridge (1984). The operation of the scheme, including its costs in terms of tax revenue forgone, has been documented by Linda McQuaig in the Toronto *Globe and Mail* (13 July 1984, p. 5; 27 December 1984, p. B1).

7 The theoretical case for free-riding by a small country is made by Berkowitz and Kotowitz (1982). Canada has maintained a system of compulsory licensing of patented pharmaceuticals at a royalty rate of 4 per cent since 1969. A royal commission recently found that this rate was not compensatory to the patentee, and suggested that the latter be guaranteed a four-year period of exclusivity and a royalty rate of 14 per cent on licences awarded thereafter (Commission of Inquiry on the Pharmaceutical Industry, 1985).

8 The role of domestic market guarantees in facilitating international market penetration by Canadian manufacturers of telecommunications equipment was recently addressed by the Restrictive Trade Practices Commission (1983).

CHAPTER 5

The original focus of this paper was on two of the net energy exporters in ASEAN, Indonesia and Malaysia; the Philippines and Thailand were included later. Some of the issues that receive cursory treatment here are examined more thoroughly in Ariff and Hill (1986). Parts of this chapter, and of that book, draw on research undertaken under the auspices of the Trade in Manufactures component of the ASEAN–Australia Joint Research Project.

1 The conventional ('narrow') definition of manufactured exports includes essentially footloose manufacturing activities, whereas the broad definition includes additional resource-processing industries. The distinction is of some importance in all four countries (see Table 5.1). The broader definition is more appropriate, but its use involves serious data problems.

2 The index is computed in the usual way; that is, $\Sigma\ (Ai2-Ai1)$ for all $Ai2 > Ai1$, where Ai refers to the percentage of industry i (at the 3-digit ISIC level) in manufacturing value added and 1 and 2 refer to periods of time.

3 This is especially true for Indonesia, where definitional changes in 1974 excluded small firms, many of which produced food products, from the 'factory sector'. Several processing activities (notably tea) have also been excluded in later years. The coverage of Philippine data, by contrast, was extended over this period.

4 In addition to the country papers in Garnaut (1980), see McCawley (1981) on Indonesia, Hoffman and Tan (1980) on Malaysia, and Bautista, Power and Associates (1979) on the Philippines.

5 Recent policy documents include Indonesia, Departemen Penerangan (1984); Malaysia, Jabatan Percetakan Negara (1984); Philippines, NEDA (1982); Thailand, NESDB (1982). The Philippine plan for 1983–87 was later overtaken by events and has been substantially modified.

6 The focus of this section is on protection policies in the four countries, rather than on those in export markets. Recent trends in the latter have been analysed extensively: see, for example, Cairncross et al. (1982); Corden (1984); and Hughes and Krueger (1984). The general conclusion of this literature is that, while protection has intensified, particularly for 'sensitive' items such as textiles and clothing, in developing countries exporters have been largely able to circumvent import barriers.

7 For an extensive discussion of the effects of the commodity-price boom in Indonesia on the rest of the economy, see recent issues of the *Bulletin of Indonesian Economic Studies*, including the 'Survey of Recent Developments'.

8 Medalla and Power (1984) suggest that in recent years the 'shadow' exchange rate has been about 20 per cent higher than the official rate. For various reasons, however, this is a conservative estimate.

9 The most thorough treatment of this subject for ASEAN is by McCawley (forthcoming).

10 These are the Boards of Investment in the Philippines and Thailand, the Malaysian Industrial Development Authority, and the Capital Investment Coordinating Board in Indonesia.

11 For example, the Indonesian government's very liberal policy towards foreign investment was substantially modified in the mid-1970s as a result of strong nationalist pressure.

12 Among the exceptions are Lall (1979) on Malaysia, and Lindsey (1977) on the Philippines.

13 For details, see the case studies on Malaysia (Ariff, 1983), the Philippines (Alburo, 1983) and Thailand (Tambunlertchai, 1983).

14 Galenson (1984) summarises the results of many studies examining these issues. Gregorio (1979) provides a detailed examination of the effects of fiscal incentives in the Philippines.

15 Data on the regional concentration of industry are not directly comparable, nor are they sufficiently disaggregated in some cases to permit firm conclusions. But the following table is illustrative.

Employment and output shares by region[a] (percentage of total for each country)

Region	Output	Employment
Capital city		
Indonesia	20.5 (1974/75)	6.7 (1980)
Malaysia	13.1 (1983)	
Philippines	56.3 (1980)	47.4
Thailand	51.7 (1980)	35.3
Capital city plus adjoining province/region[b]		
Indonesia	39.8	26.8 (1980)
Malaysia	39.7 (1983)	
Philippines	69.9 (1980)	59.7
Thailand	98.7 (1980)	65.5

Notes: a Philippine and Thai data are from the Manufacturing Survey; Malaysian data are from the National Accounts; Indonesian output data are from the Industrial census and refer only to firms employing twenty or more workers, while employment data are from the population census

b Includes West Java (Indonesia), Selangor (Malaysia), Southern Tagalog (the Philippines) and the Centre Region (Thailand)

Sources: Indonesia, Biro Pusat Statistik (1982); Malaysia, Jabatan Percetakan Negara (1984); Philippines, National Census and Statistics Office (1983); Thailand—World Bank (1983a).

16 It should be noted, though, that this protection is heavily concentrated on textiles and clothing (see Hughes and Krueger, 1984).

17 It is interesting to compare the programs in the ASEAN countries with those of South Korea and Taiwan, both of which have recently embarked on ambitious programs aiming at full local manufacture of passenger cars. By the early 1990s they aim to produce, respectively, 1.3 million and 250 000 units annually, in each case with no more than three manufacturers (see *Far Eastern Economic Review* 5 April 1984).

18 In addition to Roemer, see Wall (1980, 1984) and Yeats (1981, 1984).

CHAPTER 6

Thanks are due to Professors W. Hong and T. Watanabe for helpful suggestions and comments.

1 Furthermore, bonded warehouses could be established to avoid the cumbersome problem of assessing and refunding taxes.
2 The government abolished income-tax reductions for exports in December 1970.
3 Such a practice was not in conformity with a unitary exchange-rate system, and negotiation of retained or registered foreign exchange was terminated on 30 July 1970.
4 These schemes to subsidise exports no longer exist; for instance, the cotton-spinning scheme ended in 1972.
5 Financial deepening means that financial assets are accumulating more rapidly than non-financial wealth (Shaw, 1973: vii). Appendix Table A2.2 gives some indicators of Taiwan's progress in financial deepening by computing changes in the ratio of financial instruments outstanding as percentage of GDP. (GDP is used as the denominator because of the unavailability of national wealth statistics.) In a steady state, capital stock must grow at the same rate as output.

CHAPTER 7

The author wishes to thank Bela Balassa for comments, Paula DeMasi and Tamara Giles for research assistance, and Charlotte Kaiser and Evelyn Taylor for text processing.

1 For a more complete exposition see, for example, Meier (1980:93–101).
2 See, for example, Adams and Klein (1983); Jacquemin (1984); Pinder (1982); Sheperd et al. (1983).
4 Foreigners have frequently alleged that United States defence policies represent a covert but powerful industrial policy. There may be some merit in this argument with respect to certain early products, such as the first semiconductors and jet aircraft, but empirical investigations of the role of defence research and development on general industrial productivity growth suggest very little beneficial effect. Given the post-Vietnam reduction in defence spending in the early 1970s, the present competitiveness of the United States electronics and computer industries owes very little to defence efforts. This may change in the 1990s with the renewed emphasis on defence research and development through the Defense Advanced Research Projects Agency.
5 If the International Trade Commission makes a decision in favour of an industry, Section 201 of the Trade Act of 1974 provides industries with the remedy, chosen by the President, that is best suited to 'preventing serious injury or threat thereof to the industry ... and to facilitate the orderly adjustment to new competitive conditions'.
6 In six other cases the president of the commission recommended trade adjustment assistance for workers. (Baldwin, 1984).
7 Of the sixteen industries in the sample examined, twelve had adjusted successfully, in the sense that upon the removal of protection the industry could pay factors of production their opportunity cost without government assistance. For the remaining four it was too early to tell.
8 Indeed, the weight placed by political decisionmakers on preventing dislocation is indicated in the regulations under which the Commerce Department provides assistance for domestic industries: 'Plans involving relocation of firms which may reduce employment or otherwise adversely affect a local or regional economy will be acceptable only in unusual circumstances.'
9 The issue of whose injury protection is designed to prevent (workers? capitalists? regions?) is probably kept deliberately vague to permit maximum political use.

10   For a broader comparison of United States–European social systems, see Ostry and
     Koromzay (1982).
11   In Italy, for example, as described by Balassa (1984), employers have to follow a
     complicated legal procedure to show 'just cause' for dismissal; in France a time-
     consuming consultation with labour representatives is followed by a decision of the
     Labour Inspectorate, and is subject to appeal to the Ministry of Employment.
     Collective dismissal for economic reasons requires authorisation by the Federal
     Institute of Labour in Germany and the Ministry of Labour in Italy.
12   As Hesselman (1983) notes, in several cases the federal government overruled the
     Cartel Office.
13   In France, for example, six high-priority areas were singled out: energy conserva-
     tion, office and information systems, offshore technology, biotechnology, electro-
     nics, and textiles.
14   For example, in France a number of companies (e.g. Renault) were nationalised
     soon after the war. They were run by successful bureaucrats with a relatively high
     degree of autonomy. During the period of retrenchment they had to be highly
     subsidised.
15   Note that if private investors are systematically shortsighted there should be
     opportunities for investors to make profits by buying stocks in firms whose
     earnings are far in the future (generally those with high price–earnings ratios) and
     holding them until the market recognises their true profitability. But there is no
     evidence to suggest that such a strategy is profitable (see Lawrence, 1984:93).
16   An excellent discussion of French industrial policy is to be found in Balassa (1985).
17   For an example giving explicit estimates of the waste entailed in keeping the
     Shelton Steel Works in the United Kingdom open for too long, see Curzon Price
     (1980: 206).
18   This account relies heavily on Mottershead (1983).
19   This concentration of aid reflects political responses to regional concerns and,
     particularly with respect to research and development projects, a preference for
     larger firms, which the government has been trying to reverse since' 1979.

CHAPTER 9

The author is grateful to Prue Phillips of the Research School of Pacific Studies at
the Australian National University for her willing assistance in providing the data for
Table 9.2. Ching-ing Hou Liang and Ippei Yamazawa made helpful comments on the
paper at the conference.

1   The trade flows in this table have been converted to an ISIC basis from the original
     SITC-based trade data using a concordance. This was done in order to match
     production with trade data for the purpose of calculating import shares. The
     different classification bases for international trade and production statistics plague
     all researchers who need to match the two classifications. After many frustrations
     myself, I feel compelled to complain about the use of dual classification. In princi-
     ple, all production and trade flows should be based on a single classification derived
     from production-activity flows. International transactions in intermediate commod-
     ities are merely transfers of commodities across national borders as part of the chain
     of activities that produces final products.
2   For example, after surveying the empirical studies of the demand for clothing
     products the most precise statement the OECD could make of the income elastici-
     ties of demand was that 'directly estimated income elasticities are of around 0.4;

when demographic proxies are included, these rise to 1.0 ... Moreover, the explanatory value of the equations is much poorer after 1973, suggesting that under the perturbed conditions of the recent period, factors other than real incomes and relative prices played a significant role in determining the demand for clothing' (OECD, 1983b:30).

3   When the value added, however, is measured at international prices the relative sizes of the two subsectors are reversed (IAC, 1984:Table D1). This is due to the higher levels of effective protection in the clothing subsector.

4   The definition of the clothing industry in this study includes footwear.

5   See IAC (1984) for the details of the current seven-year program of assistance to the textile and clothing (and footwear) industries, the administration of quotas and bounties and estimates of the nominal and effective rate structure of the industry.

6   The structural adjustment problems of labour laid off or threatened with lay-off in these industries, and consequently the opposition to structural adjustments, would be eased if governments were more successful in improving the macroeconomic environment.

7   These include homogeneous labour in the industry and the existence of non-distortionary lump-sum taxes to finance the subsidy payments. Neary (1982) has shown that when unemployment arises because of fixed real wages the best policy, assuming that the rigidity of real wages cannot be relaxed, is a temporary wage subsidy decreasing over time to zero.

8   In practice the deadweight losses are not reduced to zero because the subsidy must be financed by some distortionary tax. However, most taxes are preferable to the extremely high rates exacted by tariffs and quotas.

CHAPTER 10

I should like to thank H.E. English, John Kwoka, Hiromichi Mutoh, and participants in the conference for helpful comments.

1   Perhaps the steel industry would also qualify in terms of the scope of government actions; see Robert Crandall 'Anatomy of an Industrial Policy' *Wall Street Journal* 19 June 1985, p. 30. For book-length indications of recent interest in the motor vehicle industry and its problems, see Altshuler (1984); Chang (1981); Cole (1982; 1983; 1984); Cole and Yakushiji (1984); Hunker (1983); National Academy of Engineering (1982); Rader (1980); and Sekaly (1981).

2   Though the Canadian and United States markets have, in essence, been consolidated into a free-trade area for the past twenty years (as a result of the US–Canadian Automotive Agreement of 1965), the focus of this chapter is on United States policy and therefore on United States data.

3   For further discussion of the loan guarantee program, see Reich (1985); Stewart (1983:ch.5).

4   See US Congressional Budget Office (1980); US Department of Transportation (1981); US House of Representatives (1980); US Office of Technology Assessment (1981).

5   Imported light trucks from Japan were a problem until domestic manufacturers succeeded in convincing the US Customs Service that imported knocked-down light trucks should carry the full 25 per cent duty rather than the lower duty applicable to parts.

6   All cost comparisons of vehicle manufacturers entail problems of comparing differing degrees of vertical integration and differing products and product mixtures.

For a discussion of the relative cost disadvantage, see Cole and Yakushiji (1984:ch.7); Flynn (1983); Gomez-Ibanez and Harrison (1982); National Academy of Engineering (1982:ch.6).

7 For discussion of Japanese production techniques, see Altshuler (1984:chs 6, 7); Chang (1981); Cole and Yakushiji (1984:chs 7, 8, 9); National Academy of Engineering (1982:ch.6).

8 Since the new-car component of the consumer price index is explicitly adjusted for quality changes (and for mandated regulatory requirements, such as safety features and emission-control systems), whereas most other components are not so adjusted, caution is necessary in making these comparisons. Nevertheless, the pattern discussed in the text is probably valid.

9 Not included here are general measures that assisted all industries, such as the large tax cuts and accelerated depreciation measures of 1981.

10 It was never explained why protectionist legislation could not be vetoed by the President.

11 Shortly afterwards, the Canadian government arranged for similar import limitations.

12 For a discussion of the decree, see Mills and White (1978).

13 See *Federal Register* 46 (13 April 1981) pp. 21628–29.

14 Most of the measures helped both domestic and overseas producers, but it was clear that their primary purpose and effect was to assist domestic producers.

15 For discussion of the earlier standards, see White (1981; 1982b).

16 Informational problems in the market place must ultimately involve one of the other forms of market failure.

17 Also, the terminology seems highly inappropriate for an 80-year-old industry. But the same arguments are trotted out for the steel, textile and footwear industries, which are even older.

18 The author is not aware of any data that specifically compare the income distribution of car buyers with that of automobile workers.

19 The author is indebted to Hiromichi Mutoh for these two points.

20 For discussion of the costs and perverse incentives that are created even under normal bankruptcy conditions, see Golbe (1981); White (1980).

21 These arguments draw heavily on Kwoka (1983; 1984).

22 Social insurance arrangements, though, do spread some of the costs to the general public. But the same is true of smoking and alcohol abuse.

23 A sensible compromise would seem to be State laws mandating the use of existing seatbelts and levying modest fines on their non-use. To the extent that social insurance has created an externality from the non-use of seatbelts, the fine that a non-user pays (if detected) seems to be the correct type of 'effluent fee'.

24 For a discussion of the Korean motor vehicle industry see Kim (1984).

CHAPTER 11

1 The European Community here includes seven countries: Belgium, the Netherlands, France, West Germany, Italy, Luxembourg, and the United Kingdom.

2 'Steel intensity' means the quantity of steel consumed per dollar of GNP; thus it reflects the importance of steel-intensive industries in an economy's production structure.

3 Wienert (1980). This figure includes North Korea and the People's Republic of China, the Asian centrally planned economies.

4 According to Cockerill (1974), average production cost decreases by 14 per cent

when the production capacity of a plant increases from 5 million tonnes to 10 million tonnes.

5   One estimate shows that in sixteen important developing countries about 90 per cent of steel-producing capacity was publicly controlled in 1975 (UNIDO, 1978:124).

6   During the 1960s the United States became the single largest steel-importing country in the world, whereas Japan became the largest exporter of steel; in 1970 Japan exported 17.5 million tonnes (roughly 30 per cent of world steel trade), while the United States imported 11.8 million tonnes (roughly 20 per cent of world steel trade).

7   From 1968 to 1972 investment in the United States steel industry showed a declining trend (US Federal Trade Commission, 1977:75).

8   The newly emerging steel producers are Argentina, Australia, Brazil, Canada, India, Korea, Mexico, South Africa, Spain, and Taiwan.

9   The commission is required to seek voluntary solutions (Article 57 of the European Coal and Steel Community) before resorting to compulsory measures.

10 The Aid Code, which was agreed in 1981 to be effective until 1985, was an attempt to link subsidies to the long-term restructuring objective by clearly stating the conditions under which subsidies could be provided.

11 Imports were so tightly controlled that even Korean exporters were able to fill less than half the quotas allocated to them for 1981–82.

CHAPTER 12

1   'Plastics' are high-molecular (polymer) substances having plasticity.

2   Petrochemicals capacity in the United States, on the other hand, was broadly in line with long-term demand, although a great deal of refining capacity was evident by then. Capacity in mid-1982 was judged sufficient to meet domestic and export needs until 1985, beyond which one new, full-scale ethylene plant a year would be needed to maintain equilibrium between supply and demand (see Wett, 1981).

3   The ability to deploy as feedstock natural gas that has hitherto been flared (and hence has virtually no opportunity cost) underlines the competitive edge that Saudi Arabia has in producing petrochemicals. In recent times some of this gas has been collected and used for air-conditioning and other purposes, so that its opportunity cost, though still low, is no longer zero. Offsetting this low-cost advantage is the fact that capital costs will be considerably higher in Middle East locations because extra facilities are needed to cope with the region's characteristic high temperatures and dusty, salty atmosphere. Another important caveat is that the Saudis' low-cost competitive edge depends crucially on the ability of the OPEC cartel to hold together; any future breakup of the cartel would imply a substantial fall in oil prices and hence lower feedstock costs for non-oil-producing petrochemicals manufacturers (such as those in Europe and Japan), with a consequent erosion of Saudi Arabia's competitive edge.

4   United States chemicals firms own around 70 per cent of the Canadian industry.

5   See the study by Arthur Anderson and Co., reported in *Business Week* 15 June 1981.

6   Trends in market shares held by Japanese and United States exports of plastics to Southeast Asia are as follows. For high-density polyethylene exports to eight Asian countries (ASEAN and the four Asian newly industrialising countries), the Japan–United States ratio changed from 62:38 in 1978 to 40:60 in 1980. The ratio for low-density polyethylene was also reversed, from 77:23 to 45:55, and that for

polypropylene from 70:30 to 20:80. Although Japan's shares are still higher than those of the United States for polystyrene and vinyl chloride, they are on a declining trend.

7   Because of the pollutive properties of petrochemicals, this move has also been encouraged since the 1970s, when domestic concern shifted towards greater emphasis on the quality of life and environmental issues (rather than the mere pursuit of economic growth that characterised the 1960s). These concerns have given rise to calls for a reduction of heavy chemicals industry activities in Japan.

8   As far as overseas investment is concerned, Japan has been fairly successful in establishing joint petrochemicals ventures with governments and firms in Saudi Arabia, Iran, Korea and Singapore. Most of these projects have the support of the Ministry of International Trade and Industry.

9   The project was actually conceived in 1969, but was delayed for reasons that will be discussed later.

10   The shareholding structure for the companies is as follows:

The Petrochemical Corporation of Singapore
—Japan, 50 per cent
—Singapore government, 50 per cent

The Polyolefin Company
—Japan, 70 per cent
—Singapore government, 30 per cent

Phillips Petroleum
—Phillips, 60 per cent
—Singapore government, 30 per cent
—Sumitomo Chemicals, 10 per cent

Ethylene Glycols
—Singapore government, 50 per cent
—Japan, 30 per cent
—Shell Eastern Petroleum, 20 per cent

11   Since the upstream cracker plant was designed with the four downstream plants in mind, the one-year delay in starting up Ethylene Glycols meant an underutilisation of upstream facilities, which therefore operated at about 65 per cent of designed capacity in their first year of operation.

12   Some observers believe that there are also chinks in the Saudi armour. First, there is Saudi Arabia's cash reserves position; with falling oil and gas prices, the Saudis may not be able to price their petrochemicals too low. Second, the petrochemicals produced by the Saudi plants are of unknown quality, and, like any new plants, they are liable to strike teething problems. Third, the higher construction costs in Saudi Arabia may be a deterrent to price-cutting.

13   However, observers of the industry think that there could be two obstacles to Thailand's plans to use natural gas to fuel its petrochemicals plant. First, the offshore gas fields in Thailand are quite far out, which could make the landed cost of the gas feedstock quite high. Second, there is a question mark over whether there is sufficient gas available.

14   Officials there told the Japanese that Malaysian studies showed domestic demand increasing from 70 kt annually to 195 kt in 1990. Thus the Malaysian market will be able to support a domestic petrochemicals plant producing 200 kt a year by then. Pioneer status confers the benefit of exemption from the 40 per cent corporate tax for a period of five to ten years. Export incentives in the form of a 90 per cent exemption on export profits in excess of a specified base for three years in

the case of pioneer companies are in principle applicable to the petrochemicals industry if it performs well and enjoys export profits. This was apparently not the case in the first year of operation, when losses were registered.

15 For instance, only 100 kt of the propylene produced by the Petrochemicals Corporation of Singapore can be absorbed annually by the downstream Polyolefin plant. The balance of 60 kt is sold to South Korea, Taiwan and Japan at a low price. Other surplus products from the Petrochemicals Corporation are benzene, toulene and xylene.

16 The value added per worker in the speciality chemicals industry ranges from S$200 000 to S$500 000, compared with S$34 000 in the general manufacturing sector and S$76 000 in the chemicals industry in 1983.

17 The Economic Development Board has also identified the following areas of investment opportunity in speciality chemicals: electronic chemicals, photochemicals, fuel additives, engineering plastics, and speciality polymers.

18 These include industries that will economically produce goods for domestic use in place of goods being imported in large quantities. This applies particularly to industries that will process further, and thereby increase the value of, agricultural, mining and timber products already being produced for export, or that will produce goods at costs low enough to be competitive in export markets.

CHAPTER 13

The views expressed in this chapter are those of the author, and should not be taken to reflect the official stance of the Indonesian Ministry of Industry.

1 The ASEAN Declaration (Bangkok Declaration), which established an association for regional cooperation among the countries of Southeast Asia to be known as the Association of South-East Asian Nations (ASEAN), was signed in Bangkok on 8 August 1967 by the foreign ministers of the original five member states, namely Indonesia, Malaysia, the Philippines, Singapore and Thailand. With the signing of the Declaration of the Admission of Brunei Darussalam Into the Association of South-East Asian Nations in Jakarta on 7 January 1984, Brunei became the sixth member state.

2 When ASEAN was established, the groupings included: in Africa, the East African Community, the Central African Customs and Economic Union, and the West African Economic Community; in South America, the Latin American Free Trade Association, the Andean Group, the Central American Common Market, the Caribbean Free Trade Association, and the East Caribbean Free Trade Association; and in the Middle East, the Arab Common Market.

3 With respect to the market economies, it has been suggested that there are five kinds of economic integration, with the following characteristics: the free-trade area, where tariffs and quantitative restrictions among the member countries are abolished; the customs union, where the free-trade area adopts common tariffs against outside countries; the common market, where the customs union allows free movement of factors of production; the economic union, where there is harmonisation of national policies within the common market; and total economic integration, the unification of economic, fiscal and other policies, and the setting up of a supranational authority whose decisions are binding on the member states. See Balassa (1966).

4 For a discussion of the recommended forms of ASEAN cooperation, see UN (1974:50–71).

5   Singapore's position is obvious, since it has adopted low tariffs and a liberal trade
    policy: its average level of nominal protection for the entire manufacturing sector
    has been estimated at around 5 per cent, and that of effective protection at 18 per
    cent (Chia, 1975); according to one estimate, over nine-tenths of tariff rates within
    the range of 0–10 per cent in the consolidated ASEAN schedule applied to
    Singapore. Malaysia had a low average level of nominal protection (18 per cent) as
    well as of effective protection (44 per cent), compared to the Philippines, where
    the respective rates were 30 per cent and 62 per cent (Ariff, 1975; Power, 1971).

6   On 20 January 1977, one week before the third Meeting of ASEAN Economic
    Ministers in Manila, Singapore and the Philippines signed the first bilateral trade
    cooperation pact: they agreed to implement mutual across-the-board preferential
    tariff reductions of 10 per cent of existing tariffs on all products traded between
    them. On 1 February 1977, Singapore and Thailand agreed to a preferential tariff
    agreement on certain groups of products. These preferences were subsequently
    extended to the trilateral level, providing for a tariff cut of 10 per cent for about
    1700 items traded among the Philippines, Singapore and Thailand.

7   Under the agreement two methods can be used. The first is the matrix approach: a
    country may make a specific request to and elicit a response from another country.
    The second is the voluntary approach: each country volunteers a list of products
    for preferential treatment at each round of negotiations.

8   Perceptions differ on what it signified. On the one hand, it has been suggested that
    'these preferences were considered relatively significant regional trade items ...
    These items according to 1976 trade values amounted to US$515 million in
    intra-ASEAN imports and US$501 million in intra-ASEAN exports, compared to
    US$1.55 billion in the total ASEAN imports and US$2.26 billion in the total
    exports' (Ooi Guat Tin, 1981:9). Other commentators have claimed that 'the
    recent identification of 71 products by the ASEAN Economic Ministers for pre-
    ferential tariff cuts ranging from 10 to 30 per cent does not represent a major
    break-through, after all. The items involved are either so unimportant in the total
    imports or traded intra-regionally with tariff levels which are already so low that
    the trade liberalization effects of tariff reductions are likely to be negligible' (Ariff
    and Thillainathan, 1977:9).

9   The Eighth ASEAN Economic Ministers meeting (September 1979, Manila)
    agreed to expand the number of preferences exchanged at each round of negotia-
    tions (held four times a year) from 100 to 150; to consider deeper tariff cuts; and to
    do away with lightly traded items frequently offered under the voluntary offer
    system, so that thenceforth import values of less than US$50 000 each (based on
    1978 statistics) would be automatically included under the preferential trading
    arrangements. The amount of US$50 000 was continuously increased (to
    US$100 000; to US$200 000; to US$500 000; and then to US$1–2.5 million), and it
    reached US$10 million in July 1983 and over US$10 million in May 1984, with
    preferences ranging from 20 per cent to 25 per cent, subject to an exclusion list of
    sensitive products.

10 Ooi Guat Tin's 1981 analysis of the effects of the preferential trading arrangements
    scheme on trade expansion reached the following conclusions. First, across-the-
    board tariff cuts of 20 per cent on small items are not likely to increase intra-
    ASEAN trade significantly. Second, a sensitivity analysis shows that deepening
    tariff cuts to 100 per cent and applying them to all items up to US$500 000 would
    not result in dramatic trade expansion. Third, any effect of the new procedure (the
    groundwork of which was laid down by the Eighth ASEAN Economic Ministers
    meeting) would result largely from trade diversion rather than trade creation. See
    also Naya (1980).

11 It was suggested that 'very little preliminary studies were done and the decision appears to have been taken rather hurriedly ... the industrial projects, except for the urea project allocated to Indonesia, seem to be heading towards impasse even in the initial stages' (Ariff and Thillainathan, 1977:5, 8).

12 National projects already firmly planned and in their early stages of implementation before the allocation of the ASEAN Industrial Projects were to be allowed to proceed as national projects.

13 Each shareholder entity is defined as an agency or company that enjoys support and guidance from its respective government of an ASEAN member state and is nominated by the government to participate in the ASEAN Industrial Projects scheme.

14 The ASEAN Industrial Complementation scheme is intended to involve primarily private-sector undertakings, enjoying the support of governments through the identification of opportunities, the formulation of programs, the design of projects, and agreement on measures to ensure the success of these schemes. It is realised through making tariff and/or non-tariff preferences available to Industrial Complementation products.

15 The meaning of exclusivity is as follows: for the country allocated a product, how it organises its production facilities is entirely at its discretion; other participating countries cannot set up new production facilities or expand old ones to make the same product as that already allocated to the other participating country, except when 75 per cent of its production is for export outside the ASEAN region. Nevertheless, these countries are allowed to proceed with the implementation of firmly planned projects to produce the product in question.

16 The offering countries and the indicative list of products are as follows: Indonesia—motorcycle axles, headlights for motorcycles, wheel rims for motorcycles, spark plugs; Malaysia—road wheels (5 tonnes and above), crown wheel pinions for commercial vehicles, seat belts; Philippines—automotive springs (leaf), front and rear axles and components, automotive gauges, signal lights; Singapore—fuel injection pumps, carburettors (automotive), brake systems, diesel engines for trucks, motorcycle frames, heavy-duty shock absorbers, trunnion shafts; Indonesia and Malaysia—piston assemblies (pistons, rings, liners); Malaysia and the Philippines—automotive springs (coil); the Philippines and Singapore—automotive transmissions (gearboxes).

CHAPTER 14

1 The inland area of China includes sixteen provinces: Anhwei, Chinghai, Honam, Hunan, Hupeh, Inner Mongolia, Kansu, Kiagsi, Kweichow, Ninghsia, Shansi, Shensi, Sinkiang, Szechuan, Tibet, and Yunnan.

2 A mu is equivalent to 0.0667 hectares, or approximately one acre.

3 The distinction being made here corresponds to the distinction between 'white-collar' and 'blue-collar' workers in western economies.

Bibliography

Adams, F.G. and C.A. Bollino (1983) 'Meaning of Industrial Policy' in Adams and Klein (eds) *Industrial Policies*

Adams, F.G. and Shinichi Ichimura (1983) 'Industrial Policy in Japan' in Adams and Klein (eds) *Industrial Policies*

Adams, F.G. and L.R. Klein (eds) (1983) *Industrial Policies for Growth and Competitiveness* Lexington, Mass.: D.C. Heath

Aho, C. Michael and Thomas O. Bayard (1980) 'American Trade Adjustment Assistance After Five Years' *The World Economy* 3, pp. 359–76

Alburo, F.A. (1983), Export Incentives and Manufactured Exports: Employment, Productivity and Distributional Considerations in the Philippines, paper presented to a seminar at the Free University, Amsterdam

Altshuler, Alan et al. (1984) *The Future of the Automobile: The Report of MIT's International Automobile Program* Cambridge, Mass.: MIT Press

Anderson, D. (1982) 'Small Industry in Developing Countries: A Discussion of Issues' *World Development* 10, 11, pp. 913–48

Anderson, J.E. (1985) 'The Relative Inefficiency of Quotas' *American Economic Review* 75 (March) pp. 178–90

Ariff, M. (1975) 'Protection for Manufactures in Peninsular Malaysia' *Hitotsubashi Journal of Economics* 15, 2, pp. 41–53

—— (1977) 'Trade Policies and ASEAN Industrial Cooperation' in M. Ariff, Fong Chan Onn and R. Thillainathan (eds) *ASEAN Cooperation in Industrial Projects*, Papers and Proceedings of a Symposium Organized by the Malaysian Economic Association, Kuala Lumpur and the Institute of Southeast Asian Studies, Singapore

—— (1983) Export-Oriented Industrialisation in Malaysia: Policies and Responses, paper presented to a seminar at the Free University, Amsterdam

Ariff, M. and H. Hill (1986) *Export-Oriented Industrialisation: The ASEAN Experience* Sydney: Allen & Unwin

Ariff, M. and R. Thillainathan (1977) 'ASEAN Industrial Cooperation—Problems and Prospects' in M. Ariff, Fong Chan Onn and R. Thillainathan (eds) *ASEAN Cooperation in Industrial Projects* Papers and Proceedings of a Symposium Organized by the Malaysian Economic Association, Kuala Lumpur and the Institute of Southeast Asian Studies, Singapore

Auquier, Antoine A. and Richard E. Caves (1979) 'Monopolistic Export Industries, Trade Taxes, and Optimal Competition Policy' *Economic Journal* 89 (September) pp. 559–81

Automotive News (1985) *1985 Market Data Book Issue* (April)

Balassa, B. (1965) 'Trade Liberalisation and "Revealed" Comparative Advantage' *Manchester School of Economic and Social Studies* 33, 2, pp. 99–123

—— (1966) 'A Theory of Economic Integration' in M.S. Wionczek (ed.) *Latin American Economic Integration* New York: Praeger

—— (1984) 'The Economic Consequences of Social Policies in the Industrial Countries' *Weltwirtschaftliches Archiv* 2, pp. 221–29

—— (1985) Industrial Policy in France, mimeo

Baldwin, Robert E. (1970) *Nontariff Distortions of International Trade* Washington, DC: The Brookings Institution

—— (1982) 'The Inefficiency of Trade Policy' International Finance Section *Essays in International Finance* No. 150 (December) Princeton: Princeton University

—— (1984) 'Rent-Seeking and Trade Policy: An Industry Approach' *Welwirtschaftliches Archiv* 4, pp. 662–77

Bator, Francis M. (1958) 'The Anatomy of Market Failure' *Quarterly Journal of Economics* 72 (August) pp. 351–79

Baumol, W.J. (1982) 'Contestable Markets: An Uprising in the Theory of Industry Structure' *American Economic Review* 72, pp. 1–15

Bautista, L. (1980) *Transfer of Technology Regulations in the Philippines* Geneva: United Nations Commission on Trade and Development (UNCTAD/77/32)

Bautista, R.M., J.H. Power and Associates (1979) *Industrial Promotion Policies in the Philippines* Manila: Philippine Institute for Development Studies

Bell, M. et al. (1984) *Assessing the Performance of Infant Industry* World Bank Staff Working Papers No. 666, World Bank, Washington, DC

Berkowitz, M. and Y. Kotowitz (1982) 'Patent Policy in an Open Economy' *Canadian Journal of Economics* 15 (February) pp. 1–17

Bhagwati, J. N. (ed.) (1982) *Import Competition and Response* Chicago: University of Chicago Press

Bhagwati, J.N. and T.N. Srinivasan (1983) *Lectures on International Trade* Cambridge, Mass.: MIT Press

Bhanich Supapol, A. and D.G. McFetridge (1982) 'An Analysis of the Federal Make-Or-Buy Policy' Discussion Paper No. 217, Economic Council of Canada, Ottawa

Biggs, Margaret (1981) *Adjust or Protect?* Ottawa: North–South Institute

Bishop, Paul M. and Harold Crookell (1985) 'Specialization and Foreign Investment in Canada' in D.G. McFetridge (ed.) *Canadian Industrial Policy in Action* Ottawa: Royal Commission on the Economic Union

Bowen, H.P. (1983) 'On the Theoretical Interpretation of Indices of Trade Intensity and Revealed Comparative Advantage' *Weltwirtschaftliches Archiv* 119, 3, pp. 464–72

Brander, James A. and Barbara J. Spencer (1981) 'Tariffs and the Extraction of Foreign Monopoly Rents Under Potential Entry' *Canadian Journal of Economics* 14 (August) pp. 371–89

—— (1984) 'Trade Warfare: Tariffs and Cartels' *Journal of International Economics* 16 (May) pp. 117–31

Breton, Albert (1964) 'The Economics of Nationalism' *Journal of Political Economy* 72 (August) pp. 376–89

Britton, J.H. and James M. Gilmour (1978) *The Weakest Link: A Technological Perspective on Canadian Industry Underdevelopment* Ottawa: Ministry of Supply and Services

Brook, P. (1983) *A Preliminary Assessment of Restructuring in the Textile Industry* Wellington, NZ: Department of the Treasury

Bruch, M. and U. Hiemenz (1984) *Small- and Medium-Scale Industries in the ASEAN Countries* Boulder: Westview Press

Cairncross, A. et al. (1982) *Protectionism: Threat to International Order. The Impact on Developing Countries* London: Commonwealth Secretariat

Canlas, D. et al. (1984) *An Analysis of the Philippine Economic Crisis: A Workshop Report* Quezon City: University of the Philippines

Caves, Richard E. (1980) 'International Trade and Industrial Organization: Introduction' *Journal of Industrial Economics* 29, 2, pp. 113–17

Caves, Richard E. and Masu Uekusa (1976) *Industrial Organization in Japan* Washington, DC: The Brookings Institution

Chaney, P.K. and A.V. Thakor (1985) 'Incentive Effects of Benevolent Intervention: The Case of Government Loan Guarantees' *Journal of Public Economics* 26, pp. 169–89

Chang, C.S. (1981) *The Japanese Auto Industry and the US Market* New York: Praeger

Chee, P.L. (1984a) 'Small Enterprises in ASEAN: Need for Regional Co-operation' *ASEAN Economic Bulletin* 1, 2, pp. 89–114

—— (1984b) 'The Malaysian Car Industry at the Crossroads: Time to Change Gear?' in L.L. Lim and P.L. Chee (eds) *The Malaysian Economy at the Crossroads: Policy Adjustment or Structural Transformation?* Kuala Lumpur: Malaysian Economic Association

Chia, S.Y. (1975) 'Size of Market and Export Oriented Industrialization in Singapore' in N. Susuki (ed.) *Asian Industrial Development* Tokyo: Institute of Developing Economies

Clark, Kim B. (1984) 'Unionization and Firm Performance: The Impact on Profits, Growth, and Productivity' *American Economic Review* 74 (December) pp. 893–919

Cockerill, A. (1974) *The Steel Industry* London: Cambridge University Press

Cole, Robert E. (ed.) (1982) *Industry at the Crossroads* Michigan Papers in Japanese Studies No. 7, Center for Japanese Studies, University of Michigan

—— (ed.) (1983) *Automobiles and the Future: Competition, Cooperation and Change* Michigan Papers in Japanese Studies No. 10, Center for Japanese Studies, University of Michigan

—— (ed.) (1984) *The American Automobile Industry: Rebirth or Requiem?* Michigan Papers in Japanese Studies, Center for Japanese Studies, University of Michigan

Cole, Robert E. and Taizo Yakushiji (eds) (1984) *The American and Japanese Auto Industries in Transition* Ann Arbor: Center for Japanese Studies, University of Michigan

Commission of Inquiry on the Pharmaceutical Industry (1985) *Report of the Commission of Inquiry on the Pharmaceutical Industry* Ottawa: Ministry of Supply and Services

Contractor, F.J. (1981) *International Technology Licensing: Compensation, Costs and Negotiations* Lexington, Mass.: Lexington Books

Corden, W.M. (1974) *Trade Policy and Economic Welfare* Oxford: Oxford University Press

—— (1984) *The Revival of Protectionism in Developed Countries* New York: The Group of Thirty

Corden, W.M. and R.E. Falvey (1985) 'Quotas and the Second Best' Working Papers in Economics and Econometrics No. 115, Faculty of Economics and Research School of Social Sciences, Australian National University

Crandall, R.W. (1981) *The US Steel Industries in Recurrent Crisis* Washington, DC: The Brookings Institution

—— (1984) 'Import Quotas and the Automobile Industry: The Costs of Protectionism' *Brookings Review* 2 (Summer) pp. 8–16

Curzon Price, Victoria (1980) 'Alternatives to Delayed Structural Adjustment in "Workshop Europe"' *The World Economy* (September) pp. 206

Daly, D. (1968) *Scale and Specialization in Canadian Manufacturing* Staff Study No. 21, Economic Council of Canada

Daly, D. and S. Globerman (1976) *Tariff and Science Policies: Applications of a Model of Nationalism* Toronto: University of Toronto Press

Dasgupta, Partha and Joseph Stiglitz (1980) 'Uncertainty, Industrial Structure, and the Speed of R & D' *Bell Journal of Economics* 11 (Spring) pp. 1–28

Denny, M. (1985) 'The Prospects for Productivity' in J. Sargent (ed.) *Economic Growth: Prospects and Determinants* Ottawa: Royal Commission on the Economic Union

Denzau, Arthur T. (1983) *Will An Industrial Policy Work for the United States?*
St Louis: Center for the Study of American Business, Washington University

Department of External Affairs, Canada (1983) *Canadian Trade Policy for the 1980s*
Ottawa: Ministry of Supply and Services (see also *A Review of Trade Policy*, background document to the statement)

Department of Finance, Canada (1983) *Research and Development Tax Policies* Ottawa:
Ministry of Supply and Services

Dixit, A. (1979) 'A Model of Duopoly Suggesting a Theory of Entry Barriers' *Bell Journal of Economics* 10, pp. 20–32

—— (1980) 'The Role of Investment in Entry-Deterrence' *Economic Journal* 90, pp. 95–106

—— (1984) 'International Trade Policy for Oligopolistic Industries' Supplement to *Economic Journal* 94, pp. 1–16

Donges, Juergen B. (1980) 'Industrial Policies in West Germany's Not So Market-Oriented Economy' *The World Economy* 2, 2, pp. 185–204

Dorrance, G.S. and H. Hughes (1984) Economic Policies and Direct Foreign Investment with Particular Reference to the Developing Countries of East Asia, paper prepared for the Commonwealth Secretariat, London

Eads, George C. (1981) 'The Political Experience in Allocating Investment: Lessons for the United States and Elsewhere' in Michael L. Wachter and Susan M. Wachter (eds) *Towards a New Industrial Policy?* Philadelphia: University of Pennsylvania Press

Eastman, H.C. and Stefan Stykolt (1967) *The Tariff and Competition in Canada* Toronto: St Martin's Press

Eaton, Jonathan and Gene M. Grossman (1984) 'Optimal Trade and Industrial Policy Under Oligopoly' Working Paper No. 8413C, Center for the Study of International Economic Relations, University of Western Ontario

EC Commission (1975) *Guidelines on Iron and Steel Policy* Brussels: EC Commission, COM (75) 701

—— (1977) 'Community Steel Policy' *Official Journal* C303 (Davignon Plan)

Economic Council of Canada (1969) *Interim Report on Competition Policy* Ottawa: Economic Council of Canada

—— (1975) *Looking Outward* Ottawa: Economic Council of Canada

—— (1983) *The Bottom Line* Ottawa: Ministry of Supply and Services

Ellis, N. and D. Waite (1985) 'Canadian Technological Output in a World Context' in D.G. McFetridge (ed.) *Technological Change in Canadian Industry* Ottawa: Royal Commission on the Economic Union

Emerson, C. and P. Warr (1981) 'Economic Evaluation of Mineral Processing Projects: A Case Study of Copper Smelting in the Philippines' *Philippine Economic Journal* 20, 2, pp. 175–97

English, H.E. (1964) *Industrial Structure in Canadian International Competitive Position* Montreal: Private Planning Association of Canada

—— (1979) 'Specialization and Export Agreements in Canada' in J.R.S. Pritchard, W.T. Stanbury and T.A. Wilson (eds) *Canadian Competition Policy: Essays in Law and Economics* Toronto: Butterworth

Executive Yuan (1982) *Science and Technology Development Program* (revised and promulgated 26 August)

Falvey, R.E. (1979) 'The Composition of Trade Within Import-Restricted Product Categories' *Journal of Political Economy* 87 (October) pp. 1105–14

Feenstra, Robert C. (1985) 'Automobile Prices and Protection: The US–Japan Trade Restraint' *Journal of Political Modeling* 7 (March) pp. 49–68

Flam, H., T. Persson and L.E.O. Svensson (1983) 'Optimal Subsidies to Declining Industries' *Journal of Public Economics* 22, pp. 327–45

Flynn, Michael S. (1983) 'Comparison of US–Japan Production Costs: An Assessment' in Cole (ed.) *Automobiles and the Future*

Freeman, Richard B. and James L. Medoff (1984) *What Do Unions Do?* New York: Basic Books

French, Richard (1980) *How Ottawa Decides* Toronto: Lorimer

Galenson, A. (1984) *Investment Incentives for Industry* World Bank Staff Working Papers No. 669, Washington, DC

Garnaut, R. (ed.) (1980) *ASEAN in a Changing Pacific and World Economy* Canberra: Australian National University Press

Garnaut, R. and K. Anderson (1980) 'ASEAN Export Specialisation and the Evolution of Comparative Advantage in the Western Pacific Region' in Garnaut (ed.) *ASEAN in a Changing Pacific and World Economy*

GATT (General Agreement on Tariffs and Trade) (1984a) *International Trade 1982/83* Geneva: GATT

—— (1984b) *Textibles and Clothing in the World Economy* Geneva: GATT

Gibbs, I. and V. Konovalov (1984) 'Volume Quotas with Heterogeneous Product Categories' *Economic Record* 60 (September) pp. 294–303

Glenday, Graham, Glenn P. Jenkins and John C. Evans (1982) *Worker Adjustment Policies: An Alternative to Protectionism* Ottawa: North–South Institute

Globerman, Steven (1980) *Foreign Ownership in the Canadian Economy* Montreal: C.D. Howe Research Institute

Golbe, Devra L. (1981) 'The Effects of Imminent Bankruptcy on Stockholder Risk Preferences and Behavior' *Bell Journal of Economics* 12 (Spring) pp. 321–28

Gomez-Ibanez, Jose A. and David Harrison Jr (1982) 'Imports and the Future of the US Automobile Industry' *American Economic Review* 72 (May) pp. 319–23

Gomez-Ibanez, Jose A., Robert A. Leone and Stephen A. O'Connell (1983) 'Restraining Auto Imports: Does Anyone Win?' *Journal of Policy Analysis and Management* 2, pp. 196–218

Government of Canada (1972) *Foreign Direct Investment in Canada* Ottawa: Information Canada

Gregorio, R.G. (1979) 'An Economic Analysis of the Effects of Philippine Fiscal Incentives for Industrial Promotion' in Bautista, Power and Associates *Industrial Promotion Policies in the Philippines*

Gregory, R.G. (1986) 'Wages Policy and Unemployment in Australia' *Economica* (in press)

Grey, Rodney de C. (1981) *Trade Policy in the 1980s* Montreal: C.D. Howe Research Institute

Grossman, Gene M. and Jonathan Eaton (1985) 'Tariffs as Insurance: Optimal Commercial Policy When Domestic Markets are Incomplete' *Canadian Journal of Economics* 18 (May) pp. 258–72

Grubel, H.G. and P.J. Lloyd (1974) *Intra-Industry Trade: The Theory and Measurement of International Trade in Differentiated Products* London: Macmillan

Harris, R. (1985) *Trade, Industrial Policy and International Competition* Ottawa: Royal Commission on the Economic Union

Harris, Richard G. with David Cox (1984) *Trade, Industrial Policy, and Canadian Manufacturing* Toronto: Ontario Economic Council

Hart, Michael (1985) *Some Thoughts on Canada–United States Sectoral Free Trade* Ottawa: Institute for Research on Public Policy

Helliwell et al. (1985) 'Economic Growth and Productivity in Canada' in J. Sargent (ed.) *Economic Growth: Prospects and Determinants* Ottawa: Royal Commission on the Economic Union

Hesselman, Linda (1983) 'Trends in European Industrial Intervention' *Cambridge Journal of Economics* 7, pp. 197–208

Hill, H. (1984) 'Survey of Recent Developments' *Bulletin of Indonesian Economic Studies* 20, 2, pp. 1–38

—— (1985) 'Subcontracting, Technological Diffusion and the Development of Small Enterprise in Philippines Manufacturing' *Journal of Developing Areas* (April)

Hill, H. and B. Johns (1985) 'The Role of Direct Foreign Investment in Developing East Asian Countries' *Weltwirtschaftliches Archiv* (June)

Hindley, B. (1984) 'Empty Economics in the Case for Industrial Policy' *The World Economy* 7, pp. 277–94

Hirschleifer, Jack (1971) 'The Private and Social Value of Information and the Reward to Inventive Activity' *American Economic Review* 61 (September) pp. 561–74

Hoffman, L. and S.E. Tan (1980) *Industrialization, Employment and Foreign Investment in Peninsular Malaysia* Kuala Lumpur: Oxford University Press

Horiuchi, Toshihiro (1984) 'Koka Toboshii Sangyo Chosei Saku' (Industrial Adjustment Policy is not Effective) *Nihon Keizai Shimbun* 7 June

Houseman, Susan N. (1985) Job Security and Industrial Restructuring in the European Community Steel Industry, PhD Dissertation, Harvard University

Hughes, H. and A.O. Krueger (1984) 'Effects of Protection in Developed Countries on Developing Countries' Exports of Manufactures' in R.E. Baldwin (ed.) *The Structure and Evolution of Recent US Trade Policies* Chicago: University of Chicago Press

Hunker, Jeffrey A. (1983) *Structural Change in the US Automobile Industry* Lexington, Mass.: D.C. Heath

IAC (Industries Assistance Commission) (1980) *Textiles, Clothing and Footwear. Part C: Clothing* Canberra: Australian Government Publishing Service

—— (1984) *Textiles, Clothing and Footwear Inquiry, Background Paper* Canberra: Australian Government Publishing Service

IDE (Institute of Developing Economies) (1982a) *Comparative Advantage of Manufacturing Industries in the Philippines* CAM Series No. 14, Tokyo: IDE

—— (1982b) *Comparative Advantage of Manufacturing Industries in Asian Countries* CAM Series No. 16, Tokyo: IDE

IISI (International Iron and Steel Institute) (1980) *Causes of the Mid-1970s Recession in Steel Demand* Brussels: IISI

Indonesia, Biro Pusat Statistik (1982) *Penduduk Indonesia* (The Population of Indonesia) Series S, No. 1 (Preliminary Tables) Jakarta

Indonesia, Departemen Penerengan (1984) *Rencana Pembangunan Lima Tahun Keempat, 1984/85–1988/89* Jakarta

Itoh, M., K. Kiyono, M. Okuno and K. Suzumura (1984–85) 'Economic Analysis of Industrial Policy: (1)–(4)' *Contemporary Economics* 58, pp. 73–90; 59, pp. 82–89; 60, pp. 113–37; 61, pp. 65–90 (in Japanese)

Jacoby, N.H. (1966) *US Aid to Taiwan: A Study of Foreign Aid, Self-Help, and Development* New York: Praeger

Jacquemin, Alexis (ed.) (1984) *European Industry, Public Policy and Corporate Strategy* London: Oxford University Press

Jaffe, I. (1984) 'Industrial Policies: Responses to a Common Core of Problems' *OECD Observer* 130 (September) pp. 126–39

Jenkins, G.P. (forthcoming) 'Costs and Consequences of the New Protectionism: The Case of Canada's Clothing Sector' in North–South Institute and World Bank *Canada in a Developing World Economy: Trade or Protection?* Washington, DC: Oxford University Press

Johnson, C. (1982) *MITI and the Japanese Miracle* Stanford, California: Stanford University Press

—— (1984) *The Industrial Policy Debate* San Francisco: Institute for Contemporary Studies

Johnson, Harry G. (1965) 'Optimal Trade Intervention in the Presence of Domestic Distortions' in Robert E. Baldwin et al. (eds) *Trade, Growth and the Balance of Payments: Essays in Honor of Gottfried Haberler* Chicago: Rand McNally
—— (1970) 'A New View of the Infant Industry Argument' in L.A. McDougal et al. (eds) *Studies in International Economics* Amsterdam: North-Holland
Joint Statement on Assistance for the Textile, Clothing and Footwear Industries (1980) Statement by the Minister for Industry and Commerce and the Minister for Business and Consumer Affairs (15 August)
Kamien, M.I. and N.L. Schwartz (1982) *Market Structure and Innovation* Cambridge: Cambridge University Press
Katrak, H. (1977) 'Multi-National Monopolies and Commercial Policy' *Oxford Economic Papers* 19 (July) pp. 283–91
Katz, Harry (1985) *Shifting Gears: Changing Labor Relations in the Automobile Industry* Cambridge, Mass.: MIT Press
Kemp, M.C. (1960) 'The Mill-Bastable Infant-Industry Dogma' *Journal of Political Economy* 68, pp. 65–67
Kim, Lee-won (1984) 'The Vehicle Industry in Korea' Korea Exchange Bank *Monthly Review* 18 (November), pp. 1–13
Komiya, R. (1975) 'Planning in Japan' in M. Banstein (ed.) *Economic Planning, East and West* Cambridge, Mass.: Ballinger
Komiya, Ryutaro, Masahiro Okuno and Kotaro Suzumura (eds) (1984) *Nihon no Sangyo Seisaku* (Industrial Policy in Japan) Tokyo: University of Tokyo Press (in Japanese)
Korea Iron and Steel Association (1984) *Iron and Steel Statistics Yearbook* Seoul: Korea Iron and Steel Association
Kornai, Tanos (1980) *The Economics of Shortage* 2 vols, vol. 131 of *Contributions to Economic Analysis* Amsterdam: North-Holland
Krause, L.B. (1982) *US Economic Policy Towards the Association of Southeast Asian Nations: Meeting the Japanese Challenge* Washington, DC: The Brookings Institution
Krueger, A.O. (1977) *Growth, Distortions and Patterns of Trade Among Many Countries* Princeton Studies in International Finance No. 40, Princeton University
—— (1978) *Foreign Trade Regimes and Economic Development: Liberalization Attempts and Consequences* National Bureau of Economic Research, Cambridge, Mass.: Ballinger
—— (1983) *Trade and Employment in Developing Countries* vol. 3: *Synthesis and Conclusions*, Chicago: University of Chicago Press, for the National Bureau of Economic Research
Krugman, Paul R. (1983) 'Targeted Industrial Policies: Theory and Evidence' in *Industrial Change and Public Policy* Symposium sponsored by the Federal Reserve Bank of Kansas City
—— (1984a) 'Import Protection as Export Promotion: International Competition in the Presence of Oligopoly and Economics of Scale' in Henryk Kierzkowski (ed.) *Monopolistic Competition and International Trade* Oxford: Clarendon Press
—— (1984b) 'The US Response to Foreign Industrial Targeting' *Brookings Papers on Economic Activity* 1, pp. 77–121
Kwoka, John E. Jr (1983) Memorandum to Edward Glynn, Bureau of Competition, US Federal Trade Commission (3 October)
—— (1984) Testimony Before the Subcommittee on Commerce, Transportation, and Tourism, Committee on Energy and Commerce, US House of Representatives (8 February)
Lall, S. (1979) 'Multinationals and Market Structure in an Open Developing Economy: The Case of Malaysia' *Weltwirtschaftliches Archiv* 115, pp. 325–48

Lawrence, Colin and Robert Z. Lawrence (1985) 'The Dispersion in Manufacturing Wages: An Endgame Interpretation' *Brookings Papers on Economic Activity* 1, pp. 31–62

Lawrence, Robert Z. (1984) *Can America Compete?* Washington, DC: The Brookings Institution

Lawrence, Robert Z. and Paula R. DeMasi (1985) 'Do Industries with a Self-Identified Loss of Comparative Advantage Ever Adjust?' in Gary C. Hufbauer and Howard F. Rosen (eds) *Dealing with Decline: Trade Policy for Troubled Industries* Washington, DC: Institute for International Economics

Lea, Sperry (1963) *A Canada–US Free Trade Arrangement: Survey of Possible Characteristics* Montreal: Canadian-American Committee

Lee, Eddy (ed.) (1981) *Export-Led Industrialization and Development* Singapore: Maruzen Asia

Lee, Teng-hui (1971) *Intersectoral Capital Flows in the Economic Development of Taiwan, 1885–1960* Ithaca: Cornell University Press

Lee, T.H. and Kuo-shu Liang (1982) 'Development Strategies in Taiwan' in B. Balassa and Associates (eds) *Development Strategies in Semi-Industrial Economies* Baltimore: Johns Hopkins University Press

Li, K.T. (1983) 'Development of Science and Technology in the Republic of China' *Industry of Free China* 59, 1 (January)

Liang, Kuo-shu and Teng-hui Lee (1974) 'Process and Pattern of Economic Development in Taiwan' in Shinichi Ichimura (ed.) *The Economic Development of East and Southeast Asia* Honolulu: University of Hawaii Press

Liang, Kuo-shu and Ching-ing Hou Liang (1978). Export Expansion and Economic Development in Taiwan, paper presented to Conference of the Asian Studies on the Pacific Coast, Anaheim, California (9 June)

Lieberman, Marvin B. (1984) 'The Learning Curve and Pricing in the Chemical Processing Industries' *Rand Journal of Economics* 15 (Summer) pp. 213–28

Lim, D. (1980) 'Industrial Processing and Location: A Study of Tin' *World Development* 8, 3, pp. 205–212

Lin, Ching-yuan (1973) *Industrialization in Taiwan, 1946–72: Trade and Import-Substitution Policies for Developing Countries* New York: Praeger

Lindsey, C.W. (1977) 'Market Concentration in Philippine Manufacturing, 1970' *Philippine Economic Journal* 16, 3, pp. 289–312

Lipsey, R.G. and K. Lancaster (1956–57) 'The General Theory of the Second Best' *Review of Economic Studies* 24

Lipsey, Richard J. and Murray G. Smith (1985) *Canada's Trade Options* Toronto: C.D. Howe Research Institute

Lloyd, P.J. (1983) Industrial Restructuring, paper presented to FAEA-IEA Conference on Economic Interdependence: Perspectives from Developing Countries, Manila (May)

—— (1984) 'The Australian Textile and Clothing Group: Untoward Effects of Government Intervention' in K. Jungenvelt and Sir Douglas Hague (eds) *Structural Adjustment in Developed Open Economies* London: Macmillan

McCawley, P. (1981) 'The Growth of the Industrial Sector' in A. Booth and P. McCawley (eds) *The Indonesian Economy During the Soeharto Era* Kuala Lumpur: Oxford University Press

—— (ed.) (forthcoming) *Industrial Regulation in ASEAN and Australia*

MacDonald, Robert M. (1963) *Collective Bargaining in the Automobile Industry* New Haven: Yale University Press

McFetridge, D.G. (1984) 'The Effect of the 1983 Federal Budget Amendments on the Incentive to Engage in Industrial R & D' in *Report of the Proceedings of the Thirty-Fifth Tax Conference* Toronto: Canadian Tax Foundation

—— (1985) 'The Economics of Industrial Policy: An Overview' in D.G. McFetridge (ed.) *Canadian Industrial Policy in Action* Ottawa: Royal Commission on the Economic Union

McFetridge, D.G. and R. Corvari (1985) 'Technology Diffusion: A Survey of Canadian Evidence and the Public Policy Issues' in D.G. McFetridge (ed.) *Technological Change in Canadian Industry* Ottawa: Royal Commission on the Economic Union

McFetridge, D.G. and J.P. Warda (1983) *Canadian R & D Incentives: Their Adequacy and Their Impact* Toronto: Canadian Tax Foundation

McKinnon, R.I. (1973) *Money and Capital in Economic Development* Washington, DC: The Brookings Institution

—— (1979) *Money in International Exchange: The Convertible Currency System* New York: Oxford University Press

—— (1984) 'The International Capital Market and Economic Liberalization in LDCs' *The Developing Economies* 22, 4 (December)

Magaziner, Ira, C. and Robert B. Reich (1982) *Minding America's Business* New York: Harcourt Brace

Maizels, A. (1968) *Exports and Economic Growth of Developing Countries* London: Cambridge University Press

Malaysia, Jabatan Percetaken Negara (1984) *Mid-Term Review of the Fourth Malaysia Plan 1981–1985* Kuala Lumpur

Marcus, P.F. (1982) World Steel Dynamics: The Steel Strategists #6

Martin, J.P. and J.M. Evans (1981) 'Notes on Measuring Employment Displacement Effects of Trade by the Accounting Procedure' *Oxford Economic Papers* 33 (March) pp. 154–64

Medalla, E.M. and J.H. Power (1984) 'Estimating the Shadow Exchange Rate, the Shadow Wage Rate and the Social Rate of Discount for the Philippines' Working Paper No. 84–03, Philippine Institute for Development Studies, Manila

Meier, Gerald M. (1980) *International Economics: The Theory of Policy* New York: Oxford University Press

Menon, M.G. (1966) *Petrochemicals Digest* London: Asia Publishing House

Mills, Edwin S. and Lawrence J. White (1978) 'Government Policies Toward Automotive Emissions Control' in Ann F. Friedlander (ed.) *Approaches to Controlling Air Pollution* Cambridge, Mass.: MIT Press

Mottershead, Peter (1983) 'Shipbuilding: Adjustment-Led Intervention or Intervention-Led Adjustment?' in Sheperd et al. (eds) *Europe's Industries*

Mueller, H. (1982) A Comparative Analysis of Steel Industries in Industrialized and Newly Industrializing Countries, paper presented to the Eastern Economic Association, Washington, DC (April)

—— (1978) Structural Changes in International Steel Market, mimeo

Munger, Michael C. (1985) 'A Time-Series Investigation into Factors Influencing U.S. Auto Assembly Employment' Bureau of Economics, US Federal Trade Commission (February)

Mussa, Michael (1978) 'Dynamic Adjustment in the Heckscher-Ohlin-Samuelson Model' *Journal of Political Economy* 86 (October) pp. 775–91

MVMA (Motor Vehicle Manufacturers Association) (1984) *Facts & Figures '84* Detroit: MVMA

Nambu, Tsuruhiko (1986) 'The Role of Government in the High Technology Industries' *Pacific Economic Papers* Pacific Trade and Development Conference Special Paper, Australia–Japan Research Centre, Research School of Pacific Studies, Australian National University (May)

National Academy of Engineering and National Research Council (1982) *The Competitive Status of the US Auto Industry* Washington, DC: National Academy Press

Naya, S. (1980) 'Preferential Trading Agreements and Trade Liberalization' Project

RAS/77/015/A/40, Bangkok

Neary, J.P. (1982) 'Intersectoral Capital Mobility, Wage Stickiness, and the Case for Adjustment Assistance' in Bhagwati (ed.) *Import Competition and Response*

Negishi, T. (1972) *General Equilibrium Theory and International Trade* Amsterdam: North-Holland

Nelson, R.R. (1982) *Government and Technological Progress* New York: Pergamon

Nelson, R.R. and R.N. Langlois (1983) 'Industrial Innovation: Lessons from American History' *Science* (18 February) pp. 814–18

Odaka, K. (ed.) (1983) *The Motor Vehicle Industry in Asia: A Study of Ancillary Firm Development* Singapore: Singapore University Press, for the Council for Asian Manpower Studies

OECD (Organization for Economic Cooperation and Development) (1983a) *Positive Adjustment Policies* Paris: OECD

—— (1983b) *Textile and Clothing Industries: Structural Problems and Policies in OECD Countries* Paris: OECD

—— (1984) 'The Importance of Long-Term Job Attachment in OECD Countries' *OECD Employment Outlook* (September) pp. 55–68

Okuno, M. (1985) 'Competition, Interdependence of Industries and Marshallian Externalities' Discussion Paper 85 F-1, Faculty of Economics, University of Tokyo

Okuno, M. and K. Suzumura (1985) 'Welfare Criteria for Industrial Subsidies in an Oligopolistic Setting' Discussion Paper No. 118, Institute of Economic Research, Hitotsubashi University

Ooi Guat Tin (1981) 'The ASEAN Preferential Trading Arrangement' Research Notes and Discussion Paper No. 26, Institute of Southeast Asian Studies, Singapore

Oshima, H.T. (1984) 'Issues in Heavy Industry Development in Asia' *Ekonomi dan Keuangan Indonesia* 32, 1, pp. 31–72

Ostry, Sylvia and Val Koromzay (1982) 'The United States and Europe' *OECD Observer* (May) pp. 9–13

Pack, H. (1981) 'Fostering the Capital Goods Sector in LDCs' *World Development* 9, 3, pp. 227–50

Panagariya, A. (1981) 'Variable Returns to Scale in Production and Patterns of Specialization' *American Economic Review* 71, pp. 221–30

Patrick, H. (1983) 'Japanese Industrial Policy and its Relevance for United States Industrial Policy' Statement prepared for the Joint Economic Committee of the US Congress (13 July)

Peck, M.J. and S. Tamura (1976) 'Technology' in H. Patrick and H. Rosovsky (eds) *Asia's New Giant: How the Japanese Economy Works* Washington, DC: The Brookings Institution

Peltzman, Sam (1975) 'The Effects of Automobile Safety Regulation' *Journal of Political Economy* 83 (August) pp. 677–726

Pernia, E.M. and C.W. Paderanga (1983) 'The Spatial and Urban Dimensions of Development' in E.M. Pernia (ed.) *The Spatial and Urban Dimensions of Development in the Philippines* Manila: Philippine Institute for Development Studies

Philippines, NEDA (National Economic and Development Authority) (1982) *Five Year Philippine Development Plan, 1983–1987* Manila: NEDA

Philippines, National Census and Statistics Office (1983) *1980 Annual Survey of Establishments* (Preliminary) Manila

Pinder, John (ed.) (1982) *National Industrial Strategies and the World Economy* New Jersey: Allanheld Osmun & Co.

Power, J.H. (1971) 'The Structure of Protection in the Philippines' in B. Balassa (ed.) *The Structure of Protection in Developing Countries* Baltimore: Johns Hopkins University Press

Rader, James (1980) *Penetrating the US Auto Market: German and Japanese Strategies, 1965–1976* Ann Arbor: UMI Research Press

Ranis, G. and C. Schive (1985) 'Direct Foreign Investment in Taiwan's Development' in W. Galenson (ed.) *Foreign Trade and Investment: Economic Development in the Newly Industrializing Asian Countries* Madison, Wisconsin: University of Wisconsin Press

Reich, Robert B. (1983a) 'An Industrial Policy of the Right' *Public Interest* 73 (Fall) pp. 3–17

—— (1983b) *The Next American Frontier* New York: Penguin

—— (1985) 'Bailout: A Comparative Study in Law and Industrial Structures' *Yale Journal on Regulation* 2, pp. 163–224

Reisman, Simon (1978) *The Canadian Automotive Industry: Performance and Proposals for Progress* Ottawa: Ministry of Supply and Services

Restrictive Trade Practices Commission (1983) *Telecommunications in Canada—III Vertical Integration* Ottawa: Ministry of Supply and Services

Rhee, H.Y. (1983) Protection Structures of the Developing Countries in South and East Asia, Pacific Economic Cooperation Conference Task Force Workshop on Trade in Manufactured Goods, Seoul

Roemer, M. (1979) 'Resource-Based Industrialization in the Developing Countries: A Survey' *Journal of Development Economics* 6, pp. 163–202

Rokuhara, Akira (ed.) (1985) *Kenkyu Kaihatsu to Dokusenkinshi Seisaku* (Research and Development Antitrust Policy) Tokyo: Gyosei

Ruffin, R. and R.W. Jones (1977) 'Real Wages and Protection: The Neoclassical Ambiguity' *Journal of Economic Theory* 18, 3, pp. 337–48

Sadli, Mohammed (1983) 'ASEAN Industrial Co-operation' *Indonesian Quarterly* 11, 1

Safarian, A.E. (1983) *Governments and Multinationals: Policies in the Developed Countries* Washington, DC

Salinger, Michael A. (1984) 'Tobin's q, Unionization, and the Concentration–Profits Relationship' *Rand Journal of Economics* 15 (Summer) pp. 159–70

Santikarn, M. (1984) *Trade in Technology: ASEAN and Australia* ASEAN–Australia Economic Papers No. 8, ASEAN–Australia Joint Research Project, Kuala Lumpur and Canberra

Schive, C. and R.S. Yeh (1982) 'Multinational Corporations and Host Country Technology: A Factor Proportion Approach in Taiwan' *Asian Manpower Studies Discussion Paper Series* No. 82–01 (February)

Schultze, Charles L. (1983) 'Industrial Policy: A Dissent' *The Brookings Review* 2 (Fall) pp. 3–12

Schumpeter, J.A. (1942) *Capitalism, Socialism, and Democracy* London: George Allen & Unwin

Science Council of Canada (1985) *Canadian Science Counsellors* Ottawa: Ministry of Supply and Services

Scott, B.R. (1984) National Strategies: Key to International Competition, mimeo, Harvard University School of Business, Boston

Sekaly, Raymond R. (1981) *Transnationalization of the Automobile Industry* Ottawa: University of Ottawa Press

Shaw, E.S. (1973) *Financial Deepening in Economic Development* New York: Oxford University Press

Sheard, P. (1984) 'A Case Study of the Aluminium Refining Industry' Discussion Paper, Faculty of Economics, Osaka University

Sheperd, Geoffery, Francois Duchene and Christopher Saunders (eds) (1983) *Europe's Industries: Public and Private Strategies for Change* Ithaca, NY: Cornell University Press

Spence, M. (1984) 'Industrial Organization and Competitive Advantage in Multi-national Industries' *American Economic Review* 74 (May) pp. 354–60

Spencer, Barbara J. and James A. Brander (1983) 'International R & D Rivalry and Industrial Strategy' *Review of Economic Studies* 50 (October) pp. 707–722

Spinanger, D. (1984) 'Objectives and Impact of Economic Activity Zones—Some Evidence from Asia' *Weltwirtschaftliches Archiv* 120, 1, pp. 64–89

Standing Senate Committee on Foreign Affairs (1982) *Canada–United States Relations* vol. 3, Ottawa: Ministry of Supply and Services

Statistics Canada (1983) *Federal Government Expenditures on Activities in the Natural Sciences 1963–64 to 1983–84* Cat. No. SS83–4, Ottawa

—— (1984) *Industrial Research and Development Statistics 1982* Cat. No. 88–202, Ottawa

Stewart, James B. (1983) *The Partners* New York: Warner Books

Stiglitz, J.E. (1981) 'Potential Competition May Reduce Welfare' *American Economic Review: Papers and Proceedings* 71, pp. 184–89

Stone, Frank (1984) *Canada, the GATT and the International Trade System* Ottawa: Institute for Research on Public Policy

Suzumura, K. and K. Kiyono (forthcoming) 'Entry Barriers and Economic Welfare' *Review of Economic Studies* (in press)

Suzumura, K. and M. Okuno (1985) Capacity Investment, Oligopolistic Competition, and Economic Welfare, unpublished ms

Takacs, W. (1975) Quantitative Restrictions in International Trade, unpublished PhD Dissertation, Johns Hopkins University, Baltimore

Tambunlertchai, S. (1983) Manufactured Exports and Employment in Thailand, paper presented to a seminar at the Free University, Amsterdam

Tan, N.A. (1979) 'The Structure of Protection and Resource Flows in the Philippines' in Bautista et al. (eds) *Industrial Promotion Policies in the Philippines*

Tandon, P. (1984) 'Innovation, Market Structure, and Welfare' *American Economic Review* 74, pp. 394–403

Tang, Anthony M. and Kuo-shu Liang (1973) 'Agricultural Trade in the Economic Development of Taiwan' in G.S. Tolley and P.A. Zadrozny (eds) *Trade, Agriculture and Development* Cambridge, Mass.: Ballinger

Tarasofsky, A. (1984) *The Subsidization of Innovation Projects by the Government of Canada* (study prepared for the Economic Council of Canada) Ottawa: Ministry of Supply and Services

Tarr, David G. and Morris E. Morke (1984) 'Aggregate Costs to the United States of Tariffs and Quotas on Imports' Staff Report, Bureau of Economics, US Federal Trade Commission (December)

Task Force on Federal Policies and Programs for Technology Development (1984) *A Report to the Honourable Edward C. Lumley, Minister of State, Science and Technology* (the Wright Report) Ottawa: Ministry of State for Science and Technology

Task Force on the Structure of Canadian Industry (1968) *Foreign Ownership and the Structure of Canadian Industry* Ottawa: Privy Council Office

Textile and Apparel Industry Advisory Council (1980) *Stocktake of the Textile, Clothing and Footwear Industries* Canberra: Department of Industry and Commerce

Textile, Clothing and Footwear Industry Council (1984) *Stocktake of the Textile, Clothing and Footwear Industries* Melbourne: Australian Manufacturing Council (December)

Thailand, NESDB (National Economic and Social Development Board) (1982) *Industrial Development in Thailand and Industrial Development Policy 1982–1986* Bangkok

Tolchin, Susan J. (1984) 'Air Bags and Regulatory Delay' *Issues in Science and Technology* 1 (Fall) pp. 66–83 de la Torre, Jose (1978) *Corporate Responses to Import Competition in the US Apparel Industry* College of Business Administration, Georgia State University

Trebilcock, M. (1985) *The Political Economy of Economic Adjustment: The Case of Declining Sectors* Ottawa: Royal Commission on the Economic Union

Tresize, Philip H. (1983) 'Industrial Policy Is Not the Major Reason for Japan's Success' *Brookings Review* (Spring) pp. 13–18

Tsuruta, Toshimasa (1982) *Sengo Nihon no Sangyo Seisaku* (Industrial Policy in Postwar Japan) Tokyo: Nihon Keizai Shimbunsha (in Japanese)

Turner, L. and N. McMullen (1982) *The Newly Industrializing Countries: Trade and Adjustment* London: George Allen & Unwin

Tyers, R. and P. Phillips (1984) *Australia, ASEAN and Pacific Basin Merchandise Trade: Factor Composition and Performance in the 1970s* ASEAN–Australia Economic Papers No. 13, ASEAN–Australia Joint Research Project, Kuala Lumpur and Canberra

Uekusa, Masu (1978) 'Effects of the Deconcentration Measures in Japan' *Antitrust Bulletin* (Fall)

—— (1982) *Sangyo Soshiki Ron* (Industrial Organisation) Tokyo: Chikuma Shobo

—— (1984) 'Industrial Policy Since the Oil Crisis' in Komiya et al. (eds) *Nihon no Sangyo Seisaku*

—— (forthcoming) 'Industrial Organization Since the Oil Crisis' in Kozo Yamamura and Yasukichi Yasuba (eds) *Japan's Political Economy*

UN (United Nations) (1974) 'Economic Co-operation Among Member Countries of the Association of South-East Asian Nations' (report of a United Nations team) *Journal of Development Planning* 7, pp. 1–261

UNIDO (United Nations Industrial Development Organization) (1978) *The World Iron and Steel Industry* International Center for Industrial Studies, Vienna

—— (1981) *World Industry in 1980* Biennial Industrial Development Survey, Vienna (UN Publication Sales No. E 81 II B 3)

—— (1982) *Handbook of Industrial Statistics* New York: UNIDO

—— (1983) *Industry in a Changing World* Special Issue of the Industrial Development Survey for the Fourth General Conference of UNIDO, Vienna (UN Publication Sales No. E 83 II B 6)

US Congressional Budget Office (1980) 'Current Problems of the US Automobile Industry and Policies to Address Them' Staff Working Paper (July)

US Department of Transportation (1981) 'The US Automobile Industry, 1980' Report to the President from the Secretary of Transportation (January)

US Federal Trade Commission (1977) *The United States Steel Industry and its International Rivals* Washington, DC

US House of Representatives (1980) *Auto Situation: 1980* Report of the Subcommittee on Trade, Committee on Ways and Means (6 June)

US International Trade Commission (1985) *A Review of Recent Developments in the US Automobile Industry, Including an Assessment of the Japanese Voluntary Restraint Agreements* Publication No. 1648 (February)

US Office of Technology Assessment (1981) *Industrial Competition: A Comparison of Steel, Electronics, and Automobiles* (July)

de Vries, V.A. (1967) *Export Experience of Developing Countries* Baltimore: Johns Hopkins University Press

Wakasugi, Ryuhei and Akira Goto (1985) Kyodo Kenkyu Kaihatsu to Gijutsu Kakushin (Cooperative Research and Development), mimeo

Wall, D. (1980) 'Industrial Processing of Natural Resources' *World Development* 8, 4, pp. 303–16

—— (1984) 'Reply' *World Development* 9, 5, pp. 495–98

Warr, P.G.(1983) 'The Jakarta Export Processing Zone: Benefits and Costs' *Bulletin of*

Indonesian Economic Studies 19, 3, pp. 28–49

—— (1985) *Export Promotion via Industrial Enclaves: The Philippines' Bataan Export Processing Zone* ASEAN–Australia Economic Papers No. 21, ASEAN–Australia Joint Research Project, Kuala Lumpur and Canberra

von Weizsäcker, C.C. (1980a) 'A Welfare Analysis of Barriers to Entry' *Bell Journal of Economics* 11, pp. 399–420

—— (1980b) *Barriers to Entry* Berlin: Springer-Verlag

Wett, T. (1981) 'Growth in Ethylene Capacity Slows but Plenty of Potential Still Exists' *Oil and Gas Journal* 7 September, pp. 85–90

Whalley, John (1985) *Canadian Trade Policies and the World Economy* Ottawa: Royal Commission on the Economic Union

Wheeler, J.W., M.E. Janow and T. Pepper (1982) *Japanese Industrial Development Policies in the 1980s: Implications for US Trade and Investment* Hudson Institute Research Report H1-3470-RR, New York

White, Lawrence J. (1971) *The Automobile Industry Since 1945* Cambridge, Mass.: Harvard University Press

—— (1981) *Reforming Regulation: Processes and Problems* Englewood Cliffs, NJ: Prentice-Hall

—— (1982a) 'The Automobile Industry' in Walter Adams (ed.) *The Structure of American Industry* 6th edn, New York: Macmillan

—— (1982b) *The Regulation of Air Pollutant Emissions from Motor Vehicles* Washington, DC: American Enterprise Institute

White, Michelle J. (1980) 'Public Policy Toward Bankruptcy: Me-First and Other Priority Rules' *Bell Journal of Economics* 11 (Autumn) pp. 550–64

White Paper on Science and Technology (1984) Tokyo: Science and Technology Agency

Wienert, H. (1980) World Trends in Steel Consumption and Production to 1990, Paper presented at the OECD Symposium on the Steel Industry in the 1980s, Paris (February)

Wilks, Stephen (1984) 'The Practice and Theory of Industrial Adaptation in Britain and West Germany' *Government and Opposition* 19 (Autumn) pp. 451–70

Winham, Gilbert, R. and Ikuo Kabashima (1982) 'The Politics of US–Japanese Auto Trade' in I.M. Destler and Hideo Sato (eds) *Coping with US–Japanese Economic Conflicts* Lexington, Mass.: D.C. Heath

Wong, John (1985) Issues and Problems of the Development of the Wood, Petrochemical and Chemical Industries in the Developing ESCAP Region, paper presented at the ESCAP/UNIDO Workshop on Accelerating Growth Through Co-operation in Selected Industrial Sectors in Developing ESCAP Countries, Bangkok (July)

Wonnacott, R.J. and Paul Wonnacott (1967) *Free Trade Between the United States and Canada: The Potential Economic Effects* Cambridge, Mass.: Harvard University Press

World Bank (rptd March 1982) *China: Socialist Economic Development* World Bank Report No. 3391-CHA, New York

—— (1983a) *Thailand: Managing Public Resources for Structural Adjustment* Report No. 4366-7H, Washington, DC

—— (1983b) *World Development Report 1983* Washington, DC

—— (1984a) *Korea: Development in a Global Context* Washington, DC

—— (1984b) *World Development Report 1984* New York: Oxford University Press

—— (1985) *World Development Report 1985* New York: Oxford University Press

Wright, Vincent (1984) 'Industrial Policy-Making under the Mitterand Presidency' *Government and Opposition* 19, 3, pp. 287–303

Yamazawa, I. (1980) 'Increasing Imports and Structural Adjustment of the Japanese Textile Industry' *The Developing Economies* 18 (December) pp. 441–62

—— (1983) 'Renewal of the Textile Industry in Developed Countries and World

Textile Trade' *Hitotsubashi Journal of Economics* 24, pp. 25–41

Yeats, A.J. (1981) 'The Influence of Trade and Commercial Barriers on the Industrial Processing of Natural Resources' *World Development* 9, 5, pp. 485–94

—— (1984) 'On the Analysis of Tariff Escalation: Is There Methodological Bias Against the Interest of Developing Countries?' *Journal of Development Economics* 15, pp. 77–88

Index